MODERN CHRISTIAN
REVOLUTIONARIES

MODERN
CHRISTIAN
REVOLUTIONARIES

An Introduction to the lives and thought of:

Kierkegaard

Eric Gill

G. K. Chesterton

C. F. Andrews

Berdyaev

Edited by Donald Attwater

Essay Index Reprint Series

BOOKS FOR LIBRARIES PRESS
FREEPORT, NEW YORK

THE DECORATIONS USED IN THIS BOOK ARE DRAWN BY
RUDOLPH KOCH, AND ARE TAKEN FROM *The Life of Jesus*

INTERNATIONAL STANDARD BOOK NUMBER:
0-8369-2304-9

LIBRARY OF CONGRESS CATALOG CARD NUMBER:
76-156608

PRINTED IN THE UNITED STATES OF AMERICA

Introduction

THERE is an English proverb, "Give a dog a bad name, and hang him." It is an old dodge, which can be found in action throughout recorded history. It was, and is, used with devastating effect by propagandists; it was, and is, an unconscious irrationality that plays havoc among the thoughtless and lazy-minded—and not among them alone. And it is used not only of persons and groups and policies and philosophies, but even of common words—or rather, of the concrete realities they are supposed to represent.

Such a word is *revolution,* a word rich in content and meaning, which with its derivatives takes up a column of small print in the "Shorter Oxford English Dictionary." Some time ago I was explaining in conversation the scope of the studies of contemporary Christian revolutionaries that are printed here. I was interrupted by the statement that a Christian, or at any rate a Catholic, cannot be a revolutionary. This rocked me back on my heels; but the Lord delivered the speaker into my hands—for he was an American. "There is an event in history," I replied, "that, as an Englishman, I call 'The American War of Independence.' *You,* I suppose, call it 'The Revolutionary War'; or do you, a Catholic American, repudiate that war and its name?" He did not pursue the subject further, and it left me thinking.

As I remark elsewhere in this book, the word *revolution* as commonly used connotes physical violence and the subversion of social order; both those who fear and those who welcome the thing like to think of it in terms of the barricades. Here the pertinent definition of the "Shorter Oxford" is "the complete overthrow of the established government in any country or state by those who were previously subject

v

to it: a forcible substitution of a new ruler or form of government."

But antecedent to that is given a yet older meaning, of "a great change in affairs or in some particular thing." And even today, when "all right-thinking people" and the Marxists and others have done their worst, that remains (in this connection) the basic meaning of the word. "Revolutionary" is a name that may be rightly given to anyone who seriously dissociates himself from any widely-accepted and well-established state of affairs or social or other system and the principles and philosophy pertinent to it. Since I suspect that, at its origin about the year 1850, the noun *revolutionary* (as distinct from *revolution,* which is much older) started life as a term of abuse (which would account for its popular definition in negative terms), it is better defined more positively, as, say, *"an advocate of principles and policies* which involve dissociation from and reversal of established ways of thought, systems, etc." A revolution may be good or bad, great or small, personal or widespread; it has no necessary connection with barricades or bloodshed, with *sans-culottes* or fascist marches or Red ruin, with private property or socialism or any such thing. And in the first place it is a matter of the mind and spirit: in former days one use of the word meant, "The action of turning over in the mind; consideration; reflection."

∾

Jesus Christ was a revolutionary. It was on that very charge that he was brought before Pilate. But the nature of his revolution was misrepresented by his accusers then, and it is misconceived by political *enragés* among his spokesmen today. Christ was not a political revolutionary: to forbid to pay taxes to Caesar was precisely what he did not do; that he did not lead a national rising against the Roman oppressors of his people was what lost him many supporters. He was not concerned with the Romans in Palestine (say, with the English "ascendency" in Ireland, or Mussolini in Ethiopia). Indeed, he directed what was due to the foreign and infidel tyrant should be rendered to him; and it was among the heathen Roman soldiers he found a man of greater faith than any in Israel (say, a superlatively righteous man among the Red troops in Poland).

Christ's revolution was far deeper and wider, both more far-reaching and more personal. It was of the spirit.

At any time, in any society, what could be more revolutionary, a greater change from the established ways of thought and life of ordinary people than: "Seek first the kingdom of God and His righteousness," don't worry about tomorrow, "Love your enemies, do good to them that hate you," a man is defiled by what comes out of his mouth, "Be perfect," don't lay up treasures on earth, "Judge not," "Teach all nations. . . ." Revolutionary indeed.

"I am the resurrection and the life . . . the way, the truth and the life." I, *I*, Jesus Christ, the dusty-footed prophet from Galilee. I—not Caius Julius Caesar Octavian Augustus, not Simeon bar-Kokba, the patriotic leader of a "resistance movement," not the Holy Roman Empire and the Two Swords, not the New Learning, not the prophets of the Enlightenment and the Principles of Eighty-nine, not Marx and the Nationalization of the Means of Production, Distribution and Exchange. The world's greatest revolution is not a matter of big names and big organizations and big money, it is not any political or social system or device or "ideology": it is a Man—and to the outward seeming of his day a man not essentially different from his fellows: "Is not this the carpenter's son?"

The Christian revolution can be theologized, legalized, devotionalized, modernized into "harmlessness," corrupted into propaganda and partisanry, watered down into nothingness: but it remains for all to see in the earthly life and teaching of Christ, recorded in the scriptures and tradition of the Church.

❧

That spiritual revolution has constant repercussions in all affairs of life. It constrains to feed the hungry, care for the sick in mind or body, look after the orphaned and widowed, to deal justly. In another aspect it constrains to search the things of God: not only the sacred things but also the technically profane things; for example, God manifest in "nature," what is currently called "science." It can call for the Declaration of Independence and the Bill of Rights and the freeing of the Negro slaves. There is nothing (except sin and error) profane to the Christian revolution—and that revolution is itself greater than any accidental and contingent change to which it may give rise. And it is personal; if it acts on masses, it is through individuals, and acts on each individual in the mass—he, she, is converted, revolutionized —the two words mean the same thing. And it must begin with the personal universal human things and relations; if the Christian revolution touches governments and nations it does so last, not first. Not for nothing did Father Bede Jarrett, of the Order of Preachers, use to speak of the "deadly scandal of ordinary life" among Christians. A revolutionary is by definition not ordinary.

On a later page I refer to an essay by Eric Gill, called "Art and Revolution," which is extremely puzzling to those to whom the epithet *revolutionary* is commonly applied: only at the end does he refer to them at all—and then to dismiss them as mere "progressives." "Instead of the present world," he said, "they want the world which the present one *implies.* They want the same thing only more so—the same things only more of them. . . . Merely to transfer ownership from private persons to the state is no revolution; it is only a natural development. Government by the proletariat is no revolution; it is only the natural sequel to the enfranchisement of lodgers. . . . And merely to proclaim an atheist government is no revolution—for that would be to make explicit what is already implicit in capitalist commercialism: but to return to Christianity would be truly revolutionary."

The principal current connotation of the word *revolution* is indeed a drastic change in socio-economic organization and conditions, to be brought about by "direct action" and in accordance with political, social and economic principles. But Christian social principles are personal responsibility, poverty (in the gospel sense of a decent sufficiency—no more), love of God, and therefore of man. Those principles are really revolutionary, they would really turn the world upside down; and consistently followed they would probably involve us in some very surprising and extreme political and social measures—but with that I am not now concerned. In a socialist state, socialism is no longer revolutionary; but justice and righteousness and love (in individual persons *first*) will always be revolutionary, until mankind is finally remade in the unspoiled likeness of God—and then this world and all its glory and shame will have passed.

∾

This book presents studies of five men who have, in one way or another, manifested the revolutionaryness of Christianity: namely, Charles Freer Andrews, whose ideas about India are of particular interest at this time; Nicholas Alexandrovich Berdyaev, in whose person "Russian philosophy first faced the judgment of Europe, and indeed of the whole world"; Gilbert Keith Chesterton, undoubtedly one of the best-loved public men of his time; Eric Gill, whose mind and pen were no less well-tempered than the chisels with which he carved stone; and that strange and baffling genius, Søren Kierkegaard.

This is a very mixed bag. Nobody could agree completely with the distinguishing ideas of all of them, none could share all their views and enthusiasms: but everybody can learn, and learn much, from each of them. Truth is infinitely varied and its developments inexhaustible; mistakes have their uses, even flat-out heresies are the exaggeration or misuse of a truth: our knowledge of the sublimest truths is at the best imperfect and analogical, and only in the mind of God can all our human contradictions be reconciled. And the members of this mixed company have this in common: they are Christians, men who have tried, each according to his light, to follow the teaching and example of Jesus Christ as the meaning of human life; and they are all revolutionaries, people who believe that each one of us must be born again in Christ, and to the extent of that rebirth and its consequences society must be turned upside down: not, therefore, revolutionaries who happen to be Christian, or in spite of being Christian, but revolutionary *because* Christian.

Rowland Hill in the eighteenth century did not see why the Devil should have all the good tunes. Why should Christians present him also with some of the best words, such as "revolutionary"? Or "radical"—which means one who tries to get down to the roots of things. Or "liberal"—which means one who is concerned for those things which pertain to a free man. Above all is the Christian able to be a free man. Oh yes; I know about the Spanish Inquisition and the puritans in New England. And I know about the Negroes in the United States and in South Africa. But oppressed people emigrate to the United States because of her Constitution and the Bill of Rights; England is respected because of her common law and the Habeas Corpus Act. Just so Christianity: we have to look at the essence, not at the deformations, however gross and widespread and authoritative. And her fundamental moral principle is that each person, each sacred personality, must be responsible for his own deeds and omissions—and without freedom there cannot be responsibility. "This," she says, "This is the way of the Lord. Walk ye in it." To walk in the way of the Lord Christ is to be revolutionary; it is a revolutionary way that leads to "the glorious liberty of the children of God."

❦

The contents of this volume are the first instalment of a series being published in England; and I cannot let it go before the American public without saying what a pleasure it has been to produce it. The series was conceived in mid-war, in the black summer of 1941, and the first separate little books were not born till the fall of 1945. Of the difficulties of that birth, only the English publisher is fully aware: the editor in some degree shared them, but his task was greatly eased by the friendly co-operation and patience of the various contributors. It was consoling that, in that time of bitter enmities and bloody struggle, Christians of various communions were able, amid so many pressing duties, to join in a common work of presenting the thought of other Christians.

Let me therefore end with a public giving of thanks for their labours and interest: to Mr. Chaning-Pearce, whose writings in *The Hibbert Journal* and elsewhere, as well as his published books, are so much appreciated; to Dr. Lampert, who expounds Russian thought to English-speaking people; to Mr. Lea, who has since published interesting works on Carlyle and Shelley; and to Dr. Macnicol, for thirty-five years a missionary in India, and an interpreter of Indian religion to the West. Nor must I forget my good friends the editors of the New York *Commonweal*, who have allowed me to reprint in this introduction the substance of a contribution to that review.

DONALD ATTWATER

Petersfield, England.
21 July 1946

Contents

SØREN KIERKEGAARD

by

Melville Chaning-Pearce

Matthew 2:9

M. S. CHANING-PEARCE. Born 1886. Educated at King's School, Canterbury and Worcester College, Oxford; M.A. Served in the British army and the Iraq political service, 1914-1924. Founded and directed the Alpine College, Switzerland (1925-1934) and The College, South Leigh, Oxfordshire (1936-1940). Among his published writings are Religion and Reality *(Macmillan),* The Terrible Crystal *(Kegan Paul),* Life after the Spirit *(S.P.C.K.) and* Treasures of Darkness *(James Clarke).*

2

SØREN KIERKEGAARD: TWO STUDIES

1

CHRISTIANITY is both reactionary and revolutionary. It reacts to and fulfils the 'Law and the Prophets' of religious tradition; but it fulfils them with a meaning so profound or so forgotten that, in the true connotation of the term, it is also revolutionary. It revolves the orb of an eternal Wisdom, turning darkened or hitherto unrevealed aspects of it to the light. It brings out of the immemorial and inexhaustible treasure of that wisdom 'things new and old.' Its new truths are, indeed, as old as the hills; but, seen anew, they 'turn the world upside down.' Its old truths are also eternally new. Such is the basic paradox of this profoundly traditional, profoundly revolutionary faith. Because it is so, all the most profound of Christian thinkers have been both traditionalist and revolutionary, both conservative and creative.

As Dr. Lowrie has truly said, Kierkegaard "remained a conservative to the end of his days" (L. p. 91). Nevertheless, in this proper meaning of the term, there are few Christian thinkers more entitled to the style 'Christian revolutionary' than Søren Kierkegaard. The revolutionary character of his thought was also, as he constantly insisted, a reversal to the traditional truth which, so he believed, the Christianity of his time had betrayed. But, so penetrating was his insight into the treasury of Christian truth that the apostasy of Christendom which he denounced a hundred years ago to an age, in the main, incapable of understanding his meaning, is one of which our own age has become generally and ardently aware. He was, in fact, the forerunner of a Christian revolution which is only now approaching its flood-tide.

3

But—for he saw life whole and religion for him was life—
the revolution which he heralded was one not only of religion but also of life and culture. He denounced the whole
trend of thought, both religious and secular, of the romantic,
Protestant, liberal, idealistic, pseudo-democratic culture
dominant in his day and land, and the acquisitive, callous,
comfort-loving society of *laisser-faire* individualism which it
begot in life—a way of thought and life which is only now
being seriously or generally assailed.

When to say such things seemed insane or seditious, he
declared that "Christianity does not exist" (L. p. 525), that
"parsons canonize bourgeois mediocrity" (J. 1134) and "are
trained in the art of introducing Christianity in such a way
that it signifies nothing" (Papers. p. 23), that "official Christianity is both aesthetically and intellectually ludicrous and
indecent, a scandal in the Christian sense" (L2, p. 246); he
predicted a "frightful reformation" when "men will fall
away from Christianity by the millions" (L2. p. 244). In
philosophy he not only denounced the then dominant Hegelian system of idealism but also the Cartesian logic upon
which all post-Renaissance European thought had been
built; in politics he boldly pronounced that "Christianity
has nothing to do with nationalism," that "liberal constitu-
tions" arouse "longing for an Eastern despotism as something
more fortunate to live under" and point to "the intensive
development of the state itself" (J. 657), that "ideas such as
'state' (*e.g.*, as it existed among the Greeks; 'Church' in the
older Catholic sense) must necessarily return" (J. 85); in the
field of culture he repudiated romanticism since it "implies
overflowing all boundaries" (J. 44), a vain vagueness, and
found in the humanism of his age no more than "vaporised
Christianity, a culture-consciousness, the dregs of Christianity" (J. 1209). Such criticisms are made by many to-day and
much of what he foresaw we are experiencing; but Kierkegaard's was a voice crying almost alone in a wilderness of
nineteenth-century Protestantism, progress and complacency.

Kierkegaard's revolutionary criticism of life thus included
the whole fabric of the socio-political life of the modern age
in its scope, and the majority of the institutions, ideas and

attitudes which he condemned are, though increasingly attacked, those with which we have still to deal to-day. And the revolution which he preached was radical; he laid his axe to the tap-root of the tree of life—the religious attitude in which such ideas and institutions originate. The present preoccupation with religion as the root of all political, economic and psychological problems echoes his prophetic diagnosis of our disease. He said that he "came out polemically against his age" (J. 588); his polemic applies no less to our own.

His constructive criticism was no less revolutionary and modern in its trend. His dialectical mode of thought anticipated the Marxian dialectic; his 'existential' thinking is a salient feature in modern philosophy and theology. His doctrine of the 'instant' and 'repetition' propounded a conception of time which is now to the fore. His insistence upon the 'leap' of life and faith as the way of reality as opposed to the 'gradualism' of the evolutionists corresponds to the most recent conclusions of biology and physics. In his call to 'inwardness' and awareness and his own profound psychological insight and fearless self-analysis he foreran modern psychology. His doctrines of the life and nature of spirit forecast that theology of the Spirit with which the religious thought of our own time is increasingly concerned.

Kierkegaard's thought is thus not only revolutionary and not limited to religion (in the cant and restricted sense of the word), it is also highly relevant to our own political, cultural and social conditions and problems. By temperament, moreover, he belonged rather to our than to his own age; he shared with the typical modern an acute sense of catastrophe and divided consciousness and, in his journals and other writings, gave to posterity a profound and searching record and analysis of that condition. The realization of the conditioned nature of all our thought and conduct is only to-day becoming general. Kierkegaard recognized the fact a century ago and, in his searching self-scrutiny and 'existential' thinking, applied that philosophically revolutionary conclusion to all the problems which confronted him. The sources of his thought are, therefore, in a degree rare among philosophers and theologians, to be traced to his own physical and psychological conditions and some knowledge of those conditions is essential for the comprehension of his work.

❧

His outer history was singularly uneventful. His real drama was inward and of the spirit; it was not the less dramatic, catastrophic or tragic for that. He was born in Copenhagen in 1813. His father was a prosperous and self-made merchant and was aged 56 when Søren, the youngest of seven children, was born. His mother, cousin to his father, had been his employee and seems to have exercised little influence in the family. His home conditions were thus those of the comfortable middle-classes, his psychological climate that of an urban, industrial, respectable, bourgeois and Protestant piety.

His father, a passionate, austere, guilt-haunted and, in a puritan form, deeply religious man, dominated both by attraction and repulsion, the life of his son. He was obsessed with conviction of sin and its consequent curse upon him and his family. For he had once, in his own sad and bitter boyhood, cursed God and, particularly in his second marriage with Søren's mother, was agonizedly conscious of sexual incontinence. He carried that curse and sense of sin to the grave in a tortured contrition. It was a burden which his son was to inherit and assume as his own. Søren's mother appears in the records as a somewhat wraith-like and insignificant figure, submissive, repressed and impersonal, who made little impact upon her children; the gaunt figure of the father filled the family horizon. It is not hard to reconstruct that grim and gloomy world. It is a family scene of which we have many examples in our own Victorian age; a remarkably similar situation is described in Edmund Gosse's *Father and Son*.

Søren himself, a somewhat sickly son of elderly parents and in-breeding and, as is common in such cases, hypersensitive and intellectual in bent, was acutely responsive to such oppressive conditions. The massive personality of his father imposed upon the child an adult and austere form of faith. "As a child," he has recorded, "I was strictly and austerely brought up in Christianity . . . a child crazily travestied as a melancholy old man" (L. p. 48). As he grew to manhood he fluctuated between a reverent affection for and resentment and rebellion against his father. But the latter's influence remained dominant to the end and was the mould of his piety. It was from his father that he learned how to live with God; "I have, quite literally, lived with God as one lives with one's father" (J. 771), he writes towards the end of his life. It seems certain that it was his father's costly confession to him of his own failings and faith which precipitated his own conversion and he continually testifies to the depth of his debt to him. It was undoubtedly to this dominating relationship with his father that the markedly patriarchal pattern of his piety and his insight into the mystery of the fatherly love of God are due; it seems symbolic of that relation that the only memorial of his grave is a slab which leans against his father's tomb.

Physical frailty and mental instability dogged all the seven children of this ill-balanced marriage and only two of them, the eldest and youngest sons, survived their father; it was a doom which he deemed to be a curse upon his sins. Of this frailty Søren, the youngest, had more than his share. It is probable that he suffered from spinal weakness all his life though the particular malady to which he so often alluded has never been certainly diagnosed. He was, to use his own term, an 'extraordinarius' from his school-days to his grave and his physical and psychical idiosyncrasies, combined with the unconventional clothes which he was made to wear at school, fostered a precocious brilliance at the cost of social misery. His school gave him a grounding in grammar which was to give a respect for 'the rule' and a dialectical bias to his mind, while his religious education, undertaken by his father, was a Christianity of the Cross rather than of the Resurrection, and implanted a religious melancholy which pursued him all his days. But his father seems to have given to this favoured youngest son not only his own sombre faith but also the stimulus of a teeming imagination and a powerful mind, so that Søren derived from him his aesthetic and philosophical as well as his religious bias; the double link thus forged with his father was never really broken. His favoured status as a Benjamin in the family seems also to have permitted to him a pertness to which his later love of polemics may be traced.

In 1830, at the age of 17, he proceeded from the Copenhagen high school to the university with a view to ordination—a prospect with which he flirted but never fulfilled throughout his life; he remained a student at the university for ten years. For several years he lived the life of a brilliant, wayward, dilettante, mildly self-indulgent and wild young undergraduate, and until the age of twenty-two does not seem to have desired or approached an adult attitude towards life. Until 1837 he continued to live in his father's house but his relations with him became increasingly strained. In youthful reaction from paternal domination Søren played the prodigal son, and the deepening gloom at home was aggravated by the role of elder brother which the eldest son, Peter, seems to have adopted as to the manner born.

At the university he threw himself with zest into the course of liberal studies which preceded specialization in theology, and he passed his second examination with higher honours in philosophy and science than in the classics and Hebrew. He revelled in the "up-and-down and down-and-up of thought" (L2. p. 56) for its own sake and showed an intellectual integrity which he never lost. He found passionate delight in art, particularly in music and the drama, and showed at this stage all the signs of developing into an aesthetic. He gained a reputation as a wit and exercised his polemical bent at debating societies. Like most brilliant young undergraduates he posed as a *flaneur* and, in spite of a liberal allowance, accumulated debts which his father was forced to pay.

This phase of irresponsibility terminated with his twenty-second birthday in 1835, when he experienced what he has termed the "great earthquake." In the family circle matters had been moving during the previous few years to a climax of disaster. Before 1832 two of the seven children had already died. In the following two years Søren's brother, two sisters (including his favourite Petrea) and mother died. In the next year Søren became acquainted with his father's guilty secret —the fact, it seems probable from the evidence, that he had violated his second wife when, though a relative, in a menial capacity in the house, before he had married her. In the following spring Søren met Regina Olsen, to whom he became engaged six years later.

These events violently forced the young Kierkegaard from the childish fantasy world in which till then he had lived. But it was the disclosure of his father's guilt which most of all caused for him what he has called a "frightful upheaval" in the course of which he was "inwardly rent asunder." For this indeed was ruin at the very roots of his being, so rooted, as has been seen, in his father's influence. A due appreciation of this profound psychological crisis is the master-clue to the division of consciousness which scarred him to the end and to the paradoxical mode of his thinking; here too is the *fons et origo* of his otherwise incomprehensible and, for some, reprehensible, behavior in his love-affair with Regina Olsen. In a thinly-veiled autobiographical story entitled 'Solomon's Dream' he wrote of a "rift in his nature;" it was at this time, in his twenty-second year, that this rift opened; it was a rift only to be closed by his hard-forged faith.

The immediate effect of this 'great earthquake' was to drive him to defiance, not only of his father, but also of God, and to beget in him a violent "offense at the religious" which manifested itself for several years in a bitter breach with his father, in a preference for philosophy rather than religion, and a life of increased dissipation. He was in fact in full rebellion and, as he recognized later, rebellion against his father implied rebellion against God; his infidelity at this time was a matter, not of intellect, but of will. "It is so difficult to believe," he wrote, "because it is so difficult to obey" (L2. p. 86). It was during this period that he girded at "the strange, stuffy atmosphere which we encounter in Christianity" and its "narrowbreasted asthmatic conceptions" and indulged in utopian conceptions of a "republic of science and learning" (L. p. 112). He was to some extent, plainly transferring to Christianity in general the particular stuffiness of the religion which clouded his unhappy home in such strictures, but the antipathy for this malady of conventional Christianity remained to colour his attack upon the established church at the end of his life, and the humanism which he now imbibed with such zest gave a peculiar vitality to the religion which he was later to regain.

The nadir of this phase of irreligion and rebellion came in the year 1836 when he employed himself for his thesis on 'The Concept of Irony'; it was a theme congenial to his, at this time, somewhat mordant and inhuman wit. Alienated from faith and feeling, he lived in an egotistic world of ideas and art. "I grasped solely at the intellectual side of man's nature and clung to it . . . the idea my only joy . . . men were to me indifferent" (L2. p. 92), he wrote. But in all his diversions he was deeply divided and miserable; while his mind occupied itself with irony, his heart was held by despair, and the deep knowledge of dread which he then learned was later to be written in his book *The Concept of Dread.* He sought a pose of ironical observation of life but his would-be detachment was undermined by that dread which, with a remarkable psychological acumen, he knew to be "an attraction for what one fears." He feared the absolute sensuality which was, for him, the only alternative to absolute religion, and he fell to that fear during this year in a drunken visit to a brothel, thus incurring a guilt which at once seemed to fasten more surely upon him the parental curse, bred a humility which later helped him to become reconciled to his father, and was to constitute one of the causes for the breach of his engagement.

The shock of this sexual fall called his *hubris* and humanism to a halt and the two succeeding years were a time of regress towards reconciliation with his father and religion. For, with a profound piety, he recognized that repentance implied return "into the family, into the clan, into the race, back to God" (L2. p. 101). At this time he was, moreover, profoundly moved by his reading of the journal of a con-

temporary German writer, Georg Hamann; its immediate
message to him was "Awake, thou that sleepest!" At this
time also he fell in love with Regina Olsen.

On his twenty-fifth birthday in May, 1838, he became
reconciled with his father, then an old man of 82, who took
this opportunity, it seems, to make a full confession of both
his failings and his faith to his son. Three months later his
father died, and Kierkegaard evidently believed that, by
overtaxing his strength by so costly a confession, he had
sacrificed himself for his son's sake. The reconciliation was
complete; the broken link between father and son was re-
forged more firmly than before, and the obedience and grat-
itude which Kierkegaard had latterly denied to his father
alive, he rendered doubly to him dead. He repented himself
back to his father and family; it was by the same motion and
act that he repented himself back to God, and the refound
religion which ensued was therefore the more patriarchal in
type.

With this return to his father he also accepted, with a
deep filiality, the curse which had darkened his father's faith
and which he believed that he himself must inherit and expiate. It became for him and his peculiar conditions the type
of the general guilt of mankind which each sinner shares,
and it is to this deep relationship with his father alive and
dead that his own profound sense of sin as an iron and in-
eluctable fact in life is to be ascribed. But with this sense of
sin he also inherited a knowledge no less deep of the mystery of paternal love. It was the full significance of fatherhood which his reconciliation had discovered, of the Divine
Fatherhood as of the human fatherhood which is the mortal
type of that 'great tradition.' It is in the light of this flash of
comprehension that he can say that Christian truth is true
"because my father told me so" (J. 785). He had plumbed
to a profound piety in the rich Latin sense of *pietas* and
thereby had also learned "what father-love is . . . the divine
father-love, the one unshakable thing in life, the true
Archimedian point" (L. p. 183). This conception of the full
pietas of faith and of the reciprocal love of God the Father
of men was henceforward the rock of his own religious

faith and his "new and infallible law of interpretation of life." He explored that filial relation in religion to the end.

~~

Return to religion swiftly succeeded return to his father. In May, 1838, he experienced, with a profundity reminiscent of Pascal's 'heure et demie' of 'fire,' the 'sudden,' 'inexplicable' and 'indescribable joy' (J. 207) of re-conversion to Christianity. Although he disclaimed any mystical content for that experience, and in the light of our knowledge of his precedent condition of mind it may seem less 'inexplicable' to us than to him, there can be no doubt as to its force or its reality. Or as to its joy—a fact which, in view of the prevailing grimness of much of his gospel, should be stressed: "I rejoice over my joy, of, in, by, at, on, through, with my joy" (J. 207), he wrote with obvious sincerity and spontaneity. It is to be noted also that for him return to God also implied return to his Church; in July he went to public confession and received holy communion.

His return to his father and faith also implied return to 'the race' and his engagement to Regina, also in May, 1838, seems to have been undertaken in token of this acceptance of his conditions. The feminine element in his life had faded out with the deaths of his mother and sisters; in his intercourse with Regina he seems to have sought to fill that gap and to fulfil himself in his human life. He saw in marriage the fulfilment of both natural and spiritual life, and seems, though he failed to attain to it (as to the priesthood), never to have abandoned that belief. In later years he confessed in his journal—"had I had faith I should have remained with Regina" (J. 444). But he did not do so. "The next day," he wrote later, "I saw that I had made a mistake" and just under a year later he broke off the engagement and "to save her, to give her soul resiliency" (L. p. 226), he determined to try and make her believe that he did not love her and that the rupture was due to his own frivolity and worthlessness. He believed it to be both psychologically and religiously wrong to pursue the marriage, and his reasons for that 'great refusal' have a vital relevance for his later thought.

From the sequence which has been sketched it will be seen that Kierkegaard's engagement to Regina coincided with a watershed period in his life, a phase of great inner eruption of a peculiarly catastrophic kind—in the words of St. John-of-the-Cross, "a fearful breaking up in the innermost parts," during which, in a profound conversion, "turning about," of both religion and life, he was passing from an irresponsible, dilettante and, in his own terms, "erotic" and "observer" attitude to a responsible, realistic and religious attitude and from immaturity to a rapid maturing. For her part, Regina seems to have been a girl who lived very near to nature; her world was that of (in Kierkegaard's phrase) the 'first immediacy,' of naïve feeling and the 'erotic.'

It was a world which, with a mounting realization during these years, Kierkegaard had come to realize that he must renounce. His conversion had imbued him with a deep sense of dedication and of personal mission. He knew himself to be dedicated to an 'idea'—the Christian idea, and that conversion had meant a radical change in attitude and mode of life from 'immediacy' (natural spontaneity) to 'spirituality'—a way of life which he called the 'second immediacy.' But Regina lived in a world of the 'first immediacy.' He knew that, since that inner crisis, he had become "an eternity too old for her." For, he quotes from Johan Georg Hamann, "a man who lives in God therefore stands in the same relation to the 'natural' man that a waking man does . . . to a dreamer. . . . He has been 'born again' . . . he has become an eternity older . . . he has now become spirit . . ." He knew that "essentially I live in a spirit-world" —a world of which Regina knew nothing. "So then," he comments, "she would have gone to smash" (L. p. 221). "My engagement to her," he wrote elsewhere, "and the breaking of it is really my relation to God, my engagement to God, if I may dare say so" (L2. p. 147).

This was part of the 'secret' which he could not tell her because she could not have understood. But there was more. He felt himself to be a 'penitent.' He had, so he believed,

not only inherited but incurred his father's sin and curse.
For he too had defied both his father and God. And he too,
in a sudden blind sensuality, had been guilty of lustful incontinence. "Had I not been a penitent, had my *vita ante
acta* not been melancholy," he wrote, "union with her would
have made me happy as I had never dreamed of becoming"
(L. p. 218). He was conscious too of his own dawning genius
which "like a thunder-storm comes up against the wind"
(J. 309) and of the "pale, bloodless, hard-lived, midnight
shapes" to which he must "give life and existence" (J. 345),
and of, as he believed, "the curse which rests upon me . . .
never to be allowed to let anyone deeply and inwardly join
themselves to me" (J. 379). Therefore, for God's sake, for
hers and for his own, he was driven to the conclusion that
he must not marry.

However his motives and conduct may be construed, it is
certain that it was no simple or easy sacrifice, and that for
him it was a crucial decision for a Christianity which, in
his conception, is compact of decision. "I loved her dearly,"
he declared with an indubitable sincerity, "she was as light
as a bird, as daring as a thought" (J. 363). She was, in fact,
the living symbol of all that his soul, his 'erotic' nature,
most passionately desired. And again—"there is nothing so
infinite as love" (J. 368); he could not forget her. To abandon her and, with her, his erotic desire, meant death; "when
I left her," he wrote, "I chose death" (J. 655). And he died
to more than Regina—a whole world. "Ce n'est pas Regina
Olsen seulement," comments Leo Chestov, "c'est le monde
entier qui s'est transformé pour Kierkegaard en une ombre,
en une fantôme." Whatever judgement may be passed upon
his behaviour, there can be no doubt that he acted from an
overmastering sense of compulsion. "I had not the strength
to abstain from marriage, I was compelled" (J. xxxviii), he
confessed later.

However bitter that renunciation, it was not barren; in
that sacrifice he was taught his truth and it is perhaps by
that fruit of his act that it is rightly to be judged. Six years
later he wrote, "I owe what is best in me to a girl; but I did
not exactly learn it from her, I learnt it through her"

(J. 761). The experience was crucial and formative for all his future life and thought. Here is the forge of his passionate and paradoxical faith, for a faith which could not adequately interpret that experience to him was of no avail. Here was the implacable conflict and dialectic of 'Yes' and 'No' in his actual existence from which sprang his Christian co-ordination of contraries, his 'existential thinking' and the dialectic, the poignant paradox, which he found at the heart of religious reality. And here was the knowledge of passion 'proved on his pulses' by the light of which he affirmed that "faith is a passion (though a passion which must be purified)" (J. 590). Therefore he perceived in paradox "the passion of thought" and judged that "the thinker who is devoid of paradox is like the lover who is devoid of passion— a pretty poor sort of fellow" (J. 335). Since his own faith was thus forged in this furnace of existential passion, he found no use for a religion not rooted in reality. Since the breach of his engagement to Regina was also the sealing of his 'engagement to God,' religion was for him first and foremost a "love-story." "This relationship of mine to God," he wrote ten years later, "is the experience of a happy lover" (L. p. 441).

❧

Kierkegaard's conflict and agony were poured out in books. Two years after his breach with Regina he began his serious career as a writer with four books, all written as 'indirect communication' to her: *"Either-Or, Two Edifying Discouses, Repetition* and *Fear and Trembling,* all published in 1843. In 1846, in the *Unscientific Postscript,* he published a statement of the existential philosophy which is the foundation of his religious thought; it remains one of the most 'central' (as he himself described it) and important of his books; in it he challenges the whole system of Cartesian and Hegelian philosophy. In the same year he launched an attack, in the interests, as he conceived, of public decency, upon a disreputable periodical called *The Corsair.* But he had succeeded in representing himself to the public of Copenhagen (though not to Regina) as a worthless cynic, and had provoked a publicity and unpopularity of which *The Corsair* made capital in a series of anonymous lampoons. Kierkegaard learned what it meant to be "trampled to death by geese"; for his extreme sensitivity, as he wrote, "such a galling sort of abuse is about the most torturing experience" (L. p. 358).

His work and his experience up to this point had been *prolegomena* to his religious writings and, as he said, his "education in becoming a Christian" (L2. p. 186). He was then 34 years old, an age beyond which he had never expected to live. For the remainder of his life, nine years, he devoted himself to religious writing, at first under a variety of pseudonymns and later, after his second conversion in 1848, under his own name. In 1847 the first of this series, *Edifying Discourses,* appeared. In 1848 he underwent a second crisis of spirit when, as he said, "God had run me to a standstill" (L2. p. 201), of which he wrote—"My whole nature is changed . . . I must speak" (J. 747). This second crisis seems to have convinced him of his own integration as a spirit-person and of an urgent call to action. "From now on," he said, "I shall have to take over clearly and directly everything which up till now has been indirect and come forward personally, definitely and directly as one who wished to serve the cause of Christianity" (J. 806). And from now on the note of his writing is, as was said of John Donne, that of a "dying man to dying men."

This final phase is heroic. He was, in his own words, "venturing far out." He was venturing "the burden of being and becoming spirit," into what he believed to be that new dimension of spirit-being to which the Christian is called, venturing beyond his limits and daring deeds beyond his competence or his desire "by virtue of the absurd . . . trusting in God." He was venturing beyond "the erotic," beyond the plane of the sensuous poetry in which his poetic spirit had found its delight. Such poetry of earth had now for him come to seem "wishful, infatuating, benumbing"; in comparison with that, he writes, "Christianity . . . is prose . . . and yet is precisely the poetry of eternity"; like St. Paul, he declares that now "I will sing with the spirit." He was venturing what he believed would mean martyrdom in the belief that "Denmark has need of a dead man"; in fact his venturing probably precipitated his death. He was venturing an unconditional Christianity for himself and an uncompromising attack upon the conditional Christianity of the established church, "putting a match to established Christendom." Finally, he was venturing his personal security, for he was now nearly at the end of his resources; his diminishing capital ended with his life. He did so deliberately, eschewing the security of a living in the church, of the financial prudence of which he was well aware for, he wrote, "as soon as I make my life finitely secure . . . I am finitized." He was now staking all and more than he had or was upon his faith. "I have the honour," he told King Christian, "to serve a higher power, for the sake of which I have staked my life." It is not possible to study the man and his records with care without realizing that these were no heroics; he lived out his 'troubled truth.'

The immediate fruit of this new crisis and decision is to be found in his two major religious books, *Sickness unto Death* (1849) and *Training in Christianity* (1850), and in a religious biography entitled *The Point of View* (1848); his impulse to definitive and provocative action produced a frontal attack upon the established church in *The Instant* in 1855, the year of his death at the age of 42.

His Christian thinking had grown continually more challenging and unconditional; his action as a Christian in this final phase fulfilled his thought in deeds. At the end he was able to declare, in a saying reminiscent of St. Paul's apologia for his life, ". . . I have not let go of my thought, I have not made my life comfortable" (L2. p. 226). On his death-bed he refused the ministrations of the official church since he said that "the parsons are royal functionaries, and royal functionaries are not related to Christianity" (L2. p. 254). He died in the assurance of grace and joy and with, in the words of a spectator, "a sublime and blessed splendour" of appearance.

The chief characters in this intense inner drama are few in number. Kierkegaard's retiring and introverted disposition and semi-recluse existence did not conduce to the making of intimate friendships, and Emil Boesen, friend of his youth and attendant at his death-bed, seems to have been the only person to whom, apart from his family and Regina, he gave his confidence. In his later years one Rasmus Nielsen, a professor, attached himself in the role of a follower but it was a relationship which irked the unwilling rabbi. The two public contemporaries of mark for whom he had an affectionate respect, Bishop Mynster, primate of the Church of Denmark and his father's close friend and director, and Professor Martessen, popularizer of Hegel in Denmark, became, with an irony peculiarly his own, the targets of his attack upon the established order in religion and philosophy. But, although he made few friends and many enemies, in his habitual saunterings in the Copenhagen streets and long carriage drives, he made acquaintance with nature and with all sorts and conditions of men and women—a racy actuality of which he made rich use in his writing.

In the making of his mind books played a more important part than persons. Apart from the Bible, the dialogues of Socrates (from whom his dialectic is largely derived), the works of Hegel and the Jena romantics such as Fichte, Novalis, Schelling and the Schlegels (mainly in strong reaction), the plays of Shakespeare (in particular *Richard II, Hamlet* and *King Lear,* which seemed to speak most poignantly to his condition) and the writings of Johan Georg Hamann (whose conversion and attitude towards Christianity so nearly resembled his own) were the main formative influences upon his thought. Though he repudiated the name of 'mystic' and held that "mysticism has not the patience to wait for God's revelation" (J. 321), he studied Gorres' *Mystik* and was acquainted with mystical writers such as Boehme, Tauler and the Victorines.

༚

The sources of Kierkegaard's profound and persistent sense of crisis and catastrophe are to be sought chiefly in his own inner life. But the course of public affairs in Denmark during his lifetime fomented that feeling. He had long and with

the persistence of a Jeremiah prophesied political disaster;
with the Danish-German war of 1848, as a result of which
Denmark lost Schleswig-Holstein and suffered a constitu-
tional revolution, the storm broke with a sense of catastrophe
for his countrymen and contemporaries which it is not easy
for an age attuned to disaster upon a scale so much more
vast to appreciate. Nevertheless Kierkegaard's generation in
Denmark lived with thunder in the air, and his thought was
shaped under the shadow of a catastrophe clearly foreseen
by him. Moreover, with a prophetic vision alone sufficient
to acclaim his genius, Kierkegaard foresaw what he described
as the "total bankruptcy towards which the whole of Europe
seems to be heading" (L. p. 157)—a bankruptcy of which
our world is all too well aware. With an uncanny prescience
he foresaw and foretold the whirlwind which we are reaping.
He conceived it to be his duty and destiny to sound a 'cry
of alarm.' It is rather as a 'corrective' (the title with which
he himself described his role as he saw it) and 'cry of alarm'
than as systematic theology or philosophy that his work is,
with justice, to be judged.

Kierkegaard's conditions were thus evidently of a kind to
render them a happy hunting-ground for psychologists. An
Oedipus-complex, a father-fixation, making him at once the
psychological murderer and 'spiritual wife' of his father, bi-
sexuality, homosexuality, schizophrenia, paranoia are eagerly
diagnosed by Freudian fanatics. *Cf.,* an article in *Horizon,*
by Rudolph Friedmann, Oct. 1943. It seems characteristic
of his ironic humour that he should have himself anticipated
them all, for he analysed himself throughout his life with a
pitiless persistence and acumen unparalleled in literature.
A full and modern estimate of his thought cannot indeed
omit such a mode of enquiry and it is amply evident that his
genius (like all genius) bordered upon the pathological.

Such enquiry serves rather to magnify than to minimize
the quality of the man for it illuminates from one angle the
extreme tension to which he, like all men who in Dr. Reinhold Niebuhr's words stand "at the junction of nature and
spirit," inherit "as the sparks fly upward." Save for a bigoted
and uncritical psychological dogmatism, they cannot pass any

final verdict upon the "unmapped, unmeasured, secret heart" of Kierkegaard or any other genius. Nor can they, as is sometimes so glibly assumed, denigrate the spark of spirit, the flame of personal truth born in the womb of genius from such inner conflict. In the words of Henri Massis (Les Idées Restent, p. vii) "là où l'èsprit est libre, actif, il n'y a pas de désastre irreparable" for a soul, such as that of Søren Kierkegaard, wrestling, 'free' and 'active' to the end, with its psychological contraries.

Such psychological criticism, however, serves to emphasize the kinship of Kierkegaard's spirit with the temper, so conscious of a similar division of consciousness, of our own age. It is thus with a special sense of affinity that the more aware of modern men can contemplate the inner drama of Kierkegaard's life and the knotty texture of his thought. For, with a lonely heroism of spirit which can but elicit the admiration of the understanding, he confronted, a century before its full time, a conflict of consciousness of which the majority of Europeans have only recently become aware. But it is with the wisdom born from that travail of soul and seen in the perspective of our knowledge of his conditions that we are concerned. In such a presence preconceived formulas and dogmas are best laid by.

2

THE foundations of Kierkegaard's faith were laid in his own life; the only truth which was of any value for him was that which was 'existential,' which spoke to his own suffering and corresponded with the paradox, conflict and despair so poignantly experienced in his own individual existence and passion. He had known the paradox and dialectic of life and love, the extremity of inner division and had plumbed the depths of human futility. "I stick my finger into existence—it smells of nothing," he wrote in *Repetition*. It was in this 'tension of reality' that his thought was rooted and for such a 'sickness unto death' in his own experience of human existence that he sought a 'radical cure' in an 'existential truth.' Both his need and his psychological state were thus remarkably similar to those of our own time.

Such a personal truth had always been his aim. When only 22 he had already stated his life's quest. "The thing is to understand myself, to see what God really wished *me* to do; the thing is to find *the idea for which I can live and die*" (the italics are Kierkegaard's). That truth was alone true for him which he could, in Keats's phrase, "prove upon his pulses." Such a truth he styled 'existential.' It is a term which is fundamental for his faith and now in common use—and abuse. It therefore requires careful consideration.

Although modern 'existential philosophy' largely derives from the thought of Kierkegaard, he himself never precisely defined the term. But he has stated what 'existence' implied for him. "Existence is the child of the infinite and the finite, the eternal and the temporal, and is therefore constantly striving . . . an existing individual is constantly in process of becoming" (U.P. p. 79). Existence thus implies for Kirkegaard not the calm of being but the conflict of becoming, and not life in the abstract, but conditioned human life lived in the 'tension of reality.' The 'existing individual' exists on the frontier between time and eternity, finite and infinite, a—

" . . . swinging-wicket set
Between
The Unseen and the Seen."

He is, in Dr. Reinhold Niebuhr's words, "under the tension of finiteness and freedom, of the limited and the unlimited." It is to this specifically human predicament in existence that Kierkegaard's use of the word refers, with such existence that his 'existential thought' is concerned and by such existence that he believes it to be conditioned. He thus anticipated the notion of the conditioned nature of all thought and of the 'tension of faith' upon which such leaders of modern thought as Professor Karl Mannheim and Dr. Niebuhr to-day insist.

It is thus with such actual existence that, for Kierkegaard, real thinking is alone concerned, and by its conditions that it is itself conditioned. Thinking which recognizes such existence as at once its only real subject-matter and its test of truth and that the thinker is himself, as an 'existing individual,' immersed in the conditions of his existence and therefore "in process of becoming," is for him 'existential thinking'—the thought of "the whole man facing the whole mystery of life." In Dr. Paul Tillich's definition of this type of thought, "truth is bound to the existence of the knower . . . Only so much of knowledge is possible as the degree to which the contradictions of existence are recognized and overcome" (*The Interpretation of History*, p. 63).

But it is important to observe that, for Kierkegaard, experience of existence is not limited to the experience of personal human existence apart from God; it includes the existence of God. For God has himself entered into existence and the existential experience of man; "the God-Man is himself the existential" (J. 1054). Of his existence Kierkegaard is as sure as of his own with the steadfast conviction of Browning's ". . . thy soul and God stand sure."

That initial faith in the existence of God in human history and in his own individual experience is, for Kierkegaard his datum; he accepts it as axiomatic and beyond either proof or dispute; it is, not rational, but faith-knowledge. That some such premise which is always in reality, not rational, but faith-knowledge lies at the root of all thought is obvious; the rationalist could not reason unless he believed in the validity of reason and this he cannot know, he can only believe. For Kierkegaard this dual premise of the existence of his own soul and God was his 'jumping-off point.' He believed that both existences are knowable by the individual's inner experience of existence and are, indeed, only by such an 'inwardness' to be known at all. And it is this, to reason, apparent contradiction and 'absurdity' of the entry of being into becoming, essence into existence, God into history, which constitutes the tension and paradox of life and necessitates a dialectical mode of thinking—a simultaneous Yes and No.

Therefore the datum of existential thinking and the existential test of truth are for Kierkegaard, dual—the existence and experience of, not only self, but God. It is this supremely important fact which differentiates the 'existentialism' of Kierkegaard from that of the nazis. The latter accept and affirm the existence of man (in the abstract) only; Kierkegaard accepts and afirms the existence of both man and God. Therefore the criticism of existential philosophy delivered by Miss Dorothy Emmett in *Philosophy* (July 1941) that it implies "no external standard of truth and morality above the individual decision," while true of the nazi form of existentialism, is false for that of Kierkegaard. For he, in his experience of existence, posits both the subjective standard of self-knowledge and the objective standard of knowledge of God. For him the nazi form of existentialism is unexistential since it omits the greater part of existential experience.

The test of truth for Kierkegaard and all existential Christian thinking which accepts his dual premise is thus an existential decision or apprehension of the self when confronted with the objective reality of life and God. It is not some arbitrary and arrogant 'private judgement' of the self upon life and God, and as such subject to the manifold corruption and fallibility of all human judgement. It is that truth and conviction which are struck from the meeting of the subjective and inward 'passion' or feeling of the 'whole man' with a reality and revelation which, though apprehended subjectively, are, in fact, utterly objective to him.

It is, indeed, like his own apprehension, embodied in and conveyed to him by tradition. For tradition (that which is handed across the generations to the individual) both conditions the 'passion' of the individual and confronts him in the Great Tradition of history and revelation. Thus the tradition of Christian truth is conveyed to him by the Christian Church. It is to this objective element in existential truth that Kierkegaard refers when he says that he accepts Christian truth "because my father told me so." Thus an existential decision after the pattern of Kierkegaard in fact includes "an external standard of truth and morality" as a major factor in its decision. The ultimate decision is itself dialectical;

from the opposition and meeting of the individual soul and God a new condition, that of faith, is born. To pose the process in simple Christian language, the soul, when confronted by Christ, is constrained to obey that call of reality; when it does so it becomes a 'new man' and leads a 'new life.'

Existential thinking is thus based upon a primary postulate which is the precise contrary of that of Descartes from which the whole of the Cartesian and idealistic philosophy, liberal sociology, scientific evolutionism and humanism of the modern age derive. Where Descartes declared that "I think, therefore I am," Kierkegaard retorted, "I am, therefore I think." For the one, abstract thought, for the other, concrete and total existence was the foundation of faith. Both thus accept primary postulates which cannot be proved. The Cartesian and humanist accept their fundamental faith in the validity and sovereignty of the human reason upon the supposed evidence of human experience; Kierkegaard accepts his faith in the existence of himself and God upon the evidence of an existential experience which includes both human feeling and divine revelation. His revolution in thought was thus of the most radical kind which can be conceived and one which, if accepted, must reorientate the whole course of thought and life.

This fundamental faith not only provides the ultimate criterion of truth; it also shapes to its pattern all thought and life proceeding from it. For Descartes and his followers truth is that which is true for thought; for Kierkegaard and existential thinkers it is that which is true for life. For the former, intellect, for the latter, the whole personality in its 'human predicament' is dominant and decisive. The one necessarily tends towards a predominantly rational and intellectual, the other towards a vital and intuitive way of life and thought.

The revolt against the Cartesian philosophy and that which ensued from it and dominated European thought in Kierkegaard's day is now general. It has recently been well expressed by Mr. H. J. Massingham. "What he [Descartes] did," he writes, "was to elevate man above his proper station, above, that is to say, his 'creatureliness' by his intellectual gospel of egocentricity. 'I am,' he wrote, 'because I think.' Neither God nor 'I' were realities, both being intellectual abstractions" (*The Tree of Life*, p. 109). But in Kierkegaard's day such a denunciation of the dominant dogma of philosophy was a radical revolution in the realm of ideas. It is a revolution which is still in process to-day.

This revolutionary doctrine of the nature of human truth and human thinking gives to 'existential thinking' characteristics which were quite contrary to those of the prevalent idealistic philosophy. In the first place, it is a different mode of thought and therefore begets a different type of thinker. While the tradition of Descartes produced philosophers and scientists who seek to be detached observers of life, 'above the battle,' that of Kierkegaard produced thinkers involved in the concrete battle of existence, and it is noteworthy that Kierkegaard repudiated the title of 'philosopher' and preferred that of a 'Christian thinker.'

As Professor Karl Heim has said of Kierkegaard's type of thought, "a proposition or truth is said to be *existential* when I cannot apprehend or assent to it from the standpoint of a mere spectator but only on the ground of my total existence" (*God Transcendent*, p. 75). Such thinkers are 'educated by experience' rather than by thought. Since their "concern implies relationship to life, to the reality of personal existence," they therefore renounce both "the high aloofness of indifferent learning" and "scientific aloofness from life." And since they are primarily concerned, not with thinking, but with living, their thinking is, to employ a phrase now popular in scientific circles, 'operational'; it is "drawn from life and expressed again in life" (L. p. 214).

Therefore Kierkegaard and 'existential thinking' repudiate all abstract thinking and thinkers. Thus he asserts that "the sciences . . . reduce everything to calm and objective observation" and, therefore, that "the whole of science is a parenthesis." Again he denounces "the hopeless forest fire of abstraction" and is acid in his comments upon 'dons' and 'professors.' The don is "a man in whom there is nothing human, where enthusiasm and the desire to act . . . is concerned, but who believes it to be a learned question." 'The truth' is crucified like a thief, mocked and spat upon—and dying, calls out, "Follow me." Only the 'don' (the inhuman being) understands not a single word of it all, he construes it all as a learned problem. "One is to suffer; the other is to become a professor of the fact that another has suffered" (J. 1362). "Take away the paradox from the thinker and you have the professor" (L. p. 506) 'Parsons' come under the same condemnation but, in so far as they are 'observers' of the passion of God their offence is the more rank.

Second, existential thinking proposes a different objective to that of abstract philosophy and science; it is concerned, not with intellectual proofs or certainty, but with pragmatic faith; "certainty can only be had in the infinite, where he (the existing subject) cannot remain, but only repeatedly arrives" (U.P. p. 75). For Kierkegaard this "prolix knowledge . . . this certainty which lies at faith's door and lusts after it" is anathema. Therefore abstract philosophy unrelated to life (as he conceived the Hegelian system to be) is both futile and fatal for faith, which alone matters. For while "a logical system is possible, a system of existence is impossible" (L. p. 308). "Existence must be content with a fighting certainty." The quest for certainty, which is the quest of such a philosophy, has thus nothing whatever to do with existential truth, or with Christianity as Kierkegaard conceives it, "wherein," he writes, "lies the misunderstanding between speculation and Christianity" (L. p. 301). Therefore, for him, "Christianity and philosophy cannot be reconciled" (J. 32).

Third, since existential thinking is concerned with "the reality of personal existence," it is not objective but subjective, not coldly external to life but inward with an "endless passion" of "inwardness," not impersonal, but profoundly personal. "The real task is to be objective to oneself and subjective towards all others" (J. 676).

But by 'subjectivity' Kierkegaard does not mean mere individualism or that the individual judgement is the measure of all things. The term is used by him in opposition to the Hegelian claim to objectivity or personal disinterestedness in the effects of speculative thinking. The subjective thinker, for Kierkegaard, is not he who judges solely by subjective standards and private judgement but he who is concerned with the truth for him and his own concrete situation. Moreover by subjectivity he also implies personality, a spiritual person derived from and dependent upon a transcendent God known to him in his own 'inwardness.'

This emphasis upon the personal apprehension of truth is perhaps Kierkegaard's most important contribution to modern thought; it is one which gives him a spiritual paternity to that 'personalism' which, with Berdyaev, Maritain and many more, is now in the van of philosophical and political speculation. In Professor Theodor Haecker's judgement "The being and essence of the person are the elements which Kierkegaard brought into philosophy" (*Søren Kierkegaard*, p. 29).

Fourth, existential thinking is not dispassionate (as philosophy aspires to be) but passionate. "Passion is the real thing, the real measure of man's powers." And the age in which we live is wretched, because it is "without passion" (J. 396). For him both truth and faith are passions. But he equates passion with *pathos*, in its proper Greek sense of feeling or suffering—a suffering to which mind and soul as well as body are subject. He is careful to discriminate it, in this sense, from what he calls "unshaven passion" and insists that "passion must be purified."

He emphasizes the fact that "passion and feeling are open to all men in an equal degree"; here is the basis of the universalism which he constantly and vehemently affirms. Such an exaltation of 'passion' or feeling as a primary means for the apprehension of truth is therefore profoundly democratic in tendency. For, since all can feel but few can reason in the meaning of rationalism, truth is thus within the reach, not merely of a learned *élite,* but of every man who has been schooled by suffering.

This conception of 'passionate' thinking is also closely akin to the mystic approach to reality, though Kierkegaard repudiated the pseudo-mysticism which, as he wrote, "has not the patience to wait for God's revelation" (J. 321). Thus "by love may he be gotten and holden; but by thought never" is written in the *Cloud of Unknowing*, where a form of knowledge is expounded ". . . not coming from without . . . by the windows of the wits, but from within." Such a *via mystica* is evidently of the same order as the Kierkegaardian way of 'passion' and 'inwardness.'

It seems clear, indeed that he ranks 'passion' or feeling higher than abstract reason in the scale of apprehension of existential truth. Upon the premise that it is "the whole man facing the whole mystery of life" who can alone reach reality, it must be so. For, while such reason is rare and at one remove from reality, feeling is universal and immediate.

In so far as it denies to abstract reason and intellect the monopoly of truth, existential thinking thus tends towards anti-intellectualism and even irrationalism. For Kierkegaard "the intelligence and all that goes with it has done away with Christianity . . . the fight is against intelligence" (J. 925). In the modern tendency towards irrationalism and the popular feeling against 'intellectuals' and 'highbrows' Kierkegaard's revolt against the tyranny of rationalism is peculiarly modern in its trend. But the tendency towards irrationalism in such 'corrective' sayings has been exaggerated by some of his successors. Thus a modern disciple of Kierkegaard, Miguel de Unamuno, declares that "reason is the enemy of life. A terrible thing is intelligence . . . All that is vital is irrational" (*The Tragic Sense of Life*, pp. 90-1).

It seems very doubtful whether Kierkegaard would have endorsed such statements. Intellect, abstract reason and analytical science are for him not primary, but they are secondary; they are servants of the human spirit who have usurped the sovereign seat of the existential decision of the 'whole man' and, as such, are to be fought. But he nowhere suggests that reason is not an important element in the apprehension of the whole man to which he appeals, and he himself attacks what he believes to be a false use of reason with the weapons of reason. Indeed he specifically declares that "the race must go through reason to the absolute" (J. 1256). But "Life can only be explained after it has been lived" (J. 192), he wrote, and he himself devoted his life to explaining it. He does not deny the need to explain life; he is concerned to put rational explanation in its proper place in the approach of man to reality.

Moreover, the reason which Kierkegaard attacked was neither reason in the Greek sense of *nous* nor that 'natural reason' to which, according to St. Thomas Aquinas, "all are compelled to assent"; on the contrary the 'existential thinking' which he desired had much in common with these conceptions of reason, as also with the 'understanding' of the "Wisdom literature" of the Old Testament. It was the cold, abstract, analytic and arrogant reason of the Cartesian school which Hegel, as he thought, had inherited, which he condemned.

Fifth, the whole man, by virtue of such 'passion' in existential thinking, is believed to be capable, in Dr. W. M. Horton's words, of "consciousness of an extra dimension of reality inaccessible to the cool intellect but accessible to a warmer and more vital faculty" (*Contemporary Continental Theology*, p. 90); existential thinking opens the door to new realms of reality and 'faith-knowledge' of which 'intellect' can know nothing. "With the eyes of the heart I read it," Kierkegaard declares. It is a mode of comprehension of which Pascal wrote, "le coeur a ses raisons que la raison ne connaît point"—the heart has its reason which reason knows not. For with that 'eye of the heart,' so the existentialist claims, the "world of reality" which is "the world of qualities" (not of quantities) can be perceived. By such an existential approach, in Rilke's phrase, "the heart is born into the whole."

Sixth, since man's existential apprehension of reality is that of his 'human predicament,' a state of constant and, in time, irresolvable tension between 'mighty opposites'; that tension and conflict can no more be eliminated from real thinking than from real life. He is everywhere inescapably conscious of contradiction and paradox in his existential experience; it is the paradox, the clash of contraries in life which causes its passion. Therefore, for existential thinking, paradox must also be "the passion of thought" and ". . . the thinker who is devoid of paradox is like the lover who is devoid of passion—a pretty poor sort of fellow." "Take away the paradox from the thinker and you have the professor." "The paradox," Kierkegaard writes, "is really the *pathos* of the intellectual life." It is "a category of its own," with its own dialectic.

The predominance of paradox in existential thinking and in the thought of Kierkegaard is thus, in his use of it, no wilful or obscurantist irrationalism but (since it is the very texture of the 'tension of life') also the very texture of the only real reasoning which the human mind, thus conditioned by tension and paradox, can achieve. All reasoning which seeks to smooth out that paradox is therefore both unrealistic and arrogant.

Seventh, since the speech of paradox is dialectic and "existence is surely a debate," the dialectic of paradox is the proper mode of existential thought. This dialectical mode of thought has been lucidly described by Canon V. A. Demant: "Dialectical thinking . . . bids us look for the unity behind any pair of conflicting opposites and leads us to expect a re-emergence of something which will stand in relation to the original unity of both as the same and not the same, like it but on a new plane" (*Christian Polity*, pp. 152-3). It is thus "the opposite of continuity thinking which conceived change as the sum of increments of movements in one direction."

For Kierkegaard the necessity for such dialectical thinking is proved by his existential apprehension, through passion or feeling, of the double paradox of his own experience and the Incarnation, the two axiomatic facts from which all his thinking derives. Of the paradox of his own experience he has written in *Repetition* and his journals; for Christianity "the eternal truth has to come into time, this is the Paradox" (L. p. 319). Yet "if man is to receive any knowledge about the Unknown [God] he must be made to know that it is unlike him, absolutely unlike him" (P.F. pp. 36-7). "As a sinner man is separated from God by a yawning qualitative abyss" (S.D. p. 199).

Therefore, again to quote Dr. Horton, "a truly reverent theology, which knows that God is in heaven and man on earth, must never pass directly from human thought and experience to God, as Schleiermacher and Hegel sought to do. It must reverse the Hegelian dialectic . . . look for no synthesis on the earthly plane, but balance every thesis with an antithesis, every Yes with a No, and then, standing helplessly in the contradiction, appeal to God for a revelation, and act of grace" (*op. cit.,* p. 101). The dialectic of paradox thus leads direct to a doctrine of despair—despair of all attempts of the intellect or any other human faculty fully to comprehend the paradox either of man's own existence or that of God.

Existential thinking thus leads to an abyss which thought cannot cross; Kierkegaard's conclusion is that of Jan van Ruysbroek: "we must all found our lives upon a fathomless abyss"—an abyss which can only be crossed by the 'leap in the dark' which is faith, that "happy passion." But, for existential thinking, faith itself remains a 'tension.' Existential truth is thus a 'troubled truth' which points to despair and so to the decision of faith.

In the meaning of Kierkegaard 'existential thinking' is thus a mode of thought which accepts the 'tension of life' and is therefore concrete not abstract, subjective and personal not objective and impersonal, passionate (in the sense of suffering) not dispassionate, which seeks, not rational proof for thought but the assurance of faith for life and claims to explore a dimension of reality closed to the analytical reason, which carries the paradox of life into the process of living thought and employs in that thought a dialectic which the recognition of that paradox requires, which expects its synthesis, not in time and the mind of man, but in eternity and the mind of God.

It is a mode of thought which begins, as has been seen, with a religious affirmation of the existence of the self and of God, and ends with a declaration of despair and points to the 'leap' of faith as the only 'radical cure' of that despair. It is conditioned and 'operational' thinking of a kind which completely reverses the 'continuity' systems of Cartesian, idealistic and evolutionary philosophy and science. Its fundamental proposition is that "truth is bound to the situation of the knower."

It is thus, in all respects, a mode of thought which is remarkably modern and apposite to our age. It is also one which, as Dr. Tillich has pointed out, speaks the same language of thought (though not of faith) as Marxian Communism. For such a truth, "bound to the individual situation in Kierkegaard," is of the same order as the Marxian dialectic which is bound "to the social situation in Marx" (*op. cit.,* p. 63). In the case of Kierkegaard, owing to his initial and axiomatic faith not only in the existence of self but also in that of the God-man, it inevitably leads to a Christian faith reconsidered by such an 'existential thinking.' That faith remains to be explored.

3

KIERKEGAARD's criticism of contemporary Christianity and his reconception of what he believed to be a real Christianity are based upon his principle of existential thinking. It led him to a profound religious realism which could only reject much of the religion of his time as unreal, and to what may be termed an existential Christianity of the spirit.

Whatever our estimate of his criticisms and conclusions, it is difficult at this distance adequately to estimate the lonely courage or the cost of that enterprise, or to reckon its full impact upon our life, thought and faith. It was a revolution, not only in the realm of ideas but also of faith, far more radical than that which begot the French Revolution; it is one which seems only now to be approaching its high tide in the thought and faith of the Western world.

In its heyday Kierkegaard assailed the then undisputed sovereignty of the abstract, analytical, systematizing reason which, since the Renaissance and Descartes, had increasingly dominated European thought and life. He substituted for it the existential apprehension of an existing, not an ideal, reality, not by detached and isolated intellect alone, but by the whole human person in, from and for his existing conditions. He sought a living truth for life rather than an ideal but dead truth for thought, and applied the logic of that principle uncompromisingly to Christian thinking. The task involved the reconsideration from this existential angle of the whole Christian tradition which he had inherited.

It was an inevitable stage in his own progress towards spiritual maturity and literally a matter of life and death for him. He was forced by his own existential need to find a truth by which he could live and die. As for Hamlet (with whom, in the crucial and formative phase of his thought, he felt so strong an affinity), the double discovery of the guilt of his father and the impossibility of marriage with the woman he loved had destroyed his natural zest for life and will to live—what he termed his 'first immediacy.' He had been driven inwards by his fate to the dark foundations of his being and to Hamlet's ultimate agony of "to be or not to be." He had come to the abyss at which pure thought ends and to the knowledge that "suicide is the only tolerable existential consequence of pure thought" (U.P. p. 273). He must find the "secondary immediacy" of the "new man" or cease to be.

No light humanism or hedonism could for long suffice a mind so powerful, profound and acute, a nature so passionate or an integrity so exacting. His early training in Christianity, his father's influence and the force of his own conversion in 1838 had rooted within him a fundamental faith in God and the Christian vision of life which no storm could destroy. His soul, like that of the modern Western world, was too deeply christianized to permit of any pre- or sub-Christian faith. He might rebel against the form of Christianity which he encountered; he might flirt with infidelity as a gesture of defiance, but he could not really escape from the Christian pattern of life and thought. His problem was not that of proving Christian truth, but of reconciling that truth with the reality which he knew, of finding a reconception of Christianity for which "the very being of truth is life, as the truth was in Christ" (T.C. p. 201). He must reconcile Christianity with the catastrophe which had come upon him or perish. It is a pass to which many come to-day.

To do so he was forced to a ruthless search of the foundations of his thought, his faith and himself. That search led him, by way of a profound self-analysis which remarkably anticipates modern psychology, to a radical reconception of Christianity as essentially a religion of inwardness and the spirit. But much demolition had to be done before that faith could be so reconceived and recaptured.

It was, by constraint of his own inner necessity, a faith built upon foundations of dread, despair and suffering to which (like our own age) he had been driven; his regress to religion was, in his own words, "a stern education from innate dread to faith" (L. p. 129). By temperament he was peculiarly susceptible to dread. At the age of twenty-six he had written, "the whole of existence frightens me, from the smallest fly to the mystery of the Incarnation" (J. 72). He analysed it as "a desire for what one fears . . . an alien power which takes hold of the individual" (J. 105). That dread included Christianity: "I felt a dread of Christianity and yet felt myself strongly drawn to it" (J. 321). He wrote in 'Nebuchadnezzar,' evidently out of his own experience, "my thoughts terrified me, the thoughts in my mind, for my mouth was closed, and none could hear ought but a cry like that of a beast" (J. 567).

For him there lay, upon one side of that dread, despair or utter sensuality, on the other, Christianity; each was an abyss dark with dread. "There is only one proof of the truth of Christianity," he wrote, "and that, quite rightly, is from the emotions, when the dread of sin and a heavy conscience torture a man into crossing the narrow line between despair bordering upon madness and Christianity. *There* lies Christianity" (J. 926). There, in any case, lay Christianity for Kierkegaard.

This emphasis upon suffering was no mere masochism. Of that danger he was well aware. He knew his own abnormal capacity for suffering but remained convinced that the cost of the deeper insight into the Christian mystery which could alone suffice his need was a suffering proportionately more intense. He believed too that some were elected to such a martyrdom for the benefit of mankind. "In every generation," he wrote, "there are two or three who are sacrificed for the others, are led by frightful suffering to discover what redounds to the good of others. So it was in my melancholy I understood myself as singled out for such a fate" (P.V. p. 79). Nor did he conceive such suffering to be only the precondition of Christianity; he perceived that it exacted a constant and an accumulating suffering. "This is the test: to become and remain a Christian through sufferings with which no other human sufferings can compare" (T.C. p. 194).

This stress upon suffering is evidently attributable in some degree, first, to his own abnormal sensitivity and, second, to his violent reaction from the cushioned and complacent Christianity which, in his own crisis, had been found wanting. A synthetic view of the whole of his writings suggests that, to some extent, he was deliberately stressing this feature of Christianity as a 'corrective.' He was not attempting to see Christianity whole; his existential approach precluded such a purpose. He was passionately seeking a Christianity true for him and his own problems and conditions. And he was of the 'twice-born' type. It seems therefore rather as a corrective and a particular approach than as a comprehensive *summa* of the Christian faith that his "troubled truth" is to be estimated. His word is essentially prophetic: he is rather the mountain or desert guide than the settler or cultivator of the Christian inheritance. He climbs Pisgah; he does not cultivate Canaan. The religious dialectic of twice- and once-born, prophet and priest, is one surmounted only by the saints, and in this respect also Kierkegaard was a dialectician. It is precisely because he is so that he can speak so cogently to the suffering and despair of our own age.

In his stress upon the suffering which Christianity entails he counted the cost before making the venture of faith. For he conceived that venture as an act of deliberate choice: "the decisive mark of Christian suffering is that it is voluntary" (T.C. p. 111). Despair itself is an act of decision—a voluntary awareness of self and of the real and dire issues with which the Christian challenge confronts the conscious self; "choose then despair, for despair itself is a choice." And the choice of despair is also the choice of self: "when anyone chooses despair he chooses again . . . He chooses his own self." He thus chooses both 'the absolute' and himself in his 'eternal worth.' It is a double choice—the choice, not only of conscious selfhood, but also of the reality, the not-self which confronts self. In that choice and the self born from it, freedom is also born: "the individual by persisting in his despair at last wins himself," and with self, the freedom of the spirit.

But that crucial choice in which the individual and the Christian are born is also the choice of death—the death of the pseudo-self of natural life: "death comes first, you must first die to every earthly hope, every merely human reliance, you must die to your selfishness, or to the world" (L. p. 475). The life beyond that death is the life of faith, the reborn spirit-self and eternal life. "Faith, this gift of the Holy Spirit, only appears when death has come between . . . Faith is against understanding, faith is on the other side of death . . . when it is dark as the dark night . . . then comes the life-giving Spirit and brings faith" (L. p. 477).

This death from which faith and spirit are born is the death of the 'first immediacy' that the 'second immediacy' of eternal life may come to be; its anguish is the "suffering which is involved in the dying away from immediacy." This 'self-annihilation' implied the denial of the aesthetic and speculative attitude to life, of the "sophistical pleasure of imagination," the "precious heart-stimulant of poetic illusion," the "snug delight of intellectual occupations." Since he was by nature both poet and philosopher, this was the mortification which the Christian law that "he that loseth his life shall save it" primarily implied for Kierkegaard.

By 'poetry' he seems to signify the romance of the youthful imagination and by 'speculation' the wisdom of this world. These are of time; real religion is of eternity: "poesy is youth, and worldly wisdom is the fruit of the years, and religiosity is the relation to the eternal" (U.P. p. 409). For him this was no mere pietistic gesture. Such a dying demanded the sacrifice of love; he paid the price. It meant the crucifixion of the erotic, aesthetic and philosophic desires of a profoundly passionate and gifted temperament and the abandonment of the role of 'genius' (which he knew himself by nature to be) for that of 'apostle'; from that mortification also he did not flinch.

It seems clear indeed that Kierkegaard really equates 'poesy' with romanticism; to 'poetize' is to romanticize. It is rather therefore romantic poetry and the romantic attitude to life and its substitution for religion by the Romantic movement, then so dominant and still so persistent, than poetry itself which he condemns. It is, for him, the life-attitude of the 'first immediacy.' He seems to suggest, moreover, that not only he himself but European civilisation has come to the point when it must sacrifice such a romanticism or perish: "it seems," he wrote, "as though the age of poetry were past . . . That the age of poetry is past signifies that immediacy is no more" (St. pp. 74-5). He sensed, as so many have done since his day, the end of an age. But he was primarily concerned with the relation of such a 'poesy' to religion. "Poetry is idolatry refined," he declared. He believed that in the popular Christianity of his day, "Christ has been completely poetized." Therefore, for an existential Christianity, "a man must get out of the poetical and into the existential, the ethical." "Christianity is (thus) as good as done away with"; therefore, "a poet's heart must break." "Christianity conceived, every poet-existence is sin, the sin to poetize instead of to be."

Nevertheless, though Christianity thus implied for him the crucifixion of the poetry, philosophy and romance of the 'first immediacy,' it also prefigured a poetry and romance of another order, 'not of this world.' In his discourses on the lilies and the birds published after his second conversion in 1849, he proclaimed his purpose "to make evident the conflict between poetry and Christianity." "In comparison with this [natural poetry]," he declared, Christianity "is prose." Yet, he adds, it is also "precisely the poetry of eternity" (L2. p. 211). He foresaw, though he himself hardly attained, a singing of the spirit-self, the "new song" of the "new man," of the "second immediacy." Moreover, from the pyre of unregenerate romance, the romance of the life of spirit soared like the phoenix. In a paper written in 1853 he writes lyrically of this new romance which dawns for him beyond the death of the old. Its refrain is "endlessly thou art loved."

Such was his self-criticism and self-mortification, his condemnation of himself and his world. But his drastic denials of the religion and culture of his world were no arm-chair onslaughts. His world-criticism is also self-criticism; "when I want to spit," he writes, "I spit in my own face." No student of his life can deny the truth of that statement. It was a severity to which the Erinyes, the furies of his fate, implacably compelled him. Only by the severest of judgements could he save his soul in its existential extremity. "To put an end to coquetry I had to introduce severity." And the severity which he had "proved on his pulses" to be the only cautery which could cure his own inner conflict, he believed to be that by which the Christianity of his day could also alone be cured. For, in his own soul, he beheld the microcosm and mirror of his world. "For Christianity there is only one solution—severity" he concluded. For himself and for his world he must find "religiousness absolute, of a different sort from that of the parsons." His mission to men was thus formed in the matrix of his own need and suffering. He believed that his was the task of "introducing the unconditional . . . to utter the cry of alarm." It was a cry which was first sounded in and to his own soul.

The anatomy of the life of spirit thus founded upon despair and death is stated most forcibly in his *Sickness unto Death*. The book dates from the year 1848, when at last he felt justified in speaking in his own name and abandoned the veil of anonymity which, for ten years after his conversion he had felt constrained to adopt. He is now no longer exploring or discussing; he utters forthright and freely his insight into the nature of dread and despair, of the life of spirit and faith, and the dialectic of the Christian tension.

The life of spirit which he expounds proceeds from an agony of consciousness which is itself a dying, to despair, from despair to that state of tension whence the flame of spirit (which is eternal life) is struck, and from that tension to the life of the lovers of God and so to the fruits of the

Spirit, "love, joy, peace." "A believer," he declares, "is surely a lover, yea, of all lovers the most in love" (S.D. *passim*). It is upon that final and triumphant note and not, as is so often misconceived, in the long counterpoint of conflict and paradox, that Kierkegaard's real gospel comes to rest and his ultimate word is to be found.

But it is from an agony of awareness that this procession of spirit derives: "the more consciousness, the more intense the despair." From such a consciousness self and the will to choice proceed. "The more consciousness, the more will." The individual, the self, emerges in the 'instant' of choice from that chaos of consciousness upon which spirit broods.

This law of integration in the life of spirit is integral to Kierkegaard's thought. "The Christian heroism is to venture wholly to be oneself as an individual man, this definite individual man, alone before the face of God." It is a courage which demands not only decision, but also grace, the grace which "compels him to be the self he does not will to be."

But Kierkegaard is preaching much more than mere individualism. To become individual, a self, is to become 'concrete' and "to become concrete is a synthesis." The conscious man is a "synthesis of the infinite and the finite, of the temporal and the eternal, of freedom and necessity." That synthesis is the fusion of the tension and dialectic of sin and faith, despair and hope. It is a state to which few attain or, having attained, dare to endure: "many are called but few are chosen." It is, moreover, a state which an individualistic society consistently condemns: "in our age it is a crime to have spirit." Nevertheless true selfhood and spirit are indissoluble: "spirit is the self." And it is the state of true freedom: "the self is freedom." It is the only real freedom, but it is a freedom which a man buys with all that he has and is; few desire or find it. For as Nicholas Berdyaev has written, "man is a slave because freedom is difficult, whereas slavery is easy."

Yet this individual self "gained by the infinite abstraction from everything outward, this naked, abstract self," is not the final self; it is "the first form of the infinite self," embryo self and spirit, no more. And since it involves the deliberate choice of the tension of the life of faith, it is also the choice of a deeper despair than any to which the natural man is heir—a despair which "has something of the eternal in its dialectic." For it confronts the infinite and the eternal and partakes of that which it confronts.

Here is the "sickness unto death," an "agonizing contradiction . . . everlastingly to die, to die and yet not to die." It is so because the self is, in its essence, potentially eternal. Thus "despair has entered into something which cannot burn." Here we stand upon sub-Christian ground. It is the faith of Plotinus, with his "nothing that has being is destroyed"; the faith of the Bhagavad-Gîta, "never the spirit was born; the spirit shall cease to be never." It is the point at which much modern theosophy comes to rest.

But for Kierkegaard, with his Christian pre-suppositions, such despair, being a phenomenon of spirit, merges into faith. It is, as he wrote elsewhere in his journals, "that dialectical hovering which, though in fear and trembling, never despairs." In that dialectic is the paradox upon which all his thought and faith are poised. Here is the real Christian tension, the frontier between despair and faith.

The faith which thus polarizes despair is itself eternal life. In the field of that faith we pass from sub-Christian lowlands to Christian summits. For the humanist *Cogito ergo sum*, "I think therefore I am," Kierkegaard substitutes the Christion counter-creed, "to believe is to be." Belief is being. The former lives the soul-life of natural consciousness and becoming, a life transient and perishable as the flowers of the field, the other the imperishable spirit-life of being.

None the less, for our frontier state of mortality it is a faith which remains subject to the dialectic, tension and paradox whence it derives. The Christian, so Kierkegaard conceives, swings ever between faith and unfaith; his faith too is a 'swinging wicket.'

"To reach truth one must pierce through every negativity." Faith and doubt are thus linked in this humanly indissoluble dialectic. For Kierkegaard as for Emerson, "a saint is a sceptic once in every twenty-four hours."

But beyond that "swinging-wicket" of despair and faith is

that land of light where God's lovers live in an "immediacy," a new spontaneity of reborn spirit, of which the immediacy of sense is but the reflection in time. So we reach Kierkegaard's "fundamental formula" for the life of spirit: "by relating itself to its own self and by willing to be itself the self is grounded *transparently* in the Power which posited it." It is "grounded *transparently*"; Kierkegaard strains towards the dim concept of that life of the person-self or spirit, reborn from the death of the self of nature, crystal-clear, the mirror of Eternal Being, the state of saints, which is the lodestar of his "troubled truth."

Such are the dark foundations of the starry faith to which Kierkegaard's existential thinking impelled him—faith in a life of spirit (eternal life) rooted in the dialectic of despair and faith, despair which is itself sin and yet (*O felix culpa*, "O blissful guilt") the occasion of redemption, the sin which, so he declares in defiance of the humanists, "lies in the will, not in the intellect." For the Christian, he contends, it must be so, for the self born from despair is confronted with Christ, and since "a self is quantitatively what its measure is," therefore the law of spirit that "the more self the more intense the sin" comes into fatal force.

It is a despair-born faith with an obvious relevance for our own day of despair. Kierkegaard diagnoses the dialectic of such despair with an unequalled acumen. But he does more than diagnose; he points towards a Christianity of the spirit beyond a decomposing Christianity of the soul, an eternal life beyond the 'tragic climax' of the life of nature. "First death, then life"; his own laconic aphorism is the pith of his faith; he believed it to be the pith of the Gospel.

Progress, or regress, to real religion was thus for Kierkegaard a series of 'stages,' 'spheres' or 'categories.' He has variously enumerated these. "There are three stages: an aesthetic, an ethical, and a religious" (U.P. p. 261). "The spheres are thus related: immediacy; finite common sense; irony; ethics with irony as incognito; and then finally the Christian religiousness" (U.P. p. 473. note). These 'stages' or 'spheres' are milestones upon his existential progress from the life-attitude of the natural man, the poet or aesthete, to that of the man of God as he observed them in his own case. His 'categories'—the individual, dread, guilt, repetition, the "instant"—are a specifically inward and religious differentiation. The first three lead him to the threshold of real religion. Recognition of individual selfhood leads to dread and despair, dread to the sense of guilt before God, guilt to a dying to the natural self and to the repetition of that self in the spirit-self re-born in the 'instant' which is eternal life.

It was at this stage of the consciousness of guilt—the period of his father's confession and death, his breach with Regina and the "great earthquake" of his first conversions—that he grasped the category of what he called 'repetition.' Although conditioned by his own emotional catasprophe, it was in the first place as an intellectual concept that it came to him. For one who lived so much in the mind it was perhaps inevitable that a mental should precede a moral reversal. Repetition was thus for mind what conversion and regeneration are for soul. Kierkegaard was to carry that transformation from the life of mind to that of spirit, but it was in terms of thought that it must first be seized. For the 'intellectual,' which he then predominantly was, the temptation to arrest that conversion within a mind insulated from life must have been immense; it is the mark of his calibre that he could not be content till he had lived what he had thought.

It is in this concept of repetition that the clue to Kierkegaard's reconception of Christianity is to be found. It is also here that his message comes with a special relevance to that class of 'intellectuals' who are so numerous in latter-day European culture. For such citizens of the 'kingdom of the mind' a Christianity couched in terms of emotion or morality makes no immediate appeal. They too must first be converted in mind if Christianity is to have meaning for them. The concept of repetition implies such a conversion of mind —a reversed life-view. In his book *Repetition* Kierkegaard gave to the world an intellectual's 'pilgrim's progress' or regress.

But though it leads to a primarily intellectual *volte face,* the book was forged in his personal emotional agony. He had realized, as he wrote in his journal, that he was "an eternity too old for" Regina. None the less the poet and romantic in him mourned for her loss and, recollecting his "first, fine, careless rapture" of love, longed for its repetition. In that very recollection he finds only the "rank weed of memory" which "strangled every thought at birth" (*Repetition, passim*). It is notable that it is *thought* rather than feeling which is strangled. It was thus in his thinking that he is first driven to seek deliverance. For if he could no longer think he could no longer live. By nature and nurture he was a disciple of Descartes. So fate forced melancholy to despair. While he waits and hopes, Regina marries; and, with a devastating disillusionment, he finds that "all his sentiments were bosh," and in that despair finds the type of all human despair. The "melancholy of repetition" is a mirage; repetition seems no more than myth.

The Regina episode precipitated a conflict which had long been latent; it was primarily a conflict of attitudes. "His nature," he writes, "had become split." He is two beings, the 'observer,' whom he names 'Constantine Constantius,' who tells the tale and the young man in love of whom the tale is told. These two selves contend within him and typify his own conflicting life-attitudes. The 'observer' is the "cold disciple of reflection," a stoic armed against immediate contact with life with the "elasticity of irony," who can stand aside from life and view it dispassionately. It was a pose natural and congenial to the young poet and philosopher, and one which, in his reprobate phase, he had deliberately cultivated. But the 'observer' avoids existential experience of life, therefore he cannot comprehend a religion relevant for reality. For Kierkegaard now perceives that it is only when "Stoicism has stepped aside" that a man is confronted with religious decision. And now, for him, nothing short of real religion can suffice his need.

In the 'observer' Kierkegaard is thus embodying the detached, speculative thought, culture and religiosity which he was so fiercely to assail in the professors, dons and parsons whom he denounced. The ferocity of the attack is the measure of his realization of his own participation in the guilt which he condemned. He was castigating the speculative philosopher, the romantic poet, the ineffectual don, the un-realist parson in himself. He was, in fact, denouncing the *trahison des clercs,* the betrayal of life and the unlettered by the intellectuals which Julian Benda condemned in our own day. For Kierkegaard that betrayal lay precisely in this aesthetic, philosophic, religious detachment from real life to which he himself was peculiarly prone. It is again a diag-nosis of intellectualism which anticipated the modern repu-diation of the 'highbrow.' But where most modern criticism of that disease of spirit can only condemn, Kierkegaard probes to its roots in himself and, from his own agony of self-awareness, wrests what he conceives to be the remedy.

His passion was too poignant, his despair too deep, his integrity too steely to permit him to take any final refuge in the adoption of such an 'observer' role towards life and love. The lover in him could not thus be repressed. In this intense inner drama the simple humanity of the "young man in love" is thrown into sharp contrast to the 'observer.' His 'immediacy' cannot be quelled with Stoicism; he must live, not look on at life. He retains, against all that "pure reason" may contend, his original 'immediacy,' his direct contact with life, as, within Kierkegaard's own intellectual detachment, passion burned on. Like Job, the lover will not renounce his 'integrity' or decline the conflict of life and love. He continues to yearn for the repetition of first love and to bear the brunt of recollection's melancholy and de-spair. Like Job, he endures to the end of his agony and be-wilderment and accepts a probation which he cannot com-prehend. Like Job, he receives his answer. It is, as for Job, the answer of neither logic nor morality; it is the reality of repetition.

This conflict of consciousness, so modern in grain, is so piognantly conveyed as, for the reader aware of what is involved, to be almost intolerable. The failure of love takes the dimensions of failure in life. When raised, as Kierke-gaard must raise it, to the level of metaphysics and religion, the melancholy of recollection becomes such a despair and life-loathing as that which darkens the tragic period of

Shakespeare. Mere recollection becomes a nightmare; the 'repetition' dimly surmised is beyond his reach. The tension can only be relieved by a 'thunderstorm'—an act of God—for he knows himself to be at the end of his powers. The storm breaks; he learns that Regina is married; "it came as a thunderstorm after all."

The 'thunderstorm' spells for Kierkegaard transcendence and miracle. It is that which cleaves the skies of his consciousness from beyond his ken or his expectation. The stroke which, through no volition of his own, destroys his 'first immediacy' and annihilates his dreams of repetition of love, also reveals to him the nature of the 'second immediacy,' the spontaneity of the 'new man' and the nature of a real repetition. His cleft consciousness is suddenly made whole. "I am again myself," he writes, "here I have the repetition, I understand everything, and existence seems more beautiful than ever." "The discord in my nature is resolved, I am again unified."

In this experience of repetition he knows the double benediction of Job; all that he had counted lost he finds again. He has regained his very self, his very life, out of despair and death. It is indeed a double boon, for not only has he found the 'new man,' but he has regained the 'old man' reborn; he knows both 'immediacies,' that of innocence and that of experience, in memory and in faith, in recollection and in repetition. But it is repetition in the sphere of spirit, not of flesh; "only spiritual repetition is possible." It is of eternity, not of time; "eternity . . . is the true repetition." So he can go forward, in "fear and trembling," yet "rejoicing in repetition."

Such an acutely personal experience must remain, in the main, incommunicable. Its reality can only be gauged by its results. Although emotional in origin, it was, as has been noted, at this stage chiefly as an intellectual illumination that the concept of repetition burst upon Kierkegaard's brain. Had it remained so it might well be dismissed as self-dramatization. But it did not; what he saw in mind, he lived out in person. And here is the soil from which his faith flowers. It is from this experience that his conviction of the transcendence of God seems to be derived. For he is utterly sure that the revelation which has come upon him is unconditioned and uncaused by any human causation. Like Cortez on Darien he gazes upon a new world. It is a new world of the spirit and eternity which he hails with an amazed exultation eloquent of profound conviction.

It is thus as a new vision of the meaning of life in the mind that, at first and in this book, he experiences this *volte face,* this reversal of attitude. "Repetition is a new category," he declares, a new world-view. The full significance of the Christian world-view has suddenly dawned upon his mind and he realizes the complete reversal of conception and attitude which it implies. "Recollection is the pagan life-view; repetition is the modern life view," he writes. By 'modern' he evidently means 'Christian.' "Recollection" affirms that "all that is has been"; it can therefore never be repeated; "the things which I have seen I now can see no more" (Wordsworth). "Repetition," on the other hand, "affirms that existence which has been now becomes." Essence and existence, being and becoming, are made one in Christ. For being, the Alpha and the Omega, the eternal Christ, becomes in time and flesh. Thus, in the category of repetition, "we look before and after and pine," not for "what is not" (as for Shelley and in pagan recollection), but for what "was, is and evermore shall be," by virtue of the Incarnation. The category of repetition is thus the category of the incarnate Christ.

Here is the Christian paradox which is the 'absurd' of faith, but it is a paradoxical faith which illuminates life, out of despair begets conviction and from futility meaning. He labours almost breathlessly to enumerate the attributes and implications of this Christian repetition. "It signifies freedom"; "it is consciousness raised to the second power"; it is "a *sine qua-non* of every dogmatic problem"; it is "always a transcendence." "True repetition is eternity"; it is "to receive oneself again"; it is "the life of spirit" in which "the germinal sprout comes last" (thus reversing the order of natural life); it is peace, for the "religious individual" which repetition creates "reposes in himself." In fact for Kierkegaard the category of repetition implies the second Eden, the "immediacy of the new man."

Here then is the crux of his existential Christianity, the watershed which divides the pagan from the Christian life-view. For in such Christian repetition the *Ave atque Vale,* "hail and farewell," to life characteristic of the pagan (and pseudo-Christian) attitude to life is reversed to a Christian *Vale atque Ave,* "farewell and hail." In the recollection of the former attitude man can only look back with an infinite regret to the first Eden of his unfallen state, of his innocency. But the Christian who knows repetition looks both back and forward. Recollection is thus the mode of immanence, repetition that of transcendence.

Thus out of the affirmation of the individual self which, when confronted with reality, begets dread and, when confronted with Christ, guilt, dawns the third category of repetition, and in that transition the foundations of Kierkegaard's faith are laid. It is as yet a faith of concept rather than conduct, and one of which the implications have yet to be lived out. But, having attained to this category of repetition, Kierkegaard knows his direction. He has heard his "word"; in the doing of that "word" he learns the doctrine of that Christianity of the spirit which remains to be explored.

4

KIERKEGAARD'S existential rediscovery of Christianity led him to a religion of 'inwardness' and the spirit, too, in the terms of St. Paul's antimony, a rejection of a Christianity 'after the flesh'—a Christianity come to terms with the life of this world—and the search for a Christianity 'after the spirit.' A religious realism which began with a realistic acceptance of human conditions of time and 'the flesh' led, by its own inexorable logic, to an absolute necessity for their fulfilment, transcension and transformation in the life of spirit. For a candid confrontation of those conditions and of the 'inwardness' of the human heart reveal a profound conflict and contradiction within them, a 'law of Abraxas,' [1] a "grain of evil seed sown in the heart of Adam from the beginning," a "leaven of unrighteousness" by reason of which, in their own unredeemed cycle of causality, they come, in the end, to an inevitable corruption. 'Flesh,' save for 'spirit,' is doomed. But the reality of spirit is reached, not in spite of, but through and beyond the reality of 'the flesh.' There is the core of Kierkegaard's reconception of Christianity. It was not a new but an old treasure of Christion truth newly interpreted.

Only a conception of spirit at least as concrete and realistic as the conditions and sin which it transcends and saves could suffice for such a salvation. Kierkegaard's Christianity is thus rooted in a profound realism. For him such a realism implied an inwardness growing continually more searching and intense. For he could not forget that "the kingdom of Heaven is *within*." It is a realism so distasteful to man, for whom the outward life is familiar and secure but the inward obscure and haunted, that only a catastrophe threatening his very existence can compel the soul to confront it. Such a catastrophe cleft Kierkegaard's own 'inwardness'; to-day it assails our world both without and within. In the space of a century the conflict and calamity which he divined within the soul of Western man have become externalized in a chaos of world-conditions. That is his real significance for our time. It is when we read his inward agony with reference to the radical revolution in which we live that the study of the man kindles into a biting pertinence for the problems which beset us.

His main and constant 'cry of alarm' is 'look within.' But his conception of 'inwardness' is far removed from quietism or a pietistic spirituality; it is a passionately concerned intensity which is the seed-plot of spirit. "Christianity is spirit, spirit is inwardness, inwardness is subjectivity, subjectivity is

---

[1] "The law of contradiction in all man's sublunary aims" (*Secular Despair and Christian Faith;* by Alec Vidler. p. 18).

essentially passion and in its maximum an infinite, personal, passionate interest in one's eternal happiness" (U.P. p. 33). The statement is one which calls for comment from the context of his other utterances. For Kierkegaard is constantly conscious that his experience is microcosmic, that his private happiness or suffering are also, in some sense, those of mankind; his preoccupation with his own inner drama has always this universal connotation. His real concern is always rather with man than self, but his existentialism implied that it was in the study of himself that he could best know mankind. Moreover it is no unsanctified but a holy and disciplined passion which he commends—a passion for the truth, for Christ, God only and eternal life. For what he termed 'unshaven passion'—the passion of the unbridled senses—he held no brief.

Thus the essential impulse of real religion is for him a passionate and personal concern. And passion is suffering. "Passion implies pathos, an infinite susceptibility to suffering . . . action in inwardness is suffering . . . it is for this reason that suffering is the highest form of inwardness" (U.P. p. 388). Thus inwardness spells a suffering growing ever more intense as inwardness drives more deep. It is no interior life guarded and secluded from life's storms and actuality, but a deepening, through an existential experience neither denied nor despised but embraced to the uttermost, to the essence of existence, to the quick of consciousness.

Inwardness therefore involves risk. "Without risk there is no faith, the greater the risk the greater the faith; the more objective security the less inwardness" (U.P. p. 188). "Faith is precisely the contradiction between the infinite passion of the individual's inwardness and the objective uncertainty. If I am capable of grasping God objectively, I do not believe, but precisely because I cannot do this I must believe" (U.P. 182). Inwardness demands daring: "to dare . . . is Christianity." His characteristic simile for this venture of inwardness and faith is that of the deep sea. To be "in danger, above seventy fathoms of water, many miles from all help, there to be joyful—that is great" (S.E. p. 425). For him, a real Christianity involves embarking upon an ocean of intellectual and spiritual uncertainty and abandonment of the safe ports of probability. "All religious (not to say Christian) adventure is on the further side of probability, is by letting go of probability" (S.E. p. 116).

It is significant that Kierkegaard's instinct should have chosen the simile of the sea; for modern psychology, then in its infancy, finds, like primordial mythology, in the sea the universal archetype for the unconscious; it was from the 'great waters' of the underworld that Babylonian mythology derived life and wisdom. For that which Kierkegaard styles 'inwardness' evidently in part corresponds to that which modern psychology calls the unconscious or the subconscious. He plumbed indeed to depths of spirit far below the levels of the psyche to which psychology as such can do no more than point, but that inward Odyssey, being existential, traversed regions of the subconscious to which then there was no map.

In his own existential experience he had known to his cost the perilous nature of that quest—the demonic forces of the unconscious released in such an inwardness which psychology has since more fully revealed. "What the inner voice brings close to us," Professor C. G. Jung has lately written, "is generally something that is not good, but evil . . . In a most unaccountable way the lowest and the highest, the best and the most atrocious, the truest and the falsest are mingled together in the inner voice, which opens up to us an abyss of confusion, deception and despair" (*The Integration of Personality*, passim). Such are the perils of inwardness; Kierkegaard knew them well. It is for fear of them he held that men take shelter in the security of convention, objectivity and abstract dogma which, to quote Professor Jung again, "advises us not to have an unconscious." But Kierkegaard, believing with Lascelles Abercrombie that "in the religious life, prudence is the deadly sin," scorned such securities of soul.

These were perils, now in some degree known and charted, which Kierkegaard braved a century ago. He did not escape unscathed. "I only have," he writes in his journal, "pale, bloodless, hard-lived midnight shapes to fight against to which I myself give life and existence." He is pursued by dread and lives his inner life in a constant 'fear and trembling.' "It [dread] grips me with its terror," he confesses, "I cannot and must not flee from it, I must endure the thought; then I find a religious composure and then I am as free and happy as spirit" (St. p. 340). "The whole content of my being shrieks in contradiction against itself" (R. p. 114-5). These are symptoms to which modern psychiatry is accustomed. Kierkegaard confronted them without the aids of psychiatry and found his cure in 'God only.'

In the light of modern psychological research Kierkegaard's doctrine and practice of inwardness thus assume in some degree the character of an extension of the Christian consciousness into the regions of the subconscious. With a remarkable pre-view of our own new awareness of those 'great waters' below the surface of our conscious life, it is as though he both sought and carried the Cross into that underworld and, in daring that perilous descent into his own inwardness, followed his Lord into a 'nether world,' a *She'ôl* of the soul to which then there was no Christian chart. He thus obeyed the injunction of another master of instinctive Christian psychology, St. Augustine—*descendite ut ascendatis,* "descend that you may ascend."

His intuition of the need for such an inwardness was in itself prophetic. He seems to have been aware of an impending crisis in the history of the human consciousness, that Western civilization was nearing (it is now a commonplace) the 'end of an age' and doomed either to a new mutation or to destruction. He saw that the crust of our culture, morality and religion had become too brittle to contain the mounting inner fires; he proclaimed the 'bankruptcy of Europe' and the danger of a demonic possession which has now passed into history. He was convinced that Christianity alone could control that chaos, but only a Christianity with the courage to descend and confront it in the inward world, and that the established religion of his day was selling the passes of Christendom for the sake of comfort and security. It is a diagnosis which many have made to-day. "Everywhere else," as Peter Drucker wrote in *The End of Economic Man* in 1940, "demonic forces roam outside the natural order."

Such a psychological view of Kierkegaard's word and work explains much that otherwise seems obscure—the incomprehension and hostility of a church which either would not or could not face the uncomfortable vistas to which he pointed, the mounting violence of his denunciation of an unrealism which, to his insight, was dastardly and incomprehensible, the stubborn (and still persisting) attempt of vested interests in church and state to discount the dangerous discredit to their status which is prophecy implied and to muffle his cry of alarm. For man fears nothing so much as the unknown, and they who live, both economically and spiritually, by the church are very loth to admit that its fabric is rotten. It is more comfortable to dwell in the past than to face a menacing future, and to cultivate the sown lands of the conscious than to explore the wilds of the subconscious. Churchmen can be as tenacious of spiritual as laymen of economic security. Kierkegaard had looked into deeps of the soul of which his contemporaries were either unaware or afraid; he could not go back, and they dared not go forward.

A century later the inwardness of which he was then a solitary pathfinder and herald has become an acknowledged and, to some extent, an explored area of the human psyche. But it has not yet been christianized, and it seems as true today as when Kierkegaard wrote that a Christianity which fails in that mission will have only a failing message for a world now forced into awareness of the facts which he foretold. Can Christianity overcome that inward world also? Such seems to be the essential challenge of Kierkegaard's doctrine of inwardness to the Christianity of our own as of his day. He proclaimed triumphantly that it could, but only at the price of a new and costly awareness, inwardness and religious realism.

From such an angle many of what might otherwise seem unjustifiable over-emphases in his writings become understandable. He saw that venture of inwardness as a quite blind 'leap in the dark'; for him it was so. And he believed that only a rare knightly heroism of spirit could undertake it; for such a pioneer venture into an unknown dimension it was and always is so. Such forerunners are ever "knights of infinity," Don Quixotes of the spirit, knights "of reflection . . . of the sorrowful countenance." It was indeed only such a reckless and knightly courage which could then dare such a 'leap' from the security of the conscious to the unknown deeps of the subconscious, from the dimension of soul to that of spirit, from rational and dogmatic proofs and probabilities to the 'absurd' and the 'offence' of faith-knowledge.

He is very insistent upon the "yawning abyss" between these opposites. "There is no direct transition (by logical proof)," he writes, "to the thing of becoming a Christian." "Faith is against understanding, faith is on the other side of death." And becoming Christian and faith were, for Kierkegaard, coterminous with inwardness. For him the only *vraie vérité*, the ultimate Truth, was inward. Therefore a Christianity confined to the extroverted life, the beaten tracks of consciousness and tradition and the security of convention, were for him utterly unreal. Therefore for him "Christianity doesn't exist" (S.E. p. 155).

Such intransigent declarations are characteristic of Kierkegaard's prophecy. They are doubtless in part to be attributed to his sense of urgency and the need for stabbing the Christianity of his time 'broad awake.' Prophecy and prudence rarely march together. But from the angle of the psychological *éclaircissement* since his day which has been considered, it seems possible for a balanced modern criticism to mitigate his condemnation of 'once-born,' conventional and conservative Christianity, his emphasis upon the almost impossible heroism required for the venture of faith, and the gulf between rational and faith knowledge. In a fully catholic Christianity there is room for both the once- and the twice-born types of piety, for extraverted and conservative and for an introverted and creative Christianity; it is a wisdom which is "justified of all her children." The conquest of the subconscious is no longer altogether the 'forlorn hope' which it was for Kierkegaard, and the gulf between rational and faith-knowledge perhaps less unbridgable than he assumed.

Such considerations, though they may discount some over-emphasis, do not minimize the fortitude of spirit which such a venture of faith and inwardness implied for Kierke-gaard in his "pre-psychological" age, or the significance and relevance of his conception of a Christianity of inwardness for an age committed either to a conquest of its own sub-conscious forces or to conquest by them. And while psychol-ogy wrestles with this crucial problem of the underworld of the soul of man, established Christianity to-day seems as prone to evade the issue as in his day in Denmark.

But his conception of inwardness has far more than a merely psychological content; it plumbs to deeper levels than those of the soul of man. His real and ultimate wrestling was upon the plane of spirit. He affirmed that "the move-ment of the spirit was inward," that "Christianity is precisely an affair of spirit, and so of subjectivity, and so of inward-ness," and that "to be spirit—this is man's invisible glory." Psychology can only analyse and diagnose the diseases of the soul; the synthesis, the making whole, healthy, holy, of the soul is in the power of spirit alone. "Into this night of hope-lessness," he wrote in 1851 when he had "ventured far out" in the life of spirit, "comes then the life-giving Spirit and brings hope, for according to that merely natural hope there was no hope left, and so this is hope against hope" (S.E. p. 101). It is at this point, therefore, that he has a word still more relevant for our condition for which even the 'new psychology' can offer no cure. Kierkegaard pointed to an inwardness more profound than that of psychology and pro-claimed (what Christianity has always professed) that the only salvation for soul is spirit.

In this deep spiritual inwardness it would seem that Kier-kegaard is of the company of the great Christian mystics. Yet the name of mystic was one which he hotly repudiated. For mysticism, as he conceived it, was a short-cut to salvation for which a real Christianity gave no warrant. He rejects with an equal ardour all claim to a mystical revelation on his own part. "I beg the reader," he writes in his autobiographical sketch *The Point of View,* "not to think of revelations or anything of the sort, for with me everything is dialectical."

He will not admit to any moment of mystical unity or ecstasy; for him all spiritual experience is strictly conditioned and subject to the tensions, dialectic and paradox of mortal life. The 'unitive state' which some forms of mysticism claim in the flesh is for him an arrogant defiance of the dualism which constituted man's divinely appointed probation in time.

Yet the journal entries which describe his moments of conversion suggest experiences as mystical as those recounted in similar terms by St. Paul or Pascal. In 1838 he writes, "There is an undescribable joy which kindles us as inexplicably as the apostle's outburst," and in 1848, "My whole nature is changed . . . I must speak" (J. 207 & 747). These are utterances with the authentic mystical ring. What Rudolf Otto has called "first-type mysticism . . . withdrawal from all outward things, retreat into the ground of one's own soul, knowledge of the secret depth and the possibility of turning in upon one's self" seems altogether consonant with Kierkegaard's experience and doctrine of inwardness.

A few of the characteristic sayings of the great mystics, moreover, suffice to demonstrate the affinity between Kierkegaard's inwardness and such mysticism. "The secret way lies inward . . . the swiftest steed to bear you to your goal is suffering; none shall ever taste eternal bliss but those who stand with Christ in depths of bitterness" (Eckhart). "By love may he be gotten and holden but by thought never" (*The Cloud of Unknowing*). "God works in us from within outwards . . . we must all found our lives upon a fathomless abyss" (*Ruysbroek*). "He made his understanding blind, not venturing to apply an instrument so vile to a matter so high"; "I die because I do not die" (St. John-of-the-Cross). Such sayings evidently speak the very language of Kierkegaard and echo his thought.

If the mystic, as the derivation of the word denotes, is one who closes lips, eyes and ears to outward things that he may look and hear within, then Kierkegaard's Christianity of inwardness must be classed as of the true mystical tradition. But with a more vaunting and specious form of mysticism which denies the reality of the ostensible world and

the self, and claims immediate union with Deity, Kierkegaard has nothing in common. His repudiation of mysticism
seems, indeed, like many more of his more trenchant
utterances, to be rather a corrective of a false than denial of
a true theology. In the proper, though not in the Christianly
improper sense of the term, he was a mystic. He seeks and
finds reality within, and Schweitzer's conclusion that "all
logical thinking ends in mysticism" seems accurately to describe his own attitude towards all speculative philosophy
and dogmatic theology.

The inwardness which Kierkegaard sought was thus no
fantasy-world escaping from the conditions of human existence but that of a reality more real and profound than the
established Christianity of his day (or, it may be, of our
own) could comprehend. Of an escapist inwardness he writes
with the full edge of his irony, of pseudo-Christians "christianly keeping their Christianity in hidden inwardness and
employing their natural gifts and talents to succeed in the
world" (T.C. p. 219). And again, "One should deny oneself
in hidden inwardness, in hidden inwardness renounce the
world and all that is of the world, but (for God's sake! shall
I say?) one must not let it be observed. In this way established Christianity becomes a collection of what one might
call honorary Christians" (T.C. p. 246).

Kierkegaard's doctrine of inwardness is thus, in Professor
W. E. Hocking's phrase, that of a "deepening to the essence"
of Christianity, below soul to spirit, below becoming to
being. It was a religion of the essence, the inward being, of
life that he conceived Christianity to be. It was thus not only
the unconditional which he sought through and beyond conditioned existence but also, through time, the eternal. For
him inwardness and the "instant" were of the same eternal
order. But, so he tirelessly reiterates, there are for man no
short cuts to that state of essence, being, spirit, eternal life.
To reach the unconditioned one must, in Charles Lamb's
wise words, "accept one's conditions"; to attain to eternal
life one must accept the limitations of time. An inwardness
which pretended to despise the conditions of mortal life, a
mysticism which claimed eternal life within our mortal time,

were equally anathema to his conception of Christianity. It is, again, in that existential realism that he speaks the idiom of our own age and with that conception of a Christianity of the spirit seen only "through the lattice of our flesh" (St. Augustine) that he offers the cure for its disease.

At root the two conceptions meet. For Kierkegaard the 'instant' was "not an atom of time but of eternity." But it flowers in the womb of time. "It is short, indeed, and temporal, as every instant is, gone like all instants, the following instant, and yet it is decisive, and yet it is full of eternity. Such an instant must have a special name, let us call it *the fullness of time*" (L. pp. 121 & 312). It is a conception which anticipates much modern speculation upon the relation of time and eternity. In his Bampton lectures on Time and Eternity in Christian Thought, Dr. F. H. Brabant conceived of eternity in the same sense: "In the deepest and truest sense of the word 'Eternity,' we find that the emphasis is much less upon lastingness or duration than upon completeness or perfection."

Moreover, for Kierkegaard, the 'instant,' like inwardness, also implies the 'leap' of faith. "The instant does not need to be long, for it is a leap," he writes. And, like inwardness, it also implies paradox. "If only the Instant is posited, the Paradox is granted." "An instant," comments Dr. Lowrie, "if it is only an instant in time, is 'filled with emptiness.' What fills it with eternity is the apprehension of the paradox that God became man. It is then the decisive Instant of faith." And that instant is eternity; it is the instant of repetion' in which past, present and future are fused in an 'immortal moment.'

It is a conception which, like that of inwardness, is constant and crucial for Kierkegaard. It was by this name that he called the series of pamphlets with which in 1855, the year of his death, he launched his attack upon the established church. This for him was what "to work in the instant" had come to mean; it is characteristic of the man and his thought that he should have envisaged his own ultimate 'instant' in the terms of a strictly conditioned task—that of disabusing his generation of "the illusion of being Christians and the·belief that the parson's game of Christianity is Christianity" (L. p. 577). There, at last, lay his own "leap in the dark," his decisive, existential 'instant.' It synchronized with his leap into the darkness of death.

For Kierkegaard the 'instant' thus implied, as the derivation of the word infers, a standing within. It is the opposite of 'ecstasy,' a standing outside of existence. Kierkegaard's Christianity was one of instancy, not ecstasy. In the instant a man, standing within his time and existence, takes his stand in the immutable and eternal essence or being which underlie them. Existence is a standing out or forth from that pure being; the instant is a return to it, a standing within it. Thus the existential movement, according to Kierkegaard, is from and through existence to the "instant," and that movement is one of inwardness. Both conceptions turn, like the compass-needle to the north, to the 'still Centre' of our time and existence.

For him that conversion or turning again to the soul's true north is essentially what he called "the thing of becoming a Christian"; for Christianity and for him, that true north, that 'still Centre' of the instant was, as for St. Paul, *in* Christ. But since our life here is a life of becoming, he dare not affirm that he is, only that he seeks and hopes to become a Christian. The instant is thus a fundamental Christian category. Paul Claudel wrote that "Eternity and Resurrection are ceaselessly renewed in the Instant" (*Le Père Humilié*), and in that saying epitomized what seems to have been the significance of this conception of the "instant" for Kierkegaard. In that instant the inward and the eternal meet in a timeless here-and-now reached through and within, yet ever beyond, our space-time continuum. There is the point of intersection where the longtitudinal line of human life, love (*eros*), thought and time meet the vertical line of eternity and the downpouring love (*agape*) of God. For the Christian, for Kierkegaard, that instant of intersection, is the cross of the incarnate Christ. There is the paradox of faith.

His conception of this inward meeting of time and eternity in an Instant filled with eternity, the fulfilment and perfection of time and existence, is one which grows increasingly salient in modern thought and feeling. It has been echoed and expressed in lapidary language by T. S. Eliot in his group of war-born poems, *Four Quartets*. For Eliot as for Kierkegaard, reality and eternity meet within at "the still point of the turning world" and—

> "The point of intersection of the timeless
> With time . . ."

For each the way to that instant lies inward:

> "into another intensity
> For a further union, a deeper communion."

And for each that way lies—

> "Through the dark cold and the empty desolation . . ."

And for each the apprehension (or in Kierkegaard's language, the 'appropriation') of that "timeless moment" "is the occupation for a saint." The categories of inwardness, repetition and the instant alike, for Kierkegaard, point to the necessity for sancitity and the life of spirit in existence. That is the only way to eternal life; it is the way of inwardness. It was a way which he strove to follow "not only in lip but in life." In the doing he learned his doctrine of the life of spirit.

5

KIERKEGAARD'S reconception of Christianity led him from, in his own terms, 'reflection' to the 'new immediacy,' from the region of abstract speculation to that of a dynamic and concrete faith, and from faith to following, to a way and a life. That process from thought to deed and faith to following is implicit in his existentialism, and it is in obedience to its intrinsic logic that, as he matures, his writings become increasingly concerned with, not the theory, but the practice "of the presence of God."

For his chief 'corrective' to a Christianity for which 'pure faith' (like 'pure reason') had become increasingly escapist and unreal was his passionate affirmation that "belief is being." With that truth he sought to salve the fatal spirit-matter, faith-works, contemplation-action, religious-secular dualism which, so he conceived, divided and paralysed Christendom at its source. He was not content to diagnose that disease and propound its Christian cure; he applied his 'corrective' to his own Christian living. From the date of his second conversion in 1848 till his death seven years later his prime concern is with the Christian life, the personal 'appropriation' of Christian truth and the application of his faith to his own conditions.

That faith had, indeed, originated in 'reflection' as an intellectual revelation, a world-view. But it had been forged in passion, not only of thought but also of feeling; the tempered blade was not merely a formula for mind but a living force for life. Since for him faith thus implied living and believing being, faith was also for him a thing never finished but always, like life itself, in process of becoming. Therefore he disclaimed the possession of faith just as he disclaimed the name of Christian. "I have constantly said," he wrote, " 'I have not faith'—like a bird's anxious flight before the approaching tempest, so I have expressed the presentiment of stormy confusion; I have not faith . . . there sits in a cloister cell like Luther, or in a remote chamber, a solitary man in fear and trembling. There indeed lies the truth" (S.E. p. 44).

Thus for Kierkegaard faith itself is existential—neither intellectual assent nor dogmatic acquiescence, but a life: "faith is a new life" (T.C. p. 121). It is "immediacy after reflection," the "second immediacy" of the "new man." Being a mode of life and not merely of thought, it is rooted in existential passion. "Faith is a passion," he declared, "the highest passion in the sphere of human subjectivity" (U.P. p. 118). It is a passion, not prudence, and therefore, like all passion, ready for risk; he speaks of the "foolhardiness of faith." "Without risk there is no faith, and the greater the risk the greater the faith" (U.P. 118).

He thus shares with Pascal the conception of faith as a wager. The object of that wager of faith is "the absurd"— the fact that "the eternal truth has come into being in time, that God has come into being." For Kierkegaard it is precisely this 'leap' beyond reason, this wager upon 'the absurd,' which constitutes Christian faith. More, it is the task of faith to seek 'the absurd.' "Faith has two tasks: to take care in every moment to discover the improbable, the paradox; and then to hold it fast with the passion of inwardness" (U.P. p. 209). Just as true Christianity requires a reversal, conversion, *volte face* in life, so in mind; as the 'new life' is contrary to the old life of flesh, so those who are "renewed in the spirit of [their] minds" base their thinking upon propositions which are paradoxical and absurd to unregenerate reason. They must not only accept, they must seek for a truth which offends the natural mind and the 'laws of thought.' For reason cannot grasp what faith believes" (J. 1033).

This emphasis upon the paradoxical and the absurd must, for a catholic criticism, be gauged in consideration of Kierkegaard's reaction from the prevalent rationalism of his day and his urgent sense of the need for a 'corrective' which if it were to disturb complacency, could not be couched in moderate terms. It was not his task, as he conceived it, to seek for a synthesis or *summa* of rational and faith knowledge, but to declare that which the thought and theology of his day tended to deny, that between human reason and divine truth a great gulf is fixed, that it is not by "taking thought" that man finds God, that faith is infinitely removed from mere intellectual assent or doctrine. "The object of faith is not a doctrine," he declares, "but God's reality in existence as a particular individual" (U.P. p. 290).

Since the object of faith is itself a "living God," the faith which meets such a God must also itself be a vital process, dynamic not static, compact, not only of thought, but of passion and will; "faith is self-active." By virtue of the correspondence with the Creator which it establishes it is itself creative. In a sense and from the manward (though not the Godward) angle it creates the God in whom it trusts and a co-ordination of contraries which God alone can cause.

"Faith is the anticipation of the eternal which holds the factors together, the cleavages of existence." And it is only in faith that God exists for man at all. For "God does not *exist*, he only is . . . he can only exist in faith" (J. 605).

Faith is thus the medium in which alone a God of pure being can be known in our life of becoming, of existential experience. But such an incarnation of the divine in human apprehension is something which, though he may and must go out to meet the miracle by an act of will, man cannot cause. Therefore "faith itself is a miracle." It is not gained; it is given. Miguel de Unamuno is thus echoing and amplifying the thought of Kierkegaard (whose leadership he acknowledged) concerning faith when he writes that "faith in its essence is simply a matter of will" and that "faith in God is born of love for God" and is "a movement of the soul towards a practical truth, towards a person, towards something that makes us not only comprehend life, but makes us live" (*The Tragic Sense of Life*, pp. 114, 150, 191).

It is, indeed, as an act of love, and so of passion, that Kierkegaard conceived Christian faith, and it is only by the analogy of love that it can really be interpreted. He turns, like Pascal, from the aridities of scholastic theology to the *connaissances du coeur*, the intuitions of the heart and an intelligence *vive et lumineuse*, live and luminous, by return to its existential sources. This ardent, loving and living faith in a loving and living God is, in fact, the faith of love —that new life of utter trust and new-born understanding which every lover knows, a faith which lives and feeds on love, "a love which talks with better knowledge and knowledge with dearer love" (*Measure for Measure*). Such a love-faith and love-knowledge are ever, for the uninitiated, a faith in 'the absurd' and the paradoxical; it is a faith which, in some sense, seems to create its own object and its own co-ordination of previous contraries.

Such a love-faith is therefore a living faith which must, of its own nature, reproduce itself in a life which flowers only in love and life, which harvests its own comprehension of that which, for the loveless, seems absurd as it loves and lives, which learns its doctrine not by abstract thinking, but in the doing of love's will. It is a secret wisdom common to all the wise in Christ (and in love). Kierkegaard is only repeating in the idiom of his own age a knowledge of the real nature of Christian faith which practising Christians such as Wyclif, with his "Love and good life are needful to right belief," have proclaimed throughout the Christian centuries. Therefore, for Kierkegaard, faith passes beyond the ethical to the religious category; "the oposite of sin is not virtue . . . the opposite of sin is faith" (S.D. p. 132).

It is a dynamic and existential conception of the nature of faith which seems indeed to harmonize with that of the Bible where we are told not to know, but to love God, and faith is always envisaged as a creative force. "If ye will not have faith ye shall not have staith"—so runs an early English version of the saying from Isaiah (vii. 9); faith is that which lays the foundations of life. "The just shall live by his faith," says Habakkuk in a prophecy echoed by St. Paul; faith is the fountain, not merely of thought, but of life. In the gospels and the words of Jesus faith is always the concomitant power, and the writer of the Epistle to the Hebrews chronicles the fruits of faith as not theories, theologies or dogmatic rectitude, but 'mighty works.' Like the biblical conception of the Memra-Word of God, faith, in the Bible, as for Kierkegaard, is "a concrete event, a personal communication . . . bringing salvation" (*Communion in the Messiah*, by Lev Gillet, pp. 111-113). Kierkegaard's doctrine of faith was thus no innovation but rather the reassertion of an ancient biblical truth forgotten by an age gone a-whoring after humanism.

For Kierkegaard, therefore, Christian faith not only points to but is Christian living. It is a 'new life,' born from the death of the autonomous natural self; it is a "dying into life." It is therefore, like the paradox of the Incarnation, an 'offence' for unregenerate reason. Offence and faith are, indeed, almost equated for him. "So inseparable from faith is the possibility of offence that if the God-man were not the possibility of offence, he could not be the object of faith" (T.S. p. 143). "This is the very first utterance of the New

Testament," he declares, "that Christianity, and the fact that one is truly a Christian, must be in the highest degree an 'offence' to the natural man . . . being the thing that defines man as spirit, [it] must so appear to everyone one who has not by 'dying from' been reborn as 'spirit' . . . As soon as Christianity is again presented in its true form, then the true judgement will come out: 'It is treason against humanity' " (S.E. 154-5). "The possibility of offence is the dialectical factor in everything Christian"; it is that which constitutes its constant challenge to the complacent humanism of the human heart and mind.

That offence arises from the "infinite qualitative difference" between God and man; "that there is an infinite difference of quality between God and man is the possibility of offence which cannot be taken away" (S.D. p. 209). The offence of faith is thus, for Kierkegaard, rooted in transcendence, and it seems to be from this intransigent insistence upon the transcendence of God that the 'wholly other' doctrine of Barthianism is derived. But in Kierkegaard this 'offensive' doctrine of divine transcendence is, as has been seen, coupled with an equal insistence upon 'inwardness.' This transcendent Deity, the 'kingdom of heaven,' are not only other than and above man, they are also 'within.'

Kierkegaard is thus affirming not transcendence only, but a transcendence in immanence, a Christ and a 'kingdom of heaven' which, as Blake also affirmed, are both above and within. Here too the trend of modern thought follows his lead. The 'personalism' of Berdyaev and many others to-day is based upon the same paradoxical conception of the nature of reality, man and faith. "There is a divine element in man," writes Berdyaev; "Man is a being who surmounts and transcends himself. . . . Personality is confronted by the transcendent and in realizing itself it transcends" (*Freedom and Slavery*, pp. 30, 45, 52). But Kierkegaard was chiefly concerned to counteract the overweening immanentism of contemporary thought; it has remained for descendants from his doctrine to develop the full and balancing implications of his creed of Christian inwardness.

If such a faith was an 'offence' it was also a martyrdom.

For Kierkegaard, as for most intellectuals, it was primarily a martyrdom of mind. The renewing of the "spirit of the mind," like the whole process of spiritual rebirth, was, for him as for William Law, not "a thing done, but . . . a thing continually doing" (*Mystical Writings*, p. 22). "The martyrdom of faith (crucifixion of the understanding) is not a martyrdom of the instant but precisely the martyrdom of endurance" (U.P. p. 496). For the impulses of the natural mind, like those of the will, constantly reassert themselves, and by the Christian must as constantly be mortified and reversed. Homocentric humanism dies hard in the modern mind in the texture of which its habit has been long and deeply ingrained.

For Kierkegaard Christianity implied also an external martyrdom which, in his own fashion, he endured. His journals suggest that he expected even a physical martyrdom as the reward of his Christian "contumacy" and attack upon official Christianity. But the traditional pattern of martyrdom did not fall to his lot, except in so far as a frail constitution impaired, and a perhaps premature death caused, by the prodigious labours which his faith exacted and the infirmity to which he frequently refers as his "thorn in the flesh" are concerned. He endured what he has called the "martyrdom of laughter" in his controversy with *The Corsair*. "I have been made a laughing-stock," he writes in 1849, "that is the martyrdom I have suffered . . . I am the martyr of laughter; for not everyone who suffers being laughed at, even though for an idea, is strictly speaking a martyr of laughter . . . But I am the martyr of laughter . . . I myself could have commanded laughter on an unequalled scale . . . and so have become just what the age desired . . . And quite rightly I had to command laughter to turn on me" (J. 880). In other words, he had deliberately become "a fool for Christ's sake"; for a man of his natural pride, wit and fastidious sensibility it was a persecution not easily to be endured.

In his renunciation of Regina, whatever the merits or demerits of the course which he felt constrained to adopt, he had also incurred a martyrdom of feeling far more acute

and enduring. It is impossible to read his story without realizing that, in making that sacrifice, he was losing his natural
life, his 'first immediacy,' and inviting a slow martyrdom
of that life which lasted to the end of his days. It was more
than the sacrifice of love; it was the sacrifice of life. For all
his natural human life had come to a burning point in that
passion. He at least was convinced that its renunciation and
the martyrdom of his manhood which it entailed were the
inexorable requirements for him of his Christian faith.

But his real martyrdom and the real meaning of martyrdom for him was, like his faith, a matter of 'inwardness.'
Such inwardness involved a profound inward suffering of
spirit in a continual and increasing awareness laying open
ever deeper levels of consciousness to the searching and con-
suming fire of the Spirit. He who essays to search his heart
and hidden motives invites an end to his equanimity, a
stripping of self to the buff, a despair and dereliction, an
agony of self-dissolution which those "whose sails were never
to the tempest given" can neither know nor guess. So "secret," as J. H. Mozley exclaimed, "is the system of temptation." Here is the real inward martyrdom of man. Therefore,
as Kierkegaard declared, "Christianity is the deepest wound
which can be inflicted upon a man" (L. p. 535).

That inward martyrdom and mortification is also a sacrifice, self-incurred, in which the self is both the sacrificial
priest and the victim after the pattern of his Lord. "According to the New Testament," he writes, "to be a Christian
properly means . . . to be sacrificed." That wound and sacrifice are incurred, he affirmed, in the very choice of despair
and selfhood and the aloneness which such a selfhood involves. It is a sacrifice which the Christian is called not only
to endure but passionately to desire, "When one is able to
endure the isolation involved in being a single individual
. . . alone in the endless world and the endless world of
men . . . alone before the face of God—then . . . he must
say: O my God, now I have but one wish, one prayer, one
desire, one passion, that I may experience suffering, become
hated, persecuted, mocked, spit upon, put to death . . .
Behold, this is the passion for martyrdom" (L. p. 542). It is

in that following of Christ along the way of self-sacrifice, that sanctification by his blood, that the difference (obscure to the sceptic) between masochism and martyrdom consists.

Such a voluntary self-martyrdom, such a devastating solitude and sincerity of spirit before God are, Kierkegaard affirmed, "the bold adventure which is required of us." Such sayings, emphasizing the solitude of the Christian 'venture' of spirit with which his writings are starred, have earned for him, from more gregarious and scornful critics, the stricture of 'solitudinarianism'—a wilful self-seclusion from the society of men, the saints and the community of the Church. That such an aloneness "before the face of God" was a way deliberately chosen his self-revelations amply attest. He certainly conceived such an aloneness to be incumbent upon the real follower of Christ and particularly incumbent, in his particular situation, upon him. This was the martyrdom to which he believed himself called. "What the age needs," he said, "is not a genius . . . but a martyr"; "Denmark has need of a dead man"—that is, of one really 'dead to the world.'" For he believed himself to be 'the exception,' a man chosen by God to stand out from the misled crowd of so-called Christians and sound the "cry of alarm." Such a role demanded isolation if it were to be faithfully fulfilled. "If the crowd is the evil," so he reasoned, "if chaos is what threatens us, there is salvation only in one thing, in becoming a single individual in the thought of 'that individual' as an essential category" (P. V. p. 61). The chaos, of which he beheld the threat as of a "cloud the size of a man's hand," has come upon us and the worth and freedom of the individual are assailed on every hand. That Kierkegaard, in that he thus foresaw the shape of "things to come," was an 'exception' now needs no argument.

Such a solitude of spirit is indeed the lot of all 'exceptions,' of all who are called to stem the mass-movements of a deluded majority. It is the aloneness which every leader incurs —such an aloneness as that which Bernard Shaw voices in his *St. Joan:* "France is alone; and God is alone; and what is my loneliness before the loneliness of my country and my God? I see now that the loneliness of God is his strength . . . it is better to be alone with God." So it was that Kierkegaard conceived of the essential solitude of spirit of a real Christianity. Nevertheless—it seems a paradox as existentially true of spiritual as of philosophic solitude—he who can attain and endure such a solitude finds a community with life and man in God, the All, which can be found by no way less 'strait' and can, in the end, affirm that he is "never less alone than when wholly alone." Christian solitude is the 'strait way' to true Christian community.

But his conviction that loneliness was the lot of real Christians was not limited to his own particular destiny, though that destiny made it more acute for him; it was, he believed, the "flight of the alone to the Alone" (in the phrase of Plotinus) to which a true Christian inwardness inevitably called—the way of the Cross. For he was convinced that "the individual is the category of spirit, of spiritual awakening." And "as a single individual" the Christian "is alone, alone in the whole world, alone before God." Therefore a Christianity of inwardness and the spirit required a realization and rebirth of individual selfhood which, in itself, inevitably means an inward martyrdom of the natural, the 'old man.'

Solitude and the life of spirit were thus for him a single way and life. It seems an inescapable conclusion. It is only when a man communes in solitude with his own heart and God that he can enter the dimension of spirit at all, and it is only when he can dare to be alone that he can hear the word of God or discern "truth in the inward parts." And it is upon this "naked intent," this personal 'appropriation' of the word of God in the Bible, that Kierkegaard bases his belief. Here too the affinity of his faith to that of Pascal is clear. For Pascal heard, he declares, the voice of Christ assuring him that "I am present with thee by my word in Scripture"; it was the persuasion of Kierkegaard also. But he can only know that presence and that Voice in stillness and solitude of spirit. "He who is not alone with God's Word," he wrote, "is not reading God's Word." "I have never seen anyone," he adds, "whom I could venture to believe that he had sincerity and courage enough to be so completely alone with God's Word that absolutely no illusion surreptitiously intruded" (S.E. p. 55). Thus for Kierkegaard such a solitude of Spirit, like inwardness and faith, is also a process of becoming in our life; we cannot here and now fully attain, we move towards, that final loneliness with 'God only,' following in the footsteps of the Lord.

Thus solitude with 'God only' is for Kierkegaard part of the daring, the risk, the 'leap' which he believes an essential Christianity to be. It is the essential solitude of every soul which dares to become aware of itself and its destiny. There is ample evidence that the choice of such a solitude was, for him, due to no morose self-centredness. In his undergraduate days he had been the most "clubbable" of men, the centre of a wide circle of friends, and throughout his life it was his practice and pleasure to mix daily with the Copenhagen crowds. His solitude was inward and one, not of natural predilection, but of inner compulsion; it was, for him, the 'strait way' of Christ. It was a solitude replete, not only with that "joy of the Lord" which came to him at last, but with "pale, bloodless, midnight shapes," with "dread and trembling," a solitude in which, as Gerard Manley Hopkins (in so many ways his peer in the life of the spirit) was to write long afterwards—

> "We hear our hearts grate on themselves . . .
> . . . this tormenting mind
> With this tormenting mind tormenting yet."

It is in this solitude, this "dark night of the spirit," that Kierkegaard finds the real and inward martyrdom of the Christian man. It is of such an inward martyrdom that he declares that "the nervous system of Christianity meets in the reality of martyrdom." We are here again in the presence of something which only the paradoxical logic of love can interpret. For here are the solitude and passion of the lover —a solitude which is delight and dereliction at the same time, passion which is both joy and pain. This was for him the price of love and the "pearl of great price" of ultimate, inward reality for which he gave "all that he had." It is a secret obscure for the casuist but open for the mystic.

The Christian way thus meant for Kierkegaard a passionate

following along the way of the Cross to an inward world of spirit, stripped and stark as some high glacier upland from which the life-giving waters flow down to the life of men. It is the following, not the formula, that matters. "The proof of Christianity really consists in the 'following'," he says (S.E. p. 88). "There is only one way of being a Christian— to be a disciple" (S.E. p. 215). "Save us," he prayed, "from the error of wishing to admire Thee instead of being willing to follow Thee" (T.C. p. 227). And discipleship requires renunciation. But renunciation is the lover's own reward. He speaks of "the delight of renunciation" as "simply a lover's understanding with God . . . it was as though God had whispered the secret to me. Renunciation is a higher relation to God, it is really a love-relationship: and for me at least an enchantment was spread over renunciation" (J. 1279). It is the very language of love.

In his conception of the way and the life of a real and existential Christianity, the thought, feeling and language of Kierkegaard are thus always and, as he moves towards spiritual maturity, increasingly those of a lover. There is the heart of his mystery, of his inwardness, his agonies, his solitude, his dyings, his martyrdom, his emphasis upon now the severity and now the gentleness of Christianity. It is a note which sounds more and more clearly through his later writings, such as *Training in Christianity, Discourses at the Communion on Fridays, For Self-Examination* and *Judge for Yourself.* These books are devoted not to the theory but to the practice of the Christian life—the mystery, following and discipline of love.

Thus the lover's life, he writes in the preface to his Discourses, "is my very life, the content of my life for me, its fullness, its happiness, its peace and contentment" (S.E. p. 11). "Love's judgement is the severest judgement," he writes. "Learn to fear, not the severity of justice, but the gentleness of love." "Love pierces far more deeply into life, to the very issues of life, than does justice"; "love, whose condemnation is (óh, frightful condemnation!) 'Thy sins are forgiven thee' "; "of one fault we are all guilty more or less: of loving too little" (S.E. 12, 13). Just so St.-John-of-the-Cross declared

"in the evening they will examine thee in love." And it is
with the eyes of love that the word of God can alone rightly
be read. "Think of a lover," he says, "who has now received
a letter from his beloved—as precious as this letter is to the
lover, just so precious to thee, I assume, is God's Word"
(S.E. p. 51). These are intimations and insights with which
all existential experience of the life of love is familiar; they
are only comprehensible in that light.

It is thus in love that he finds "nature's profoundest myth"
and in religion "the highest love." "This God-relationship
of mine," he declares, "is the 'happy love' in a life which has
always been troubled and unhappy" (P.V. p. 64). For a certain school of psychological criticism a spiritual love thus
derived from a frustrated physical love is readily written off
as "compensatory illusion." But in this case, such a conclusion seems to incur the criticism of being itself unrealistic.
For reality does not arise from the unreality, and it is impossible to study Kierkegaard's life and work without prejudice
and fail to realize the ardent reality of this love-relationship
to which, in the end, Christianity resolved itself for him. It
was inescapably and ruthlessly real and was itself the crown
and consummation of the exacting existential realism which
was his first principle.

Moreover Kierkegaard's interpretation of the Christian
mystery as essentially a 'love-story' penetrates far beyond the
romance of "love's young dream" to the fulfilment and realism of marital love and fidelity. In view of his own renunciation of the state of marriage, his estimation of the real meaning and worth of marriage for the life of religion is a surprising token to his genius and charity. A bitter cynicism
or a blindness to the true significance of marriage might
have been expected; in fact we find precisely the reverse.

He was fully conscious of the apparent and difficult Christian dilemma which sexual and marital life present, and of
the merits and demerits of the classic solution of that
dilemma by the medieval church of celibacy for saints but
marriage for sinners as a remedy against being "burned,"
and of the apparent impossibility of reconciling the life of
generation with that of regeneration. "The unmarried man,"

he wrote, "can make greater ventures in the life of spirit than the married man, he can stake everything" (St. p. 244). And "it is quite certain and true that Christianity is suspicious of marriage" (T.C. p. 119).

Nevertheless it was in marriage that he perceived the true completion of the Christian life and in a comprehension to which only the well married can attain the true meaning of its mystery. A paper on marriage written late in his life contains some of the most penetrating of his utterances on this matter. "Every other sort of acquaintance with life," he declares, "is superficial in comparison with that acquired by the married man, for he and he alone has thoroughly fathomed the depths of life." "Only a married man is a genuine man." It is, he affirms, in this wisdom of marriage that the Christian excels the pagan comprehension of life; "in paganism there is a God for love but none for marriage; in Christianity there is . . . a God for marriage and none for love." Like Christianity as he conceives it, marriage is "the synthesis of love and resolution," for marriage, like faith, demands decision. Marriage is "the beauteous mid-point and centre of human existence." It is more; in marriage he perceives what he means by the 'instant.' "Marriage is the fullness of time." And marriage gives access to the deepest reality possible for mortality; a mother "belongs completely to reality."

Kierkegaard never explores the full spiritual significance of these insights into the crucial importance for Christianity of the fact and concept of marriage, or the nature, in that context, of the true ultimate Christian resolution of the generation-regeneration dilemma. It may be surmised that he felt that his own experience, frustrated of that fulfilment, disqualified him for such a task. But there can be no doubt that he saw in marriage the type in tune of the true Christian consummation and in a psychological and spiritual marriage the supreme co-ordination of our existential contraries.

In that insight he is at once with a great crowd of Christian witness. No realistic reading of the Bible can evade the realization that the marriage-motif is dominant throughout that book. A continuing Christian tradition, of which St. Bernard, St.-John-of-the-Cross, Ruysbroek and St. Teresa are

salient exponents, has found in the *Song of Songs* the perpetual prototype and symbol of the 'spiritual marriage.'
Origen wrote of the "intercourse of the Word, the Bridegroom, with the soul, the bride" and St. Augustine that "the
soul hath in God her lawful husband." "I cannot contain
myself for joy that the Divine Majesty disdains not to . . .
enter into marriage with a soul still in exile," wrote St.
Bernard (*Canticle* lii. 2). For Ruysbroek the "Bridegroom
is Christ, and human nature is the bride" and "nothing is
more joyful to the lover of God, than to feel that he belongs
wholly to his Beloved" (*Adornment of the Spiritual Marriage*). St.-John-of-the-Cross speaks of "the consummation of
this most happy state of marriage with Him" (*Spiritual
Canticles*) and sees in "this flame of love . . . the Spirit of
the Spouse—that is, the Holy Spirit" (*The Living Flame of
Love*). In our own age Coventry Patmore wrote that "God
has declared to us his mystic rapture in his marriage with
humanity . . . This is the burning heart of the universe"
(*Aphorisms and Extracts*). Comparison of such sayings with
those of Kierkegaard leaves little room for doubt that for
him also in this concept and fact of the 'spiritual marriage'
was the "burning heart" of his faith, and that in this respect
also he was rather rediscovering a repressed Christian realism
than departing from the great tradition.

Here too, though concerning this aspect of Christianity
he rather points than explores, Kierkegaard's existential
Christianity speaks to a real and deep need of the consciousness of our own as of his day. For, as with regard to the subconscious, so with regard to sexuality, established and 'safe'
Christianity has signally failed to confront the real issues or
to proclaim the real remedy for psychological and sexual ills
which the Christian treasury of truth contains. It is only, as
Kierkegaard saw and insisted, upon the plane of spirit that
these inner and corroding conflicts of consciousness can be
co-ordinated and to that co-ordination the Church, so he
believed, holds, but, from failure of realism and nerve, hides
the key. "Ye have taken away the key of knowledge: ye
entered not in yourselves, and them that were entering in
ye hindered." Such was, in effect, Kierkegaard's indictment

of the Christianity of his day. It remains his challenge to
our own.

The tortured division of consciousness, dialectic of thought
and life, despair, gloom and rigour which characterize Kierkegaard's first arduous wrestlings with religious reality thus
led him at last to the gentleness and simplicity of a Christianity which is essentially a 'love-story.' It is perhaps in part
due to the fact that the majority of his critics have not themselves passed beyond that grim first phase that our world
wanders yet in its own 'waste land,' that the prevailing conception of the man and his thought is one of conflict, despair
and austerity and the "love, joy, peace," the "simplicity
which is in Christ" to which he won and in which his real
gospel for our condition is to be found, are normally neglected. His initial desperate struggle was as grim as that
which racks us to-day; but the faith which overcame that
world of woe was as gay, as radiant and as simple as that of
the first followers of Christ.

For Kierkegaard the simplicity and gentleness of Christ
are not prizes easily won; they are the hard and high reward
of strenuous spiritual endeavour and discipline. From the
first he had recognized that simplicity as the hallmark of the
true wisdom; it was as a "simple wise man" that he venerated
Socrates. But for him "the movement is not from the simple
to the interesting but from the interesting to the simple."
That movement is itself the "thing of becoming a Christian." "To become again a child . . . to *will* to . . . retain
youth's spontaneous enthusiasm with its spontaneity un-
abated, to *will* to reacquire it by valiant effort . . . that is
the task" (T.C. p. 190). "In a Christian sense simplicity is
not the point of departure from which one goes on to become interesting, witty, profound, poet, philosopher, etc. No,
the very contrary. *Here* one begins (with the interesting,
etc.) and becomes simpler and simpler, *attaining* simplicity"
(P.V. p. 148). Such, at all events, was his own course, and
here too, it would seem that he has a special leading for
intellectuals "bowed with the infirmity" of a complex and
disintegrated consciousness, unable to be "made straight" in
simplicity and so glorify God. That Kierkegaard himself

attained to a large measure of the loving simplicity which he had seen afar off and sought his latest utterances testify.

His attitude towards the contrasted severity and gentleness of Christianity is the same. He believed that Christianity had become corrupt with a false gentleness—the sickly gentleness of the Victorian "gentle Jesus, meek and mild." "Christianity was abolished in Christendom," he wrote, "by gentleness . . . there is only one salvation; severity" (T.C. p. 222). But he knew that severity and gentleness or 'leniency' were as dark and light, night and day, of the single orb of the paradoxical Christian reality. "In my presentation," he says, "severity is the dialectical moment in Christianity, but leniency is just as strongly represented . . . If I had understood only its frightful severity—then I should have kept silent . . . For a merely negative result . . . **one** must not communicate" (L. p. 448). He never wavers in his certainty of the gentleness of God and of a real Christianity, and as his life moves towards its close, and especially after his second conversion in 1848, his assertion of that verity grows more constant and emphatic. In 1843 he had written, "God is certainly love, but not love to sinners" (J. 442), but in 1849, "God is gentle. That I have always understood. My own life shows me that" (J. 1005). And in 1850, "This is all I have known for certain, that God is love . . . His love is a spring which never runs dry" (J. 1102). And at last, in 1853, in a rapturous repetitive refrain, "how endlessly thou art loved" (J. p. 563). To such a childlike simplicity, love and peace had his conflict and complexity come.

For Kierkegaard the pith of the Christian way and life was thus a dynamic faith in a divine Spirit transcendent in our immanence, belief which is also being, a Christian realism of inwardness and reborn individuality ever deepening to the essence, to an inward martyrdom of 'dying into life,' to a personal 'appropriation' of the word of God, to a conception of real Christianity as a 'love-story' and so to its consummation as a 'spiritual marriage.' It was thus to a Christianity of the spirit that his existential conceiving came.

But, the inner conflict resolved, an outward conflict came upon him. For this was a faith which inevitably involved

conflict with an established Christianity confined, so he believed, to the 'letter' of the Christian law. His conception of
a Christianity of the spirit, of the nature of the Church and
the apostasy of the churches are the sequel to the personal
faith which has been considered.

6

IN THE course of his religious expe-
rience Kierkegaard had come to discriminate between what
he termed "religiousness A and B." By 'religiousness A' he
intended, in general, a religion of immanence and the 'first
immediacy' of nature; and by 'religiousness B' a religion of
transcendence, the 'second immediacy' and grace. The conflict between these two forms of 'religiousness' in his own
case had been acute. It was inevitable, therefore that when
his own faith and conception of a real Christianity had crys-
talized as 'religiousness B,' his inner conflict should become
externalized in an attack upon the 'religiousness A' which, so
he believed, the established church in Denmark was purvey-
ing to the "hungry sheep" of its flock as Christianity.

He was, in fact, assaulting that which, 'writ large' in popular and officially-sponsored 'religiosity,' he had fought and
overcome in his own soul. Until the second spiritual crisis
of 1848—when he heard the call to action, believed himself
to be at last made whole in spirit and wrote, "I must speak"
—the war with religion A had been confined to his own
consciousness. After that date it became increasingly a war
waged against the same foe in the outward world. It was, in
little and in anticipation, the conflict with which all Christendom is confronted to-day.

It was no merely theoretic distinction which he drew between these forms of religion, but one based upon personal
and poignant experience—an arduous and perilous migra-
tion from an old to a new world of the spirit. He had him-

self passed from the one world of consciousness to the other. It had meant for him no smooth passage, no continuity from one way of life and form of thought and faith to another more mature and profound, but a "leap in the dark," a catastrophic dying to the "first immediacy" of nature and an anguished rebirth "from above" into the "second immediacy" of grace, of the 'new man.' He knew well the lure of the religiousness which, by every shift and sleight of self-justification, seeks to evade that catastrophic 'instant' of judgement and 'dying into life' in which religion A is reborn into religion B and, in a counterfeit Christianity, to escape the perils and ardours of that new life of spirit and real Christianity which, for him, constituted religion B. He knew too, in his own soul, the unceasing trend and temptation to "revert to an earlier condition," to relapse into the comfortable religiosity of "religiousness A."

For Kierkegaard these two contrasted forms of religion are divided and distinguished, first, by the historical fact of the Incarnation and, second, by the realization of sin (in distinction from the sense of guilt) caused by confrontation with that fact. It is the coming of the God-man into our actual human existence and history which sets a wall of fire between these two forms of faith. "In religiousness A," he writes, "there is no historical starting-point"; the eternal, the God-man, has not entered into history but only into imagination. Religion A is therefore a religion of recollection and immanence. "In time the individual recollects that he is eternal" (U.P. p. 508). And, since for such religion God and eternity dwell, not in his existence, but in his imagination, it is only in man's own imagination and will that he can seek salvation by "the individual's own pathetic transformation of existence" (U.P. p. 515). Since such a God is not a person, but an idea, and sin can only exist in relation to a person, such religion knows guilt but does not yet know sin. Such a religion is thus, in Dr. Lowrie's words, "simply a heartfelt expression of a sense of God, or of the numinous" (L. p. 325).

Religion A—commonly called Christianity in Christendom—is thus a religion between which and other 'high religions' there is no essential difference. Modern attempts (such as those of Count Keyserling, Rudolf Steiner or Gerald Heard) to blend a basic wisdom common to all the wise among men and a 'basic Christianity' in a 'Federation of Faiths' are thus of this order. For Kierkegaard this is genuine religion—'religiousness A'—and it may be magnificent; but it is not Christianity.

Into religion B, however, to which for Kierkegaard real Christianity is confined, the Incarnation, the God-man, Christ has come. God has become man, eternity has entered time, being has invaded becoming and essence existence at a precise historical time and place. This is the crucial paradox and 'offence' which differentiates religion B absolutely from religion A and fixes a great gulf between them. Therefore the individual for whom the Incarnation has become fact and no longer fancy is immediately confronted with God and eternity, not in idea only, but in his actual existence. "As the eternal came into the world at a moment of time, the existing individual does not in the course of time come into relation with the eternal and think about it (this is A), but *in time* it comes into relation with the eternal *in time*" (U.P. p. 506). In that relation and context the individual is reborn into the dimension of spirit and eternal life. "The individual who was eternal now becomes such, and so does not recollect what he is but becomes what he was not" (U.P. p. 508). In fact, in Kierkegaard's terminology, he has entered the category of 'repetition'; "what has been now becomes."

But this new life of selfhood, spirit and eternity is not an abstraction from but concrete (growing with) within existential reality. It is in our actual existence, not in some 'other world,' that this new and eternal life is born and becomes. Since the eternal has entered time, therefore, for religion B, "only in existing do I become eternal." Moreover, here, in this direct relation of eternity with time, God with man, in our existence, guilt becomes sin. For while man in religion A knows guilt towards an 'Unknown God,' sin is offence against a person and, in the Incarnation and religion B, the self is confronted with the person of the God-man, Jesus Christ.

Religion B is thus, by virtue of the Incarnation, a faith

peculiar to Christianity; it is therefore unique among religions, 'high' or 'low,' and in this crucial respect 'wholly other' than they as a religion of and in history. The possibility of 'federation' with other faiths and forms of religion A is therefore excluded, for the federation (though not the marriage) of God and man, eternity and time, spirit and flesh is no more than fantasy.

Christianity is thus the only example of religion B. Its real power and challenge consists in that uniqueness. Again to quote Dr. Lowrie, it is a religion of "eternity *in* time, challenging time, conflicting with time, and looking forward eschatalogically to the termination of time" (L. pp. 323-4). It is "essentially paradoxical"—no 'faint trust' in some 'larger hope,' no mere numinous memory or apprehension of God and eternity, no human attempt to transform existence, but "the paradoxical transformation of existence by faith through relation to an historic fact" (U.P. p. 515). Here alone sin becomes a reality and such a "sin-consciousness is the breach with immanence"—and with religion A. And not only is existence transformed by this faith, the self which thus confronts Christ in existence is reborn, not from within by its own effort, but 'from above.'

Kierkegaard is no bigot; he does not suggest that these two forms of religion are absolute and irreconcilable contraries; he seems to conceive rather of the transcendent "paradoxical religiousness B of the second immediacy" as proceeding, reborn, from the "religiousness A" of immanence and the 'first immediacy.' And, for him, with his insistence upon the 'inwardness' of real religion, the transcendence of religion B is a transcendence in immanence; it is within existence that this transcendent kingdom of the God-man and eternal life comes to pass.

But he insists upon the absolute distinction between them, upon the fact that, by virtue of the paradox of the Incarnation, properly speaking real Christianity is confined to religion B and upon the catastrophic (not continuous or evolutionary) character of the 'instant' in which A is transfigured, reborn into B. His primary quarrel is with an aesthetic, speculative, erotic travesty of real religion (whether A or B), which eludes any real confrontation with the 'offence' and judgement of the Word, the God man, and abstracts religion from reality; his secondary quarrel is with a 'religiousness A' which, though aware of the "infinite qualitative difference" between the two, masquerades as 'religiousness B,' as real Christianity, from cowardice, complacency or love of ease. It is upon both these counts that he indicts the established, official Christianity of his day.

Religion B, which he thus identifies with a real Christianity, is not only unique among religions by virtue of the Incarnation; it is also the only real religion 'after the spirit.' For, in religion B, the concept of spirit is something quite distinct from that which the term connotes for religion A. For the former it is both transcendent and concrete, for the latter it is abstract from and immanent within man and his world; for the one spirit is a Person, for the other it is a ghost, a fairy-tale or a dream. Spirit, he declared, "is the negation of direct immediacy"; it is that which mortifies the life of nature and, in that dying and self-losing, regenerates it to eternal life. "Into this night of hopelessness—it is in fact death that we are describing—comes then the life-giving Spirit and brings hope—the hope of eternity" (S.E. p. 101). On the other hand the religion A of 'direct immediacy' is a religion of and in time and, according to Kierkegaard, "the temporal never is and never will be the element of spirit" (P.V. p. 82).

For Kierkegaard, moreover, spirit is no phantom, no "visitor within this creature," as for Neo-Platonism and non-Christian mysticism. Man, he says, "is a synthesis of the soulish and the bodily. But the synthesis is unthinkable where the two are not united by a third. This third is spirit." He equates spirit with the 'self,' the reborn individual; "spirit is the self." Spirit is both that which begets the self upon the natural consciousness or soul of man in a fusion or marriage of the "synthesis of the infinite and the finite, of the temporal and the eternal, of freedom and necessity" which, by nature, man is, and the being of the reborn self which is begotten from that marriage. Spirit is thus that which begets the real and eternal self and, in that new birth 'from above' (which is also 'within'), transfigures soul into spirit. But, in that transfiguration, man and matter, though thus transfigured into spirit-being and eternalized, remain man and matter. The life of spirit is that of humanity and the world redeemed, transfigured, not annulled, and that redemption is only possible by virtue of the paradox of the Incarnation and for religion B. The life of grace and spirit is thus, not abstract from the life of nature, but concrete, growing within it—that life fulfilled. Therefore real Christianity (confined, for Kierkegaard, to religion B) is life 'after' (or in the power of) spirit, while religion A is life 'after the flesh.'

Kierkegaard's antithesis is thus substantially the same as that of St. Paul in the Epistle to the Romans. For him as for Paul, that deep difference is a matter of mortal urgency. For he, like Paul, believed passionately that "if [we] live after the flesh [that is, a life limited to the 'first immediacy'] [we] shall die" (as all flesh must die), but that if "we mortify the motives (or impulses) of the flesh (in inwardness, aloneness with God and the life of spirit), in the power of the Spirit, we shall live—the life of the 'second immediacy' which is eternal life. It is thus an issue of eternal life or death. Therefore he dare not compromise or fail to "speak with boldness" what he has seen and heard. Therefore he was constrained to assail that which he most cherished—his own Mother Church. It was with the anguished austerity with which Hamlet was impelled by his own integrity to upbraid his mother Gertrude for her betrayal of his father that he did so. Just so, it seemed to Kierkegaard, his Mother Church of Denmark had betrayed God the Father with the treacherous Claudius of a counterfeit Christianity.

But his astringent criticism of his church—*a* church—was no denial of the claims of *the* Church. From first to last Kierkegaard was, indeed, a devoted church-man, a faithful attendant at the services, and especially at the communions, of the Church. It was only at the last and as a final gesture of protest, that he refused the communion from a clergyman of the established church. He not only attended, he also assisted the services of the church as his *Religious Discourses* attest. And, throughout his life, he contemplated ordination.

That he never actually took that step was due rather to an exalted conception of the office of priesthood, an acute contrition for past sin and sense of his own inadequacy for so high and holy a function and to an integrity which refused the material security which a 'living' offered, than to any depreciation of its importance.

He held, indeed, at all events at one time, an extreme 'Catholic' view of the character of the priesthood. A priest, he wrote, "is essentially what he is through ordination and ordination is a . . . paradoxical transformation in time, by which he becomes, in time, something else . . . ordination constitutes a *character indelebilis*" (U.P. p. 244). There seems some reason to suppose that he afterwards modified this extreme view of the priestly 'character,' but none that he reduced his veneration for the office. He held a view no less 'high' of the authority of the priesthood. "A priest *must* use authority, he *must* say to men: *You shall;* he must do that even though they put him to death" (J. 716). But he finds that "alas, a true priest is even more rare than a true poet" (S.D. p. 166).

His own vocation to the priesthood never ceased to sound in his ears. His sacrifice of that deep desire was as bitter—and, indeed, of the same nature—as his sacrifice of his hopes of marriage; in each case it was dictated by his overmastering sense of mission and of unfitness. In 1846 he writes, "The wish to be a priest in the country has always attracted me." In 1847 financial stringency suggested a 'living' as a means of subsistence and security and in 1848 he writes, "Now by God's help I shall become myself . . . and then I will become a priest." But, his congenital melancholy, an exaggerated remorse for the sins of his youth and fear of causing scandal to the Church deterred him, and he was not the man so to purchase material security. Moreover he seems to have felt that, if he were to fulfil what he believed to be his mission to sound a 'cry of alarm' and denounce what he believed to be the counterfeit Christianity of the established church, he must remain free and unfettered by professional loyalties.

It was not, therefore, from any underestimate of the cruciality of the Church for a real Christianity that he either refrained from taking holy orders himself or attacked the established church in Denmark. He was, indeed, a staunch Catholic in his attitude towards the "Holy, Catholic and Apostolic Church." Nevertheless, for 'churchianity' he had no sympathy; "the deification of the Church," he wrote, "is nothing but permanent rebellion against God" (L. p. 428). Protestantism, on the other hand, was for him not a faith or a church, but a 'corrective.' He wrote in 1838 that "there are on the whole few men who are able to bear the Protestant view of life"; it was an attitude towards Protestantism to which there is no good reason to suppose that he did not adhere for the remainder of his life.

It was, in fact, on behalf of the Church of Christ that he attacked the established church of Denmark. And by establishment he meant more than the English technical connotation of that term—a church come to terms with secular society, become static rather than dynamic and conservative rather than creative, "settled on its lees," corrupted by the enjoyment of place and the corruption of power. He speaks of "the ungodly veneration of the established church divine," declares (with a strangely prophetic voice) that "the deification of the established order is the secularization of everything" and that "the established order desires to be totalitarian" (T.C. p. 92). He saw his stigma of 'establishment' seducing the established church from her chastity in Christ and her duty to 'God only.' "In established Christanity," he wrote, "the natural man manages to have his own way"; in other words, established Christianity tends always to relapse from religion B to religion A, from the second to the first 'immediacy,' from a Christianity 'after the spirit' to a Christianity 'after the flesh.' Therefore, for him, "established Christianity simply doesn't make sense"; it is a contradiction in terms, and "established Christendom . . . might be called the caricature of Christianity" (P.V. p. 77).

He saw the officials, the parsons, of such an established Christianity as quite inevitably to some extent infected by that corruption, however saintly in character they might be. For they were, *ipso facto*, servants of the state rather than of the spirit, professional men always liable to be concerned rather with 'livings' and making a living than with the gospel of eternal life, and officials caught up in the spirit-quenching busy-ness of a bureaucratic machine. They were doomed to become more or less hypocritical or (as the Gospel word correctly implies) unrealist, alienated by temporal and worldly appearance from eternal realities.

His indictment, his declaration of 'Woe unto you' is as bold and severe as that of his Lord in what he conceived to be similar circumstances. For he stood for "religiousness absolute (*i.e.,* religion B), of a different kind from that of the parsons. He speaks forth boldly, as he believes that he ought to speak. "What concerns the clergy is their livings . . . official Christianity is both aesthetically and intellectually ludicrous and indecent, a scandal in the Christian sense" (L2. p. 246). He adds his irony to his invective. "Had St. Paul an official position? No. Had he any means of livelihood? No. Did he make a lot of money? No. Did he marry and have children? No. But in that case St. Paul was not a serious man" (J. 686). "Truly and seriously to give up all things is not a joke, like the parson's trash." *"Parson:* Thou shalt die unto the world.—The fee is one guinea."

But it is not so much simony as that with which simony adulterates Christianity which he assails most vehemently. For the parson, whose priesthood is his career and means of livelihood, is sorely tempted to accommodate his Christianity to worldly caution. "The modern clergyman is trained," he declares, "in the art of introducing Christianity in such a way that it signifies nothing" (J. 1305). "The so-called Church falsifies Christianity by watering it down" (J. 1358).

His mind was not lightly or swiftly made up on this matter. In 1849 he writes that he is "in the midst of the strain, of the struggle with ideas and questions of principle, whether, from the Christian point of view, there should be official Christian offices" (J. 928). In 1854 he thanks God that "he has prevented me from thoughtlessly becoming a parson in the sense that people here, nowadays, are parsons, which is to make a mockery of Christianity"; he believes it his duty to declare that "official divine worship is a mockery of God, and to take part in it a crime." (J. 1405). At the end of that year and a little less than a year before he died he at last launched a public attack upon the established church in the course of which he cried, "One thing I adjure thee for the sake of God in heaven and by all that is holy, shun the parsons" (L2. p. 252).

In this matter again his language must be read in the light of his conviction that it was his task to utter, not a cautious and considered judgement, but a 'corrective,' and in a form which would gain a hearing. Nevertheless his challenge still stands, for the corruption of Christianity and Christendom which he foresaw and prophesied is to-day a fact which none can deny. But the corruption has spread since his day like a black-death; his challenge is now not merely to a church but to a world. He foresaw the judgement of Europe: it has come upon us. He proclaimed that in "religiousness absolute," religion B, a Christianity 'after the spirit' and therefore a radical Christian revolution, lay its sole salvation. His challenge remains; it seems not less but more relevant for our own day.

Kierkegaard's attitude towards our hollow civilization and Christianity has been allegorized by Franz Kafka in the opening to his novel *The Castle:* "It was late in the evening when K arrived. The village was deep in snow. The Castle hill was hidden, veiled in mist and darkness, nor was there even a glimmer of light to show that a castle was there. On the wooden bridge leading from the main road to the village K stood for a long time gazing into the illusory emptiness above him." So "late in the evening" of the first Christian age, Kierkegaard gazed into the "illusory emptiness" of Christendom and cried out with a loud voice that "Christianity no longer exists." His existential thinking denied its existence in our world; his faith stedfastly affirmed and reaffirmed its eternal and incorruptible essence, and its 'strait way.'

G. K. CHESTERTON

by

F. A. Lea

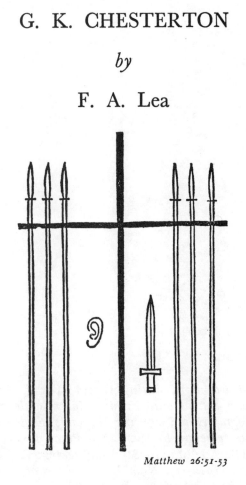

Matthew 26:51-53

*F. A. LEA was born during World War I. Educated at
Charterhouse School and Trinity Hall, Cambridge, where
he read geography and won the Members' Essay Prize; M.A.
Was private secretary to Mr. J. Middleton Murry, assistant-
editor of* The Adelphi *(1938-40) and secretary of The Lang-
ham Centre (1940-42). Now head master of Burgess Hill
School. Author of* Carlyle: Prophet of To-day *and* Shelley
and the Romantic Revolution; *the last had an almost sensa-
tionally good reception from English critics.*

1

It was G. K. Chesterton's life-long fate to be taken seriously when he was being flippant, and flippantly when he was being serious. Since he very seldom was flippant, he was nearly always laughed at, alike by his friends and enemies. They admired or admitted him as a "character," and there, too often, criticism has been allowed to stay. The memory of him cherished by the world is summed up in Mr. Walter de la Mare's portrait of Falstaff:

"He smiled, compact of loam, this orchard man."

Reformers shook their heads over him: he seemed constitutionally unable to treat reform as the serious matter it was; conservatives applauded his "magnificent common sense": they who would never have dreamed of trying to revive the village-community, let alone wearing sombrero hats. The solemn were offended by his frivolity; the frivolous were shocked by his solemnity: neither knew what to make of him. Both seized on the aspect of his writing that appealed to them, called that the "essential Chesterton," dismissed the rest as playful perversity; neither could escape an uncomfortable suspicion that the essential Chesterton was all the time chuckling at them from behind another tree, while they clasped his empty coat in their hands. He fell between dozens of stools. His friends, seeing him fall, rushed to the rescue, to plant him firmly on the stool nearest themselves. But he did not seem to appreciate their help; he only fell over again on the other side, like the White Knight; and in the end they also gave him up as a bad job. They left him to the multitude; and the multitude, which has no ideas, was content to look up to him as a huge, benign figure; a sort of universal uncle officiating at a never-ending Christmas party; an old gentleman so obviously charming that, said they, he must really be like themselves, whatever quaint views it might amuse him to profess.

However, to be a character is by no means the same thing as to have one. Indeed, university dons make a point of metamorphosing themselves into "characters" expressly in order to conceal the fact that they have none. It is the only way they can draw attention to themselves. They inhabit universities for the same reason: they are the only places where they would be noticed. Even to have "no character" in the poet's sense may be a potent incentive towards becoming one. For to lack identity is to be the plaything of other people's opinions; it is to be acutely sensitive to other people's regard: and one so sensitive cannot but hold his popularity a matter of life and death. A "character" is a passport to popularity, a nickname the first step on the way to a name.

That Chesterton was a character is a truism. That he was enormously popular is equally true. And the essays which, more than anything else, established his fame are reminiscent of Mr. Dick's soap-bubbles, alike in their iridescence and their reflection of a child-like personality. It is impossible to dislike Mr. Dick, even when one of his soap-bubbles gets in your eye. It was equally impossible (for most people) to take offence at G. K. Chesterton, exulting in the *Daily News* over dragons, Easter-eggs and Christmas. Like Browning, "He delighted, with a true poetic delight, in being conventional. Being by birth an Englishman, he took pleasure in being an Englishman; being by rank a member of the middle class, he took a pride in its ancient scruples and its everlasting boundaries. He was everything he was with a definite and conscious pleasure" (*Browning*). He enjoyed his popularity, and enjoyed himself—literally, as one might enjoy a glass of ale or a circus: nobody can laugh at Chesterton without laughing with him. And it was by this "ardent and headstrong conventionality" that he fulfilled that ambition to "belong" which must have been with him even as a boy, when he strove manfully to remain at the bottom of his form at St. Paul's.

Nevertheless, the laughter and applause that warmed his heart never went to his head. He began his career, like Gabriel Syme in *The Man who was Thursday,* by "revolting into sanity," for the sake of revolt, and because there was nothing else left to revolt into. But this youthful pose was quickly superseded by a real and deep-seated revolution and reorientation of his whole standpoint. His "character" was at no time afterwards the most important thing about him in his own eyes, whatever it may have been in others'. Before he had a public, he had ceased to depend on public opinion. Underlying all his apparent perversities was the consistency of a real conviction, without which they would have been as empty, as well as brilliant, as soap-bubbles. "I know nothing," he wrote, "so contemptible as a mere paradox; a mere ingenious defence of the indefensible . . . Mr. Shaw is cruelly hampered by the fact that he cannot tell any lie unless he thinks it is the truth. I find myself under the same intolerable bondage" (*Orthodoxy*). Mere consistency is essential to a "character"; conviction of truth is not. Consistency in perversity would have been enough to ensure Chesterton's popularity. He was not perverse. If he attacked what he believed to be the pedantry of Prussian professors, when public opinion held them in esteem, that did not prevent him from continuing to do so after the whole populace had rallied to his flag. His books, he said at the end of his life, he had never taken seriously: his opinions he had. Since one of the first of these was that an artist's success must be judged by his own standards, and not by what his critics think ought to have been his standards, Chesterton's must be measured at least as much by his wisdom as his wit.

❧

He was one of the last important English men of letters to embrace orthodox Christianity *in toto* at an early age, and grow up inside it. That is the first essential fact about him. The book *Orthodoxy* was his confession of faith. It appeared as early as 1909, when he was thirty-five, and it contains

nothing that he would have repudiated at any time afterwards. It was not, however, till long afterwards that it began
to be taken seriously, and even then not by everybody. As
late as 1929 he found it necessary to refute a critic in some
modernist newspaper, who had said that "for all he knew"
Mr. Chesterton was "modernist enough in his own thoughts."
He shared the general fate of poets and prophets, and all
who are pre-eminently gifted with the power to say what
they mean: nobody would believe that he meant what he
said. He told rationalists that they were irrational, but they
only laughed; he told them that there was nothing to laugh
at, and they laughed all the louder; then he grew angry, and
they were hurt; they felt that he was letting them down. To
dismiss Chesterton's conversion as a joke which may be carried too far, however, or as an elaborate parody on more
solemn ecclesiasticism, is to make nonsense of his whole
achievement; and though there are some who are quite prepared to do this, and even to justify their action on the
ground that nonsense is what one looks for from a humorist,
it must be insisted firmly that this conception of humour is
too narrow: that there is a kind of humour that is not nonsensical—and also a kind of nonsense that is not humorous.
One can always forgive a man for not immediately locating
the Great Nebula when a rocket is fired to show him where
it is, or for losing sight of the argument of *Orthodoxy* in the
illustrations; but no one who has himself experienced that
sudden co-ordination of intuitions which we call conversion
can really mistake the authenticity of the description of it
contained in that book, or fail finally to sympathize with
the author when he throws in his hand in gay despair over
the impossibility of expounding it: "There is, therefore,
about all complete conviction, a kind of huge helplessness.
The belief is so big that it takes a long time to get into
action. And this hesitation chiefly arises, oddly enough, from
an indifference about where one should begin."

In *Orthodoxy* "the main problem for philosophers" is
defined as "how we can contrive at once to be astonished
at the world and yet at home in it." Not many philosophers,

I think, would acknowledge that as their main problem, or even as a problem at all. At any rate, they would say, it is necessary first to decide whether the world exists or astonishment is a possibility, and, if it is, whether it needs anybody to be astonished or anything to be astonished at. Chesterton poured ridicule on such enquiries. "Most modern philosophies," he said, "are not philosophy but philosophic doubt; that is, doubt about whether there can be any philosophy" (*St. Thomas Aquinas*). He accepted the old idea of philosophy as the pursuit of wisdom; and it is only within the circuit of that idea that his problem has any meaning. The question whether it is, in fact, "the main problem for philosophers" remains to be discussed. But one thing is certain: it had been the main problem for Chesterton himself.

He himself had never ceased to be astonished at the world. He had, he said in his *Autobiography,* preserved into manhood something of "the romance of receptivity" of a child. He had not come to take the world for granted. But he had, in growing up, been confronted by a system of reasoning, apparently impregnable, which denied the validity, and even the actuality, of his wonder. How, it challenged, could he be thankful for creation when there was nobody to thank, or be astonished at what was only a projection of his own imagination? It is hard to picture Chesterton at any time deeply impressed by the arguments of "nihilists"; yet he has left a record in two of his romances, *The Man who was Thursday* ("thrown up in the nihilism of the nineties") and *The Poet and the Lunatics,* of that "mood of unreality and sterile isolation" which, as he says in the autobiography, settled upon him under their influence. Says Gabriel Gale in *The Poet and the Lunatics:*

"I also dreamed that I had dreamed of the whole creation. I had given myself the stars for a gift; I had handed myself the sun and moon. I had been behind and at the beginning of all things; and without me nothing was made that was made. Anybody who has been in that centre of the cosmos knows that it is to be in hell."

Chesterton's had been a peculiar, but authentic, case of that division between the deductions of reason and the certainties of intuition which is the precondition of genuine conversion.

He had not ceased to be astonished at the world; but he had ceased to be at home in it. And this alienation, this sterile isolation afflicting him, was ended by one thing—Christianity. It was Christianity, or Christian theology, that supplied him with a system of reasoning as compact and comprehensive as anything the nihilists could offer, which yet had a place in it for all the experiences he valued: a place of honour indeed. It was Christianity that reconciled his reason with his intuition; and a Christian philosopher whose works he read, so he declared, with a pleasure "definitely not only of the reason, but also of the imagination."

The chapter in *Orthodoxy* entitled "The Maniac" is the most appropriate commentary on *The Poet and the Lunatics*. *Orthodoxy* itself is the record of Chesterton's conversion. And the *St. Thomas Aquinas* contains an account of the kind of life that sprang from it. If we accept his conception of philosophy as the pursuit of wisdom, there is but one way of answering the question whether "How we can contrive at once to be astonished at the world and yet at home in it" is really what he called it, "the main problem for philosophers": and that is by deciding whether this kind of life made him wise.

❧

It was the life of the "great contemplative." The great contemplative, he said, "is the complete contrary of that false contemplative, the mystic who looks only into his own soul, the selfish artist who shrinks from the world and lives only in his own mind." He is one who faces outwards, and surrenders himself to each fresh object in turn of the outer world.

"According to Aquinas the object becomes a part of the mind; nay, according to Aquinas the mind actually becomes the object. But, as one commentator acutely puts it, it only becomes the object and does not create the object. In other words, the object *is* an object; it can and does exist outside the mind, or in the absence of the mind. And *therefore* it enlarges the mind of which it becomes a part. The mind conquers a new province like an emperor; but only because the mind has answered the bell like a servant."

One is reminded of the poet, who "is the most unpoetical of anything in existence, because he has no identity—he is continually in for and filling some other body" (Keats: Letter of Oct. 27, 1818). And it is just this attitude of more than intellectual humility, which he equated with the spontaneous "wonder" of children—the vision uncorrupted by theory or convention—that Chesterton made it his life-work to preach and practice. He continues:

"Note how this view avoids both pitfalls; the alternative abysses of impotence. The mind is not merely receptive, in the sense that it absorbs sensations like so much blotting-paper; on that sort of softness has been based all that cowardly materialism which conceives man as wholly servile to his environment. On the other hand, the mind is not purely creative, in the sense that it paints pictures on the windows and then mistakes them for the landscape outside. But the mind is active, and its activity consists in following, so far as the will chooses to follow, the light outside that does really shine upon real landscapes. . . . In other words, the essence of the thomist common sense is that two agencies are at work; reality and the recognition of reality; and their meeting is a sort of marriage. Indeed it is very truly a marriage, because it is fruitful; the only philosophy now in the world that really is fruitful."

We can see how it was that the thomist philosophy came to Chesterton as a liberation, that it made "a very peculiar and powerful impression" upon him "analogous to poetry." It enabled him to adopt consciously towards the world an attitude that had previously been unconscious, or rather, instinctive and at variance with his intellect. Thereafter he could, and did, spend his life answering the bell like a servant and conquering innumerable provinces like an emperor. We can justly apply to himself his own further words concerning St. Thomas: "He was a man who always turned his full attention to anything; and he seems to fix even passing things as they pass. To him even what was momentary was momentous. The reader feels that any small point of economic habit or human accident is for the moment almost

scorched under the converging rays of a magnifying lens."
And furthermore: "It is impossible to put in these pages a
thousandth part of the decisions on details of life that may
be found in his work. . . . We can only touch on one or
two obvious topics of this kind." This is to be an introduction to Chesterton and not a dissertation.

 ❧

But, it will be said, there is nothing peculiarly orthodox about the attitude he has been describing. And that
is true. There is a palpable equivocation contained in
the passage we have just quoted. It is not the philosophy
that is fruitful but the way of life promoted by it; and
it is quite possible, nay, it is certain, that other philosophies besides the thomist (or Chestertonian) may solve
the same problem and promote the same attitude. But
Chesterton's intuitions, prior to his acceptance of orthodoxy, had been manifold: this had been only one of them.
There had been others, demanding a far more elaborate
rationalization. "This, therefore, is . . . my reason for
accepting the religion and not merely the scattered and
secular truths out of the religion. I do it because the thing
has not merely told this truth or that truth, but has revealed
itself as a truth-telling thing" (*Orthodoxy*). It substantiated
and coordinated *all* his intuitions—and for a very obvious
reason: because they were precisely the intuitions to substantiate and coordinate which it had originally been designed.
It fitted him, because it had been measured to fit—like
Cinderella's shoe; he did not have to chop off his toes or pad
it with paper before he could get into it. He could wear it
naturally—far more naturally than most theologians. He
could, and did, caper in it, whilst they hobbled and limped;
and when he wanted to use it as a weapon, he kicked with it:
he did not have to take it off first and throw it. It had been
the key to his difficulties, and when he saw others in the same
difficulties he used it as a key: he did not knock them down
with it, like St. Peter in the *Vision of Judgement*.

Naturally, he was misunderstood. People had grown so
used to hearing church dogmas propounded dogmatically

they had ceased to believe that they could really mean anything to anybody; they had grown so used to seeing them accepted as superstitions, they had forgotten that even superstitions often have a foundation in fact. "We and our critics have come to talk in two different languages; so that the very names by which we describe the things inside stand for totally different things in the absurd labels they have stuck upon the wall outside. Often if we said the great things we have to say, they would sound like the small things they accuse us of saying" (*The Thing*). He had to explain patiently to Mr. H. G. Wells that the dogma of The Fall rested on realities of experience, and could not be confuted simply by saying, "Where is the Garden of Eden?"

"There ought," he observed once, "to be a real study called anthropology corresponding to theology" (*St. Thomas Aquinas*). Orthodoxy interpreted his own nature to himself and thereby detached him from it. It was for this reason that he was able to call Aquinas an anthropologist: he had "a complete theory of Man, right or wrong." In his *St. Thomas Aquinas* Chesterton deplores the too exclusive attention given by modern anthropologists to the study of anthropoids. The science of man as it exists, he complains, leaves out of its scope precisely those features of man that are distinctive: those that distinguish *homo sapiens* from *simius insipiens*. Yet, "it is necessary to know whether he is responsible or irresponsible, perfect or imperfect, perfectible or unperfectible, mortal or immortal, doomed or free: not in order to understand God, but in order to understand Man. Nothing that leaves these things under a cloud of religious doubt can possibly pretend to be a Science of Man." In orthodoxy, and orthodoxy alone, he found these questions answered. They were answered so completely, and so completely to his satisfaction, that he concluded right away that the pronouncements of the Church on other issues, which had not yet faced him, were probably satisfactory also. At the end of *Orthodoxy* he declares that he is willing to accept them tentatively, until he has proved them by experience. By the time he had written *St. Thomas Aquinas* he had accepted them absolutely, without the proviso.

He became a Roman Catholic in 1922. Thereby he bound himself to accept as just and true whatever the supreme authority of the Roman Catholic Church pronounced— within however circumscribed a sphere—to be just and true. And thereby, I think, he made his first great error. He set himself apart from the religious tradition of his own country, and glanced aside the impact of his influence on its religious and political thought. Nor would he have repudiated these charges; he would only have added that they were not charges at all, but a commendation and a comparison. Nevertheless, his action betokened a certain insensitiveness to the ethical advances and contributions that really have been made by the Protestant churches in England: contributions which have no parallel within the Roman church, and which are, in fact, incompatible with its pretensions.

He was one of the most brilliant controversialists who have ever lived. In the *St. Thomas* he states the principle upon which his controversies were conducted: "We must either not argue with a man at all, or we must argue on his grounds and not ours." He was, in fact, continually engaged in cutting their ground from under his opponents' feet. While they aimed their big guns at some distant, and generally illusory, target, he would rise up suddenly behind them and turn their artillery upon themselves. Did they challengingly assert that "Living religion is not in dull and dusty dogmas"?—Of course it is not, he replied: but our dogmas are neither dull nor dusty. Did they arraign him as a reactionary, because he argued against their socialism?— "I do not object to socialism because it will revolutionize our commerce," he would answer blandly: "but because it will leave it so horribly the same." He always knew the standpoint of his opponents better than they knew it themselves— and far better than they knew his. Therein lies the advantage of being a controversialist of imagination: he had entered into their minds, and sympathized. None the less, on the one issue of ecclesiastical authority he was unable to employ his accustomed tactics. When he was told that he had surrendered his freedom of conscience, by subscribing in advance to the dictates of the infallible pope, he evaded the charge, first by proclaiming that there was as much, if not more, variety of opinion among Catholics than other men—*upon topics to which the dogma of infallibility did not extend;* and secondly, by asserting that he did no more in taking the verdicts of the Church on trust than other men did in accepting the facts laid out in a Bradshaw—an analogy too obviously false to need refutation.

Chesterton's allegiance to Rome was, we believe, his first great error. Nevertheless it was, in a sense, inevitable. He had one of the most naturally Catholic minds that have appeared in England during this century. That is to say, not only was he naturally religious, in the highest sense, and therefore bound to be attracted by the magnificent breadth and almost unlimited provisions of the Roman Catholic Church; but he was inclined from the first to submit his conscience to authority. We can detect this in his attitude to orthodox theology itself; it is epitomized in that little phrase, parenthetical in the passage we have quoted from his *St. Thomas,* "so far as the will chooses to follow."

We have said that he knew his opponents' viewpoints better than they knew them themselves. This is strictly true, so long as his opponents were rationalists, modernists, progressive humanitarians and so forth. He reasserted and substantiated repeatedly his claim that "the modern world, with its modern movements, is living on its Catholic capital"; that is to say, that one "progressive" movement after another since the Reformation has seized upon some single element out of the old Catholic synthesis, and built upon it as upon a self-evident truth; whereas, not only was it already contained in Catholicism, together with many other elements equally important (without which it was itself no more than a half—or even quarter—truth), but that apart from the total philosophy it was not self-evident at all. For example:

> "The Calvinists took the Catholic idea of the absolute knowledge and power of God; and treated it as a rocky irreducible truism so solid that anything could be built on it, however crushing or cruel. They were so confident in their logic, and its one first principle of predestination, that they tortured the intellect and imagination with dreadful deduc-

tions about God, that seemed to turn Him into a demon. But it never seems to have struck them that somebody might suddenly say that he did not believe in the demon" (*The Thing*).

Similarly Shelley and Whitman and the revolutionary optimists of the eighteenth century:

> "They also, though less consciously because of the chaos of their times, had really taken out of the old Catholic tradition one particular transcendental idea; the idea that there is a spiritual dignity in man as man, and a universal duty to love men as men. And they acted in exactly the same extraordinary way as their prototypes, the Wesleyans and the Calvinists. They took it for granted that this spiritual idea was absolutely self-evident like the sun and moon; that nobody could ever destroy that, though in the name of it they destroyed everything else. They perpetually hammered away at their human divinity and human dignity, and inevitable love for all human beings; as if these things were naked natural facts. And now they are quite surprised when new and restless realists suddenly explode, and begin to say that a pork-butcher with red whiskers and a wart on his nose does not strike them as particularly divine or dignified, that they are not conscious of the smallest sincere impulse to love him, that they could not love him if they tried, or that they do not recognize any particular obligation to try" (*op. cit.*).

The modern world "is using, and using up, the truths that remain to it out of the old treasury of Christendom." The point itself is urgent. For, as Chesterton did not fail to point out, this process may well be carried to its logical conclusion, in the repudiation of pity itself, the last of the traditional virtues. It is a conclusion that does not seem so remote from us to-day as it may have done ten years ago. And there is nothing, nothing whatever, to prevent it, except the promulgation of a true philosophy in which all these truths and virtues find their place and their justification. If they are to be challenged by reason, they must be reasonably defended: the unaided instinct can no longer be trusted to uphold them. Yet, just when they are most needed, because they are most needed, there is a real and desperate danger of the world's losing sight of *all* the forms and systems in which they have hitherto inhered, and all the symbols the past has established to convey them to the imaginations of men. Of this danger Chesterton was acutely aware. It was because he was aware of it that he pitted himself hand and foot against all the partial and logically indefensible positions taken up by his Protestant and humanitarian critics. It was *not* sufficient, he saw clearly, to take this virtue or that virtue out of the treasury of Christendom and call it the one thing necessary: it was not sufficient either to earn the title of "Christian" or to save Christianity itself. It was a case of all or nothing. And we can see how truly great must have been the temptation to him of an authoritarian church which, as he believed, stood for the all, and used its authority to enforce it. The Roman Catholic Church may possibly thrust itself in the way of new and acceptable ideas; but it does certainly stand out against the endless proliferation of old and unacceptable ones. The papacy has never tolerated, as the Protestant churches have had to tolerate, the anti-intellectual pragmatism of Buchman.

Still, Chesterton's assumption that the Catholic theology was "all" remained an assumption—and one which he refused to question. That is the crux of the argument. He had no difficulty in dealing with the representatives of movements based on scattered and secular truths out of his own religion: because he accepted their basic principles himself, and a great deal more besides. But he could not, or would not, admit that there was any positive significance in the original repudiation of the Catholic synthesis from which they sprang. Yet it was not mere perversity that brought about the Reformation; it was not even sheer indignation alone, against the monstrous iniquities of the papal curia at the time of the Renaissance. It would be truer to say that it was the Renaissance itself. Chesterton could point out the need of a complete anthropology, corresponding to theology, and demonstrate that all his opponents' were incomplete; but he would not allow that such a complete anthropology might really be found outside Catholicism. From the first he followed only so far as his will chose to follow the light outside that did really shine upon real things; and his will did not choose to follow the light that shone upon certain things. He acknowledged the existence of a complete anthropology that rested on faith in the supernatural, and of many incomplete anthropologies that repudiated the supernatural; he never seriously admitted the possibility of an anthropology that repudiated the supernatural and was yet complete. When he was faced with what some would regard as the potentiality of such a thing, he averted his eyes.[1]

It is significant that he at no time faced up fairly to the pantheist position. He was continually referring both to pantheism and Buddhism. In the *St. Thomas Aquinas* he repeatedly contrasts them with thomism: and always he dismisses them upon the same ground—that they deny the multiplicity whilst exalting the unity of creation. Had he ever submitted himself to the writings of either the pantheists of the western world or the Buddhists of the eastern, he might have discovered some things that would have made him pause. He might, for example, have discovered the following passage from an old *zen,* which, were the word "Catholicism" only substituted for "Buddhism," might easily be mistaken for one of his own familiar pronouncements:

> "To a man who knows nothing of Buddhism, mountains are mountains, waters are waters, and trees are trees. But when he has read the scriptures and knows a little of Buddhism, mountains are no longer mountains, waters are no longer waters, and trees no longer trees (*i.e.,* they are *maya,* or illusion). But when he has thoroughly understood Buddhism, mountains are once again mountains, waters are waters, and trees are trees" (Quoted in *The Legacy of Asia and Western Man,* by A. W. Watts, Murray, 1937).

One is tempted to draw a further comparison between Chesterton's "wonder" and the "awe before the pure phenomenon" of the spinozist, Goethe; and between the attitude of "the great contemplative" and that "true process of subjective growth through objective experience," which has been ascribed to Goethe by Mr. Middleton Murry. But there is no object in emphasizing further what we believe to have been the limitations of Chesterton's Christianity.

[1] See Note I at the end of this book.

Whether we call it "awe" or "wonder," the recognition of whose importance he called the "chief idea" of his life, he himself certainly possessed it; and it is upon his manifestation of it, and the unique quality of that manifestation, that his claim to greatness reposes.

∾

Chesterton, in *The Victorian Age in Literature,* once provoked a storm of indignation by likening Thomas Hardy to "the village atheist brooding and blaspheming over the village idiot" (a writer in *The Adelphi* called it a "most profoundly irreligious criticism"). To his accusers, however, he replied characteristically that this was not an attack on Hardy but a defence of him: for "the whole case for him is that he had the sincerity and simplicity of the village atheist." We might, I think, without being one whit more insulting, compare Chesterton in passing this judgement to the village idiot brooding and blaspheming over the village atheist. For it was precisely his truth and his triumph that he himself possessed something of the naïvety of the village idiot. Indeed, one might go so far as to draw a parallel between the English expression "a natural" and Goethe's *eine Natur.*

Another characteristic of the "natural" is often his irrepressible hilarity in grave situations. It is a characteristic that has been known to cause considerable resentment in the more solemn quarters of the community. Chesterton's much-needed emphasis on the place held by "wonder" in Christianity was his first important contribution to contemporary thought. His second, and more original, was the equation of wonder with humour.

It would nearly be true to say that this was his unique contribution. It is certainly true that no Christian philosopher has given it a more prominent place in his system. Goethe would probably have repudiated it altogether. Yet it is a great and necessary element in Christianity. Humour is, indeed, allied to forgiveness, because it is, as Clutton Brock once said, a "joyful sense of the imperfections of this life." Jesus's own love is hardly more perfectly manifested than in his nickname for James and John, "the Sons of

Thunder." When he laughed at their ambition to call down
fire from heaven upon the Samaritan village, he forgave in
them what was nothing less than their complete incomprehension of everything that he stood for. He was laughing at
his own despair.

It is by this quality of joyfulness that humour is distinguished from satire. Satire is essentially joyless. It is a bitter,
merciless *denunciation* of what is imperfect; and it is the
work of a man who is at heart miserable, because he is alone:
as Swift and Byron and Heine were alone and miserable. It
is the work of a man who has identified himself with the
good, aspired to the loneliness of God—and found the everlasting solitude of Satan. Satire is not life-bringing, however
often it may deceive itself into thinking it is. It is deathly,
because it calls into being the resentment it is bred of, and
perpetuates it.

All this stripping away of illusions which is the principal
occupation of "intellectuals" to-day is, in fine, but an indul-
gence of the supreme illusion: that of their own superiority.
"The poetry," said Wilfred Owen, "is in the pity." Cynicisms
of this sort cannot even be called pity turned rancid, for
those who exhibit it have never attained to pity—or charity:
they are the same thing. "They have not gone off their
heads," one can hear Chesterton saying: "they have gone off
their hearts; they have gone onto their heads: probably they
were dropped on them in infancy—and they have been
swollen ever since." To meet what is hateful with hate is to
meet it on its own level, and duplicate it. Only by loving
it, in all its hatefulness, can we hope to triumph over it, in
spirit or in fact: for it is true, as Chesterton maintained—
and he never uttered a truer paradox—that "until we love a
thing in all its ugliness we cannot make it beautiful"
(*Twelve Types*).

Thus he was unjust in calling Dickens "a violent satirist":

"Nearly half-way through the nineteenth century there
came out of England the voice of a violent satirist. In its
political quality it seemed like the half-choked cry of the
frustrated republic. It had no patience with the pretence that
England was already free, that we had gained all that was

valuable from the revolution. It poured a cataract of contempt on the so-called working compromises of England, on the oligarchic cabinets, on the two artificial parties, on the government offices, on the J.P.'s, on the vestries, on the voluntary charities. This satirist was Dickens, and it must be remembered that he was not only fierce, but uproariously readable. He really damaged the things he struck at, a very rare thing" (*Dickens*).

Chesterton here is plainly thinking at least as much of himself as of Dickens. These were the abuses he also struck at. His "fiercest mood" also was "reserved for methods that were counted scientific and progressive." [2] It is possible that he also really damaged them. He was certainly uproariously readable. But it is just this quality of uproariousness in his work that distinguishes it from satire, in the sense in which we have been using the term. He laughed at the evils he decried even while he was tilting at them. Swift could never do that.

༝

So Chesterton wrote *The Napoleon of Notting Hill*. It is the epic of the reconquest of London by humour and love, personified in Auberon Quin and Adam Wayne respectively. And the first important thing to notice about them is their child-like character—it is a feature that is repeatedly stressed; the second is the quality of vision with which both are invested. This is how Quin is introduced:

"So the short government official looked at the coat-tails of the tall government official, and through street after street, and round corner after corner, saw only coat-tails, coat-tails, and again coat-tails—when, he did not in the least know why, something happened to his eyes.

"Two black dragons were walking backwards in front of him. Two black dragons were looking at him with evil eyes. The dragons were walking backwards it was true, but they kept their eyes fixed on him none the less. The eyes which he saw were, in truth, only the two buttons at the back of a frock-coat: perhaps some traditional memory of their meaningless character gave this half-witted prominence to their gaze. The slit between the tails was the nose-line of the monster: whenever the tails flapped in the winter wind the

2 Especially *Eugenics and other Evils* and *The Fallacy of Divorce*.

dragons licked their lips. It was only a momentary fancy, but the small clerk found it embedded in his soul ever afterwards. He never could again think of men in frock-coats except as dragons walking backwards."

The passage deserves to be quoted at length, because it illustrates a reservation we must make before going farther. "It was only a momentary fancy," says Chesterton. It would have been truer to say that the impression was only a fancy. For this seeing of things as *other than they are* is not what is meant by imaginative vision at all; it is not what he himself had meant by it. The alliance of Adam Wayne and Auberon Quin is capable of two, quite distinct, interpretations. Chesterton seldom separated them. Under the grave, yet humorous, seeing of a child he grouped a whole assemblage of attitudes, most of which may be valuable, but only one of which is indispensable.

In his second collection of essays, for example, there is a third: "Now I deny most energetically that anything is, or can be, uninteresting. So I stared at the joints in the walls and seats, and began thinking hard on the fascinating subject of wood. Just as I had begun to realize why, perhaps, it was that Christ was a carpenter . . ." (*Tremendous Trifles*). Blake is reported to have said that he could stare at a knot in a piece of wood until it terrified him; and Chesterton is fond of applying the adjective "terrible" to things: to pillar-boxes, railway-signals, human nature, etc. (In fact he did so far too often: the mannerism soon ceases to surprise and only irritates the reader). But in this case he is not *contemplating* a piece of wood at all—as Blake was, imaginatively; he is *thinking about* it; and not even thinking about a particular joint or knot, but about wood in general. The distinction is important; but it was not until the end of his life that he made it unequivocally. In his *Autobiography* occur the finest of his descriptions of childish vision. In this book occur also the following words:

"I am much more disposed *now* to fancy that an apple-tree in the moonlight is some sort of ghost or grey nymph; or to see the furniture fantastically changing and crawling at twilight, as in some story of Poe or Hawthorne. But when I was a child I had a sort of confident astonishment in contemplating the apple-tree as an apple-tree."

The distinction was made too late. The "chief ideas" of Chesterton's life had, in fact, been two: first to reveal the necessity of direct perception; and secondly to disguise the revelation as completely as possible by confounding it with something totally different. No one would wish to conjure his fancy, any more than his character, out of existence. But, if the truth he proclaimed is to be allowed its full potency, they must be distinguished.

The purpose of these pages might be defined as that of rescuing Chesterton from "G.K." For I believe that Chesterton unconsciously distorted the doctrine of "becoming as a little child" to suit the exuberances of his character. It was "G.K.," the "orchard man," who rode through Beaconsfield breaking eggs down his shirt-front in the likeness of Dr. Johnson; who declared, and demonstrated, that direct was crooked seeing, that becoming child-like meant being childish; and who would, if he could, have equated the Kingdom of God with the nurseries of Heaven.

THERE was a time when one of the regular Saturday afternoon entertainments arranged for Englishmen was a debate between G. K. Chesterton and Bernard Shaw. It is not recorded that agreement was ever reached on these occasions. Wine and water mingle badly; and it is, in fact, still a subject of dispute which rose to the top. Whatever the ultimate verdict, however, Chesterton's critical study of Shaw will remain a masterpiece. Nobody who has not read the whole of this book can fully appreciate the humour of the "defence" with which it ends: "To represent Shaw as profane or provocatively indecent is not a matter for discussion at all; it is a disgusting criminal libel upon a particularly respectable gentleman of the middle classes, of refined tastes and somewhat puritanical views."

Unless the truth in that description is recognized—and the rest of the study is written to substantiate it—the humour is lost. This points to the error of those who call Chesterton "perverse." Perversity by itself is not humorous at all. It only becomes so when it is consistent, with itself and with the truth. Neither Chesterton nor Shaw would have been wits had they not first been crusaders—any more than Johnson or Voltaire: or, if they had been, their aphorisms would long ago have been lost sight of, as have all but a few of Oscar Wilde's. Their settled convictions alone gave them the high and and secure vantage-ground from which to shoot: and held between their two fires, it would have been a hard road that journalists trod—had either of them ever been taken seriously.

Describing the impact of Bernard Shaw upon the literary world left over from the 'nineties, Chesterton compressed books into one phrase: "The single eyeglass fled before the single eye." Were we to describe his own collision with a world that centred upon Shaw, it could hardly be done better than by saying that the single eye itself recoiled. For that was the eye of an intellectual; and Chesterton came armed with the two eyes of a child. The decadent with the single eye-glass had been doubly removed from reality; but the progressive with the single eye was still removed. He could see things from one side only—from the left. A child sees them from the left and right simultaneously.

Chesterton possessed the direct, imaginative vision of a child, and it is this that makes his greatness, as it does that of nearly all really great men: for the power to see things, not as we have been brought up to see them, nor as our preconceived theories demand that we should see them, but as they actually are, is the privilege of creative genius. Many have seen that this is true in the realm of art; and it was in that realm that Chesterton himself most often emphasized the truth.

"The arts exist, as we should put it in our primeval fashion, to show forth the glory of God; or, to translate the same thing in terms of our psychology, to awaken and keep alive the sense of wonder in man. The success of any work of art is achieved when we say of any subject, a tree or a cloud or a human character, 'I have seen that a thousand times and I never saw it before'" (*The Thing*).

Nevertheless, the power to see things as they are is not confined to artists. Those who have the "vision and the faculty divine" are far outnumbered by those who have the vision only. And strange as it may seem, it is to the latter that I would most naturally assimilate Chesterton.

∾

That Chesterton possessed genius is unquestionable; that he possessed an incomparable and astonishing eloquence nobody who has read or heard him would be prepared to deny; that he possessed that gift which, in poetry, Robert Bridges called the "highest of all"—"the power of concentrating all the far-reaching resources of language on one point, so that a single and apparently effortless expression rejoices the aesthetic imagination at the moment when it is most expectant and most exacting and at the same time astonishes the intellect with a new aspect of the truth" (*Collected Essays*, iv. "Critical Introduction to Keats")—that, I do not think anyone would claim for him. Chesterton astonishes the intellect often enough—too often, indeed, as I shall try to show: the final felicity is wanting.

He himself might have found it hard to admit this fact. He very often undertook to describe simple objects—a bird, a house, a chair—and very often he succeeded in describing them in such a way as to arouse our dormant imaginations: a bird he would define as "a blossom broken loose from its chain of stalk"; a house as "a gigantesque hat to cover a man from the sun"; a chair as "an apparatus of four wooden legs for a cripple with only two." In all these fantastic comparisons we can trace his effort to communicate his own renewed delight in everyday things. But it is precisely because we can trace his effort that Chesterton fails in his purpose. It is the author who startles us by his ingenuity, not the object by its novelty.

As with simple objects, so with the scenes in his romances. Let us take an example:

"The man still holding the sword cast it down with a wordless sound more shocking than a curse. He was a tall, elegant man, with an air of fashion even in his duelling undress; his face, with a rather fine aquiline profile, looked whiter against red hair and a red pointed beard. The man beside him put a hand upon his shoulder and seemed to push him a little, perhaps urging him to fly. This witness, in the French phrase, was a tall, portly man with a long black beard cut as if in the square pattern of his long black frock-coat, and having, somewhat incongruously, a monocle screwed into one eye. The last of the group, the second of the slayer's formal backers, stood motionless and somewhat apart from the rest—a big man, much younger than his comrades, and with a classical face like a statue's and almost as impassive as a statue's. By a movement common to the whole tragic company, he had removed his top-hat at the final announcement" (*The Man Who Knew Too Much*).

It is when we read such passages as this that we are reminded that their author began his career by being an artist. There is about the picture a singular and surprising clearness: the whole scene is vivid to the mind's eye. The *mind's* eye it is, however. In trying to analyse the impression it makes, one is driven inevitably into comparing it to that of a toy theatre, such as Chesterton loved all his life. Those beards, we feel, were stuck on; that gesture common to the whole company was as automatic as it was unanimous. Oddly enough, Chesterton seems to have felt the same:

"They followed his glance down to the garden by the wall, and the first thing they saw was that the rusty old garden door was standing open, letting in the white light of the road. Then they realized that a few yards within it was a tall, lean, grey-bearded man, clad completely in black and looking like some puritanic minister. He was standing on the turf looking down on the dead. A girl in grey, with a black hat, was kneeling by the body, and the two seconds had, as by an instinct of decency, withdrawn to some distance and stood gazing gloomily at the ground. *In the clear sunlight the whole group looked like a lighted scene on a green stage.*"

To point out the all but childishly simple way by which this effect has been achieved—the meticulous building up of the picture, item by item, without much regard for realism (the open gate would hardly have been observed before the people inside it); the rejection of all half-tones (as from "the white light of the road"); the characteristic repetitions —this is not in the least to disparage it. Such a style, individual chiefly through the absence of individuality, might profitably be copied by any apprentice to story-telling. But it is important to realize that it exhibits the simplicity of simplification, rather than that of simplicity itself. The world portrayed by Chesterton is not the real world, seen through the eyes of "second childhood," not even that of his own infancy, when men really wore beards and frock-coats, but a world of abstractions. It appeals neither to the senses nor to the imagination, but to the mind: it is poster-painted in words.

He could not turn words into a medium like light, which illuminates what it falls upon while remaining invisible itself: the spectrum of his own idiom was too diverting. The attraction of his most realistic tale lies not in its truth to life but in its style and moral. He was, in fact, less of an artist than a dialectician. It is not the material of poetry— concrete objects, scenes and characters—that reflects his imaginative genius to the best advantage; it is the relatively abstract matter of philosophy.

❧

Chesterton the philosopher is one of the most captivating, and at the same time one of the most bewildering writers in the world. To open any one of his books is to be caught, as securely as a fly in a spider's web—only rather more pleasantly. Imagine yourself, like a fly, entangled in a web. You are held by a mesh of interwoven threads, all glittering with dew-drops, all stretching far away to some end beyond your sight; you are aware of a pattern uniting them, but what it may be you have no idea. You try to free yourself. If you are impatient you begin by fluttering about, buzzing frantically —and find yourself all the more firmly held. Then you consider the best means of unravelling the knot. The first necessity is to find an end; and with that view you start following one of the threads that envelop you. But as with the threads composing a web, so with the strands of Chesterton's thought: if you want to find an end, you must needs wind all round the spiral until you reach the middle. Only when you have found that will you be able to break away—and the middle happens also to be the one place from which you may discern the pattern of the whole.

Chesterton spent a lifetime arguing (he said once that his occupation in life was "catching flies")[1]; he threw out his lines of argument in every direction: but he always threw them out from the same standpoint. It was the standpoint of an imaginative vision. There is no direct communication of that vision in his works. What there is is an endless series of rationalizations of its component parts (the rationalization of the whole being thomist). If we wish to share the vision, therefore, we must follow the arguments; but we shall in all probability be unable to follow the arguments unless we share the vision, in some measure, already. "To him that hath shall be given, and from him that hath not shall be taken away, even that which he hath."

This is a paradox. But things discerned by the imagination can only be formulated, intellectually, by means of paradoxes. That is why Chesterton's own writing abounds in them. The body of his wit is parodoxical, because the soul of it is truth. That is why, also, some of his most brilliant epigrams were made to crystallize the views of other imaginative men, the most brilliant of them all to crystallize those of the most imaginative of them all; the marriage of wit and insight in his remark concerning Middleton Murry—"He is a voice crying in the wilderness, 'There is no God, and Marx is his prophet' "—was surely made in Heaven.

This is, in my opinion, the most perfect of Chesterton's paradoxes, because it is at once the most startling and the most searching. He saw things with both eyes—stereoscopically, so to speak; but his mastery of language is shown, not by his power of re-creating them before us, in all their con-

[1] "On Thoughtless Remarks" in *All I Survey*.

crete and complex simplicity—so that we too may perceive them as if for the first time—not by this, but by the rapidity with which he can expose them from the right and left by turns. Sometimes he does it so deftly that an illusion of direct seeing is obtained; and sometimes so fast that the illusion becomes truth. He presents a thesis, antithesis, and the mind combines them. Shaw, as he observed, is not paradoxical; wit of this kind, no less than humour, rests on an imaginative apprehension of the truth.

For what is, in fact, the essence of this paradox? One could go on trying to expound it for ever, and yet come no nearer to a definition. One might say that it involved a simultaneous denial of the God of anthropomorphic theology and reassertion of the God of experience: with an additional clause to the effect that Karl Marx was a vehicle of this God. But such an exposition would bring no conviction to those who know of no other God than the deity of anthropomorphic theology—whether they affirm his existence or deny it; and to those who do not know the God of experience, it must appear for what it is—the clumsiest possible paraphrase for a perfect paradox.

Considering Chesterton's aversion to pantheism, it is rather surprising, when one comes to consider it, that he should have shown so much insight into Middleton Murry's creed. On other occasions, indeed, he resolutely refused to understand it. He refused to penetrate to the heart of what he called that "mystical paradox about losing freedom in order to be free" ("On Fate and a Communist" in *All I Survey*), which is Murry's solution to the problem of necessity and free will; he would not see that the pantheist who denied his charge, that "no special impulse to moral action" can possibly arise from a belief in absolute determinism, was asserting a contradiction neither more violent nor less defensible than he himself was doing, when he upheld "the complex God of the Athanasian Creed": and might in fact have used his own words to justify it—"This thing that bewilders the intellect utterly quiets the heart." The fallen angels were baffled by the problem, precisely because they were fallen angels—because they had lost the imagination, which is love.

To the imagination it is self-evident that the pantheist contention is not a contradiction at all, but what Chesterton actually called it, a paradox; that it involves, in other words, a simultaneous denial of one sort of free will and reassertion of another. Its illogic, like that of the Trinity, and of all the highest truths of high religion, is its most triumphant vindication.

For reality itself is illogical. Being a developing process, it is, and is not what it is, at any given moment. That process of denial in one mode and reassertion in another, which is the very heart of paradox, is also the very heart of all "becoming" or growth. That is why the thought that is loyal to it, formulated intellectually, can only be formulated in contradictions; the truth is always either self-evident or it is incomprehensible. It is self-evident to the imagination—and paradoxical; to the intellect it is incomprehensible—and a contradiction in terms. From the sublime to the ridiculous, all Chesterton's paradoxes may be cited in illustration of this fact. What does his reference to a man "proud of his humility" reflect, but the insight of a psychologist who knows the subtle and interminable process by which the *ego* arrogates to itself the virtue of the soul, or of God? What does his demand that "the democracy be taught democracy" imply, but an analogous recognition of the negation of the spirit by the letter? Even his amusing words about the necessity of being unpractical involve the denial of one end in life and the reassertion of another. His wit and his philosophy are inseparable.

❧

Chesterton's vision is imaginative, his expression of it intellectual. This is the central fact that explains nearly all the contradictions in his work. Not only the superficial and profound contradictions of his paradoxy, but the rather less amiable one, which repels many a serious reader, between the solemnity of the truth he is uttering and the overt vulgarity of its utterance.

This vulgarity of his—which, let it be said at once, is occasional only and has nothing to do with his gaiety—arises from an insensitiveness to the subtler emotional quality of words. He was insensitive to this in his own writing; and sometimes he proved himself unresponsive to it in the writing of others. In his own writing we find him indulging frequently in rhetoric. Now rhetoric is simply emotion become self-conscious, and is not by any means always a vice. The modern attitude of contempt towards it, at all times and in all circumstances, is an absurdity which should be dispelled by a single perusal of *Lepanto*. But the tawdry crescendoes that end one chapter after another of Chesterton's *Chaucer* can leave a very sour taste in our mouths. They are incongruous, and to a sensitive and interested reader they may be intolerable.

Equally incongruous are some of his references to the sayings of greater men than himself. When he dubs the sombre and magnificent paradox of Jesus, "He who loseth his life, the same shall save it," "not a piece of mysticism for saints and heroes, but a piece of everyday advice for sailors and mountaineers" *(Orthodoxy)*—we realize that there are moments when Chesterton "seems to debase and flatten everything he touches; and most of all when he touches worthy and exalted things" ("On Vulgarity" in *Come to Think of It*).

Fortunately these are not many. As we have suggested, to blame him for the hilarious incongruity of his similes in all his books would be to blame him for the chief strength of his style. It is just these that make him so vastly more readable and popular than almost any other writer of comparable significance. For if he did by his apparent flippancy drive away more than one serious (he would have said "solemn") seeker after truth, it is at least questionable whether they were not made up for by the hundreds who came to him for a laugh and stayed for the lesson. It is at least arguable whether his pamphlets were not as effective as the clarion-calls of the present *Weekly Review,* or even the audacious alarums and excursions of Mr. Pepler.

∾

Moreover, between the highest form of art and mere artifice there are innumerable degrees; and in some of these

Chesterton excelled all others. Mastery of language in any form, quite apart from subject-matter, may be considered artistry; and he was, indisputably, both one of the greatest essayists and one of the most successful humorous poets in our language.

Of Chesterton's light verse I will say little, except that it stands in a class by itself. The glorious fantasy of his best ballads was something new in English literature; nothing more riotously ironical than his songs for bank-clerks and post-office workers had ever been penned; nothing more sublimely crushing than the lines to F. E. Smith. His humour is not a sly smile, but a broad grin. All the features of his style which are defects in his more serious compositions— the tub-thumping rhythms, the glaring colours—are sources of strength to his humorous and satirical ones; and, as Mr. Julius West long ago pointed out (in *G. K. Chesterton: A Critical Study.* Secker, 1915), every advantage that the verse-form can offer, for sharpening antithesis or developing a refrain, Chesterton exploited to the utmost, with unerring felicity and inescapable effect.

But the essay was his literary form *par excellence.* Not only did he write more essays than anyone before or since; he wrote better ones. Even if he had written nothing else but essays his works would still be impossible to read in their entirety; even if he had written nothing else, his place in English literature would be assured. More than any other writer of the first thirty years of this century, he kept alive the English tradition of essay-writing; and not only did he keep it alive—and what an achievement that was!—but he invented a new kind of writing which his essays exhibit to the best advantage. Paradox and irony, antithesis and a gentle humour, combine to produce a work of art, the distinctive quality of which can only be suggested by saying that, in some of the best examples, the manner of its presentation *is* the subject-matter.

Often it is said that Shaw's plays owe more in their structure to music than to literature. There is an analogy between the arrangement of Chesterton's early essays and that of some musical compositions. They remind one of Dohnani's "Nursery Suite," or Weinberger's variations on a familiar theme. "A series of paragraphs on some topical subject, with little spaces between them in order to encourage the weary reader" —so Julius West described them: but each paragraph is a new development of the original subject; and the reader is never weary. For the essay suited perfectly both Chesterton's temperament and his style. It must have appealed to his partiality for small things—even his longer discursive works, like *The Outline of Sanity* and *What's Wrong with the World,* tend to fall into a series of essays, just as his novels, like *The Man who Knew too Much* and *The Poet and the Lunatics,* fall into a series of short stories. And it suited his style because, in these longer works, however well it is sustained— *because* it is so well sustained—it palls or even insults. He who could be one of the most exhilarating, could also be one of the most exhausting of authors.

◆

This introduces a much more serious charge against Chesterton's practice than his occasional vulgarity. It can and should be acknowledged that his wit was too exuberant. His parallels are too often real parallels, pursuing a course of their own, independent of the main argument, which is all but lost sight of in their proliferation. Moreover, although he never indulged in paradoxes for their own sake, in the sense of striking them regardless of the truth, he did, very often, insert them where they were superfluous. In a writer less prodigal the compression into a single, arresting phrase of an argument that might take pages to unfold could only be looked upon as a virtue. But the reader of *Orthodoxy* knows a point of saturation, beyond which the mind calls out for a respite from epigrams. They no longer startle, only weary it. The writer alone seems never to have wearied. Towards the end of his life, he was still quite content to publish a book whose whole *raison d'être* seems to have been its paradoxes.

Reading *Four Faultless Felons* one cannot escape a suspicion that the title of the book was thought of first, suggesting in its turn the four sub-headings: "The Moderate Murderer," "The Honest Quack," "The Ecstatic Thief" and "The Loyal Traitor." The tales to fit these have been worked out with amazing ingenuity (though never, perhaps, with complete success). In each case the simple unfolding of a complicated plot, a detective story which is at the same time a paradox and a lively parable; the subtle interweaving of one *motif* with another, is carried out with a skill that cannot but command our admiration. Chesterton exactly described his method in such stories when he wrote of Shaw's plays that each is "an expanded epigram. But the epigram is not expanded (as with most people) into a hundred commonplaces. Rather the epigram is expanded into a hundred other epigrams; the work is at least as brilliant in detail as it is in design. But it is generally possible to discover the original and pivotal epigram which is the centre and purpose of the play" (*G. B. Shaw*). And yet, to measure the gulf that separates artifice from art, one has only to compare any one of these tales with one of his essays, or with an essay by Middleton Murry. The sheer brilliance of Murry's style, at its infrequent best, has seldom, if ever, been appreciated. It would be a bad sign if it were: for it exists as a means to an end, and not as an end in itself. In his "From the Lamb to the Bull" (as in Chesterton's "The Wind and the Trees," which is not one of those essays in which the manner is the matter) a multitude of threads of thought and feeling are woven into an organic unity so complete that such felicity, we feel, could never have been thought out: could only have come "as naturally as the leaves to a tree." Where the paradoxes of G. K. Chesterton startle us by their agility, Murry's astonish with their profundity. On this level there is all the difference between wit and wisdom, novelty and originality.

Novelty calls for mental acrobatics; originality demands a *katharsis*. Those who fancy it was the novelty of their technique that made the greatest of the Romantic poets and philosophers unpopular during their lives are far astray. They may seek to guard against the old error of Lockhart and Croker by an indiscriminating eulogy of everything unusual flaunting itself in the literary world to-day—they take for a resurrection the maggots heaving in the dead carcase of poetry. Mr. T. S. Eliot has more penetration than most of his following (which would be considerably reduced if it had to take his words seriously: unfortunately, that is the necessity obviated by its own theory). Wordsworth, in his letter to Charles James Fox, Mr. Eliot writes, "proceeds to expound a doctrine which nowadays is called distributism," and in so doing,

> "He was not merely taking advantage of an opportunity to lecture a rather disreputable statesman and rouse him to useful activity; he was seriously explaining the purpose and content of his poems. . . . It is Wordsworth's social interest that inspires his own novelty of form in verse, and backs up his explicit remarks on poetic diction; and it is really this social interest which (consciously or not) the fuss was all about" *(The Use of Poetry and the Use of Criticism).*

Similarly Chesterton himself:

> ". . . the old quarrels were quarrels of quite a different sort. The motives of the attack on Keats were almost entirely political and social. The motives of the attack on Swinburne were almost entirely moral and religious. But it is not true, of either of these great poets, that they seemed utterly unreadable or unintelligible to those who had formed their taste on the older poets. Gifford was a low Tory hack, who hated and feared the little group of Radicals associated with Leigh Hunt and Shelley, and who regarded the very appearance of an apothecary's apprentice as a new poet in this group as a menacing sign of Jacobinism" ("On Mr. Epstein" in *Come to Think of It*).

The Romantics, even Keats, were hated because they were revolutionaries; and there is nothing men fear more than revolution, whether within themselves or without. Few really great men have ever been popular except through a misunderstanding. Murry is out of fashion to-day principally because he has dared to tear away the trappings from men's heroes, and reveal them as heroic. Only when the astringent of the Romantic movement had been turned into a narcotic, its vision into a dream, did it become possible to represent Shelley's war on society as a passionate indictment of the stopped couplet.

Chesterton was misunderstood, with his own connivance.

There are three ways of making a revolutionary innocuous; by making him a god, by calling him a genius and by turning him into "a character." The first is out of date; the second is wearing thin; the epoch of the third seems to have dawned. The last recorded act in the life of Adam Wayne, provost of Notting Hill, was the single-handed up-rooting of an oak-tree. After that he and King Auberon Quin set out through the world together in search of adventure: "Humour consists in the reversal of the obvious." In this sense, during forty years spent in almost unremitting reversal of the obvious, Chesterton uprooted a good many trees, and orchards too. In the end the occupation lost some of its original novelty in the eyes of the public. The crash of branches striking the ground became so familiar to men's ears, they scarcely bothered to turn round to see once again roots wriggling in the air, and the woodman contemplating his handiwork with the same quiet enjoyment as at first. They merely murmured to themselves smiling, "G.K. again," and continued on their daily round. So that, when the crashes abruptly stopped, and the woodman was no longer to be seen at his accustomed post, they found it hard to believe that the end of that great felling had really come, and that many rank growths were already bursting their pods and creeping up between the fallen trees. Chesterton, who spent a lifetime preaching the necessity of seeing things as though they had never been seen before, lived to be one of the few features left on the landscape so well-known that it was unnoticed. The irony would have pleased him.

3

"*To see the thing simply as it is, not as it is traditionally or conventionally supposed to be, is a gift of the 'daemonic' man, the creative spirit. . . . The fresh, direct and uncorrupted view of the situation, whether in science, or art, or history, or politics is the privilege of the 'daemonic' man. . . . Thus the 'daemonic' is essentially revolutionary in appearance, in whatever province of human activity it manifests itself*" (J. Middleton Murry, "*Heaven and Earth*").

To one approaching Chesterton's
works for the first time, perhaps the most striking thing
about them is the versatility they display. There seems, at
first sight, to be only one province of human activity which
he left exclusively to Mr. Belloc, and that was science. He
was, as a matter of fact, always inclined to be less than just
to both science and scientists. It is possible that he was no
more able than his friend to recognize the vision he preached
when it expressed itself through facts and figures: though
this failure is curious when we remember the nature of his
insight elsewhere.

In one of the first of his poems, which, he said, contained
the "foundation of the philosophy of his later years," there
occurs the following verse:

> "The sun was black with judgment, and the moon
>   Blood, but between
> I saw a man stand, saying, 'To me at least
>   The grass is green.'" [1]

Now it is perfectly true, as D. H. Lawrence declared, that
a child, when it cries, "Why is the grass green?" is not enquiring but exclaiming; and they are dull pedants who seize
on the pretext for prating about chlorophyll. But when a
naturalist says, "Why is the grass green?" he is both exclaiming and enquiring. Admittedly the exclamatory element is
often lost sight of. There is a type of scientist (usually conspicuous at meetings of the British Association) who regards
everything explained as something explained away. Often
he is the same who looks upon some acquaintance with
pachyderms or plankton as a passport to theology: and Chesterton held him, justly, in low esteeem. The greatest scientists, however, from Aristotle to Freud, have not been of this
breed. Darwin might have described his sublime synthesis
of a thousand minute and loving observations [2] in the very
words used by Chesterton of his conversion to Christian

[1] "Femina contra Mundum" in *The Wild Knight*, see note to 2nd edn.
[2] *Cf., Reminiscences of my Father's Everyday Life*, by Sir Francis Darwin
(Watts, 1929): "Thus in the *Origin*, p. 440, there is a description of a larval
cirripede, 'with six pairs of beautifully constructed natatory legs, a pair of
magnificent compound eyes, and extremely complex antennae.' We used to
laugh at him for this sentence, which we compared to an advertisement."

orthodoxy. And so might Freud; for the dynamic of psycho-
analysis derives from Freud's seeing as apparent miracles,
demanding explanation, a host of phenomena which all
others had taken as matters of course.

Chesterton left science to the scientists. But he wrote plays
and novels, poems and detective-stories, pamphlets, procla-
mations and epistles on every subject under the sun, and
some over it. He was not a great playwright, novelist or poet,
nor a supreme master of the short story: but he was never
a dull one; and he did succeed in doing what very few
writers since Dickens or Stevenson have done—he created a
character lively enough to roam beyond the wide circle of his
own readers. Nor can there be much doubt who was the
spiritual ancestor of Father Brown: "The round, moon-like
face and round, moon-like spectacles of Samuel Pickwick
. . . move through the tales as emblems of a certain spheri-
cal simplicity. They are fixed in that grave surprise that may
be seen in babies; that grave surprise that is the only real
happiness that is possible to man" (*Dickens*).

The art at which Chesterton excelled was literary criticism.
In calling criticism an art we are, of course, using the term
in a sense broader than hitherto in these pages, and perhaps
too broad. Criticism is really a halfway house between art
and philosophy: that is why so many social and political
philosophers have begun their careers as critics. Nevertheless, the affinity between art and criticism is very close: how
close Chesterton himself revealed in the casual phrase, "After
all, what we want is direct and individual impressions of
primary objects, *whether poets or pine-trees*" ("On the Standardization of Stevenson" in *All I Survey*). Literary criticism
demands of its exponent a readiness for self-obliteration of
exactly the same quality as poetry or painting: not merely a
"willing suspension of disbelief," but a suspension of belief.
The critic approaching his object must be able to make a
holocaust at once of conventional prejudice and the more
intimate bias of his own convictions, if he is to approach it
imaginatively, from within outwards. His mind must be a
"thoroughfare for all thoughts"; his reason and sensibility

alike on tip-toe for their quarry—"that strangeness of things which is the light in all poetry, and indeed in all art" (*St. Thomas Aquinas*), otherwise his appraisement will stop short at externals, attentive only to the logical content of the lines, or else become, like much of Swinburne's, a thing that is neither prose nor poetry, appreciation nor exposition. Chesterton's studies, with a few significant exceptions, such as his *Blake,* are always of this character. And of course they are saturated through and through with his own peculiar and Christian humour. It may be confidently asserted that only a great critic could have composed his parodies on Tennyson and Walt Whitman.

OLD KING COLE

Me clairvoyant,
Me conscious of you, old camarado,
Needing no telescope, lorgnette, field-glass, opera-glass,
    myopic pince-nez,
Me piercing two thousand years with eye naked and not
    ashamed;
The crown cannot hide you from me;
Musty old feudal-heraldic trappings cannot hide you from
    me,
I perceive that you drink.
(I am drinking with you. I am as drunk as you are).
I see you are inhaling tobacco, puffing, smoking, spitting
(I do not object to your spitting).
You prophetic of American largeness,
You are anticipating the broad masculine manners of these
    States,
I see in you also there are movements, tremors, tears,
    desire for the melodious;
I salute your three violinists, endlessly making vibrations,
Rigid, relentless, capable of going on for ever;
They play my accompaniment; but I shall take no notice
    of any accompaniment;
I myself am a complete orchestra.
So long.

Chesterton never came nearer than that to direct revelation. That *is* Whitman, seen with the understanding that is love, and the love that is laughter. The same insight characterizes his studies of Shaw, Dickens and Chaucer.

Because his criticism is of this quality, deriving from an imaginative apprehension of primary objects, it avoids all classifications. Delighting in diversity, Chesterton had no hankering after the specious uniformity imposed by such terms as "classical" and "romantic." He was free to acknowledge that there are as many different kinds of poetry as there are poets, and to enjoy each for its own merits. These terms are useful within limits, so long as they are kept as classifications. But they are for ever being turned into judgements, by one party or another, because they are for ever being used by men of one idea—"single-eyed" intellectuals. The Romantic poets descended to this level, when they denounced the eighteenth century for not conforming to their own, quite inapplicable canons; the self-styled "classicists" of the present day do likewise, only with less excuse. Few of them thank G. K. Chesterton for the first effort of this century towards a rehabilitation of Pope. "Judge not that ye be not judged": refusing classifications, he became unclassifiable himself.

A critic more in vogue to-day than Chesterton ever was accustomed himself and his readers to drawing a hard and fast distinction between the formlessness, the dreamy sensuality of Romantic art, and the purpose, unity and decorum of the Classical masters. The most remarkable thing about this antithesis is that the late eighteenth and early nineteenth centuries themselves were quite unconscious of its existence. For the essence of the Classic spirit Mr. Irving Babbitt saw exemplified, not in the Italians of the Renaissance, the followers of Daniello, nor the Romans, their models, but the Greeks; yet they, so far from being spurned by the Romantics with a characteristic immoderation, as we should expect if his hypothesis were true, held a positive fascination for them. In Germany, indeed, as Miss Butler has recently shown (E. M. Butler: *The Tyranny of Greece over Germany*), it amounted to nothing less than a tyranny; for not until it had claimed for tribute the poetic life of the unhappy Hölderlin did a Theseus arise strong enough to vanquish it. Heine broke the spell and banished the gods from Olympus: Hermes to a ferry-boat, Bacchus to a monastery, and Zeus to an Arctic *igloo*. In England, however, even so esoteric a genius as Blake conceived it as his mission to "renew the lost art of the Greeks"; Keats prayed for the "old vigour" of their bards; and to Shelley, who welcomed the Greek war of independence with a drama modelled on Aeschylus, it appeared that "no other epoch in the history of our species" had left "fragments stamped so visibly with the image of the divinity in man." To Babbitt all this was but one more illustration of the Romantic nostalgia—and "nostalgia I have defined as the pursuit of pure illusion." Yet it was at least as much Greek art as the isles of Greece that these poets revered, as their words show, and Babbitt would hardly have called the Hermes of Praxiteles a "pure illusion." Did it never seem to him strange that, with every period and place in history at their disposal, these "aimless and lawless" Romantics, these sensual rebels against "all the formal boundaries and limits that the past had set up," should have chosen classical Greece for their Arcadia? (*Cf.,* I. Babbitt: *The New Laocoon* and *Rousseau and Romanticism*.)

The truth is that the familiar distinction has no significance at a certain level: and to that level Chesterton by imagination belonged. From the one side he was deprecated as "romantic," because of his fondness for the colourful and Catholic middle ages; from the other rated as "classical" since he accepted the external discipline of a church. He was neither, and both. Eventually Rousseauists and neo-classicists alike solved the problem of his position in English letters by leaving him out of their histories altogether. He, however, had room for them in his superior vision even when they had none for him in their classifications. The wise words of Lord Hugh Cecil, which Chesterton quoted in his autobiography, have a wider application than to *Orthodoxy* and its critics: "Truth can understand error, but error cannot understand truth." [3]

[3] An aphorism which aptly summarizes the chapter in *Orthodoxy* itself entitled "The Maniac."

It would, we feel, be faintly extravagant to speak of G. K. Chesterton as a "daemonic" spirit, or even to refer to his vision as "daemonic": there is too much of high seriousness implied in that term. It would, however, be still more extravagant to deny that his vision had much in common with that of the "daemonic" man. Like his, it was direct and uncorrupted; and like his, it was revolutionary—or it would have been, if ever it had been heeded.

In studying Chesterton it is always necessary to remember that he became both a revolutionary and a Roman Catholic long before it was the fashion among the intelligentsia to be either. Either, but seldom both. His own revolutionism, no less than his Christianity, sustained itself from a real contact with real things. With the Communism and Catholicism of intellectuals he can have had but little sympathy: both being based on abstractions. The Marxian proletariat is an abstraction; and so is the Kingdom of Heaven that is within men and yet seeks no revolutionary embodiment in the social system of which they are a part. For it is as true that there is no individual apart from society as it is that there is no society apart from its individual members. It is curious, as well as significant, that Marxists are seldom paradoxical. At the very heart of their philosophy lies the truth that reality, being a developing process, cannot be apprehended logically, only dialectically. Yet their philosophy can have no vital meaning for them. Perhaps if it did they would cease to be intellectuals. It is accepted as dogma, as theirs is accepted by the Catholic intellectuals; and therefore any suggestion that the two systems, understood in the spirit, would cease to negate one another, converge and be confirmed in a higher synthesis is, though dialectical to the depths, regarded with abhorrence by both.

It was, however, for just such a synthesis that Chesterton stood. His profound saying, that "until we love a thing in all its ugliness we cannot make it beautiful" is naturally complemented in the realm of politics by his contention that a revolutionary movement, to be successful, must be inspired by the rights of man and not downcast by his wrongs. He understood and disclosed thirty years ago, far more nakedly than the "dialectical materialists" of the present day, the true connection between art and politics. He understood that the dynamic of each, when it is dynamic, springs from an identical imaginative vision. The self-forgetful contemplation of the artist, the Christian reverence for the individual, is the "democratic emotion" of the true revolutionary.

> "The thing which is really required for the proper working of democracy is not merely the democratic system, or even the democratic philosophy, but the democratic emotion. . . . It is a certain instinctive attitude which feels the things in which men all agree to be unspeakably important, and all the things in which they differ (such as mere brains) to be almost unspeakably unimportant" (*Heretics*).

It is not irrelevant to point out that Chesterton would certainly have condemned that last sentence had it been uttered by a Buddhist or pantheist. Much more important is it, however, to grasp his meaning firmly with all its implications, for this is a truth that has repeatedly, and fatally, been lost sight of since the war of 1914-18.

> "Democracy is not philanthropy; it is not even altruism or social reform. Democracy is not founded on pity for the common man; democracy is founded on reverence for the common man, or, if you will, even on fear of him. It does not champion man because man is so miserable, but because man is so sublime. It does not object so much to the ordinary man being a slave as to his not being a king, for its dream is always the dream of the first Roman republic, a nation of kings" (*op. cit.*).

In the epilogue to his brilliant book *Plato To-day*, Mr. R. H. S. Crossman reaches the same conclusion, with a different emphasis. "True democracy," he says, "is un-Platonic, because it springs from the Christian notion of personality"; and "as the true democrat must start with the assumption that the world has still to be made democratic, so the Christian must assume that it is still pagan, despite the existence of 'democratic' institutions and 'Christian' churches." For fundamentally both Christianity and democracy are assertions of incredibles: "Against the realism of those who accept the existing order and seek to maintain it, they preach an impossibility and try to make it come true."

In this perspective lies the true notion of the equality of man, which is not a mechanical but a mystical conception. Equality, in the eyes and on the lips of its first great champions, never meant equality in "mere brains" or talent, any more than in physique; nor can it be exorcized (as Professor Haldane and others suppose) by disproving these claims that were never made. The equality of men resides in something far more fundamental than these, something allied to that beauty beyond beauty which the artist reveals even in ugly things—a universal dignity manifest to an all-comprehending love. The philosophy that can provide a foundation for democracy must be one that has room in it for this love— which is only another name for "the democratic emotion"; no other will suffice: and such a philosophy will necessarily involve a theology, for this love is all that men really know of God.

This was Chesterton's consistent reply to those who, like Father John O'Connor, assailed the doctrine of the equality of men on the ground that it was illogical: "true equality was a mystical fact, only divinely revealed, that all men are equal only in the sight of God" (O'Connor: *Father Brown on G. K. Chesterton*). In one of his essays he points out how faith in democracy and faith in God have declined concurrently in the western world:

> "All men are equal because God loves all equally: and nothing can compare with that equality. But in what other way are men equal? The vague Liberals of the nineteenth century cut away the divine ground from under democracy, and democracy was left to stand by itself. In other words, it is left to fall by itself. Jefferson said that men were given equal rights by their Creator. Ingersoll said they had no Creator, but had received equal rights from nowhere. Even in the democratic atmosphere of America, it began to dawn on a great many people that it is very difficult to prove that men ever received the equal rights at all" ("On Romanticism and Youth" in *All I Survey*).

It was another example of the world's "using, and using up, the truths that remain to it out of the old treasury of

Christendom." But, as before, we need not agree with Chesterton that the only way to arrest this deterioration is by returning to a full profession of Christianity. The way to arrest it is by advancing to an equally comprehensive pantheism. For, after all, it is not a transcendental, but an immanent God whom men participate in and perceive, when they acknowledge the divine particularity of the world.

The democratic emotion aspires naturally to its embodiment in a society of human brotherhood: which means a society of universal spontaneity, for brotherhood is love, and love can only be spontaneous. Such a society is what most of the great democrats have meant by "democracy" itself; and, with the vision of it clearly before their eyes, they have known how to value existing institutions. They have revered the "democratic system" because it reflects an approximation (however remote) to the ideal, inasmuch as toleration, whether of religious or political opinion, finds expression in its laws; and trust, which is allied to toleration, in its constitution. Those who ridicule democracy, ridicule toleration; and those who ridicule toleration, ridicule love, of which it is an essential component. Therefore, respect for what has been achieved, no less than ambition for what has not, characterize the true democrat in a "democratic" society. Chesterton was a liberal before he became a socialist.

∿

Naturally, he rejected the "economic interpretation of history." For that theory, as it is understood by most of its exponents, rests on the abstraction of one element from the complex whole of history, and its promotion to a position of absolute responsibility for all the rest. Chesterton had no use for absolutes. The faculty that can grasp only one aspect of a phenomenon at a time—the continuity, but not the diversity of the colours in a spectrum—Bergson calls the "intellect." Most socialist theoreticians are intellectuals. They suffer, as Chesterton thought the Arab metaphysicians suffered, from "a lack of the vitality that comes from complexity, and of the complexity that comes from comparison" (*The New Jerusalem*). To the power that can grasp all at once Bergson assigns the name of "intuition." Chesterton had intuition—which is also direct perception. For the economic determinist there are but two paths open at this moment of history: to co-operate in the automatic development of productive technique, or be superannuated. He cannot admit the possibility of reversing it, because the denial of any effective reality to the individual as such is knit into the very fabric of the theory of Marxist socialism.

Chesterton's criticism of economic determinism was the same as his criticism of every other sort of determinism. It was that propounded in the *St. Thomas Aquinas:*

> "The mind is not merely receptive, in the sense that it absorbs sensations like so much blotting-paper; on that sort of softness has been based all that cowardly materialism which conceives man as wholly servile to his environment. On the other hand, the mind is not purely creative, in the sense that it paints pictures on the windows and then mistakes them for the landscape outside. But the mind is active. . . ."

He said of Bolshevism that it did not "seek to establish a complete philosophy such as Aquinas founded on Aristotle." This is true. Marxism, in its crude Russian form, which is the form most widely popularized in this country, has no place in it either for Marx or Lenin, except in the capacity of undistinguishable economic units. Chesterton's criticism is, however, inadequate when applied to the early philosophy of Marx himself. In the third of the *Theses on Feuerbach* occur the following words:

> "The materialistic teaching that human beings are the products of circumstance and education, and changed human beings the products of changed circumstances and education, leaves out of count the fact that circumstances themselves are changed by human beings; that the educator must himself be educated."

It was this young Marx also who uttered the maxim to which Chesterton is at this moment giving so perfect an illustration, "The criticism of religion is the necessary pre-condition of all criticism." It is the teaching of the later, messianic prophet that needs to be completed by another, less famous

G. K. CHESTERTON

dictum, from *The New Jerusalem* (significant title): that self-criticism is the necessary condition of all criticism.

> "A thing like the Catholic system is a system; that is, one idea balances and corrects another. A man like Mohammed or Marx, or in his own way Calvin, finds that system too complex, and simplifies everything to a single idea. . . . He naturally builds a rather unbalanced system with his one definite idea" ("On the Open Conspiracy" in *Come to Think of It*).

Marx-Leninism, by excluding the democratic emotion, ultimately excludes the democratic ideal. A book which gained considerable notoriety in 1937 was called *The Road to Wigan Pier*. It was by a socialist, George Orwell, and purported to be an accurate portrayal of the condition of the working class in Great Britain. Probably it was accurate, though there was something in the tone of the book which offended more than one working-class reader, in a way in which Chesterton's pamphlets never did. What is of more importance in this connection is that this author faced up to the prospects which an unlimited expansion of mechanical technique involves. Socialists, as Chesterton remarked in *The Outline of Sanity*, are not fond of looking at their utopia closely. The only important exception is William Morris, and his England of the twenty-second century bears a near resemblance to that of the fourteenth: a fact which a modern communist finds "irritating." [4] George Orwell does, however, glance into the future—only to avoid drawing the logical conclusions from his material. Finding that the prospect is anything but alluring, he turns hurriedly away, with the observation that the time has not yet come for such speculations; the social ownership of the means of production must be established. The time has not come to decide what is desirable; our duty is to desire it.

Chesterton began his original development where the modern socialist leaves off. He understood the economic element in history as well as most; he recognized also the moral, or human: and this he believed to be determinant. The supreme factor was not "the bodily framework, or the frame-

4 J. Strachey: *The Theory and Practice of Socialism* (Gollancz, 1936). "Morris's mediaevalism and his generally anti-scientific attitude may make some parts of his account of a communist Britain irritating to-day."

work of environment, but the frame of mind" ("On Suicide, North and South" in *All I Survey*). Development of productive methods gave the opportunities for new approximations to the ideal; it did not automatically give rise to the morality capable of making use of them. He was, in fact, a "possibilist." History, as Edward Carpenter remarked, is a difficult horse to ride; but the possibility of curbing it admitted, the necessity of a moral dynamic to that end propounded, and Chesterton at least was proof against the absurdities of those who, whether "bourgeois" or anti-bourgeois, "talk about Efficiency without any criticism of Effect" (*The Thing*).

Once again, there was nothing essentially new in his criticism of the Marxist socialist viewpoint. As early as *Orthodoxy* itself he had written:

> "We have said we must be fond of this world, even in order to change it. Now we add that we must be fond of another world (real or imaginary) in order to have something to change it to. . . . Progress should mean that we are always changing the world to suit the vision. Progress does mean (just now) that we are always changing the vision."

He himself was fond of another world, and it was partly real and partly imaginary. His ideal was, of course, the democratic ideal—a society of human brotherhood. But he believed such a society to have been more nearly approached at a certain period in the past than it is anywhere in the world to-day. The men who followed Constantine, he said, passed through the tunnel of the dark ages and "came out into a world more wonderful than the eyes of men have looked on before or after; they heard the hammers of hundreds of happy craftsmen working for once according to their own will, and saw St. Francis walking with his halo a cloud of birds" (*The New Jerusalem*).

By this vision Chesterton is triply assimilated to the great prophets of the Romantic movement. Again and again his drum and fife are to be heard where their organ sounded, playing the identical tune. Rousseau himself had made the child the focus of his philosophy: "the age at which the individual man would like to stop" is the starting-point for his consideration of the "natural man" (that final synthesis between our "natural" and Goethe's *Natur*); all the Romantics had been ardent classicists; and what the older of them (the *ältere Romantik* of Germany) had seen in Greece, the younger had discovered in the middle ages also.

Like the medievalism of the Romantics, Chesterton's was, and still is, often derided, or else laughed at as though it consisted of nothing but a fondness for bugles and bright colours. It is, however, fundamental to all his thinking; and it illustrates the constructive side of both his historical and political criticism. In a sense he regarded the medieval as the norm of a human society. It was the same sense in which a gardener may regard the full-blown rose as the norm, even though flowers stunted by frost or starved by bad soil may be much more common. He saw in it a society of men all of whose faculties were constantly employed to the full.

"The peasant does live, not merely a simple life, but a complete life." He is always in touch with real, individual things, that keep alive both his senses and his imagination; he is never in danger of mistaking the abstractions of the intellect for the particularities of experience. Similarly the craftsman: in the middle ages he was not starved of his creative satisfaction, as the modern factory-operative is, who spends his life turning a single wheel or screw. Chesterton believed that both peasant and craftsman, moreover, felt themselves to be parts of an organic whole: indeed, without the security and demand which that sense gave him, the craftsman would never have achieved what he did. In medieval, as in Greek society, men were not aware, as they are now, of an "immense distance between the craftsman and the crowd." If they had been, "they would never have set the craftsman to work solely for the crowd. In that case there would never have been any such trifles as the Parthenon or the cathedral of Seville" ("On Mr. Epstein" in *Come to Think of It*).

To those who accused him of "escaping from reality into the past" (as if "reality" were confined to factories and films and newspapers) Chesterton might have retorted that there was, in a very real sense, *more* reality in the life of a medieval villager than in that of the average modern townsman. His medievalism, like William Morris's own, was the longing for a society in which the human relation between man and nature, and between man and man, had never been obscured by the intermediacy of machinery and the "cash-nexus." The mention of these things, however, recalls a difference between their cult of the middle ages and that of the other great Romantics to whom we have referred. Chesterton and Morris were not philosophical idealists; they both realized that the economic bases of society would have to be changed before their ideal could become a reality.

∿

"Ideal" is perhaps the wrong word, if it is taken to refer to the middle ages themselves. Chesterton's ideal society was based upon the medieval, but based upon it, like M. Maritain's, according to the *analogical* principle of Aquinas; he did not desire a return to the past. Nor did he ever overestimate the happiness of the hundreds of craftsmen, though the passage quoted above from *The New Jerusalem*, taken by itself, would suggest that. "Men with medieval sympathies are sometimes accused, absurdly enough, of trying to prove that the medieval period was perfect. In truth the whole case for it is that it was imperfect." "It is bound up with the quality of the civilization in question that it was potential rather than perfect; and there is no need to idealize it in order to regret it." He had more historical imagination than most of his critics, more of that "historical humility" without which, as he said, "no great works will seem great, and no wonders of the world will seem wonderful" (*The New Jerusalem*).

Agreeing with Rousseau (of whom he wrote one of the few sensible criticisms that have appeared in the last twenty years) that "democracy is never quite democratic except when it is quite direct; and it is never quite direct except when it is quite small," he could appreciate the real virtues of the village-community, including the sense of mutual responsibility which it involved. But he believed that it might have developed into something far finer, combining with these the positive elements of individualism. "As a fact, of course, this system throughout Christendom was already evolving into a pure peasant proprietorship; and it will be long before industrialism evolves into anything so equal and so free." All that had been required was a disinterested party prepared to make it its duty to safeguard the right of the peasants, at the time when the feudal system was decaying. But the Church, which was committed by its teaching to such a course, and alone had the authority to enforce it, joined hands with the oppressors, exploited the peasantry itself, and failed to set its face determinedly against usury while its determination might yet have prevailed. The irresponsible element of individualism got the upper hand, and it has held it to the present day. This was what Chesterton believed; he could believe it only by rejecting the theory of economic determinism. For him it was not inevitable that the Church should have betrayed its trust. Had its morale not been sapped by the Black Death and the failure of the Crusades it might have done otherwise, and the evils of competitive industrialism have been spared. By the development of the powers of production a choice had been set before men, and they had chosen wrongly. It might have been turned to the advantage of the whole community, and was made use of for the enrichment of the few. "Medievalism died, but it died young."

And now, Chesterton believed, the wheel had turned full circle, and another choice was being set before men, by the development of competitive industrialism itself. The historical imagination which had played upon the past he turned upon the present also; and this was the greater achievement. For objectivity towards the present means objectivity with regard to one's own interests; means, in short, what Godwin meant by disinterestedness. Chesterton's evolution from Liberalism into Socialism was perfectly natural. He saw that the work of the former had been accomplished, when equal political rights were accorded to all men. The democratic emotion must find a new outlet; it found it in Socialism.

"We have now to assume not only that all citizens are equal, but that all men are citizens. Capitalism attempted it by combining political equality with economic inequality; it assumed that the rich would always hire the poor. But Capitalism seems to me to have collapsed; to be not only a discredited ethic but a bankrupt business." (*op. cit.*).

This was written after he had come to call himself a distributist. But Chesterton "saw our industrial civilization as rooted in injustice long before it became so common a comment as it is to-day" (*Autobiography*). The truth and courage of his revolutionary vision were never more surely demonstrated than in his refusal to take even usury for granted. But because he was aware that direct seeing had been demanded of him at his own cost—it is not comfortable nowadays to realize that the acts we perform as social units are no less our own than our personal relationships—he was proof from the first against the deception of socialist caricature. What he beheld was not the calculated exploitation of one class by another, but an all-pervading injustice accepted as a matter of course nearly as much by the "proletarian" as the capitalist. What he strove to create was a general consciousness of its existence, equal to his own, so that it must either become deliberate and challenging, or else be rectified, by the substitution of co-operation for competition.

The fundamental socialist demand for the communal ownership of industry Chesterton never relinquished. He was not such a medievalist as to believe in a total abolition of factories; and it is important to realize that his Distributism was in no sense a going back on his Socialism. He never went back on anything. All that was of positive value in Socialism he incorporated in the distributist programme. Where he differed from most socialists was in the genuineness of his belief in "turning the inventions of the age of machinery to the benefit of the community as a whole." He understood men; and thereby knew what actually was to their benefit, and what to their ultimate dehumanization. "Instead of the machine being a giant to which man is a pigmy, we must at least reverse the proportions until man is a giant to whom the machine is a toy" (*The Outline of Sanity*). In fact he was in a position not unlike that of the solitary professor in *Erewhon*, who suggested that the machine might be regarded as an appendage to mankind, instead of mankind as an appendage to the machine; only whereas the latter theory was, very logically, made a pretext for the destruction of machinery by the Erewhonians, by the modern socialist it is used as an argument for its retention. The professor in the story was not listened to by many, nor was Chesterton.

Commerce was made for man, and not man for commerce. Chesterton was never tired of upholding this thesis. It is the dominant theme of the whole of one of his most masterly works, *What's Wrong with the World*. In fact its contrary *was* what he believed to be wrong.

> "This is the huge modern heresy of altering the human soul to fit its conditions, instead of altering human conditions to fit the human soul. If soap-boiling is really inconsistent with brotherhood, so much the worse for soap-boiling, not for brotherhood. If civilization really cannot get on with democracy, so much the worse for civilization, not for democracy. Certainly, it would be far better to go back to village communes, if they really are communes. Certainly, it would be better to do without soap rather than to do without society. Certainly, we would sacrifice all our wires, wheels, systems, specialities, physical science and frenzied finance for one half-hour of happiness such as has often come to us with comrades in a common tavern. I do not say the sacrifice will be necessary; I only say it will be easy."

From the beginning to the end of his career he laboured this point, on one pretext after another; contemporary England did not leave him in want of pretexts. Towards the end, indeed, he seems at times to have become almost obsessed with it. Some of the initial buoyancy and freshness are absent from his later essays; a note of angry reiteration creeps into them; and I am told that the same note became apparent in his conversation. But we should not find fault with him for this. Rather it is a tribute to his sense of the paramount, crying evil of our time and nation: for, as Mr. R. H. Tawney has declared, industrialism in England is a national vice, equivalent to, and not less sordid than, the militarism of Hohenzollern Prussia.

The problem with which he was grappling was the same

as would confront an honest Socialism in this country: namely, how to reconcile the value of individual liberty, which has been the positive contribution of the age of individualism, with that sense of social responsibility which vanished with the village commune. He was not insensitive to the difficulties involved. The whole atmosphere of a mechanized society, with its depersonalized mode of living, is hostile even to the preservation of such true democracy as exists, let alone to its extension on the economic plane. It is more hostile to the establishment of Socialism than the village commune itself would have been:

> "Feudal manorial life was not a democracy; but it could have been much more easily turned into a democracy. Later peasant life, as in France or Switzerland, actually has been quite easily turned into a democracy. But it is horribly hard to turn what is called modern industrial democracy into a democracy" ("On Industrialism" in *All I Survey*).

Nevertheless, Chesterton had hope: because he believed that the wish for security, and not ambition for superior wealth, was really the abiding motive of the human heart. This he revered, and this he trusted. It was by virtue of this that he was enabled to believe in the restoration of a peasantry to England, not collectivized like the Russian, but independent like the French.

❧

It is an attractive ideal, the distributist—the most attractive political ideal known to me. And it is not in the least utopian; it depends, for its realization, on no impossible change in human nature as we know it. As it was expounded by Chesterton, indeed, the distributist ideal is almost identical, in its main features, with that *idéal historique* which another thomist, M. Maritain, has sketched, and which he distinguishes absolutely from the *idéal utopique* (*Cf.* Maritain: *Humanisme Intégral*). Nor has it anything in common with totalitarianism, though it is often enough labelled fascistic or reactionary by muddled left-wing thinkers. The very title, "Distributism" is the antithesis of "totalitarianism"; and this antithesis is maintained on every level of its programme, economic, political and religious. Only those who are so ignorant as to call Fascism (that utterly modern manifestation) a "return to the middle ages," and imagine that they are thereby insulting it, could confuse with it the Distributist Commonwealth.

Chesterton, like Maritain, believed that the centralization of large-scale industry, its communal, co-operative or state control, was natural and desirable; but he was not, as most communists are, bemused by the abstract idea of collectivism; he regarded the decentralization of agriculture as no less natural and desirable. He looked, moreover, for a vast multiplication of small stores—a nation of shopkeepers. Totalitarianism betrays its urban origin at once in its drive for collectivism in industry, where it is inevitable and beneficent, and its incapacity even to imagine an humane individual proprietorship. In its fascistic guise it appeals to the desperate shopkeeper—he who is being crushed between the pincers of monopoly capitalism and the menace of Communism—but it appeals to him only to betray him: for it cannot grasp the idea, or ideal, of a unity in diversity. Its instrument is the intellect—the only faculty left unatrophied in a mechanized society; and the only unity the intellect can grasp is a uniformity—in this case the uniformity of collectivism.

As on the economic, so on the political level: it is uniformity that totalitarianism aims at. The changes it brings about, the liquidation of vast anti-social interests, the organization of a nation for aggression or defence, may demand intolerant methods; but intolerance itself can be exercised only upon an abstraction, whether it be called the class or the race. And here also Distributism confronts it in an attitude of defiance: for Distributism is democratic through and through; it springs from the imagination as well as from the intellect. Moreover, because it is imaginative, it is truly religious; and because it is truly religious, it is truly catholic. That deification of the exclusive state, which is the "religion" of totalitarianism, is utterly repugnant to it.

It is catholic, but it is not necessarily Roman Catholic. Chesterton was beyond sectarianism when he became a distributist. When he called on volunteers to begin the good work of restoring an independent peasantry, he knew that only the imaginative would respond: for they alone would appreciate the necessity of re-personalizing social relationships; and the imagination can be trusted, in whatever forms it may express itself. (No doubt he thought that it could be trusted to express itself ultimately in his own form also—but that is a different matter.)

The campaign which occupied the later years of his life had for its aim this restoration, to be accomplished by the road of moral resolution, lest it be compelled along the road of ruin.

> "I think it is not unlikely that in any case a simpler social life will return; even if it return by the road of ruin. I think the soul will find simplicity again, if it be in the Dark Ages. But we are Christians and concerned with the body as well as the soul; we are Englishmen and we do not desire, if we can help it, that the English people should be merely the People of the Ruins."

The Outline of Sanity, in many respects his most perfect book [5]—the one in which his humour and insight are most exquisitely balanced and blended—was published in 1926, the year of the general strike; and it is clear from the context that Chesterton was thinking, when he wrote these words, of an internal collapse of the nation. He accepted the Marxian diagnosis of the contraditions in capitalist economy. In fact he used the concentration of capital in progressively fewer and fewer hands as a text for turning their own ideology against the capitalists. He pointed out, as ever, what those who saw things only as their fathers had seen them altogether failed to perceive: that it was equally ridiculous either to defend or attack modern "capitalism" on the ground that it was competitive, when the whole trend of the system was towards the extirpation of competition through the growth of monopolies. He pointed out that private property itself was already almost a thing of the past: "The same industrial individualism which set out with no thought except private property has produced a new world in which private prop-

[5] The most perfect of his books in all respects seems to me to be his *St. Francis.*

erty is hardly ever thought of, or at least not primarily as private" ("On Education" in *All I Survey*). Emperor and spectators alike were disgraced by the voice of a little child, crying, "But he has no clothes on!"

The collapse he foresaw, however, has not come to pass. Instead, in the two countries from whose circumstances Marxists would have predicted, and did most confidently predict, upheaval, an unprecedented degree of economic and political integration has been achieved: integration totally focused upon international war. Of the fascist states, those incarnations of abstractionism, what had Chesterton to say? "I do not think much of Hitler's funny little crooked cross, and his ranting and romantic quotations from Nietzsche, yet there is a great deal to be said for poor old Hitler. It is part of a great movement for return of order to human government" (G.K.C. reported in *The Morning Post*, May 25, 1933). Even in the political realm his "character" obtruded, challenging people not to take him seriously and clouding over his real democratic vision. Nor can it, I think, be denied that his Roman Catholicism perverted his judgement of political events. He was right in insisting on the divergencies that exist between Nazism and Italian Fascism; still more in pointing out to those who would damn both with the one facile adjective "undemocratic" that an authoritarian régime of one kind or another may at times be the only alternative to anarchy that faces a country. Yet only the concordat between Mussolini and the Holy See can have led Chesterton to overlook the Duce's deliberate and avowed subordination of the human personality to the state, and to condone the brutal invasion of Abyssinia.

There was, however, a deeper reason than this for his failure to start a dynamic political movement. The internal collapse which he predicted has not come to pass; and it will not. But a far greater catastrophe and a far darker dark ages were at hand. Yet in face of the prospect of the international war which even now threatens to turn the English into a people of the ruins, Chesterton had nothing to offer; and all that the common man asked of politics was a way of escape from this doom.

4

CHESTERTON accepted the Marxist
analysis of the contradiction of the capitalist economic system; in *The Outline of Sanity* he laid it bare with a clarity
often unknown to professional economists:

> "Capitalism is contradictory as soon as it is complete; be-
> cause it is dealing with the mass of men in two opposite ways
> at once. When most men are wage-earners, it is more and
> more difficult for most men to be customers. For the capitalist
> is always trying to cut down what his servant demands, and in
> doing so is cutting down what his customer can spend. As
> soon as his business is in any difficulties, as at present in the
> coal business, he tries to reduce what he has to spend on wages,
> and in doing so reduces what others have to spend on coal.
> He is wanting the same man to be rich and poor at the same
> time. This contradiction in capitalism does not appear in the
> earlier stages, because there are still populations not reduced
> to the common proletarian condition. But as soon as the
> wealthy as a whole are employing the wage-earners as a
> whole, this contradiction stares them in the face like an ironic
> doom and judgement."

We must be forgiven for starting a chapter with such a
long extract, since it conveys so clearly what far longer books
have failed to convey at all. Chesterton accepted the Marxist
analysis of the contradiction of capitalist society, up to the
point at which trusts emerge as the characteristic features of
the industrial landscape; and from this he deduced the
approaching collapse of the system. Unfortunately, when that
collapse did not take place, he forbore to pursue the argument further. When, in Germany, things reached such a pass
that the German people in despair put themselves and their
economics alike into the hands of a dictator; when that dictator solved the problem of stagnation and unemployment
by the simple method of massive rearmament—when, in
other words, he set the wheels of industry turning again by

the production of goods that no one need buy—all Chesterton could see was the resurrection of "Prussian" devildom. No country had shown itself capable of finding a creative way out of the impasse; when the waving of the Swastika gave it the excuse it was with an audible sigh of relief that the rest of Europe set about overcoming the same problem in precisely the same way; but all this was nothing to Chesterton. Seeing nothing in "Hitlerism" but the reappearance of the hereditary Prussian disease, he could see nothing in Baldwinism but the sharpening of the surgeon's scalpel. He would, had he lived, have welcomed the operation at present being repeated.

Thereby he dammed up the hopes of Distributism. Since the bankruptcy he predicted did not come to pass in the way he predicted, his message lost all its urgency in the ears of the common man; he abandoned the influence he might have exerted over those who grew up in the despondency of the 1920's to—of all people—the communists. For Communism did promise, at one time, a way out of war: and it was for this reason that the postwar generation turned to it. Its historians declared, and appeared to demonstrate, that there were forces at work in the world making irreversibly for good, that is, for peace: and so great was the intoxication of surrender to these forces that few realized at once whither they were being borne; few realized that the triumphal arch which seemed so near lay beyond the very chasm it was thought to span, and that the communist was indeed, as he proudly proclaimed, not a Christian—because he was not "concerned with the body as well as the soul."

But Chesterton was compelled to dam the hopes of Distributism in another way than this. It is impossible to advocate the manufacture of armaments *and* the abolition of industrialism, the centralized control by the state demanded of modern war *and* the decentralization of community; it is impossible to support at one and the same time rearmament and Distributism. If rearmament is an immediate necessity, then the distributist programme must be deferred indefinitely. If Distributism is an immediate necessity, then some means of national defence other than war must be devised. One contemporary writer, who preaches, under the name of "anarchism," an ideal rather similar to Chesterton's, goes so far as to say that "the abolition of the state and the creation of a co-operative commonwealth" naturally imply pacifism: "if pacifism is not possible, then anarchism is not possible" (Herbert Read: "The Necessity of Anarchism," in *The Adelphi*, Sept-Nov., 1937). This conclusion Chesterton rejected; he preferred rearmament to Distributism.

To represent his choice in such terms, however, is of course to misrepresent it. What he really preferred was the England that actually exists, with all its imperfections and possibilities of improvement, to an England subordinated to the imperialism of Germany; and he believed that only by a temporary intensification of armaments, if need be by war, could this England be saved.

☙

Chesterton was a patriot in the highest and truest sense. No understanding of him is possible unless this is understood. But true patriotism is a very rare thing—so rare that it is generally mistaken for unpatriotism. True patriotism has nothing to do with racialism, or imperialism or the idolatry of the nation-state. The ideal of all these things is a uniformity, and is derived from the abstracting intellect; but patriotism springs from the imagination and delights in particularity. "If patriotism does not mean a defined and declared preference for certain traditions or surroundings, it means nothing whatever" ("The Patriotic Idea" in *England a Nation*, edited by L. Oldershaw). It is not a devotion to something afar, but to something very near: the very essence of patriotism is that the traditions and surroundings should be those which a man knows best—those in which he was brought up. Therefore it cannot be an uncritical devotion. True patriotism is intensely critical; it judges the traditions of its country continually, and is as unsparing in its denunciations of the bad as it is passionate in its loyalty to the good. If patriotism demanded a wholesale approval, if it demanded a blinding of eyes to the truth, if it demanded of men that they should perform acts abhorrent to their consciences, then no good Christian could be a patriot.

Chesterton was both a good patriot and a good Christian. It was for this reason that he detested imperialism—and not only German imperialism. When he denounced the German invasion of Belgium in 1914, he was in a far stronger position than most of those in this country who did so, because he had already denounced the British invasion of the Transvaal. "The annexation of the Transvaal," he had written ten years before, "was a crime committed against the European virtue of patriotism. For a man has clearly no more right to say that his British patriotism obliges him to destroy the Boer nation than he has to say that his sense of the sanctity of marriage makes him run away with his neighbour's wife" (*op. cit.*). Naturally, he had been stigmatized as "unpatriotic."

"A thing like the British Empire," he had written, "which contains Dutchmen and Negroes and Chinamen in Hong Kong, may be a perfectly legitimate object of a certain kind of intellectual esteem, but it is ludicrous to call it patriotism, or invoke the ancient deities of the hearth and the river and the hill" (*op. cit*). As it was this intellectual esteem that distinguished imperialism from Chesterton's patriotism, so it was this that distinguishes what has come to be called nationalism from what he meant by the word. When he spoke of nationalism, and called it the spiritual demand of a healthy man, he meant "a particular relation to some homogeneous community of manageable and imaginable size, large enough to inspire his reverence by its hold on history and small enough to inspire his affection by its hold on himself" (*op. cit.*). The nation was, for him, essentially a community small enough to be experienced—the smaller the better. It was a unity that appealed not so much to the intellect as to the heart and the imagination. As such, it might well be a unity in multiplicity, like a work of art. Nor would it, I think, be unfair to Chesterton to define the England he loved as a multiplicity of local traditions bound together in one common tradition—of freedom. As he was the lifelong champion of the rights of small nations themselves, so he was the

champion of local patriotisms within the nations: for he perceived in both a return to personal and immediate relationships with people and things, from that impersonal and
mechanized relationship which is the curse of the modern
world:

> "We have reached in the modern world a condition of
> such appalling unreality that everything is done on paper.
> Men know the destiny of countries when they have never
> met a native, and profess love and hatred for men whom,
> if they saw them in the street, they could not tell from Poles
> or Portuguese" *(op. cit.).*

It is another example of that all-pervading "abstractionism" to which we have referred already. And the cure?—

> "We must at all costs get back to smaller political entities,
> because we must at all costs get back to reality. We must get
> nearer and nearer again to love and hate and mother-wit, to
> personal judgements and the truth in the faces of men"
> *(op. cit.).*

It was in loyalty to such a view of nationalism that Chesterton supported the war of 1914-18, and would have supported a greater. No stronger case against pacifism has ever
been voiced than that which is to be found in his *Autobiography*, because it is based upon facts and sentiments which
the average pacifist ignores almost as completely as the average nationalist. The war, he said, was not fought to end war;
it was not fought to make the world safe for political democracy; it was fought to defend the local customs and immemorial traditions of England: and it succeeded in its object.

The natural retort to this argument, that the war was, in
fact, fought to defend and extend vested interests in the colonies, is obviously inadequate. That the war of 1914-18 was
the natural outcome of the economic situation of the world
at that time is true: but if it can be shown that it defended
other things besides vested interests—valuable things—the
things, in fact, for which the actual soldiers actually killed
and were killed, then that truth is irrelevant. If it can be
shown that the victory of 1918 was a dual victory, for Allied

patriotism as much as for Allied finance, still it is irrelevant: the victory would have seemed worth while to those who won it. The economic argument only becomes all-important if it can be shown that Allied patriotism won less than Allied capitalism. If that is the truth, then the war was, indeed, from the standpoint of those who won it, a ghastly failure; for capitalism, as Chesterton demonstrated and patriotism knows, is the mortal enemy of all local customs and immemorial traditions whatever; it is the enemy of all creative life.

The demonstration of such a truth, however, can never be conclusive; and from the experience of the past twenty years different conclusions may, perhaps, be drawn. One conclusion only is unavoidable, and that is that in her relations with the defeated countries England betrayed the ideals of those who had fought in the name of patriotism more grossly than a nation had ever betrayed the ideals of its youth before: because never before had a nation's youth been so decimated that few or none were left to arraign it. France and England after the war set out, deliberately, to reduce the German people to penury, to ignominy and at last to despair. "The men whose names are written on the Beaconsfield War Memorial died to prevent Beaconsfield being so immediately overshadowed by Berlin that all its reforms would be modelled on Berlin, all its products used for the international purposes of Berlin, even if the King of Prussia were not called in so many words the Suzerain of the King of England. They died to prevent it and they did prevent it" (*Autobiography*). True, but they did not, because they could not prevent Berlin from being so overshadowed by London and Paris; they did not, because they could not prevent Germany from being reduced to a vassal state, "retaining merely a formal independence, and in every vital matter steered by the diplomacy and penetrated by the culture of the conqueror" (*op. cit.*). If England committed a crime against the European virtue of patriotism when she annexed the Transvaal, how great was the crime committed when she so treated every just demand of the German people, when they were beaten and unarmed, that they finally became convinced that all morality between nations was a fraud, and that nothing of their own would ever be had that was not had by force?

But patriotism is not an occasional virtue; and it is inherently impossible that a nation should act so unpatriotically in its foreign relations as England did after the war, and yet remain patriotic in its domestic concerns. For, whatever jingoes and cosmopolitans may say to the contrary, Chesterton was right when he declared that true patriotism and true internationalism are complementary. As a fact, in the Hall of Mirrors at Versailles England saw herself as she really was. The imperialism which, when the evil traditions of Germany were destroyed, trampled the innocent underfoot, had its counterpart in a commercialism at home that left, where it left them at all, the local customs and immemorial traditions of our country as survivals merely. There is only one way of saving these, and that is by means of a social revolution; but there was not the moral energy left in England after the war to carry such a revolution through; and by the time that a new generation had arisen, the fatal actions of the old were bearing their fruits—in the nemesis we are confronted with to-day.

❧

To Chesterton, labouring almost alone to awaken his country to the need of undoing, and not over-doing, the evil of capitalism, the truth should surely have been plain, that modern war, the war in which a whole nation's energies are unremittingly engaged, so decimates those who wage it at the front and corrupts those who support it at the back that nothing, save by a miracle, can result from it but an endless moral deterioration. And yet he was blind to this corruption. What he would not admit on the economic level, he could not perceive on the spiritual: namely, that war is the extension and intensification of capitalism. It is in time of war that the depersonalization of society, which is the spiritual concomitant of capitalism, reaches its maximum; it is in time of war that creative activity is everywhere at a nadir; above all, it is in time of war that men are stirred up as at no other to regard whole nations of men, women and children whom they have never seen as superhuman, worthy only of love, or sub-human, worthy only of hate.

Could he have seen it, however, he would have seen his own campaign in its true perspective, and thereby restored to it all the urgency which it had lost in the ears of the common man. "The only way out of danger," he had written in *The Outline of Sanity,* "is the dangerous way. The sort of call that must be made on the modern English is the sort of call that is made before a great war or a great revolution." That is truer to-day than when it was written; and never before has the course he advocated, for withstanding "the lifelessness which the machine imposes on the masses," been more imperatively demanded. For, whether the international war we are waging results in barbarism or totalitarianism, whether it turns the English into a people of the ruins or England into a servile state, there is no way to cure or prevent it save by such a return to reality and personal judgements as Chesterton held to be the one necessity. Voluntary communities of men and women, dedicated to re-establishing a right relationship with the earth and with one another, may prove nuclei for a new colonization of a wilderness, or they may provide the dynamic for a repersonalization of the social machine, but in either case they are the best hope of resisting the advance of moral degeneration. In such communities at least an effort can be made, however desperate or forlorn, to declare the validity of the individual in the very ecstasy of self-immolation, and in the very teeth of destruction to create.

But such a course of action in time of war implies a refusal to take part in war; it implies pacifism—and that, as we have seen, Chesterton rejected. For reasons which should now be obvious, that rejection seems to us to have been his greatest mistake. Pacifism was, we believe, the logical outcome of both his politics and his patriotism; and it was more than that: it was the natural consummation of his ethics. In pacifism not only his reason but his imagination might have been satisfied, his activity have been totally suffused by his religion. His refusal of it places him in sudden contrast to the only other churchman of his day with whom it is at all natural to compare him: the late Canon Sheppard. There is more than a superficial likeness between them in other respects. Both owed their popularity and influence largely to their humour; and their humour was of fundamentally the same kind—the kind that Carlyle called "the purest effluence of a deep, fine and loving nature." Both built up quasi-political movements on an unsectarian religious basis, and in doing so, each was consciously emphasizing an element of Christ's teaching. The elements are complementary, as the parts of an organic whole must always be; and in practice each is the justification of the other. A complete pacifism in capitalist society can be nothing less than revolutionary: a revolutionary movement that does not abjure violence becomes an accomplice in the thing it abhors.[1]

Nevertheless, Chesterton refused the pacifist solution, as Sheppard appears to have refused the distributist. "Refusal," however, is really too positive a name for his reaction. The truth is that he never faced up to the pacifist position at all. Throughout the collection of essays entitled *The End of the Armistice,* he treats under the name of "pacifism" that mere reluctance to make war, that sentiment for peace, which was in this country the backwash of 1918. Chesterton knew the meaning of love; and knowing it could only have been repelled by this simulacrum of it that used to prevail so widely in circles calling themselves pacifist: the self-mortification that passed for self-sacrifice: the turning of the other cheek which was farther from forgiveness than is anger: for anger has this at least in common with genuine compassion, that it is spontaneous. As Keats said, "a quarrel in the streets is a thing to be hated, but the energies displayed in it are fine." No doubt Chesterton would have relished a street-fight. Indeed, he described one with gusto in his autobiography. No doubt he respected the anger and defiance that find expression in battle, just as he respected the desire for security that exists in every man. Yet one of his supreme achievements was his discovery of the injustice to which this last, in itself innocent, desire was leading, in a competitive, mechanized society; and he showed that a new consciousness was necessary

[1] See Note II at the end of this book.

to man if he was not to be made the slave of the machine: a giant's awareness to manipulate the limbs of a giant.

A new consciousness will indeed be required. But it is the machine linked to anger and defiance, and not directly to the desire for security, that is destroying the remains of Christian civilization. It will be the executor of an injustice, and one intolerable to the democratic imagination, but one far greater than Chesterton dreamed. For there is no crime of oppression, destitution or unemployment that can compare with that wholesale massacre or starvation of the innocents, which is the quintessence of modern war. It was his sense of this violation of the democratic emotion that made Canon Sheppard a pacifist; and his pacifism, and that of the best of his followers, differs by a whole world of religious experience from the false "pacifism" we have been discussing. It differs from it in being prepared for the most radical sacrifices known to man: in being prepared, if need be, to lay down its life not only for its friend but for its enemy.

&

"We have used fire and sword, death and destruction, slander and surrender, diplomacy and flattery, suspicion and oblivion, to solve the supposed problem of Germany; and we find that we still have not solved the problem of Prussia. The reason is that the thing involved belongs to the history of thought, to the thousand sects and philosophies, rather than to the relatively recent imperial divisions of history. The thing is not a nation; it is rather a religion or perhaps an irreligion."

Thus wrote Chesterton in *The End of the Armistice:* and is not the corollary obvious? If all these methods have failed, would it not be wiser, not to say more Christian, to try the method of generous treatment? That was Canon Sheppard's conclusion.

It may or may not be true that Prussia stands for the evil element in Germany, inasmuch as it has long embodied the particular antichristian temptations that haunt that country. Probably it is true, since, for good geographical and historical reasons, Prussia was always less exposed than any other part of Germany to the civilizing influence of Rome. But the question, which Chesterton never attempted to answer, is why this element should at times—and especially at the present time—be allowed by the rest of Germany to "become its spearhead, or to use it like a spear"; on his own admission, the tribal element "only occasionally drives the Germans." This question Chesterton never answered, because to have done so would have meant admitting, not merely the inefficacy of the methods he had listed for exorcizing prussianism, but their absolute antagonism to the true ones. The nearest he came to admitting it was when he declared that prussianism was an idea or irreligion, that could only be countered by a truer idea or a real religion: in other words, by a "change of heart"—to use the expression beloved of those English journalists who pressed for an even harsher treaty and more prolonged starvation of Germany after the last war. But when he showed that Christendom was faced in these latter days by the same challenge of paganism that it had overcome in its earliest, he would not allow that the methods used to overcome it by the early Christians might still be the best.

"Truth can understand error, but error cannot understand truth." That phrase has for its natural counterpart another: "tout comprendre, c'est tout pardonner"; and these two between them sum up, for me, all that is most vital in Chesterton's genius. He could laugh at his opponents, because he loved them; he loved them because he forgave them; and he forgave them because he understood them: he had room for them in his superior vision even when they had none for him in their inferior. But if this is the truth, he betrayed his genius by his attitude towards Germany. It is no accident that there is little humour in *The Barbarism of Berlin* or *The End of the Armistice*. He made no attempt to understand Germany; he treated it always as a *deus*, or rather a *diabolus ex machina*, projecting on to an abstraction called "the Prussian" all the tendencies he despised. No wonder he was unable to perceive the corruption spread by war!— And yet, to see how that Germany came into being, to see the causes, spiritual and economic, that precipitated it, is to be so tempted to repentance and forgiveness that the reaction which, we have said, Chesterton's politics alone would have dictated, becomes the natural emotion of our hearts.

Pacifism is the politics of forgiveness—of forgiveness raised, as Mr. Middleton Murry has said, "from a private virtue to the virtue of nations" (in *The Brotherhood of Peace*, Peace Pledge Union, 1939). Had Chesterton given his allegiance to the great English pacifist movement, his life-work would, I believe, have been fulfilled. It was his triumph that he remained, nearly always, the spokesman of the highest aspirations of his country: it is in virtue of this fact that he can be called, at one and the same time, a conservative like Browning and a revolutionary like Blake—he was, in fact, his own supreme paradox. It was his tragedy that he did not aspire beyond those aspirations, to become the prophet of a perhaps unrealizable attainment: if, indeed, forgiveness does lie beyond the realization of England. There is no one who can be sure even of that; and certain it is that no great moral advance has ever been made by the mass of mankind that was not expected of it almost as a natural consummation by the few. Had Chesterton given his allegiance to pacifism, his genius would finally have prevailed over his "character," the Christianity he served over the common sense for which he was admired: for it is Christianity, and not common sense, that "preaches an impossibility and tries to make it come true."

POSTSCRIPT

WRITING about G. K. Chesterton is like climbing a mountain. The end seems continually to be in sight, or to lie just over the next crest; always when the crest is reached another unfolds itself beyond that. And at last one is forced to leave off out of sheer fatigue, and because the daylight is all but spent. Yet with every fresh ridge surmounted a new and wider prospect is opened up, until all that has been accomplished seems, in the fresh perspective.

narrow and insignificant. Chesterton is like church doctrine itself: he can be participated in on many different levels of understanding. At the lowest, his truths shatter into contradictions, acceptable only as perversities. At the highest, they are discovered to be, if not completely comprehensive, within their limits perfect, portions of an organic whole.

Tolstoy once said that there were three things necessary to an artist: "that he should stand on a level with the highest life-conception of his time, that he should experience feeling and have the desire and capacity to transmit it, and that he should moreover have a talent for one of the forms of art."

In the first section of this essay I suggested that Chesterton, by giving his allegiance to the Roman Catholic Church, fell below the level of the highest life-conception of his time and country. For that only is the highest which comprehends all knowledge and all experience, however contradictory. Religion, like wit, "sees the consistency in things"; it is the discovery of a unity in diversity; the final reconciliation of contraries. Chesterton did in some measure what he accused the Buddhists of doing—and in the measure to which he accused them of doing it—he restricted the diversity to preserve a unity.

In my second section I contrasted Chesterton's desire with his capacity to transmit feeling: asserting, nevertheless, that he did often succeed in his purpose, which was the purpose of all art—for art is a paradigm of religion—that of revealing the unity in multiplicity. Each of his works is an organic unity: the whole is implicit in each one of its parts.

But what applies to his individual productions applies to his achievement as a whole. To present his viewpoint becomes, therefore, inordinately difficult; "a kind of huge helplessness" overtakes one. Since to separate any one strand of his thought and treat it in isolation is immediately to impoverish it. Yet to link up each with all the others, save by implication, would be a superhuman task, involving endless repetition and final formlessness. In my third section I called criticism the art for which Chesterton had the greatest talent, and implied thereby that a work of criticism is a work of art. It cannot therefore be formless. What the imagination discovers imagination must reveal; and imagination cannot work freely on the particulars until it sees them in the perspective of the whole.

Not only literary, but social criticism was the chosen field of Chesterton's genius. In my third and fourth sections I have studied the application of his principles, first to the domestic and then to the foreign concerns of his country. The topic has proved more topical than I anticipated when I began. On all sides now (1939) people are quoting an observation of Chesterton's posthumously republished:

> "The Prussian patriot may plaster himself all over with eagles and iron crosses, but he will be found in practice side by side with the Red Flag. The Prussian and the Russian will agree about everything; especially about Poland" (*The End of the Armistice*).

Not everybody who has quoted these words, however, has remembered those which immediately follow them: "They may differ in many things, but in hatred of the Christian civilization they are truly international"; yet without these, his prophecy is insignificant. We have to know all that Chesterton implied by the term, "Christian civilization." My object has been to throw some light on this. If, in doing so, I have seemed to take Chesterton more seriously than he took himself—at least I am unlikely to be accused of trying to break a butterfly upon a wheel!

As my understanding of him has grown, and my imagination been enriched by it, so has my admiration. Now that this essay is finished, I see him towering before me, a figure of portentous stature; and I know not only that what I have written is woefully inadequate—that was inevitable—but that all I have tried to write is inadequate, too. The most fundamental, the unique quality of his genius has eluded my clumsiness to the last. The light which he turned upon the world he turned upon himself also: not merely its objectivity and charity, but its humour. His "character" at its best was, in fact, of the same order as his art and wit. It was the delight of a great man in his own personality.

NOTES

NOTE I (Pages 97-102).

The "complete anthropology repudiating the super-natural," which I had in mind when writing this essay, was that sketched by John Middleton Murry in his book *God: an introduction to the Science of Metabiology* (Cape, 1929). Although my criticism of Chesterton's standpoint still seems to me substantially correct, I would not now express the un-qualified allegiance to Mr. Murry's Metabiology that I did seven years ago.

In the recently published Letters of Max Plowman (*Bridge into the Future,* Dakars, 1944), I find the following state-ment: "Blake was a supernaturalist in the sense that he could see Nature as the expression of something greater than itself; but Murry wants Nature to be self-sufficient, which to my mind is just like wanting a work of art to disown the hand that made it. It *is* itself and in a sense self-sufficient. It is also the expression of something greater than itself" (Letter of Nov. 20, 1933). This seems to me a true criticism of Murry's former Pantheism—unsatisfactory word!—and it implies a faith more nearly akin to Orthodox Christianity than Max Plowman himself may have realised: how nearly I have tried to define in a forthcoming book, *The Tree of Knowledge.*

This essay on Chesterton was completed during the early months of the War, and bears traces of its date both in its references to public events and the absence of reference to several valuable works on Chesterton published since—Maisie Ward's monumental biography in particular. I hope the reader will take this as a partial excuse for the many defects which only a drastic rehandling could set right.

NOTE II (Pages 148-153).

The synthesis between the intuitions of G. K. Chesterton and Canon Sheppard, suggested in this section, was perfectly achieved by Eric Gill, whose writings were virtually unknown to me when this book was written. Gill was both a distributist and a pacifist professed: and a great Christian into the bargain. A remark of his recounted to me by the late Max Plowman may perhaps appropriately be put on record here. Gill was at work on his autobiography at the time. "I cannot imagine," he remarked to Max, "a more fitting end to the life of a great man than Gilbert Chesterton's, whose autobiography was only just completed when he passed away." It was less than three months later that, having just put the final touches to his own lovely record of a creative life, Eric Gill went to join the friend whom he had described in it as "a writer and as a holy man, beyond all his contemporaries."

ERIC GILL

by

Donald Attwater

Luke 15:4

DONALD ATTWATER. *Born in Essex, England, 1892. Translator of the earlier works of Nicholas Berdyaev. Editor of* The Vision Concerning Piers Plowman *and Butler's* Lives of the Saints. *Writer on behalf of war-resistance and Christian reunion. Author of books on the Eastern churches and a Life of St. John Chrysostom. Contributing editor to* The Commonweal *and* Orate Fratres (*U. S. A.*)
160

1

ARTHUR Eric Rowton Gill was born
on February 22nd, 1882, at Brighton, and his first home was
in a suburban street of this town which he afterwards characterized as a shapeless and meaningless mess. He was the
second of thirteen children. His father was a minister of that
small sect, "connection," called after its foundress, Selina,
Countess of Huntingdon, and he was a man of earnestness,
culture and probity, of a type very common in nineteenth-
century England. Eric had other ecclesiastical associations:
not only did he marry the daughter of the sacristan of Chichester cathedral, but his paternal grandfather and great-
uncle were missionaries in the South Seas, as were two of
his brothers and one sister. When the present writer first
knew him, after the war of 1914-18, he would often disclaim
any missionary enterprise for his own convictions, but as the
years passed he became in fact more and more of a missionary, "publicist," and would sometimes with a wry smile refer
to his family tradition in playful extenuation.

But this was not the only, or the most important, thing
concerning which early influences persisted. Unlike so many
"rebels" from the English middle and professional class,
Eric Gill never (except possibly for a brief period in his
youth) deliberately cut himself off from his origins; particularly did he never foul the nest of his own family and
upbringing. I have said that his father was a typical Victorian, and it has been acutely noted by David Jones that
Eric himself was, in a way, a Victorian person—not least in
his solid sincerity and high seriousness, combined with a gay
frolicsomeness such as is found in the mathematician Dodg-

son or in Lear (Edward, not the Shakespearian king). The Gill household was a happy one, and it was poor, really poor, from the point of view of ways and means; so far was this from having an embittering effect on Eric (or, I believe, on any of them) that it was the practical starting-point of his own repudiation of worldly wealth and his attachment to a decent poverty as a fundamental necessity for any good revolution, personal or social. It was a cultured family—the father had some skill as a painter, the mother as a singer, and a glance at their children's names shows their literary interests (Eric, "or Little by Little," Kingsley, Carlyle, Maurice, MacDonald, Roberston, Enid from Tennyson). But above all it was a religious family: "We took religion for granted just as we took the roof over our heads. . . . But taking things for granted doesn't mean you aren't interested in them or that, on occasion, you won't be very interested indeed" (*Auto.*, p. 59). And the religion was that combination of evangelical doctrine and upright conduct, combined both with strict domestic discipline and dissenting independence, that at its best has been so valuable a factor in making the modern English character: the "nonconformist conscience" is despicable only in its decay. The young Gills were brought up on virtuous principles, and "these principles were put before us in such a way as to win our assent to them —assent both notional and affective" (*Auto.*, p. 56).

Eric's schooling lasted some half-dozen years, in a private school at Brighton, and consisted solely of "learning things out of little books and being able to remember enough to answer questions." It made no particular impression on him, and he showed no special aptitude for book-learning: his real enthusiasms were cricket and football, not as competitive contests but as things worth doing for their own sake—games, and drawing locomotive engines. In later life he made no complaints against the sort of teaching he had received: rather was he thankful that his schoolmasters had been too timid or too uninterested to try to coerce his mind or to mould him against his proper nature. Naturally he came to have ideas on schooling: these he never had the opportunity to work out and develop (though he used them

ERIC GILL

with startlingly good effect in bringing up his own family),
but their foundation was that children should be given a
good comprehensive view of the world in general, showing
the growth and decay of peoples and nations in the light of
man's spiritual nature and eternal destiny; and that the
amount of formal learning to be done should be kept down
to the lowest possible minimum, for we are educated, not by
learning, but by *doing*—"that is, in my mind, the whole
secret of education, whether in schools or in workshops or in
life." He did not think it really matters much whether a person can read and write, and it seemed to him unreasonable
"to burden the budding mind of a child with too much high
intellectual stuff" about duty and culture and all that sort of
thing. Mathematics was the school subject that most appealed
to him: it called for that accuracy and precision that had
already been inculcated at home, it ministered to an appetite
for orderliness that was to increase with his years. The *Autobiography* gives a strong impression that the young Eric
was an intelligent, observant, sensitive boy, in no way "freak-
ish," healthy in mind and body, whose favourite author was
G. A. Henty.

> "The children of large families, especially when the parents
> are poor, do not complain with bitterness because they go
> short of clothes, firing or food. Unless their minds are pois-
> oned by jealousy or covetousness, they regard all such hard-
> ships as being part of the game of life, and, as is well known,
> no people are happier than the children of the large families
> of poor parents when those parents are engaged in humane
> occupations, even under hard conditions, provided that the
> parents are examples of justice and charity" (*Belief*, p. 222).

When he wrote those lines Eric Gill certainly had his
own early home in mind. "The shepherd boy who helps his
father in the cold nights of the lambing season does not curse
the physical universe and refuse to attend church or chapel
on Sunday." During the past couple of generations many
comfortably-circumstanced (and other) people have refused
to attend church or chapel—"abandoning institutional religion" it is called—for various reasons, often cogent, often
not; parallel with this phenomenon has been another, much

smaller, less picturesque and fashionable and therefore less talked about, of people abandoning unbelief or an elastic undogmatic form of religion for one more vigorous, exacting and authoritative, in other words, seeking for a teaching church. When Eric Gill became a Roman Catholic in 1913 he went on from where his father had left off. Mr. Gill senior had resigned from the Congregationalists because he, the shepherd, would not have his religious message dictated to him by his flock; the Countess of Huntingdon's Connection received its doctrine "from above" ("which is the proper place for doctrine to come from"), embodied in the Anglican Book of Common Prayer; then, in 1897, he took the next step in the same direction and joined the Church of England, taking his family with him. This was an important date in his eldest son's life, not simply because Eric was taken away from school, at the age of fifteen, but because they all went to live at Chichester, and the effect of this city on the growing boy's mind was profound. Not because it was old (which it is) or "picturesque" (which it isn't) but because it was an ordered human thing: not a disorderly mess made by the speculative builder, like the Brighton suburb, but "a place, the product of reason and love. . . . Here was no dead product of mathematical calculation, no merely sanitary and convenient arrangement. Here was something as human as home and as lovely as Heaven. That was how it seemed to me. . . ." (*Auto.*, p. 77). For a time he studied drawing and lettering at the local art-school, but got considerably more out of his own drawing and exploration in the cathedral and from the wise friendship of one of its prebendaries, Doctor Robert Codrington. It was a time compounded of "rapture and rebellion"; the mental and physical surge of adolescence was disturbing him. So he became dissatisfied and unhappy, and after two years he was sent off to London to be apprenticed in the large drawing-office of an ecclesiastical architect.

The first three of the next five years was a period of disillusionment, disintegration and revolt, first against religious mugwumpery, then against social and political perversions, lastly against the fatuity and play-acting that passed for architecture. Eric Gill began to be interested in "revolution." "Religion in St. Saviour's, Clapham, and irreligion in the architect's office were unequally matched. Nothing in the outward show of that Christianity could possibly hold me—the frightful church, the frightful music, the apparently empty conventionality of the congregation. And nothing that the parson ever said seemed to imply any realization that the Church of England was in any way responsible for the intellectual and moral and physical state of London" (*Auto.*, p. 108). So he slid out of Anglicanism into a vague and hungry agnosticism, and seeing that most professional politics was as much a sham as a great deal of professional religion, that Parliament did not represent the people and laws were really made in board-rooms and private gatherings, he became in an equally nebulous way a socialist. But he kept his head. Youthful "emancipation" not seldom dissolves into licence, liberty is made a cloak for malice: young Gill did not take that easy path, if only, as he modestly implies, it did not look all that easy to him. As for architecture—and here too he owed much to the sensitive conscience and clear mind of a fellow draughtsman, George Carter—he soon saw that it was not the same thing as building and that the tyranny of the architect in his office had reduced the working mason and builder to the mere copying of things designed on paper in the smallest detail by other people. Such irrational and inhuman division of labour was not for him: he wanted to be a workman, with a workman's rights and duties, to design what was to be made and make what he had designed. What work that he could do was wanted? He soon found it—letter-cutting in stone. In the evenings he went to the writing-classes of that great man Edward Johnston; after twelve months he got his first small commission, and from that day forth was never out of a job. He just walked out of the architect's office.

In 1904, at the age of twenty-two, Eric Gill married, and set up house in a block of workmen's dwellings in Battersea. Before very long, after the birth of two daughters, they removed to Ditchling in their native county. There was no "back-to-the-land" sentiment behind this, though Eric always

loved the life of the earth—and especially "the earth that
man has loved, for his daily work and the pathos of his
plight"—and Mary his wife was a farmwife by second nature.
What was behind it was the conviction from experience that
a big city was no place in which to bring up children. ". . .
we were not only able to marry young . . . but also . . . I
was subjected to the influence of marriage without the
complications of suburban snobbery and domestic indignity.
. . . Marriage meant babies—if it weren't for babies there
wouldn't be marriage. . . . But the consequences are momentous. You are no longer simply concerned to discover
what conditions are best for your work (that which you do
for your living—*i.e.,* in return for the bread and butter you
eat) and what conditions are best for your comfort, you are
concerned to discover what conditions are best for a growing
family" (*Auto.,* pp. 132-34).

Meanwhile the inscription-cutting and tombstone business
was prospering, and Gill's skill brought him to the notice of
such as Roger Fry and found him a friend and customer in
Count Kessler, of Weimar. In 1909, with much diffidence and
trepidation, he made his first essay in stone-carving, a female
figure, and this new venture at once drew more attention
to him. Sculptors nowadays mostly *model* their statuary,
building it up in clay, and then have this model reproduced
in stone by a professional carver with various machines and
gadgets: here was a man who carved his thing himself directly out of the stone; one, moreover, who thought in terms
of stone (not of clay) and of carving (not of modelling). "So
all without knowing it I was making a little revolution. I
was reuniting what should never have been separated: the
artist as man of imagination and the artist as workman . . .
I really was like the child who said 'first I think and then
I draw my think'—in contrast with the art-student who
must say, 'First I look and then I draw my look.' Of course
the art critics didn't believe it. How could they? They
thought I was putting up a stunt—being archaic on purpose.
Whereas the real and complete truth was that I was completely ignorant of all their art stuff and was childishly doing
my utmost to copy accurately in stone what I saw in my

head. . . ." (*Auto.*, p. 162). Despite this misunderstanding the "art world" opened its doors to receive him; Epstein and John, Ambrose McEvoy and William Rothenstein were among his friends; he was "given the opportunity to become acquainted at close quarters with the leading intellectual and artistic folk of our great empire"—and then, not for the first or last time, Gill saw himself standing at the edge of a yawning pit of danger, and drew back: or rather, not scorning the tactics of the Desert Fathers or St. Benedict, he ran away, "escaped."

Among the artists "there was no smell of burning boats— burning boats was the one thing no fellow should do. I think it might not unfairly be said that they all believed in beauty, were interested in truth and had doubts about the good. . . . I was so very much not the artist as they were artists, and though I was an agnostic in those days I was so very much not the sceptic as they were sceptics. . . . They most certainly believed in something called Art and I most certainly did not, and I came more and more to detest the whole art world. I believed in religion and was desperately trying to find it, and they seemed to regard religion as being essentially nonsense but valuable as a spur to aesthetic experience and activity. . . . I say I did not believe in Art or the art world. But of course I believed very much in the arts—with a small a and an s— whether it be the art of cooking or that of painting portraits or church pictures. But that's a very different matter and puts the 'artist' under the obligation of knowing *what* he is making and *why*. It ranks him with the world of workmen doing useful jobs. And as for the art *world,* well, that is even more sickening, especially when all the snobbery of intellectual distinction comes in. . . . Everybody was extremely kind and refined —and distinguished, but 'I'd rather be a heathen suckled in a creed outworn. . . .' On the other hand, in yet another sense, I believed in art very much indeed. The artist as prophet and seer, the artist as priest—art as man's act of collaboration with God in creating, art as *ritual*—these things I believed very earnestly. But here again I was generally at variance with my high-art friends. Their views were both more simple and more mysterious than mine. They were essentially aesthetes: that was the awful truth. They played about with religion and philosophy and labour politics, but that was all very superficial; what they really believed in and worked for was aesthetic emotion as understood by the art critics. But art as the ritual expression of religion I did indeed believe in and they did not. . . . So I gradually escaped from the high-art world which for a time seemed to be closing round me. Doubtless I never was a serious artist as serious art was understood in that world. I was the son of a nonconformist parson, the grandson of a missionary. Life was more than art" (*Auto.*, pp. 172-74).

The last two sentences are among the most significant pieces of self-revelation in all Gill's *Autobiography*. But before that repudiation could be complete, before he could become a citizen of a new and whole world, another and final crisis—"the end is the beginning"—had to be passed.

◆

Gill was in process of solving—*solvitur ambulando*—the problem of work; but he was also faced with the problem of social injustice, and that depended on religion. There was the evil of having too little material goods and the evil of having too much, of bossing and of being bossed: where did this evil arise and what was the remedy? He knew that socialism could answer neither question correctly, but was convinced that somewhere, somehow, religion could. But he had cut himself off from the religion of his childhood, and had no reason to suppose that Christianity could be the cure for the world's sickness.

"The churches seemed to be concerned solely with their sectarian games—they hardly seemed to be interested even in feeding the hungry. And if you could not count on the parsons to help to redress even common cruelties and injustices, how much less could you count on them in deeper matters? For that was how it struck me, and that was why eventually I had to leave the Fabian Society also, for I could not believe that charity was the flowering of justice, but, on the contrary it seemed to me, all inarticulate though I was and quite utterly unable to express the matter, that justice was the flowering of charity." Hunt's Abu ben Adhem was all wrong. "You couldn't profess to love your fellow men and know no more. It was damned impudence to start with—damned pharisaism too. I give tithes of all I possess; I give alms—see, boys, in short, how I love my fellow men. That was not at all what was meant when it was said: How can you love God whom you have not seen, if you do not love your neighbour whom you have seen? It means that you must *start* by loving God and, in the light of that love, in that light of love—for God *is* love—and as its necessary and inevitable fruit, you must love your neighbour. But you must love God first. Otherwise your neighbour-love would be a wrong kind of love; it would turn out to be no love at all or simply self-love" (*Auto.*, pp. 151-52).

The churches "seemed to be doing precisely what was forbidden—professing to love God whom they had not seen and yet bearing no fruit in love of neighbours. Their God-love was suspect. Their God himself was suspect. But, on the other hand, my friends, the socialists, were in no better case." They professed love of their neighbour and nescience of God's existence, so how could their love be well founded? Their concrete demands were endless, from higher wages to higher studies, from baths to abolition of privilege; and this conception of a "soup-kitchen world" was opposed, not because it was godless, but because it would cut down profits.

"You can't just demand justice for the poor and leave it at that. You must find out who are the poor and what is 'who,' and what is justice that the poor should be given it." It's no good agitating for municipal housing till you have made up your mind what sort of a being it is that has got to be housed. "Is it conceivable that he is a temple of the Holy Ghost? But what the devil is that? And what kind of housing can possibly be his suitable shrine?" (*Auto.*, p. 154). Religion is the first thing necessary; without it there is no answer to the primary and fundamental questions, What is man, and why? But Gill had no religion, and all the ready-made ones were wrangling among themselves, so that even of the Christian churches no two seemed to answer the questions alike. There was therefore nothing for it but for him to make up a religion for himself, or rather a metaphysic, a preamble to religion (considering it schematically).[1] And then he began to discover, very slowly and gradually, that his new invention was an old one. "To invent" means to come upon, to find, to uncover; and what Gill was inventing was, to his surprise and indeed alarm, stripped of all real or assumed irrelevancies, Roman Catholicism.

[1] For more particulars of these conclusions the *Autobiography* gives a reference to *The Highway*, organ of the Workers' Educational Association, November 1910 to February 1911.

"I did not think so to start with. In fact I thought I was doing quite the opposite. I thought the Christianity of the churches was dead and finished, and surely one can be forgiven for thinking so. The effect of Christianity in the world seemed non-existent, and I knew of Roman Catholicism only by repute. I did not know any Roman Catholics and I hardly ever went into any Roman Catholic churches or even read Roman Catholic books; moreover what little I knew of Roman Catholicism from outward appearances was, in a general way, revolting. . . . I suppose nothing on earth is more completely and efficiently camouflaged than Peter's 'barque,' which, from a short distance, looks exactly like the Ritz Palace Hotel." But "I found a thing in my mind and I opened my eyes and found it in front of me. You don't become a Catholic by joining the Church; you join the Church because you are a Catholic" (*Auto.*, 166, 93, 170).

And so in 1913, on his thirty-first birthday, Eric Gill and his wife and three children were received into the Roman Catholic Church.

I am not writing an *apologia pro vita sua* in the sense of that phrase canonized by John Henry Newman (or, for that matter, in any sense). But Gill's becoming a Catholic (or as I, writing as a Roman Catholic, would prefer to put it, his coming into visible fellowship with the Church) was certainly the most important, the most formative, the most integrating and creative factor in his life: [2] and I say this not as a pious *cliché* or expression of sectarian partiality, but as a plain fact which must be patent to anyone who knew him or who studies his work. Moreover his action in this regard has at times been misunderstood or even, in perfect good faith, misrepresented. A little more must therefore be said about it, and first, that Gill was never, at any time of his life, an ecclesiastically-minded layman, in the depreciatory sense of that expression; I would even dare to say, at the risk of being misunderstood, that he was not "interested in religion"—but he was passionately in love with God.

"I was never interested in all the stuff my high-church brothers and their friends went in for—synods and councils and the thirty-nine articles of religion, and ritual and vest-

[2] Gill ends his autobiography with it: the remaining ninety-one pages, one third of the whole book, are labelled "postscript."

ments and the episcopal succession. That all seemed twaddle to me, and I wasn't interested in the anti-catholic stuff either —Pope Joan and Maria Monk and the Spanish Inquisition, medieval corruption, cardinals' mistresses, superstition and pious frauds. I knew, surely everyone knows, that a man can be a holy man, a good man and an intelligent man, and yet be covered with sores, have a shocking temper and be subject to all the temptations of the flesh" (*Auto.*, p. 170). Religion means the rule of God, and Gill had a vision of a holy church ruling the world in the name of God—not a theocracy in a political but in a personal sense; speaking as one having authority—not authoritarian in principle (whatever the appearance and practice to the contrary), not answering every difficult or tom-fool question, but saying quietly and firmly "*This* is the way of the Lord," and putting the responsibility on her children to walk in it. So it was not professional apologetics or intellectual wrestling or that mythical[3] "aesthetic appeal" or that desire to "escape into an imposed certainty" (of which so much is heard) that persuaded Gill he had found the Church of God: like many another, he found as many problems to cope with after he became a Catholic as before, only they were different problems; as for books, "if any mere book did do anything to make me a Catholic, it is *Bishop Blougram's Apology*," which had been put before him as an anti-Catholic tract. How then did he become convinced? His own account tells us little and that little is not very clear—as is to be expected, for faith and the coming of faith are little more "patient of dialectical exposition" than is God himself. "I would not have anyone think that I became a Catholic because I was *convinced* of the truth, though I *was* convinced of the truth. I became a Catholic because I fell *in love* with the truth, and love is an experience. I saw. I heard. I felt. I tasted. I touched. And that is what lovers do" (*Auto.*, p. 247). Certainly he was deeply impressed

[3] As will be seen in a subsequent paragraph, this epithet does not call in question the beauty of Roman Catholic services, which with the liturgies of worship of other ancient churches form a supreme work of art. But in the average Roman Catholic church they come in for some rough handling, and are disguised by a layer of commercial fripperies, "devotional" externals, and a lack of really corporate approach that faithfully reflect the contemporary world.

by the fruits that Christianity had borne amid the corruptions of the dark and middle ages—and there was the Gospel.

"I had been brought up on the Gospel, so of course I can't say what effect that book would have had on me if it had been possible to approach it entirely from outside. It might be more impressive or it might be less. It is impossible to tell. But the mere fact that you've been brought up with a thing doesn't necessarily give it an unfair pull over your mind. I don't see why it should. It might work just the other way. All I know is that I felt like the prodigal son. I had been away, squandering my substance in riotous living—not with women and wine, though that would have been nice, but with riotous young minds and the wine of strong words— and now I was, in a manner of speaking, coming home. . . . 'The Church proceeds confidently in her doctrine of God'— and not only that, but her doctrine of God inspires confidence. Perhaps the reader doesn't think so. To me it was obvious. The Christ of the Gospel was the Christ of the Church in spite of all the funny stuff—Vatican paraphernalia, 'repository art,' and heathen superstition masquerading as Christian revelation. I boasted to myself that I could see the wood quite plainly in spite of the trees" (*Auto.*, pp. 182-3).

But on pages 193-4 of the *Autobiography*, in the course of an account of a visit to the Benedictine monastery of Mont César at Louvain, there is what seems to this writer a most significant passage. Eric attended one of the conventual offices in the church.

"At the first impact I was so moved by the chant, which you must remember I had never heard a note of in my life before, as to be almost frightened. . . . This was something alive, living, coming from the hearts and minds and bodies of living men. It was as though God were continuing the work of creation here and now, and I was there to hear, to see—even almost to touch. . . . There, at Louvain, after the slow procession of incoming monks and the following short silence when I first, all unprepared and innocent, heard 'Deus in adjutorium . . .' I knew, infallibly, that God existed and was a living God—just as I knew him in the answering smile of a child or in the living words of Christ."

Many would set this down simply as emotionalism, therefore unreliable and of uncertain value, if not valueless: especially might this be said by those who do not know the timeless, "unearthly" quality of the chant of the Roman church—had it been the "Gloria" of the B-minor Mass or the "Credo" of Gretchaninov the objection would be weightier. And Gill seems to have anticipated the objection, for he goes on: "There is a palpable righteousness in the things that God has made and that man is God's instrument for making. Emotion follows—of course, inevitably, naturally, but emotion is that which is suffered. It is the suffering that follows knowledge. We may, and often do, forget the knowing and wallow only in the emotion. It is better to forget the emotion. And when I got home from Louvain I did forget it and I remembered only that Christianity was 'pas symbolique.' "

I know the man; I know the music; I know the occasion: I do not believe that that was emotionalism. The Spirit bloweth where and how he listeth; God is not bound by his own sacraments, he can make a sacrament, an outward vehicle of inward grace, of any created thing: and surely Eric Gill received a sacrament, a "charismatic sacrament," if such an expression be allowable, bearing the grace of light and faith, there in the abbey church of Mont César; the bodiless finger of God, clothed in the materiality of public corporate worship, touched him.

It has been said that all of the "denominational" disagreements of Christians flow from one fundamental disagreement about the nature of the Church. It seems that they can indeed be reduced to that and it is therefore worth looking at how the Church appeared to Eric Gill, a man whose convictions attracted people of widely differing views.

> "It has been said that the Church exists in order that words may have a meaning. That, in its ultimate essence, is what a church is, that by which how, when and why cease to be pragmatical catcalls and become intelligible symbols, symbols patient of interpretation" (*Belief*, p. 310). The Church is "a perfectly human institution, matter and spirit, and the primacy is of the spirit, therefore guided by the Holy Ghost, therefore the bride of Christ, therefore a divine institution also. . . . Just as, in my mind, the Christianity enunciated by St John and St Paul is the necessary complement of the Christianity enunciated by the other evangelists, so the Church as sacrific-

ing priest is the necessary complement of the Church as the living voice. And just as Calvary was the necessary consummation of Christ's life, so the Eucharist is the necessary consummation of our life in him. . . . Our earthly life is symbolized by the bread and wine. Under the appearance of bread and wine God gives himself to us. Thus are we made sharers of his divinity who saw fit to share our humanity. Thus man, who was made in the beginning with the dignity of God's image, is yet more wonderfully renewed" (*Auto.*, pp. 190, 246).

Gill was the last man to confound things that should not be mixed up, to confuse the Church of God with the life and opinions of people, clerical or lay, who profess her membership. None saw more clearly than he the sectarianism (historically explainable) of many Roman Catholics in England, their obsession with such secondary issues as the "schools question," the efforts of their politics to convince an unnecessarily unbelieving generation that Catholics were as keen on the British Empire, mass-production, money-making and wireless culture as anybody else; their shocking complacency: "We alone were good and intelligent, and everyone else was in outer darkness: Protestants, heretics, and either fools or knaves. It was assumed that the Church was hated and Catholics absolutely basked in that hatred, wallowed in it." [4] But he saw no less clearly that the Roman church in England is "a living member of the Universal Church and knows a greatness and a wisdom and a holiness which is entirely unknown to the majority of English people" (*Auto.*, 209, 198).

The Church for Gill, then, was the church of the oldest Christian tradition—something which teaches the necessary truths about man's first beginning and last end, wherein fallen and divided man is united, restored and divinized, particularly in the sacramental meal which commemorates and continues the redeeming sacrifice of her Master and Lord.[5] No simply human assembly can do these things; she

[4] It must in fairness be recognized, as Gill recognized, that these things have been considerably modified in the past twenty years.

[5] To discourage individualistic devotion and to emphasize the corporate nature of this act, Gill advocated the putting of the altar in the middle of the church with the congregation all around. See "Mass for the Masses" in *Sacred and Secular*.

is divine. Her members on earth, members not in the sense of members of a club, but as a hand of the body or a branch of the tree, visibly or hiddenly united with her, are human: she is human.

Of what can be said against the Roman Catholic Church on her human side he was only too well aware—but "the world" was painfully apparent, even to the length of apostasy and betrayal, among the first Twelve themselves, yet who now would choose the alternative of following Herod and Pilate?

> "When you think of St Peter's and the toy soldiery, and the purple and lace of its fat wordly-looking prelates, and when you think of the subtle intangibilities and intransigencies of its diplomacy, it is not difficult to understand why people run away in a panic—what's it all got to do with the Man on the Ass, anyway? But to me the alternative was too clear to be missed or to be run away from. In fact both alternatives were too clear. The frightful, the truly frightful, horror of the corruption of the ancient Church was as nothing to the essential dirtiness, dirtiness in its very being and nature, of the industrial-capitalist world" (*Auto.*, p. 189).

So he answered the question, the "all-inclusive and final question," "Do you believe all that the holy Church teaches?" with an unhesitating "Yes." "But as to *what* she teaches on all the multiplication of funny subjects that we worry ourselves about, well, at the great risk, or rather, certainty of being thought both lazy and unscrupulous, I made up my mind to confine my attention to things that seemed fundamentally important and things that intimately concerned me" (*Auto.*, p. 191). Not for him to trouble his head about whether Jonah really lived inside a fish or whether Pope Honorius I taught heresy or whether Anglican orders are valid—or what "valid" means in that connection.

He had a strong glowing faith, but it was not the faith of a child or of the proverbial Breton peasant—because he was not a child or a Breton peasant. His was the faith of a man of more than common fineness of spirit and intellectual ability, and he had put away childish things. But his understanding of what are and what are not childish things differed greatly from that of the more complacent or unimaginative who quote St. Paul on that head—with the result that he was childlike in the sense of Christ's admonition. Playfulness was a trait in his character, "play" was one of his sacred words, and he loved to think of children—and grownups—playing before their Father in the streets of the Heavenly Jerusalem. But he would tolerate no prettifying of or toying with the majestic mysteries of the Christian faith and life: in his *Sacred and Secular* can be read a manly and adult application of the "little way" of St Teresa of Lisieux, and a book about the same simple young nun provoked him to a blistering review that was probably as near vituperation as he ever got.

❧

For the next four years Gill was principally engaged in carving the fourteen panels called stations of the cross for Westminster Cathedral, the work which put him definitely in the front rank of contemporary English sculptors. Then— it was September, 1918—he was conscripted for the army. He was, of course, by now under no illusions about politics, but he had paid no particular attention to the causes and conduct of war or to the congruity or otherwise of Christians engaging in organized violence at the behest of the civil power: his attitude was that warfare and fighting was not his line of business, that if he were really wanted he would be fetched, and then he would go quietly. So he was drafted into the mechanical-transport section of the R.A.F. His military service lasted under four months, but it was a "monstrous and momentous experience." After four years of war the "people's army," especially on home-stations, had been thoroughly militarized and dehumanized, the recruits were unwilling and fed-up from the start (at one camp at which he was stationed there were several suicides a week), and Gill found himself, not with young rustics or tradesmen (in the proper sense of that word) or others with whom he had common interests, but with men from the suburbs of industrial towns, under the worst sort of n.c.o. "If I had not had that brief taste of army life I should never have known what it is like to be one of the 'submerged tenth,' an under-dog, a person of no use to anyone but as an instrument, a unit on a pay-sheet . . ." (*Auto.*, p. 205).

After his release Gill returned to work at Ditchling Common, where with friends and their families living in neighbouring houses there was in process of formation a society of Roman Catholics, a gild, bound by their common faith and common ideas about work and society: printing, stone-carving and carpentry were among their trades. The six years that followed are passed over in a very few pages of the *Autobiography*, but they were important in that they saw the beginning and development of Eric's association with the Order of Preachers. The members of the Ditchling gild, though living in independent households, soon found the need of some limited rule of life to be followed by all, and one or other of the third-orders, founded by the friars in the middle ages, was obviously indicated: their choice fell on that one which forms part of the Order of Preachers, "Black Friars," founded by St Dominic in 1215.[6] The principal work of this order is sufficiently indicated by its name: the Dominicans are essentially teachers, and in particular they are exponents of the philosophical and theological teaching and method of St Thomas Aquinas, himself a Dominican, the fine flower of the colossal Christian and intellectual rebirth of the thirteenth century.

Eric became an enthusiastic disciple of Aquinas. This must not be misunderstood. He was never an accomplished thomist, he was not even deeply read in St Thomas's works; he learned his teaching principally in the old way, by word of mouth, from the several Dominican friars who were his life-long friends and admirers. "The starting-point of human progress," says Christopher Dawson, "is to be found in the highest type of knowledge—the intuition of pure being . . . man's development is not so much from the lower to the higher as from the confused to the distinct." The first need

---

[6] A third-order, whose members are called "tertiaries," is an association of lay people, not normally living in community, who follow a private rule of life under the direction of an order of mendicant friars. To-day they hardly differ in practice from any other similar religious society; in the middle ages their obligations and significance were more serious.

of our time, says Jacques Maritain, is an intellectual need, the need for clarity of understanding. "Good will is not so obviously wanting as good sense," glossed Gill, and agreed with Dawson and Maritain with passionate intensity. St Thomas as the philosopher of being, as pre-eminently the philosopher of common sense, as a mind of almost unearthly clarity, with a method to match it—that was what first attracted him; and then he found in St Thomas, stated and argued clearly and succinctly as nowhere else, the principles of God and man which Eric used with such devastating force (but not, alas! with corresponding effect) against the politico-industrial set-up of contemporary society. That, I think, both in life and teaching, was the principal preoccupation of the Ditchling days, to show Catholics in particular that the material basis of what is called twentieth-century civilization is fundamentally incompatible not simply with Christianity but with man's natural good: the groundwork was laid of that social teaching which for the rest of his life he put tirelessly, not only before his co-religionists, but before all who were willing to listen. And while Aquinas helped him with metaphysical and psychological principles, he found masterly statements of principles of practice and analyses of the evils of the day in the social pronouncements of two popes, Leo XIII and Pius XI, notably the encyclical-letters "Rerum novarum" and "Quadragesimo anno"; documents which, translated into turgid italianate English, explained and explained away time and again, used as slogans and stamping-ground for study clubs instead of springs of action, have lacked the influence they ought to have had in this country.

When his vigorous and mathematically-inclined mind first came under the influence of the presentation of Christianity which owes so much to Western medieval rationalism and Counter-reformation juridicism, when he was first entranced by St Thomas's use of aristotelian logic and categories of thought, Gill ran some danger of becoming too exclusively engrossed in man's rational powers,[7] of believing that all

[7] But, as Gill often pointed out, the use of reason is not to be identified with the process of ratiocination. And "the senses are a kind of reason" (he did not invent that saying, he found it in St. Thomas).

truth can be expressed in syllogistic terms, even of ultimately bogging-down in the morass of legalism: [8] he was in
violent revolt from the confused thinking and aesthetic emotionalism of the "art world," from the relativist opportunism
of socialist politics, from excessive dependence on religious
experience that was not necessarily religious. And he was
now coming into contact with people many of whom, with
sneers at the alleged muddle-headedness, illogicality and
compromise of their fellow Englishmen, continually lauded
the alleged realism and logical consistency of Frenchmen and
Italians and Roman Catholics in general. But Gill was too
fearless, too wide-spirited, too mentally alert to succumb to
the danger; if he had too much good sense to confuse prejudice or arbitrary judgement, wishful thinking or emotion,
with intuition, so was he too whole a character to underrate
the intuitive, the charismatic, the prophetic. This became
more pronounced as he got older, and in the year before he
died he wrote:

"The best and the most perfect way is the way of love.
This applies not only to life but also to teaching. The best
and most perfect way to inculcate, for example, the virtue
of honesty is to shew that love implies it. It is probable that
no other method can ever be successful; for though we are
rational beings, inasmuch as we are persons . . . yet we use
our reason so rarely and fitfully and with so rash a carelessness, without training or discipline; we follow our prejudices
and predilections with such confidence and impudence that
any appeal based upon rational argument is unlikely to be
successful. Moreover the lovely has a wider reference than the
reasonable: what we love we do not merely desire—it is something that, whether consciously or not, we recognize to be
right as well as good, not only desirable but also as it ought
to be; and the fact that this recognition is arrived at by that
leap of the intelligence that we call intuition, and not by
discursive reasoning and the painful process of thinking it out
step by step by logical argument, seems to show that reason-

[8] Early in our friendship he surprised me by saying of the Church's condemnation of a certain action as sinful in essence that "I can't understand
why. I'm always rebelling against it. Now if it were merely a disciplinary
rule, imposed for reasons of expediency, I'd be quite happy about it." Years
later he told me that his attitude had become quite the opposite: he had
learned to be critical of the desirability and efficacy of rules and regulations
and the ingenuities of casuists and canon lawyers. "The more canon law, the
less religion" (it was not Gill but an ecclesiastic who said that).

ing is both unnecessary and absurd . . ." *Seems to be,* not *is;* and, not *or.*

And, as Walter Shewring has emphasized (*Blackfriars,* February 1941, pp. 87-89), Eric increasingly disassociated himself from that strong obscurantist party that refuses to look outside the Roman Catholic Church for any assistance whatever in the pursuit of truth. "He accepted every consequence of the Ambrosian principle embraced by St Thomas, that *all* truth is from the Holy Ghost." No one was to think that "when I affirm the truth of Christianity I am therefore denying the truth of other faiths—at the most I am only denying their denials" (*Machine Age,* p. 19). There was no question of minimizing Christian doctrine: "Of all truths, the truth dearest to Eric Gill was that of the Incarnation. . . . But he responded eagerly to the call of such exponents of Eastern wisdom as Ananda Coomaraswamy (a venerated friend) and René Guénon"; and the present writer can testify to his eagerness to learn from the Eastern Christian tradition and mentality, with which, indeed, he came to have some close affinities.

Gill and his family left Ditchling Common in 1924 [9] for a more remote and undisturbed home in a valley of the Black Mountains in Breconshire. Two other families accompanied them from Ditchling and there was another of friends already there, but no attempt was made at any organization or communal living beyond what is necessarily involved by common interests and close contiguity. Here, at Capel-y-ffin, he did little stone-carving but a lot of lettering and wood-engraving and there was the beginning of his great work as a designer of printing-types, work which brought him into association with that "business-world" he so often attacked: it is an appreciative reference to the Monotype Corporation in the *Autobiography* that brings forth his disclaimer (often repeated elsewhere) of any intention to impute malice and wickedness to any individual man of business, so many of whom he had met were "more than nice," men with inher-

[9] The Ditchling gild still exists. Its press published the first work in English of that great Frenchman Jacques Maritain, viz., *Art et Scolastique,* translated by the Reverend John O'Connor under the title "The Philosophy of **Art.**"

ited traditions of honesty and good service trying to maintain those traditions within a system that must prove fatal to them sooner or later. However strongly he spoke of the business world or "the rich" or the sufferings of the workers, what he really had his eye on was not the iniquities of individual persons but an organization of society in which they are all unavoidably tied up, which, whether he knows it or not, bears in its way as hardly on Henry Ford as on Bill Jones: there must be justice for dukes (if there be any) as much as for dustmen—and in either case justice is due to them precisely as men, human beings. In another section of this book F. A. Lea writes of G. K. Chesterton that, "What he beheld was not the calculated exploitation of one class by another, but an all-pervading injustice accepted as a matter of course nearly as much by the 'proletarian' as the capitalist. What he strove to create was a general consciousness of its existence, equal to his own, so that it must either become deliberate and challenging, or else be rectified, by the substitution of co-operation for competition." This is exactly true of Gill (though he would not refer to his "revolution" in such equivocal terms: competition is sometimes good, and there can be co-operation for evil).

လ

As he grew older Eric Gill gave more and more attention to the problem of man in society, the question both social and religious of how persons can lead a whole, and therefore at least potentially holy, life on this earth. He was always a most strenuous and fully-occupied worker, but latterly screwed out ever more time for books, articles and lectures directly or indirectly concerned with this theme. With, I believe, very little conscious missionary purpose, this son of missionaries and brother of the Friars Preachers expounded Christian principles and practice in places where they would otherwise hardly, or never, have been heard.[10] He accepted invitations to speak or write, on this or that aspect of work and art or on social problems or on peace and war, indifferently for Catholics and Quakers, capitalists and communists,

[10] "The deep religion of his teaching has been to me literally the revelation of a new gospel," wrote Dr. Mulk Raj Anand in his *Hindu View of Art*.

official bodies and obscure groups. This high-tide of lecturing came later, but it was at Capel-y-ffin that writing began to have a notable part in his activities, his pamphleteering, as he called it. His earlier publications were single essays; then came collections of articles reprinted from numerous periodical publications, many of them little known; and then longer single essays, *e.g.,* on clothes, on typography, culminating in two full-length books, *The Necessity of Belief* [11] and the *Autobiography.*

These writings give a very clear and, on the whole, adequate account of Gill's ideas and arguments; and they are remarkable not only for their internal consistency but for their consistency and correlation as a whole: from the few paragraphs on Slavery and Freedom written in 1918 down to the posthumously published autobiography he was "telling the same story," often in the same words. He was not afraid of repeating himself: "It has been said that I am one of those writers who can only keep to the point by returning to it. I may say in self-defense that there are many readers who can only remember the point if it is repeated often enough" (*Beauty,* p. 5); in particular, certain pregnant "sayings" and quotations with which every reader of Eric Gill is familiar occur in the earliest writings as in the latest: such, for example, are "Look after goodness and truth, and beauty will look after herself," "Man is made up of body and spirit, both real and both good," St Augustine's "Love, and do what you will." The same basic ideas are always there—the nature of man and his relation to God, the Christian revelation, human responsibility and therefore the necessity of freedom, human sin and divine grace, man's work as a calling to collaborate with God in creation—and it seems to me that in general their application underwent but little real development: what did develop was Eric Gill himself; he saw the same things but saw deeper into them, he saw farther and he saw more clearly, and in that vision he wrote about the same things again.

[11] He disliked this title as pretentious, and wanted to call it "Believe It or Not." His publishers, Messrs. Faber & Faber, would not agree, but he had his way with the subtitle. *See* bibliography.

There can also be found in Gill's writings, especially the *Autobiography*, about as good a picture of what a man was like as can be got without knowing him in person—except in one particular (and here I except the *Autobiography* and, in a measure, *The Necessity of Belief*): his actual style of writing and expressing himself was not always *l'homme même*, it was often misleading. It is sometimes said by those who did not know him personally that Gill was intolerant, dogmatic (in the vulgar sense) and contemptuous of those who disagreed with him: an obituary-writer who ought to have known better attributed to him a mythical "rich flow of invective." It is easy to see how hasty readers formed this misconception: as he often admitted, in and out of print, his manner of writing could give an impression of cocksureness, of laying down the law. But it was a laughably wrong impression, for not the least remarkable thing about Eric was his humility and a diffidence that was sometimes staggering. While never deferring to an opinion, by whomever expressed, unless and until he came to agree with it, he would ask and listen to the opinion of all and sundry on whatever topic turned up, even on technical matters of his own work. I have seen him bring a handful of engraving proofs in to the evening meal and ask for the criticism of all present— the family, visitors, servants: and next morning some of the suggestions of those inexpert critics were carried out. This humbleness of mind is well illustrated by the following passage from a letter written only a few weeks before his death.

"I've been in bed off and on since April 15 and never anything very serious . . . Old age coming on I guess. Anyway it gave me time and opportunity to write book for Cape as ordered—100,000 words about my so-called 'life.' He asked for an autobiography but I told him it couldn't be done: it would have to be an 'autopsychography,' and that's what it is. . . . Really it amounts to a 'search for the City of God,' but of course I can't give it a fine title like that. . . . It feels to me as though I ought really to die now. I don't know how I shall be able to face the world after stripping myself more or less naked as I have done."

Since the publication of that 'autopsychography' there is no longer any excuse for thinking Eric Gill bumptious and intolerant.

Gill had hammered out in his mind and tested by practice certain principles, and these he put forward tirelessly for consideration and debate. But he hated to appear to be taking upon himself what he regarded as an office primarily of the clergy, and for that reason, as well as for the sake of first principles and of those who do not accept Christianity, he would appeal to natural reason as often as, or more often than, to divine revelation, to justice rather than to charity: charity he lived, his passion for justice was a fruit of his intense lovingness, and in more intimate private talk he would speak of God and of love more often than of either justice or reason. His intellectual judgements were downright ("We are told not to cast pearls before swine," he said, "And to adjudge persons swine in this sense necessitates making an intellectual judgement of them"), but he was always scrupulous to try to avoid making, or seeming to make, moral judgements of persons. I do not recollect ever hearing him utter a word intended to wound, and time and again I have watched him trying to find a worthy explanation of someone's apparently indefensible action, or gently changing the conversation when another's character or deeds were coming in for rough handling. Some years ago he and I were invited to speak in support of the war-resisters' candidate for the lord-rectorship of Glasgow University. The audience was extremely disorderly and Gill (who had a poor delivery) was hardly heard: I, by hardening my heart and being rude, forced some sort of hearing. "The difference between the two speakers," commented a Presbyterian minister afterwards, "was that Gill was forgiving those hooligans all the time, whereas Attwater did not forgive them till he had finished." Very characteristic of Gill; so, too, was his bewilderment that intelligent young people (he was extremely sympathetic towards the young, but without a trace of the "Youth" ramp) could come to a serious meeting only in order to make a din.

The last twelve years of his life Gill lived in Buckinghamshire, twelve full and fruitful years in which, by unflagging work and perfect order in the conduct of his affairs, his thought, writing and lecturing were enabled to keep pace with his stone carving and typography.[12] One of the carving jobs was ten panels for the new museum at Jerusalem, which involved two longish visits to Palestine, which must be spoken of here because his stay there was the last of several things in his life that he regarded as "revelations."

Many people go to Palestine and come back having apparently seen nothing but flies and touts, dirt and "backwardness," the rivalries of religions and the quarrels, emulations and meannesses of their sects. All these things are there and in good measure, and Eric saw them, but there are other things to be seen, and he saw them too. "In the Holy Land I saw a holy land indeed; I also saw, as it were eye to eye, the sweating face of Christ. . . . To me it was like living with the Apostles. It was like living in the Bible." And the beauty he saw was of people, of the Palestinian "Arabs" living without pride and with dignity in their poverty, sinful but humanly sinful; of places, Galilee and the Jordan wilderness; of the work of men's hands, above all of that Moslem shrine, the Haram as-Sharif at Jerusalem, which he declared to be the most beautiful place he had ever seen, the most spiritually pervaded. "Tell me where there is another. Is it in London, in Trafalgar Square? Is it the Place de la Concorde? Is it on the Acropolis at Athens? They tell me that is very lovely, but at Jerusalem living men worship the living God; at Athens there is but a memory of what was. Is it even in the piazza of St. Peter's? No, not there. . . ."

As for the shrines of Christendom, the basilica of Bethle-

12 Among his stone works (not all at this time) were stations of the cross in churches at Bradford and Leatherhead, the Leeds University war memorial, and carvings for the underground station at St. James's Park, at Broadcasting House, and for the League of Nations building at Geneva. He was also commissioned for work on the new Anglican cathedral at Guildford. He designed eleven faces of printing type, including a Greek, a Hebrew and an Arabic face. He engraved (on wood) many decorations for the books of the Golden Cockerel, Count Kessler's, and other presses. He was made an associate of the Royal Academy, an honorary member of the Royal Institute of British Architects, an LL.D., *honoris causa* of Edinburgh University, and was one of the original recipients of the new designer-for-industry honour (!). Some even of his friends did not know of these recognitions, which he regarded simply as manifestations of the uncritical kindness of the public bodies concerned.

hem, reminder also of the pride and glory of blood-stained Byzantium, the church of the Holy Sepulchre, reminder also of the brutalities and arrogance of Western Europe breaking in on Asia—these he would rather have as they were, half-ruinous, cluttered with the ecclesiastical junk of half a dozen churches, dirty and profaned, than restored and polished up by Caesar's building-contractors. "By the inscrutable decree of God the sweat is not thus to be wiped from His face"; the squabblings of Catholics and Orthodox, Armenians and Greeks, do less dishonour to Christ than if they should abandon his cross entirely and "hand the whole notion of salvation to the sanitary authority," as our civilization seeks to do. Jerusalem has "not yet rendered to Caesar the things that are God's" (*Auto.*, pp. 281, 257).

Blessed are the poor, for theirs is the Kingdom of God: that truth was first taught in the Holy Land and Gill found that it can still be learned there to-day, and he came back with his mind made up. "Henceforward I must take up a position even more antagonistic to my contemporaries than that of a mere critic of the mechanistic system. I must take a position antagonistic to the very basis of their civilization. And I must appear antagonistic even to the Church itself. Of course that is all nonsense but that is how it must appear. For the Christians everywhere have committed themselves to the support of capitalist industrialism and therefore to the wars in its defence, mechanized war to preserve mechanized living, while I believe that capitalism is robbery, industrialism is blasphemy and war is murder" (*Auto.*, p. 257). It was with these convictions, more or less clearly envisaged, that Eric Gill had lived most of his life; and with them thus reinforced, seen as it were from a Pisgah height between the hill of redemptive Death and the tomb of bodily and spiritual Resurrection—the spot in which Palestinian folk-wisdom so aptly recognized the centre of the world—he worked out his few remaining earthly years.

He died in a hospital close to London, in the night of November 17-18, 1940. An air raid was going on.

2

CHRISTIAN revolutionary. It was characteristic of Eric Gill that when something came up for discussion he would seek at once a definition of terms, and that as a starting-point for such definition he would consult the dictionary for the etymology and current meanings of the words concerned—the "Concise Oxford" was always kept handy. Turning, then, to the "Shorter Oxford," I find under *Christian,* "one who follows the precepts and example of Christ"; this, with the addition of "tries to" before "follow," is very suitable for my purpose. Under *revolutionary* I find "[one who works for or advocates] the complete overthrow of the established government in any country or state by those who were previously subject to it: a forcible substitution of a new ruler or form of government."

That Gill was a sincere and fervent *Christian* in the above wide sense needs no demonstration, nor that he was one in a more strict sense; for he voluntarily united himself with the Roman Catholic Church: and, whatever may be thought of some passages in her history, of some of her teaching and still more of the teaching of some of her theologians, of some of her practice and still more of the practice of many of her members, that church as a whole must be recognized as an unflinching upholder throughout the centuries of the traditional fundamental truths of Christian faith and life. Gill, therefore, professed no eclectic or dilettante Christianity: he sought to follow Christ, not, for example, as the world's most attractive or convincing ethical teacher, but because he believed him to be the One God, clothed in human flesh, with all that follows from that stupendous concept.

Two possible misunderstandings may here be cleared up. On the one hand, he was no doctrinaire religionist, no sectarian peddler of the beliefs of his church as a sort of spiritual and religious patent-medicine which would cure all ills by the simple swallowing; he never flourished the Catholic faith like a tomahawk. He believed that faith with all his heart and soul, and he never forgot it is part of that faith that its dogmas must be lived as well as assented to before they can bear fruit. "To be religious means to believe in order, and order implies a person ordering"—God: and "a great religious period is one in which men proceed confidently in a doctrine of God." He believed ("We do not claim that what we believe is true because we believe it, but simply that what we believe is what we hold to be certain"), he believed that God ordained a teaching church on earth—but that does not involve belief in every word that proceeds from the mouth of her theologians (who in any case not seldom contradict one another): "theologians have not infrequently made confusion where their job was to clear things up. They have collected the butterly only to kill it and pin it down, and the meaning they have pinned down has turned out to be not the real meaning but only that one which was suitable for such pinning."

On the other hand, neither was Gill "anti-clerical." In the continental sense of the expression, which involves opposition to a given church or even to Christianity itself, obviously he was not: in the English sense, which seems ultimately to convey the idea that clergymen necessarily know less about true religion than anybody else, his words sometimes appear to be strongly imbued with it. I do not refer to such good-humoured digs as that "[the problem of evil is such that] even theologians have been humble before it," but to harder sayings: for instance, that the swagger, human prowess and greatness implied by the church architecture of Renaissance Rome is more defiling to the face of Christ than our contemptuous spittle. "The nonsensical and illusory grandeurs of Rome, Rome, the Holy City, decked out in the finery of ballrooms and banks, the soul-ensnaring magnificence of statistical display, the grand appearance of doctrinal and ethical unity . . . it seemed to me that we should do better to eschew our grandeurs and forget our numbers—and brag less about unity while, to the heathen and the pagans and the infidels, the most conspicuous thing about

Christians is their sectarian disunity. . . . For while we fight among ourselves about doctrine, we are united in the common worship of money and material success. Here I do not exaggerate. That is the awful thing" (*Auto.*, p. 254). "The clergy are in the position of men standing on the brink of a frozen pool and shouting to men drowning under the ice that they should take good deep breaths if they want to be healthy" (*M. & M.*, p. 36). "The clergy are everywhere acknowledged to be custodians of faith and morals—the faith is what you more or less blindly believe because your school-teachers taught it during 'religious instruction,' and morals are little more than a list of things you mustn't do. Man as an intelligent and intellectual being is hardly mentioned, and never expected to function" (*W. & P.*, p. 100). "It must be a commonplace of our experience that the widespread scepticism of our time is as much the consequence of loss of respect for the preachers of Christ as it is of the writings and teachings of unbelievers, and that that loss of respect is a necessary preliminary" (*Auto.*, p. 104). Many clergy (and others) don't like people to say that sort of thing: the fact that it is true makes it worse.

For the teaching office of the Church, for the priestly office of its ministers, Gill had the profoundest reverence and respect, because it is a special participation in the one true universal priesthood of Jesus Christ (and he was very alive to the truth that every Christian in his measure shares in that priesthood). But this is not to say that the mistakes, exaggerations, deficiencies of persons exercising authority in holy orders should be extenuated or ignored, that as a matter of discipline it is good to treat clergy as outside criticism: that is obscurantism, weakness, laziness, and produces that "clericalism" of which a French archbishop has recently declared, "the Church disapproves of it and we don't want any of it at any price." Moreover, accusations against churches and ecclesiastical authorities can be substantiated only by Christian doctrine. "If you are amazed by the policeman-like frame of mind of many of the clergy and their apparent conviction that the spirit killeth but the letter quickeneth (so that you would think getting to Heaven was a business of going by the book!) you must still remember that the opposite doctrine is Christian teaching, and that it is the authority to which they themselves appeal who is the judge" (*Auto.*, p. 255).

The above-quoted definition of *revolutionary* would certainly never fit so gentle and unpolitically-minded a person as Gill, but in our day the scope of the word has been much extended, to include those who seriously oppose any widely-accepted and well-established state of affairs or social or other system and the principles and philosophy pertinent to it. I suspect that the word started life as a term of abuse, which would account for its definition in negative terms: now that it has become domesticated it is better defined positively, as, say, "an advocate of principles and policies which involve the overthrow or reversal of established systems, etc." And in this wider sense Gill was unquestionably a revolutionary. Not that he used the word much or thought of himself in such terms: in *Work and Property* is an essay called "Art and Revolution" which would be extremely puzzling to most revolutionaries: only at the end does he refer to them at all —and then to dismiss them as mere "progressives"! His reference to his own "little revolution" has already been quoted (p. 166); nevertheless to bring that about would mean "the complete destruction of a civilization in which money is god and men of commerce are our rulers." But "this destruction will come about without any need for 'revolutionary' activity. Let no one suppose I propose to wave a red flag. The present civilization is founded upon an unnatural condition and will come to a natural end. If there are battles, murders and sudden deaths it will not be the fault of" [1]—men like Eric Gill. "A kingdom not of this world"; "Poverty, chastity and obedience"—such were the slogans on the banners of *his* revolt. "These may sound strange watchwords for revolutionists. Consider then the alternatives: Riches, pleasure and irresponsibility, and a kingdom not founded in Heaven!" (*Art Nonsense*, p. 108).

The word "revolution" as commonly used connotes physical violence, and both those who fear and those who welcome

[1] He wrote this in 1928 (*Art Nonsense*, p. 291); I quote it in 1941.

the thing like to think of it in terms of the barricades. But the dictionary gives also a more fundamental meaning, "The action of turning over in the mind; consideration; reflection." And it is here that Gill really belongs: "the spirit has the primacy." What he fought for was a "unanimous society," one in which there is unity of *mind* among the people, "who know the same truth and will the same good": what he fought against was the evil *frame of mind* in contemporary society, one that is radically unchristian and antichristian, therefore contrary to nature and to nature's God, "as anti-God as any atheist could wish."

Yes, a Christian revolutionary. And not a revolutionary who happened to be a Christian, or in spite of being a Christian, but revolutionary *because* Christian.

◆

Gill being so many-sided a person (each side marvellously correlated with each other), and we humans having a boundless capacity to misunderstand and misinterpret one another, it may clear the picture somewhat to state and explain some of the things that he was *not,* or that he was not in the usual sense of the terms used. The use of labels, especially of ill-defined labels, to tag on to people, whether to express a judgement, favourable or unfavourable, or to pigeonhole them away in what are assumed to be meaningful categories, is one of the minor pernicious diseases endemic in our time.

"The individual rebel, however unspotted from the world he may keep himself, is bound to be tainted by idiosyncrasy and eccentricity; he is likely to be both a prig and a faddist. He will set up for himself a standard of his own making, unless he first ally himself to truth, and truth is a 'who' and not a 'what'!" (*Art Nonsense,* p. 123). Eric did not "ally" but submitted himself to Him who is Truth, and thus was his mind kept purged of idiosyncrasy and eccentricity, priggery and faddism—he was no individualistic crank (certain peculiarities of dress and the like to the contrary notwithstanding). But more of this will be said when I come to speak of his ordinariness and feeling for the "common man," as also then of his freedom from that lop-sided mental superiority that we call "being highbrow" and the fidgety self-conscious "culture" that goes with it.[2] "We are all," he said, "so many sweethearts to God. Are we going to fob him off with borrowed kisses—with even the best Elizabethan love-songs? Would he not rather have the vulgar endearments which are our own?" Gill mixed much and sympathetically with cranks and highbrows and *exaltés* of all kinds, and it is not surprising that he has been labelled (sometimes mutually exclusively) with some of their enthusiasms.

He is, for example, commonly regarded as a back-to-the-lander, and it is true that he lived by choice in the country, had the deepest regard for its people and their work, and said, not once but repeatedly, that "The salvation of England cannot be brought about by town improvement; it can only come by the land." But precisely because "the town, the holy city, is nourished upon elements drawn from the soil. The modern towns of our industrial England have no such nourishment."

> "It *is* a lot of nonsense, all this cackle about the beauty of the country. And the cackle would never have been heard if the towns had not become such monsters of indecency and indignity. The town properly thought of is the very crown and summit of man's creativeness. . . . The countryside exists to support and uphold and nourish and maintain the city. . . . Thus the call to the land, to the earth, is the necessary first call. We must be born again, and we must be born again on the land, to dig the earth, to plant and cultivate, to be shepherds and swineherds, to hew wood and draw water, to build simple dwellings and simple places of prayer. But we need not therefore be blinded to what is the truth. Because Babylon is vile it does not follow that Jerusalem is vile also" (*Auto.*, pp. 230-8).

That is not the language of that often rather sentimental state of mind that has earned the contemptuous epithet "back-to-the-landery"; and Gill, while sympathizing with and admiring the heroism of those who follow a call to undertake an agricultural "simple life" in groups and associations, refused the gross over-simplification of regarding this as a

---

[2] Gill might well have echoed Göring's famous remark about culture and a revolver. But whereas Göring would shoot down the good men, Gill would shoot down the bogus things. *See* again later.

cure-all to be urged on people indiscriminately: in particular did he protest against any "attempt to make out that a certain kind of simple, self-supporting country life is the only life for good Christian people" (*Beauty,* p. 34).

Gill had a great appreciation of "that most manly of great men," William Morris (as for Ruskin, who spoke the truth "more eloquently than Cobbett or Disraeli, and more solemnly"), and he was inevitably mixed up in the arts-and-crafts movement. But he had to repudiate it—and was told by the late W. R. Lethaby ("Who shall measure the greatness of this man?") that he was "crabbing his mother." But Gill was not begotten of that movement, and he saw unerringly its two great weaknesses: being unable to compete with mass-production, its products were luxury articles, bought only by the well-to-do; and it positively helped the industrial producers, who copied its designs in their factories and thus started a flood of shams that still further corrupted people's judgement of the times. So Gill escaped from arts-and-crafts: "I'm no gentleman and I don't understand loyalty to lost causes when the causes deserve to be lost."

And he was no medievalist, in the common sense of an uncritical admirer who sees in the middle ages an ideal of life and achievement—Merrie England and all that—which we should in some mysterious way seek to restore or at least approximate to. He associated himself with a religious order medieval in its origin and some of its existing customs—but it is also one of the most up-to-date; he sat at the feet of Aquinas —but Aquinas was a man of universal and timeless mind; he often referred to medieval conditions and practice for illustration, contrast and commendation—but there was nothing specifically medieval about his own dominating ideas. "I do not cite the middle ages because they were good ages or because, in those ages, a certain set of ideas were held to be just and seemly. I do not 'cite' them at all. I am merely describing. . . ." (*Art,* p. 37). Christianity teaches that the enemies of peace and good order are self-seeking and injustice, and for centuries that teaching bore fruit in the subordination of commerce, the outlawry of usury, the upholding of law that defended persons and families as such and evolved the noble concept of the *liber et legalis homo,* "free and lawful man" (now being rapidly superseded, as Richard O'Sullivan, K.C., pertinently remarks, by that of the "insured (or insurable) person"). Gill did not say that that teaching never failed in its effect or that its fruit was always plentiful; but it was after, and with the help of, the Renaissance and the Reformation that commerce and mercantile imperialism became insubordinate and the results of money-lending were honoured, poverty became a disgrace and the rich man as such was esteemed, the workman became on the one hand the artisan and on the other the artist, men gave God's glory to man. Nevertheless, "I am not advocating any indiscriminate praise of pre-Renaissance or pre-industrial works. The seeds of our worship of riches were sown long before Luther or James Watt. A great deal of medieval cathedral-building was no more than human swank and aggrandizement" (*W. & P.,* p. 136), and the religion and law of the middle ages were disfigured by any amount of wickedness, superstition and violent tyranny.

There was a time when Gill could hardly bring himself to use the word "artist," otherwise than as a term of opprobrium; the artist as a special kind of man, the lap-dog of the rich and great, the aesthetician ("relations of masses" and all that), the exploiter of temperament and sensibility, the beauty-wallah—he was certainly not that kind of artist; he was a workman, a carver of stone. The beauty of God is the cause of the being of all that is, said St Thomas, and earthly beauty is no mere delightfulness, or its perception a matter of emotion: it is "that order in things which we perceive to be in itself and at once both right and good. It is perceived by intuition and the knowledge of it is developed by contemplation" (*Art Nonsense,* p. 102); it is the splendour or radiance by which being is manifest, the shiningness perceived in things which are made as they should be; all well-made things are beautiful. "A beautiful thing is that which, being seen, pleases," and there is a whole essay in *Art Nonsense* (pp. 143-158) expounding this apparently simple, if not jejune, definition of Aquinas. "Beauty cannot be taught, and it is best not talked about. It must be spontaneous. It cannot be imposed. . . . Its enemies are irreligion and the offspring of irreligion—commercialism and the rule of the trader" (*Art Nonsense*, p. 94). To recognize it we must use our minds: just as a good life is a mortified life, so "good taste" (as we say) is mortified taste, that is, "taste in which the stupid, the sentimental, the irrelevant is *killed*."

This is not the beauty, this is not the culture, talked about in the "art world" and the welfare departments of philanthropic industrialists and the caverns of the B.B.C. Human culture is the product of necessary work, not of formal education or the activities of leisure hours ("hobbies"): it cannot be plastered on to mankind like an "ornament" glued on to a Woolworth mirror. "To hell with culture, culture as a thing added like a sauce to otherwise unpalatable stale fish! The only culture worth having is that which is the natural and inevitable product of an honourable life of honourable work" (*S. & S.*, p. 173). The divorce of beauty from usefulness and work from culture is an achievement of the bourgeois mind "and there will never be an end of the bourgeois until we have abolished Art," the art of the "art world."

It has been said (*Blackfriars*, February 1941, p. 26) that "one of the difficulties of Eric Gill's position (it was also his strength) was that in his social writings, and increasingly in the later works, his preoccupation was moral, and, if we understand his metaphysics rightly, exclusively moral." That is perfectly true; and yet Gill was emphatically not a moralist in the vulgar sense. He did not go around telling people what they should or should not do, deciding what was right or wrong, sinful or good; he did not identify religion with personal rectitude alone. He knew perfectly well that they cannot be separated, that his own teaching on this, that and the other had immediate and far-reaching implications for personal morality; but his shyness, his humility and his fear lest he trespass on another man's job made him time and again repudiate any intention of talking about morals: his appeal was to good sense rather than to good will, and it was not till comparatively late that he found himself unable to keep silent when silliness, culpable ignorance, falsity or unlovingness had to be identified with sin and that he would refer boldly to the pertinent words of St James or St Paul of our Lord himself.

" 'Patriotism is not enough'—morality is not enough. Man is not merely a moral being. He is not merely moral or immoral. He does not merely will good or evil. He also knows true or false: at least he is capable of doing so. And not only does man know and will, he also loves" (*W. & L.*, p. 115). That was a common approach. In one of his attacks on the idea of the "leisure state" he declared: "It is not a moral problem. Leisure is not a problem because people are not good enough to use it properly"; it is an intellectual problem, of what to do that is worth doing. He deprecated the moral fervour that was mixed up with the arts-and-crafts and land movements: morally the handicraftsman or farm-labourer is in precisely the same position as any responsible chemist or engineer. When he deplored the deceits and shams of gothic-revival architecture he was accusing nobody of sin; his appeal was to reason—such things are foolish: "My indignation is not so much a product of moral rectitude as of intellectual exasperation." Nor did he fail to note the weak ineffectiveness of religiose moralism: "Instead of doing anything about economics the moralists fulminate against the murder of unborn children and the selfishness of modern young people [in the practice of birth-prevention]. As somebody said: 'The drains are smelling—let's have a day of intercession.' And as another said: 'The economic depression is a good thing—it is sent to try us' " (*M. & M.*, p. 28). No wonder Pope Pius XI had to mourn that the people at large are estranged from the Church. It is not by moralism or formalist dogmatism, any more than by socialism or the "first-aid" of humanitarianism, that a sick world can be brought to health: "No 'welfare-work' in East London slums will supply religion with a reason of being otherwise lacking. No distribution of property or nationalization of the means of production, distribution and exchange will produce Jerusalem in England's green and pleasant land if the earthly paradise have no City of God for its model. No truth, no good, no beauty will shine out of human handiwork unless the truth that 'whosoever will lose his life shall save it' be known, willed and loved" (*Belief*, p. 304).

Repeatedly from 1936 onwards Eric Gill spoke and wrote against war, on the platforms and in the publications of the Peace Pledge Union, of Pax and of other associations of war-resisters—yet, though he freely used the term of himself for convenience, he was no pacifist as the word is currently understood. He held that taking part in warfare is not of itself and essentially at variance with a profession of Christianity, that the concept of the possible just war is a valid one, in the conditions commonly received (and usually very imperfectly examined) by Roman Catholics and others: this position Gill held *ex animo,* it appealed to him as traditional, authoritative, reasonable and true. But the more he saw of the contemporary world, the more he learned about political and economic forces, the more that "scientific" means of warfare developed, so much the more he became disturbed in mind. Gradually he began to realize that, as Lord Grey had said, "War is the same word as it was a century ago, but it is no longer the same thing"; the spiritual insight and logic of the medieval and seventeenth-century theologians had been applied to a quite different thing: is it possible to fulfil their conditions for a justifiable war in the new conditions? Gill decided that it is not (and here he parted company from the great majority among those of his co-religionists who have given the matter a moment's thought). He still did not say that no war has ever been justified, that the use of military force is always wrong: he said that war as we know it to-day is such that no human being, much less a Christian, should take part in it; it has become bestial, inhuman, and to talk of patriotism and the defence of civilization by such means is irrelevant. "Modern war is a remedy worse than any conceivable disease"; it is no remedy at all for the congeries of diseases which at present afflict the world: it is an extension and amplification of them. Whatever high-minded, great-souled, public-spirited combatants may intend or do, war is supremely harmful to man's love of God and his fellows, to the spirit of truth and righteousness and justice, to human responsibility and to creative work: depersonalization is at its height and at no other time are men so stirred to undiscriminating hate and abandoned to irrational processes.

"What is the alternative of which we are so afraid? . . . Are we afraid of national humiliation, are we afraid to be humbled? But it is written 'Blessed are the meek, for they shall inherit the earth.' Are we afraid of poverty? But it is precisely poverty which as Christians we should welcome. There will be no peace, there can be no peace, while wealth, comfort, riches are the ideal we set before ourselves" (*Peace*, p. 11). This had been a foremost idea in his mind when he came back from Palestine: "It became clear that it is no use renouncing war unless we first of all renounce riches. That is the awful job before us. . . . A whole world doomed to perpetual fighting—and no remedy but to persuade it to renounce riches. What a forlorn hope!" (*Auto.*, p. 256). Indeed, Gill was more interested in the causes of war than in the strictly moral problem of war itself: all over his later writings are scattered references showing the inevitability of the sort of wars we have in the sort of world we live in— and we all help to make that world.

"Let peacemakers remember above all that it is no manner of good preaching peace unless we preach the things that make for peace—that even the love of our fellow men is no good unless it means giving rather than taking, yielding rather than holding, sharing rather than exclusive possession, confederation rather than sovereignty, use rather than profit. And it means the subordination of the man of business and the dealer and moneylender, both in the world and even more in our own hearts" (in *The Christian Pacifist*, January 1940).

Gill's thought on war, coming later in life, is set out with less system and detail than his other dominant ideas. His insistence on the foulness and shameful vulgarity in all departments of war as waged to-day laid him open to the charge that he was letting his feelings of disgust run away with him, and he was sometimes misunderstood in this way: it is therefore necessary to emphasize that he did not condemn modern war simply because it is horrible. It is a question of means: he denied that spiritual goods can be obtained by killing and hate and destruction, and he vindicated the right of any man to refuse to take part in such an undertaking. "Could not Christ have called on twelve legions of angels to fight for him? And he did not. And shall we think to make a Christian triumph by calling up twelve armies equipped with all the products of our commercialism?—guns, bombs, poisons! (We can only obtain such things by calling in the financiers and borrowing their money.) Shall we thus 'make the world safe for Christianity'?" (*Stations*, p. 5.)

In this context, of the horrors of war, it may be noted in passing that Gill's treatment of the problem of evil is far from satisfactory. He devotes a special chapter to it in *The Necessity of Belief*, and it contains some most valuable analysis and observations, especially the emphasis on the necessity of the distinction between moral and physical evil. There is also a third kind, which may be called spiritual evil, but to treat them, as he seems to do, as being in watertight compartments is bad psychology (and incidentally weakens his own arguments against modern war). The whole thing is badly oversimplified. "There is no problem of evil," he concludes, "There is only the intellectual difficulty of understanding the physical universe and the moral difficulty of withstanding our own appetites and lusts." But surely that precisely is the problem of evil.

❧

Having, I hope, cleared up a few possible misunderstandings by this brief reference to some negatives, I turn to a single, and more persuasive and significant, positive: Eric Gill was an "ordinary man," a man-in-the-street, both in his estimate of himself and in fact. "I am," he said, "an ordinary person who refuses to be bamboozled. . . . What concerns me first of all is what man, the common man, the man in the street, the man in the workshop, the man on the farm, claims for himself. After all, I believe it is true to say that the philosopher and the prophet do not claim for man what he does not claim for himself" (*Belief*, p. 227). He assumed no authority to teach: "The most I claim is to speak as one of the people, and as one for whom *vox populi* is *vox Dei*.

It is not my voice, it is the people's voice. I claim that what
I say is what mankind says. It is no little flock that proclaims
man's free will. It is no minority of peculiar persons that
asserts man's being" (*Belief*, p. 331). Worms are apt to get
the best view of the roots of things, and the important criticism of things as they are to-day comes not from princes and
bishops, poets and politicians, but from "man the worm,
man the proletarian, man the delectable whore." Early in
1939 the Royal Institution of Great Britain invited four
well-known people, of whom Gill was one, to address its
members on the relations of art and industry; and he told
the assembly that it was a pity that a labourer from a factory
had not been asked to speak as well (the address is reprinted
in *Sacred and Secular*). On all sides we see men in revolt,
and the principal instigators of rebellion in our time have
been, not the professed revolutionaries, however important,
but those "little men" who "wrote, in cheap books and parish
magazines, or preached, in nonconformist chapels, country
churches or inconspicuous papist pulpits, the humane doctrine of responsibility for sin and the dual but individual
nature of man."

> They were not conscious agitators, "but they did in fact
> prevent the entire submergence of the proletariat in the non-
> human system of industrialism. They did preserve as matters
> of common knowledge and common belief the common man's
> idea of himself: that he is a unique individual and uniquely
> valuable. If this idea persists as a commonplace of Christian
> doctrine, if Christianity persists as a commonplace profession,
> it is not due to the splendid writings, great speeches or heroic
> behaviour of one or more magnificent Christians—though
> such there were and such played their part—but to the wide-
> spread unheroic efforts of little men, little pastors, little sheep.
> There can be no rebellion without grounds of rebellion. It
> is the grounds of rebellion of which the little men have pre-
> served the knowledge. There can be no rebellion except
> against wrong. It is the idea of right and wrong which the
> little ministers have kept alive" (*Belief*, p. 267).

All this did not arise from any doctrinaire democracy, any
sentimental regard for "the masses," any invertedly snobbish
contempt for learning and experience; the human perfecti-

bility of man was a heresy that had no attraction for Gill, and his comments on "the suburbs" were exceeded in pungency only by his comments on workers' ambitions to emulate the suburbs. No. Just as man's chief means to culture, worship and the contemplation of being have from the beginning been the necessity of providing himself with food, clothing and shelter—ordinary things—so wisdom, knowledge and understanding derive and ramify from fundamental truths discernable, whether through reason or revelation, by the ordinary man, man the tool-using animal, such a man as Eric Gill. In England at the end of the nineteenth-century there were thousands of obscure families like the Brighton Gills; Eric's schooling was rather below the average in such families; he had no advantage of upbringing and the rest that he did not share with thousands of other young men; he was for years no more than a letter-cutter and stone-mason, living as such; when he found himself in a so-called superior environment for example, among artists and literary people, he did not like it and cleared out; he had no high and overmastering ambition; he was not endowed by nature with any abnormal intellectual ability, he read widely, but enthusiastically or critically rather than studiously: in a word, he was quite an ordinary man—but one who used to the utmost his mind, his will and his heart.

This is one of the reasons why Gill's criticism is so important. He was not like so many philosophers who argue from the abstract to the concrete without any practical experience of the concrete. In the order of time, Gill started with the concrete; like the carpenter in Miss Sackville-West's poem (I quote from memory and perhaps inaccurately), he knew what it was to "hold down Reality, struggling, to a bench": when he expounded a philosophy of work and art, it was, for once, a working artist speaking. He slowly worked from the concrete back to the abstract and, used to dealing with real things, he found that abstractions too are realities (in the measure of their truth)—and he handled them accordingly. It is sometimes necessary to screw a piece of wood tightly in a vice to keep it still: Gill found it is sometimes necessary metaphorically to screw an idea in a vice, for a similar reason and however impatient it may be of the treatment.

Eric lived for, worked for and spoke for and to his own kind. I have heard it said that, if he begins at the beginning, reads with attention and does not skip, any person of ordinary intelligence can understand the dozen volumes of St. Thomas Aquinas's monumental *Summa*, but that no one without special training and knowledge can understand the works of Descartes and Comte, Kant and Berkeley. I have not attempted either exercise, so I do not know if this be true. But I do know that any simple fellow can read the writings of Eric Gill and find intelligible and convincing exposition of such daily and practical problems as God and man, matter and spirit, belief and science, personality, free will and responsibility, art, work and industry—all those things that are, whether we know it or not, of the first importance to every man jack of us. Gill wrote and spoke deliberately "on the level of ordinary human speech and thought," and so for the man Jack and the woman Jill, with no long words or technical jargon, no vague uplift or recondite notions, no metaphysical flights beyond the range of the kitchen and the bar (if only the kitchen and the bar would turn off the radio and pay attention thoughtfully for a bit): not these, but a straightforward examination of what are really everyman's problems, in language that everyman can understand, usually with illustrations that are at once familiar to him. And not only did Gill write what the ordinary person can read: he wrote what the ordinary person knows—but does not always know that he knows.

3

NICHOLAS BERDYAEV has said somewhere that Christian theology needs to be complemented by a Christian anthropology. He does not, I suppose, imply that there is no such thing, but that it needs to be studied more deeply and intensively and (especially in view of current theories and practice) brought before the people at large, non-Christian as well as Christian, with the earnestness and perseverance that has hitherto been reserved for theology. Eric Gill was in explicit agreement. His own most outstanding characteristic was integrality and completeness: he was a whole man, and every aspect of himself, his work and his beliefs, was integrated and interdependent, fused into one shining personality. He was a living and amazingly successful example of what he was always trying to do, what he called "my difficulty and my enthusiasm"—"to discover how things are related and to discover a right relation where a wrong one exists." It appeared to him that lack of integralness is *the* disease, the master disease, from which civilized mankind is suffering: we are not simply uprooted, we are torn to pieces.

The God of Christianity is the source of all being, Being itself, He Who Is, the God of Abraham, Isaac and Jacob. But this conception has been weakened and watered down till he is thought of merely as the Author of Nature or the Supreme Lawgiver or even—Heaven help us!—the Great Artificer who "made my mate": that is, if he is not simply the Unknown God. Just so with the Christian concept of man. He has been almost lost in a Heraclitan flux, become a creature who does, acts, becomes: "the doing is all." The concept of being has to be recovered also in relation to man. To-day it is no longer the personality of God alone that has to be upheld, but the personality of man as well. Each and every man and woman is an individual person to start with, who takes on communal functions; he is not a "functional unit which may or may not end up by developing individual idiosyncrasies." As an object of God's love his value is, as we say, absolute: he is an end, not a means. The state is a means to an end—man's good life and convenience: the Bible is a means, to the end that man may know and live the truth; Christ's resurrection was a means, to "our rebirth into the living hope." But man is, like the daisy in its eternal quality, or Dame Julian's nut, "a thing, a being in itself. It is not a means to an end. 'It lasteth and for ever shall, for

God loveth it.' " And it is not only in the face of such philosophies as fascism, nazism and communism that these
things have to be maintained, that we have to uphold that
man is "a creature who knows and wills and loves: a rational being, responsible for his acts and the intended consequences of his acts . . . made in the image of God (child of
God and, if he will, heir also), a creature who loves" (*Machine Age,* p. 26).

Eric Gill based himself ultimately on man's consciousness;
that consciousness testifies to his personality, and divine
revelation enlarges and infinitely enriches that truth. And
fundamental to the Christian idea of man is the further truth
that he is made up of matter and spirit, both real and both
good, manifestations of the same one reality, a figure of
our theandric life with all its glories and trials that Eric
constantly returned to. And in his thirst for right relations he
never allows us to forget that "though there is a distinction
of category between matter and mind, and though the mind
is the ruling partner, the body and mind do not act sep-
arately. . . . And so in man's history it is not possible to
think that this or that was simply the product of environment, economic circumstance or material force, nor is it
possible to think that such and such was simply the product
of his spirit. The two parts or principles of man's being are
inextricably intertwined and death for man is precisely the
disintegration of matter and spirit" (*Belief,* p. 273).

Throughout Christian history there has been a tendency
to belittle, or worse, the material side of human life, a tendency varying in strength from the formal heresies of encratic
gnostics and manicheans, catharists and puritans, to the sometimes hardly less mischievous exaggerations of those orthodox
people, of all denominations, who seek to keep themselves or
others from sin, or to answer the question of evil, or to ensure a godly detachment from this world, by an attitude that
seems to imply the essential evil of created matter, especially
of the human body: so widespread and continuing is this
manichean dualism (by no means confined to Christians)
with its corollary of seeing asceticism as an end and not
simply a means, that it looks as if it is a specific result of

that spoiling of human nature that Christians call The Fall. Against it Gill struck hard and often, directly or indirectly, sometimes so regardlessly of contemporary convention that some were shocked to silence and others provoked to calling him names, from "pelagian" and "antinomian" to less "polite" expressions. But he went deeper than his critics, he saw the ultimate term of the false mysticism that would have us behave as pure spirits while yet inhabiting bodies: "The 'degradation' of making anything useful—the 'sordidness' of child-bearing—the 'mere animality' of digestion: such are the phrases of Sodom and Gomorrah. Such are the phrases of aesthetes, and they disclose the root ideas of puritanism. Matter is not good enough for man" (*Beauty,* p. 107). He was far from oblivious of the disorders that so properly alarm the moralist, but he did not trust for their remedy, humanly speaking, in mere negation, "Thou shalt not." God is the source of all enjoyment, and when we enjoy his creation in the way he intended we share his enjoyment.

"Adam could not see the Wood for the Tree. Adam sinned when he fell from contemplation (as the theologian says): that is to say when he saw himself as self-satisfactory, when, like Herod, 'he gave not God the honour.' There is indeed this danger. It is of course, and obviously, man's besetting sin. It is pride, the root of all sin. But the remedy is not the denial of enjoyment but the giving of thanks. The remedy is not the denial of material goods, but the recognition of material goods as gifts, and not only as gifts, but as gifts which signify the Giver" (*W. & L.,* p. 112).

And many of Gill's critics on this head failed to notice that, if he emphasized the goodness of material things strongly and often, he emphasized the primacy of spirit more strongly and more often. Sensual pleasures are called enthralling because they can make slaves of men, "and the worse slavery is the subjection of mind to matter, of the spiritual to the material, of the immeasurable to the measurable, of the infinite to the finite . . . Materialism spells slavery. Freedom, they say with one voice (Italian, German or Russian) 'freedom is a concession of the state.' " Other tongues besides Italian, German and Russian go to make up that ghastly voice. Man is enslaved thus to-day to a terrifying degree, and this success of the materialist philosophers and propagandists has depended upon a monstrous suppression of truth, the truth about man's real nature and significance among created things.

> "No religion has ever been such a 'dope.' Priests have endeavoured to make men think themselves worms before God. They have exploited men's sense of responsibility and their consequent sense of sin. But those who in their enthusiasm oppose religion have gone further still. Men are no longer worms before God. There is no God who could desire the death of a sinner. Man is of no importance to God, because he is of no importance at all. Man's appetite for abasement cannot be further exploited. However much Christian men have been taught to grovel before their Creator, they were at least taught as a dogma that God died for their redemption —they had that much intrinsic importance. The materialist does not grovel before his Creator; he just simply grovels, because grovelling is all he can do. He is a worm and no man. . . . We crawl on the face of the earth because our presence here has no other significance" (*Belief,* p. 150).

Nevertheless, materialism too is a philosophy—without a metaphysic, and a religion—without the infinite. The fact that more attention is paid in England to-day to banks and insurance-offices than to churches shows, not a loss, but a change of religion—ultimate reality is sought in material things rather than in things of the spirit; the productions of modern Europe are as much an index to dominant religious ideas as are those of the middle ages or of India; an aeroplane is no less the work and expresses the genius of a whole people than the cathedral at Chartres. And a decisive factor in riveting Gill's attention on Christianity in general and the Roman Catholic Church in particular was her age-long struggle against these two excesses, belief that the material life is all and belief that it is nothing; whatever the aberrations of some of her members and of unorthodox sects, she has been unwavering in her affirmation that matter and spirit are both real and both good, and that spirit has the primacy. Thus the Church rejects both Western materialism and Eastern idealism, and emerges as "the arbiter of East and West because she refuses the denials of either."

The principal connotation of the word "revolution" to-day
is a drastic change in socio-economic organization and conditions; and Eric Gill's social principles can be summed up
in these words: responsibility, poverty, love of God. On the
last I need not dwell: if what I have already said does not
persuade the reader that to Gill the one thing necessary is
love of God and his Christ and a humble listening to the
promptings of the Holy Spirit, then that reader must turn to
Gill's own writings (as I hope he will in any case). Let him
read the essay on art and holiness in *Work and Leisure:* I
quote at random, from page 121: "Man is a creature who
loves. Ultimately he can only love the holy. . . . Is the word
'holy' a stumbling-block (to the Jews a stumbling-block, to
the Gentiles foolishness)? Why be afraid or shy of the word?
Primarily it means hale and hearty, whole, unsullied, perfect
and therefore of God—godly, sanctified, sacred; and therefore gay and light and sweet and cheerful and gracious. 'Oh
taste and see how *gracious* the Lord is.' But gay—above all
things gay. . . ."
Man has free will. "The freedom of the will, whether
proved by argument or not, is a fact of human experience,
and to be accepted as such. . . . Pathological states of mind
apart—and let the psychologists enlarge the sphere of pathol-
ogy as much as they can—the free will remains and man is
master, captain of his soul." To have free will involves having responsibility, being responsible for what one chooses
to do: "We know, we affirm, I know and I affirm that at the
very core of our being, of my being, there is the fact of
responsibility." Gill did not say much about freedom or
liberty but was constantly referring to responsibility, and the
one involves the other: responsibility cannot be used unless
there be freedom. He quotes Aquinas: "The free man is
responsible for himself, but for the slave another is responsible. . . . The highest manifestation of life consists in this:
that a being governs its own actions. A thing which is always
subject to the direction of another is somewhat of a dead
thing. . . . Hence a man in so far as he is a slave is a verit-
able image of death." Christianity imperatively demands
responsibility: profession of it must be freely chosen by a

free act, it must be lived equally freely. The Church and slavery could not permanently co-exist, and this was a major factor in eventually bringing formal slavery to an end; where there is a diminished responsibility there Christianity cannot be fully developed or fully effective.

Gill was sometimes criticized for apparently making too sweeping generalizations about "the rich." The same objection can be (and has been) raised against many good Christians, such as St. Basil and St. John Chrysostom, and for that matter against the gospels themselves. In speaking of the hidden power of liturgical Latin, Gill says he does not believe that the words *Divites dimisit inanes* can in their English form, "The rich he hath sent empty away," convey "such a stupendously revolutionary threat as that which they do in fact convey." Obviously he did not take upon himself to make moral judgements on rich people, whether individually or collectively; he was concerned with what St. Paul was concerned with, that revolutionary threat and the truth which lies behind it, which Gill stated in as forcible a half-dozen lines as he ever wrote: "There is no idolatry so destructive of charity, so desolating, there is nothing which so certainly obscures the face of God, as the desire of money—the root of all evil. 'The root of all evil!' Did I make up that phrase? No; it is the word of God to man. The root of all evil, the *root*. The root of all *evil*" (*Auto.*, p. 194).

"The principle of poverty," he declared, "is the only one consonant with the nature and destiny of man and his material environment and condition." What is meant by this poverty? Not, of course, indigence, destitution, evil poverty; but good poverty, that spiritual thing, explicit in Christian teaching, which bears fruit in human life and works. "To go without, to give up, to lose rather than gain, to have little rather than much—that is its positive teaching. Blessed are the poor in spirit; the humble, the common man, the common woman, simple women, mothers of children—'How hard is it for a rich man to enter Heaven'. . . . But it is only in love that this poverty can be embraced" (*S. & S.*, p. 56). "Is it not clear, beyond any possibility of doubt, that what-

ever other things may or must be said of the teaching of
Christ and of the witness of his saints, it is the blessing of
poverty which is the central fact of Christian sociology?"
(*Machine Age*, p. 13). And our present organization, while
it keeps many in dire want, insufficiency or grinding insecurity, holds up for our admiration and effort the pursuit
of wealth and luxury; while many are ill-clad and ill-fed and
ill-housed, many (and not only, or even principally, "the
rich") have a standard of living that is absurdly high. It
was this, the standard of living which the middle class and
the emulators of the middle class consider their due, that
specially outraged Eric's doctrine of poverty: when a trade-
union might be expected to be discussing work it is found
trying to shove or bolster up the standard of living, however
much too high it may be already (see *Belief*, p. 61 *et seq.*).

If "money" is the ruling influence in the state, if production for profit rather than for use rules in industry, the fault
is ultimately ours, because "money" is the ruling power in
our hearts.

❧

Responsibility is of two kinds. There is moral responsibility for what we do and intend or refrain from doing, and
there is intellectual responsibility for the kind and quality
of what we make, "make" being understood in no narrow
sense. Gill constantly returned to the theme of how deeply
the idea of "making" enters properly into man's life and in-
forms his work (*cf.,* the popular "What has he *made* of his
life?"). "Deeds done, when viewed in themselves and not
simply as means to ends, are also to be regarded as things
made."

Work, says the dictionary, is "the exertion of energy,
physical and mental" otherwise than for purposes of recrea-
tion. God has made the world and man such that work is
necessary for life and, since nothing that truly subserves our
life can be bad, there can be no form of necessary work
which is in itself degrading. Nevertheless, an idea is now
very prevalent that physical labour is bad, a thing to be
avoided so far as possible, though even in the most mechan-

ized conditions there must be a basic element of such labour. In a Christian society there should be no kind whatever of physical work which is either derogatory to human beings or incapable of being ennobled and hallowed; therefore, said Gill, "at every turn our object must be to sanctify rather than to exclude physical labour, to honour it rather than to degrade it, to discover how to make it pleasant rather than onerous, a source of pride rather than of shame. . . . There is no kind of physical labour which is at one and the same time truly necessary to human life and necessarily either unduly onerous or unpleasant."

Our industrial civilization fosters and encourages the notion that much manual work is, of itself, sub-human drudgery; when the working life of thousands of factory "hands," shop-assistants, clerks, domestics, navvies and transport workers and labourers on our pitiful farms is considered, this seems to be true; and it appears obviously a good thing that, by the use of more machinery, more of this drudgery should be got rid of. Thus it has come about that people have come to believe that all physical labour is in itself bad. We seek to reduce it to a minimum and we look to our leisure time for all enjoyable exercise of our bodies. (The contradiction has been overlooked that if physical exercise be bad in work, then it is bad in play also.)

"It should be obvious that it is not the physical labour which is bad but the proletarianism by which men and women have become simply 'hands,' simple instruments for the making of money by those who own the means of production, distribution and exchange. And those who argue in favour of the still further elimination of physical labour on the ground that much manual labour is, of itself, sub-human drudgery are playing into the hands either of those for whose profit the mechanical organization of industry has been developed or of the communists and others who look to the 'leisure state' as the *summum bonum*. We must return again and again to the simple doctrine: physical work, manual labour, is *not* in itself bad. It is the necessary basis of all human production and, in the most strict sense of the words, physical labour directed to the production of things needed for human life is both honourable and holy."

Having through our cupidity and indolence degraded most forms of work, domestic and other, so that they are no longer to be viewed as pleasant, still less as sacred, having made men and women into "hands" and profit-making instruments, herded together in monstrous cities, "we turn round and curse the very idea of labour. To use the body, our arms and legs and backs, is now held to be derogatory to our human dignity. . . . It is at the very base of the Christian reform for which we stand that we return to the honouring of bodily work."

The contempt shown for manual work has not been extended to those activities which in modern times are distinguished as the "fine arts"; on the contrary, their practitioners are excessively honoured, and a kind of mythology or mystagogy has grown up which Eric Gill castigated under the name of "art nonsense": he devoted a whole book, *Art and a Changing Civilization,* to what he called "the debunking of art." The isolation of something called Art (with a big A), especially pictorial art and the aesthetic chatter that goes therewith, the putting of the artist on a pedestal as someone apart from and above other men, the cultivation of an absurd artificiality called the "artistic temperament," such things, he said, imply "a bourgeois frame of mind, and are a notable product of a bourgeois society."

All the arts, whether "useful" or "fine," have their origin in man's fundamental needs, to supply himself with food, clothing and shelter, to pray to and praise God, to recreate himself; and accordingly Eric, putting aside all irrelevancies about emotion, self-expression, and the like, defined art simply by its earlier meaning, as "the well-making of what needs making," thus vastly extending its scope as commonly understood to-day. Time and again he quoted the words of Ananda Coomaraswamy: "An artist is not a special kind of man, but every man is a special kind of artist"; it was on the artist as workman, as a "collaborator with God in creating," that his thought on this matter was centred, the objective approach to work that was destroyed in so many arts by the Renaissance. "I would rather have brick-laying and turnip-hoeing done well and properly and high art go to the devil (if it must), than have high art flourishing and brick-laying and turnip-hoeing be the work of slaves" (*Auto.*, p. 177). It was again to the common man that he looked; his revolution was again away from the specialist, the expert, professionalism, towards the ordinary person and his needs.

"I have no use at all for 'Art' as commonly understood to-day. . . . I would abolish the fine arts altogether. Music—let us sing in church and at work and at harvest-festivals and wedding parties and all such times and places. But let us abolish the concert-hall. Painting and sculpture—let us paint and carve our houses and churches and town-halls and places of business. But let us abolish art-galleries and royal academies and picture-dealers. Architecture—let us employ builders and engineers, and let them be imbued with human enthusiasms and not be moved merely by the desire for money or by merely utilitarian standards. Poetry—let those who can, write our hymns and songs and prayers. Let them write dirges for funerals and songs for weddings, and let them go about and sing to us or read to us in our houses. But let us abolish all this high nonsense about poets who are 'not as other men.' And let us abolish all the art-schools and museums and picture-galleries" (*W. & P.*, p. 87).

Fountain-pens, motor-cars and the like are as much works of art as pictures and carvings, the bridge across the Saint Lawrence river at Quebec would stand comparison with any medieval cathedral or castle; the difference between them is that the pictures and castles are the work of an individual artist—responsible workman—or a number of them working together, whereas the only artist concerned with the production of the motor-car or the bridge is the *designer*, architect, thereof, the others concerned being mostly willing or unwilling proletarian "hands." And each method faithfully reflects the philosophy and religion and life of a society: Chartres cathedral, simply as a building, could arise from none other than an ultimately spiritual background, the Canadian bridge is as clearly a product of the materialistic enthusiasms of the times in which we live.[1]

[1] It may be noted in passing that Gill did not entertain the delusion that the culture of the past was Christian in the sense that it was in any way a direct product of the Church or of ecclesiastics. Medieval bishops, priests and monks were clergy and customers, not workmen and producers (with individual exceptions, of course). "In fact, the civilizing power of man is a lay

"Work itself becomes a game, and the curse of Adam—
'in the sweat of thy brow thou shalt eat bread'—is turned to
blessing, for man has found joy in his labour and that that
is his portion. Thus, while the necessity remains and use is
neither denied nor condemned, all things made become works
of love, all .deeds become things in themselves, all means
become ends. This is the basis, the concreted and untrembling
foundation of human art. This is man's response to his responsibility—that he freely wills what is necessary, he makes
what must be into a thing he has chosen.

"These are the things which the materialism of our time
denies and derides. By its separation of work from pleasure,
its divorce of use from beauty and of beauty from meaning,
it has produced a real disintegration of humanity, and on the
basis of its materialism there is no remedy for its sufferings
but a more efficient organization of material. Let there be
plenty for all and no parasites. Let all the milk be sterilized.
They say: Let thought be free and let all work be commanded.
We say: There is no such thing as free thought and let all
works be free offerings. Materialism spells slavery. . . . 'Freedom is a concession of the state' " (*Belief*, pp. 330-1).

And the ultimate slavery and degradation of the artist is to
be "freed from the necessity of making anything useful."

4

SOME Christians made it a matter
of reproach against Gill that *apparently* he did not pay
enough attention to the cruelties and injustices of communists and their implacable persecution of all religion or to
the cruelties and injustices of fascists and nazis and their
subtle efforts to nullify the Church's influence.[1] They over-

power—fostered, encouraged, nursed, petted by the Church but, in its own
sphere, independent. . . . [The Church] takes what she is given" (*Beauty*, p.
32). Strictly speaking, there is no such thing as a Christian or Catholic or
Protestant culture: there are the various cultures which grow up in societies
of people who are Catholics or Protestants or what not, which reflect the
corresponding ideas more or less faithfully.

[1] It is true that for a long time he held the view that militant godlessness
is only an accident of marx-leninist communism, provoked by the insufficiency

looked that in his writing and public speaking he was concerned more with diseases than with symptoms; and they
were incredulous when assured that he did not believe that
fundamentally and potentially the societies of Great Britain
and the United States and France were much better than
those of Russia and Italy and Germany; that, in effect, respectable "democratic" capitalist-industrialism is as atheistic, as destructive of responsibility and liberty, of holy poverty and the human person, of hope and love, as is communism itself; that its practical materialism has precisely the
same effects as the dialectical materialism with which marxists oppose metaphysical and spiritual truth; that, in fact,
totalitarian stateism, particularly in its communist form, is a
logical development of the civilization of "the democra-
cies." [2] No wonder communism seems the only just politics
for the "beehive state" that most people seem to want and
few try to prevent, for if all things are to be made by machines within a "rationalized" system there must naturally
be more and more standardization.[3]

Fascism and socialism and marxism do not offer holiness:
they offer more physical convenience and psychological satisfaction (by flattering human sensibility) in return for the
obedience of their citizenry. They tell us they are going to
cure a disease—by aggravating it. "Had it not been for the
spur which trade-unionism gave to human inventiveness
and the consequent development of machinery it would very
certainly have been necessary either to repeal the Factory
Acts, and all acts designed to protect the animal classes, or
else to abandon the ambition of being a first-class multiple-
store and shop-keeping nation." The socialist movement "of-

of and support of bourgeois exploitation by so many Christians. Later, I
think, he came to realize that the destruction of spiritual religion is essential
to marxist theory. In any case, it may be questioned whether stoning the
prophets is worse than ignoring them altogether.

[2] He did not of course, as some fanatics do, claim that in the present war
there is nothing to choose between the combatants. He saw many reasons why
a victory for Great Britain and the United States and the defeat of the Axis
powers offers hope for a desperate world, whereas the reverse would increase
the desperation of our state. But that is little enough without a real "revolution."

[3] But, like so large a number of people of very different views, Gill tended,
I think, to exaggerate the popularity of communist views (even as vague
aspirations) in England.

fered nothing in the way of divine inspiration, nothing beyond the ideal of a world in which all should be hygienically
and warmly clad—with a sort of B.B.C. 'culture park' loom-
ing in the background; as though to say: When we've properly got going with the love of our fellow men, then we'll see
what we can do about culture and, well, you know, religion
and art and stuff" (*Auto.*, pp. 141, 163). The marxists go one
worse. "They have thrown away the God whom the capitalists profess to worship and do not, and have accepted the
servitude which capitalism has developed and perfected but
whose existence the capitalists deny. Thus they have not emptied out the baby with the bath water. They have retained
the bath water while emptying out the baby. They have
emptied out the Baby of Bethlehem only to swallow the foul
and befouling bath water of London and Manchester" (*Belief*, p. 271). And not simply the slums and misery of those
cities, which are accidental to our materialism (Are we not
getting rid of them?), but its substance—its philosophy, its
reversal of human and spiritual values. If capitalism is as
irreligious as socialism, socialism is as inhuman and enslav-
ing as capitalism. For all its lip-service to the spirit, its church
on Sundays, and museums and art-galleries and "Shakespeare
for the workers," "business" is materialist. "For all their real
devotion to pure art, pure science, or pure what-not, the reformers are as much materialists as the men of business. The
communists among them are clearheaded enough to recognize this; they are honest enough to proclaim it and glory
in it."

"Workers, throw off your chains!"—and then put them on
again. No revolution that accepts materialism and its modern social incarnation, industrialism, can really be a revolution.

It was, then, central to the social-revolutionary aspect of
Eric Gill's teaching that industrial capitalism implies a way
of life and work that is inconsistent with man's nature and
with the Christian religion. Capitalism is a social theory
based on the profit-motive, and its essence and object is production for profit; both "labour" and "products" must be
looked at primarily from the point of view of saleability, and

not from that of their intrinsic quality and man's real needs.
Its method is that of industrialism, which had three main
processes, viz., the proletarianization of the craftsman, of the
agricultural worker, and of the "small man" generally, the
concentration of production in factories, and the use of
machines, leading to mass-production by the division and
sub-division of labour.

"Eric Gill," wrote Father Kenelm Foster, O.P., "holds
things together. He is our great *pontifex*, bridge-builder.
Spirit and matter, body and mind, knowing and loving: he
distinguished them with exquisite clarity, and then held them
together. He did it *in practice;* wherever he went he made
matter alive with rational beauty. Why did he loathe industrialism?—fundamentally because he thought that *in practice*
it separates what God has joined together, the body and the
mind." That was indeed the main point among his many
serious charges against industrialism: not its cruelty (for it
is now realized that too obvious unkindness "does not pay"),
but "the change which it has brought about in the nature of
the work to be done and therefore in the minds of the men
who do it"; it produces a world wherein "on the one hand
we have the artist concerned solely to express himself; on
the other is the workman deprived of any self to express."
He did not assert that this was anything new in the world's
history: the attempt to divorce art from work and use from
beauty has been made—and resisted—from the beginning.
But industrialism leads so clearly to the separation of mind
and matter, which spells death to man, that death may be
said to be its very object.

"It is only as persons that we serve one another, and when
personal control is divorced from ownership it is only with
great difficulty that men retain responsibility for the form
and quality of what is done or produced . . . the men have
no responsibility whatever, except a moral responsibility to
obey the terms of their contract, *i.e.*, to do what they are
told. Thus the craftsman is finally degraded—he ceases to be
a person who in any way designs what he makes and makes
what he designs; he is no longer even a hand: he has become
a tool, a sentient part of the machine" (*Machine Age,* pp.

34, 38)—and this without overlooking the real love of machines and the great skill and craftsmanship displayed both
by machine-makers and machine-minders. "Our industrial
system does not enslave the workers in any legal or technical
or political sense. It does not necessarily maltreat their bodies
or coerce their minds. It simply reduces the workman to a
subhuman condition of intellectual irresponsibility.[4] It simply separates, divorces, the material and the spiritual." More
and more workmen are being deprived of intellectual responsibility, becoming automatons in their work, prevented
from being artists.

> "And in their leisure, the time when they are not working
> they must be content to be amused; for industrialism has de-
> prived them of the necessity of making anything useful."
> "The value of the creative faculty derives from the fact that
> that faculty is the primary mark of man. To deprive man of
> its exercise is to reduce him to subhumanity. . . . A man is
> as out of place in a factory as in a lightless dungeon. . . .
> If the populations of our factory-towns were not constantly
> recruited from the country they would wither intellectually as
> certainly as they wither morally and physically" (*W. & P.*, pp.
> 84-85).

Intellectual responsibility the concern of a few, or one; for
the rest, obedience: the idea has become painfully familiar
in other spheres besides industry.

It is more horrible, wrote Gill, that men of business should
rule us through the profit-making system they have perfected,
and impose their foul view on the world, "than it would be
if the whole race of men and women should rot their bodies
with lechery and drunkenness." It produces things which, in
their nature, because of the manner of their production,
are unsuitable for the use of human beings: "We are
making a bee-hive when we should have a house. We are
making an apiary when we should have a motherland." The
thing and its results have been summed up in words that
might have been spoken by Eric Gill but, in fact, came from
Pope Pius XII: "In this age of mechanization the human per-

---

[4] Gill quoted this aphorism so often that he made it his own. It originated,
I believe, with Father Martin d'Arcy, S.J.

son becomes merely a more perfect tool in industrial production and . . . a perfected tool for mechanized warfare."

Eric did not deny the impressiveness of the powers which
industrialism has helped to confer on us, or seek to decry
them. He had no romantic ideas about the "immorality" of
using machinery, nor did he suppose its use was likely to be
noticeably lessened in any foreseeable future. "It is art-non-
sense to say that because the Forth Bridge is made of iron
it is not a work of art. . . . It is no more immoral to make
things by machinery than by hand. It is immoral to make
things badly and pretend that they are good, and no amount
of 'hand' is an excuse for stupidity or inefficiency" (*Art Nonsense*, pp. 313-14). The trouble is that machines are not simply complicated tools designed by workmen to help them in
their work. "They are things designed to enable their owners
to make things in great quantities in order to make great
quantities of money. No definition of machinery and no
description of machine industry can neglect these facts. . . .
The real distinction between tools and machines is discovered in the sphere of control and responsibility. Who is
responsible for the thing made or the deed done?" (*Belief*,
pp. 103, 88).

It was characteristic of his all-roundness and freedom from
"teetotalism" that Gill was interested in machines (*e.g.*, the
internal-combustion engines of the lorries he drove in the
R.A.F.) and appreciative of their beauty—so like the beauty
of bones and crystals and insects' wings; I have seen him
stand entranced before a shop-window full of useful gadgets
and neatly-fitting boxes and files. It was not for nothing that
for ten youthful years he drew nothing but locomotive engines, held by the "character and meaning that were manifest in their shape." Need it be said there is no inconsistency
here? On one occasion, asked by the proud owner of a sham-
gothic residence how he liked the building, Eric replied
that he liked the electrical switchboard in the hall. His ques-
tioner expressed surprise. "Oh, I like anything reasonable,"
explained Eric, to which his host replied, "That's too abstruse for me." When it is added that the owner was a scientist that anecdote becomes even more significant.

Eric Gill's indictment of industrialism has been widely misunderstood, and his sweeping generalizations of its evil effects sometimes gave understandable offence. When he said time and again that it reduces the workers to a subhuman condition of intellectual irresponsibility, the word "intellectual" was not always heard; when he said so often that the industrial population is dehumanized he did not always add that he meant dehumanized as workmen, as makers of things: machine-minding is often very skilful work and many mechanics are highly skilled and responsible workmen, but they are so in relation to the machine and not to the thing which the machine turns out. It would have been well had he more frequently and clearly stated his recognition of "the many men, and women, who in spite of the inhuman nature of their employment, retain the notions which properly belong to private and personal enterprise" (*Machine Age*, p. 35). Even so, from our own personal experience of people, we may think that he exaggerated, and in respect to present actuality perhaps he did: but he was looking also to the future—and he was a far-seeing man.

Again, when in answer to the oft-made objection that "A man can be a good Christian in a factory," he replied, "Yes; and St. Agnes was a good Christian in a brothel—but that was no reason why she should stay there!" it is not surprising that the objector should not be silenced, for the analogy between a factory and a brothel does not go very far. Of course he knew perfectly well, he never forgot, that Christianity can enable us to lead godly, righteous and sober lives amid any conditions: his point was that some conditions are more favourable than others. "A social order cannot in itself force any one to do anything, but it can be such as to place many obstacles in the way" of those who would live in a human and Christian manner: in a score of places (*e.g.*, *Art Nonsense*, p. 132), he sets out briefly, clearly and cogently why the conditions of industrialism are so bad in this respect, and it is only common prudence to remove removable handicaps. His case is most forcibly and brilliantly set out in *Money and Morals*, but its presentation there also showed most manifestly an element of exaggeration. It is gravely false, it is shocking, to say that "It is waste of time teaching Christian morals in the present condition of things," as he himself at once goes on to admit; but his admission is too reserved. It is true that the exercise of heroic virtue can't be counted on—but the grace of God can. He is on surer ground when he declares that "truth and error cannot permanently lie down together and Christian morals cannot *permanently flourish* in the same bed with a life contrary to nature" (*italics mine*).

That just as right thinking precedes right faith, so a certain way of living is the necessary preamble to Christian morals, is quite true if rightly understood; but it can be distorted, and it is easy to overlook that if Eric set that "certain way of living" very high it was because he was also looking at a very high and enlightened and unrestricted standard of life and conduct. And why should he not? Are we not bound to? "Be ye perfect. . . ." Moreover, on the psychological side, there was the factor of reaction. In his dealings with his fellow Christians he was met on all sides by clergy, the shepherds of the flock, who seemed to seek every excuse to avoid finding fault with industrial capitalism: among Catholics, in spite of the outspoken social encyclical-letters of Pope Leo XIII and Pope Pius XI, he did not find "clergy and laity all agog for social or any other reform, and in general the clergy seem to regard it as their job to support a social order which, so far as it is possible, forces us to commit all the sins they denounce" (*Auto.*, p. 214). What seemed to him so unbelievable, shocking and blasphemous was the complacency of apparently the majority of Christians, not only about the purity of their faith and practice, but also about the *kind* of world in which they live and which they have co-operated in making.

In any case, it seemed to Gill, the Christians who ask the question, "Is communism (or capitalism or nazism or whatnot) compatible with Christianity?" are approaching the matter from the wrong end. The proper question is, "Is Christianity compatible with the industrial and authoritarian development of society?" And the answer is certainly, "No"; for at the root of Christianity is the doctrine of individual personal responsibility. "Man is man all the time, and not only in his spare time."

In *The Problem of Pain* C. S. Lewis has given us a timely warning against "making use of the idea of corporate guilt to distract our attention from those humdrum, old-fashioned guilts of our own which have nothing to do with 'the system' and which can be dealt with without waiting for the millennium." In *Christianity and Crisis* Reinhold Niebuhr writes: "We do not find it particularly impressive to celebrate one's sensitive conscience by enlarging upon all the well-known evils of our Western world and equating them with the evils of the totalitarian systems." Substituting "capitalist-industrial" for "totalitarian" in the second quotation, no one who knew him or attentively reads his writings will imagine for a moment that Eric Gill stood in need of such warnings: but they do indicate very real dangers for those of us who share his thought. He was a man of peculiarly well-balanced mind and sensitive conscience, and all those of us who would follow him are not similarly well equipped: it was said by a friend precisely of Gill and a third party that "God sends disciples to geniuses to keep them humble." It is not given to everyone who sees the evils and abuses of industrial capitalism to see them in their setting so clearly or to examine them and their possible remedies with such precision as did Eric Gill; and very few of us are enabled more or less to escape them (though we shall be wise to do so if we get the chance, as St. Benedict escaped from the evils of sixth-century Rome).[5] But we can safely and surely do what Eric writes of so movingly and delicately in quite another context on pages 223-27 of the *Autobiography,* we can take the delights and dangers and evils of the society in which we live and, following the words of that same St. Benedict in the prologue to his *Rule,* "cast them on the rock which is Christ."

In face of industrialism, as of every other similar question, we have to beware of the exaggeration contrary to the exces-

[5] Eric defined the chief aim of his life's work to be "to make a cell of good living in the chaos of our world"; to do something towards "reintegrating bed and board, the small farm and the workshop, the home and the school, the earth and Heaven."

sively moralistic interpretation of Christianity: it must not be obscured that the Christian religion has directly to do with only two problems—sin and virtue. It can be applied to ploughing up pasture or to poetry only through being effectively applied to the problem of sin and virtue in farmers and poets. It can be applied to society only through the individual members of society: the disappearance of industrial capitalism, the establishment of one of these "Christian orders" we hear so much about, could by themselves effect little for the kingdom of God. "The holiness of God is something more and other than moral perfection"—but without moral goodness there can be no holiness at all, no wholeness. Eric Gill tried to live in the light of "Seek first the kingdom of God, and his righteousness" [6] and, as has been said before, he more and more found the way to that kingdom to be through the word of St. James, "pure religion and undefiled is this, to visit the fatherless and widows in their affliction and to keep unspotted from the world."

❧

"No individual Christian in our society is to be condemned except in so far as he approves or promotes the evil thing. And, again, no individual, in relation to our society, is to be praised except in so far as he promotes the Christian revolution (*i.e.*, 'turning round') by which once more a Christian society may be revived" (*W. & P.*, p. 6). In his article in *Blackfriars* already referred to, Bernard Kelly remarks that: "The categories in which Gill lived, worked, and wrote were absolute: religious, moral, metaphysical. They were not the categories of political expediency. Thus he was eminently qualified in the critique of social programmes, Catholic and not, put forward to restore a tolerably Christian social structure, but he was not qualified to judge them precisely as politically feasible." Or, as Eric put it, politics are not my line of business; if he agreed with the Reverend F. H. Drinkwater that "the economic problem fills the whole

[6] In reading Gill it must be borne in mind that the Rheims-Douay version of the Bible translates $\delta\iota\kappa\alpha\iota\sigma\sigma\acute{\nu}\eta$, *iustitia*, not by "righteousness" but "justice." This is rather misleading, since in current use the connotation of the word "justice" is almost entirely rational and juridical.

sky," yet the only socio-economic reform he put forward
(apart from his insistence on production for use and not for
profit, and with one notable exception to be mentioned
later) was the abolition of the middleman and the financier.

Way back as an architect's pupil in London he had realized
that "it was not so much the working *class* that concerned me
as the working man—not so much what he *got* from working
as what he *did* by working," and had got hold of the notion
that "a good life wasn't only a matter of good politics and
good buildings and well-ordered towns and justice in economic relations." Social reform is the business of those who
know the nature and destiny of man, he declared, and "the
trouble with the present age is that it is just the knowledge
of those things which it is most uncertain about, and consequently politics and social guidance are left to a crowd of
amateurs—novelists, multiple-storekeepers, manufacturers of
motor-cars or chemicals—whose profession of disinterestedness is only slightly more credible than that of thieves and
robbers" (*Art Nonsense,* p. 315); and in the first essay of
Work and Property he conveniently summarized some of the
things that these amateurs ought to know.

As for the professional politicians—"Liberals and Conservatives—Labour! All these parties wish to preserve the
status quo. But it is just the *status quo* which is in question."
People of all kinds toy with communism both because it
seems better politics than *that* and because it seems to offer
an approximation to absolutes in a world wherein religion
has grown cold: afraid to face Love, too tired to rebuild his
house, they "fall back on an 'economic interpretation of history,' and are satisfied to live by bread alone." It was in
Palestine that Gill fully realized in all their beastliness the
materialism, exploiting imperialism and mechanized labour
in which England has been a pathfinder and pioneer, and
he came back determined to keep clear of all politics and
politicians.

> "For . . . politics is beyond me. Politics is . . . outside my
> scope, something I can't do. Moreover I do not believe polit-
> ical arrangements and rearrangements are real. It is all a
> confused business of ramps and rackets—pretended quarrels

and dishonest schemings, having no relation to the real interests of peoples. . . . The prestige of Parliament is an empty
fraud. It is not too much to say that [parliamentarians] are
not and never have been anything but agents for the defence
of monetary interests. Such was the origin of parliamentary
representation, such is its very soul. . . . And, particularly, do
not believe politicians. By the nature of their trade they have
no professional pride and can have none. The phrase 'professional politician' has brought the very notion of professionalism to dirt" (*Auto.*, pp. 259, 148).

Again there is an element of exaggeration, but it would be
pharisaical to stress it. Years before Eric had been strongly
impressed by Julien Benda's book, *La Trahison des Clercs*
(called in the English version *The Great Betrayal*); he came
to see even more clearly that the poet, the artist, the scholar,
the "clerk," who should be a disinterested [7] man, is indeed a
traitor if he puts himself almost unreservedly at the service
of the relative and contingent: and if it be a question of professional politics, he will be buried under a mountain of
mud, "whereas it is necessary that he should keep his feet on
the earth and his head above ground." In the words of The
Preacher, without the craftsmen and the husbandmen the
city cannot be built or flourish, "but they shall not dwell
or go up and down therein; nor shall they go up into the
assembly or sit among the judges." In other words, let them
keep out of politics. "Nevertheless they shall strengthen the
state of the world, and their prayer shall be in the work of
their craft. . . ."
The increasing "politicization" of people in these latter
days was very grievous to Gill; for himself he hardly ever
adverted of his own accord to such concepts as democracy,
dictatorship and the like. A man who was about to address
a meeting of war-resisters asked him for a message to them.
"Tell them to keep clear of politics," was the reply.
Politics even at its best is quite insignificant beside Christian doctrine and its implications. The "Magnificat" is irrelevant in our dirty struggles between "interests" and classes

---

[7] In view of an increasing misuse of this word it seems desirable to point
out that it is *not* a synonym for "uninterested." I think Eric himself defined
the saint as "the wholly disinterested man."

and nations and political programmes—so it must be the struggles themselves that are really irrelevant. "Religion is politics, and politics is brotherhood," said William Blake—"and brotherhood is poverty," added Eric Gill.

"All our politics," he wrote in a publication of the Cotswold Bruderhof, "are based on a denial of the Gospels. Our capitalist society is founded solely upon the notion that those who have money have the duty to get more, and that those who have none must be enslaved or exploited or 'employed'—until machines make their existence unnecessary. The fascist societies want to create empires and become as rich and great as the others. The communist societies want to make the rich poor in order that the poor may become rich. But the Church of God wants to make the rich poor and the poor holy.

"This is the circle of human politics: When we have accepted poverty there will be peace among men. Only when we make peace shall we become the children of God. Only when we love God shall we love our fellow men. Only when we love our fellow men shall we have peace. When we have peace we shall have poverty, and when we have poverty we shall have the kingdom of Heaven."

∿

Remembering that by poverty Gill meant, where material goods are concerned, not less than a reasonable sufficiency for decent human life, it need occasion no surprise that he saw the chief "practical" means to the restoration of the dignity of physical work, and of the quality of things made, in the ownership of property; and he came to advocate as a practicable necessary reform the ownership of the means of production by the workers (*not* by the state; "workers" means all who work in a given enterprise, including the managing director if he works and if there is a job for him to do). This can be found set out in the essay on Work and Property in the book of that name and in another, "Ownership and Industrialism," in *Sacred and Secular;* but here I follow mainly a letter to the *Catholic Herald* newspaper in which he summarized his argument.

The right to property, he said, is not primarily a moral right, one due to man on account of his free will, but is, so to say, an intellectual right, due on account of his intelligence: it follows from man's material necessities and intellectual nature, deriving not from his need to *use* things but from his need to *make* things. As a moral being purely as such, man has no right of private ownership; he quotes Pope Leo XIII and Aquinas on the duty to possess things not as one's own but as common. (Incidentally, Christians, especially the Catholic clergy, have made a big mistake in presenting the right to private property as apparently simply a matter of morals, "a thing good men believe in and bad men deny, and that's all about it." We have sought to defend the institution of private property by the very arguments which are our opponents' strongest line of attack: "the earth is the Lord's," his gift to us is for our "individual appropriation and public use"—and we have done our best to destroy both, and so allowed such miseries to be heaped upon man that the socialist says, "Destroy private property!" to which the communist adds, "And religion with it," for it has been made to look as if the Church herself were on the side of big business and exploitation.)

It is, then, to man as workman, as an intelligent being who must manipulate things in order to make them serviceable, that private ownership is both necessary and a natural right, and only when there is full control of the means of production can there be proper and efficient manipulation. Unless the farmer own the fields (or have a tenancy on terms nearly equivalent to ownership) he cannot exercise his best skill and intelligence upon them; unless the carver own the tools and stone he cannot properly exercise his skill and intelligence therewith; unless the miner own the mine, individually or jointly with others, he or they cannot properly control the job of mining. This necessity of manipulation it is which gives the right of private property in the means of production: "The exercise of art or work, whether it be that of a craftsman or a manual labourer, is the formal reason of individual appropriation," as Maritain observes.

It is obvious that, as things are, the ground upon which alone a claim to private property in productive goods can be validly made has to a considerable extent been destroyed. The factory "hand" can make no claim to private ownership in his work and the big-machine industries and transport are no longer in any true sense private enterprises: they are (as their directors boast) public services. Hence the moral force of communism: what are public services should be publicly owned for the profit of all. There no longer remains any rational and Christian objection to communal ownership, since the only reason for private ownership, the intellectual operation of the workman by which he imprints on matter the mark of rational being, has been destroyed by the development of machine industry.

The conclusion is inescapable. We cannot have any right to private property in the means of production unless we are prepared to abandon industrialism; most people are not so prepared, and even if they were, it would be impossible to return immediately to pre-industrial methods.

> "Let us resolutely put away all dreams of that sort. Let us abandon the coteries of vegetarians and nut-eaters and artist-craftsmen. . . . Politics deals with things as they are. . . . Ownership is necessary to human happiness, to human dignity and virtue, and ownership means control. A share in profits is not ownership. Money in the savings-bank is not control of the means of production. The only desirable and at the same time the only possible reform of 'our world' is distribution of ownership" (*S. & S.*, p. 168).

Capitalist organization implicitly and communist organization explicitly lead to public ownership for private use. This is the exact opposite of Christian society, where there should be private ownership for the sake of common use. In our existing society we have degraded nearly all production and transport to being huge impersonal and therefore sub-human enterprises—and yet we have the insolence or folly to endeavour to maintain private ownership in the use of productive things and to declare that this sort of "private property" is a principle of Christianity which must be defended against ravening "reds" and subversive "leftists." "The newspapers and politicians and big-businessmen talk as though everybody in England had private property, and enough private property to make complete human beings of themselves, and as though it was only in wicked Russia that no one was allowed to own anything privately" (*Unemployment*, p. 27).

Workers' ownership of the means of production, then, was what Gill put forward as a practicable, perhaps the only practicable, step towards the Christian society in which there shall be private ownership for the sake of public use, a private ownership not asked for "on the selfish ground of private enjoyment, but for the sake of the good of things to be made and in order that the public use which morality demands may be a use of good things." The alternative we shall have to accept is in all probability some form of communistic industrialism and the "leisure state," wherein man's intelligence will wither away in highbrow snobbery or mob vulgarity.

> But "that alternative is no revolution, it is simply *progress*. In fact so-called revolutionaries are simply 'progressives.' They want, instead of the present world, the world which the present one *implies*. They want the same thing only more so—the same things only more of them. . . . Merely to transfer ownership from private persons to the state is no revolution; it is only a natural development. Government by the proletariat is no revolution; it is only the natural sequel to the enfranchisement of lodgers. But to abolish the proletariat and make all men owners—and to abolish mass-production and return to a state of affairs wherein 'the artist is not a special kind of man but every man is a special kind of artist'—that would be a revolution in the proper sense of the word. And merely to proclaim an atheist government is no revolution— for that would be to make explicit what is already implicit in capitalist commercialism; but to return to Christianity would be truly revolutionary" (*W. & P.*, pp. 53-54).

❦

Meanwhile—let us lift up our hearts to the Lord.

"I am quite perfectly certain that the ultimate truth of the created universe is that which is implied in the saying of Julian of Norwich: 'It lasteth and forever shall, for God loveth it,' and that as the actuality of everything is dependent upon God's will, so everything is sustained in being by his love."

In that belief Eric Gill lived, and in that belief he died.

C. F. ANDREWS

by

Nicol Macnicol

Matthew 5:3-10

NICOL MACNICOL. Born 1870 in Catacol Manse, Arran, Scotland. Educated at Glasgow University; M.A., D.Litt., Hon. D.D. His published writings include Indian Theism *(Oxford University Press),* The Living Religions of the Indian People, *and* Is Christianity Unique? *(both Student Christian Movement Press). He was a missionary of the Church of Scotland at Bombay and Poona from 1895 to 1930. He now resides at Edinburgh, Scotland.*

1

CHARLES FREER ANDREWS was born at Carlisle on February 12, 1871, the fourth child in a family of fourteen. The stock from which he came on his father's side belonged mainly to East Anglia. He himself looked back to them as being "religious leaders and preachers of the strict Puritan faith." Of his father he says, "Following the dictates of conscience as a minister of religion, he spent himself night and day during the whole of a long lifetime in a crowded Midland town, where there was no comeliness of nature, no beauty of the countryside, no leisure for mystical contemplation" (*What I Owe to Christ*, p. 32).

The town described in such unflattering terms was Birmingham and there his early life after the age of six was spent. His father was a minister of the Catholic Apostolic Church, a religious body that derives from the remarkable personality of Edward Irving, a prophetic figure who for a few years until his early death in 1834 obtained by his eloquence a great position, numbering among his admirers such men as Canning and Carlyle and Coleridge. Andrews came to recognize long afterwards that one thing at least that the Catholic Apostolic Church bore witness to was urgently required by the world—what he describes as "a renewal of those excellent gifts of the Holy Spirit which the Apostolic age had received in fullest measure." In spite of elements in his parents' church that repelled him, he agreed with it in his desire for a return to "first-century Christianity" (*op. cit.*, p. 209).

But deep as was Andrews's reverence for the devout lives that his parents lived and for their loyalty to the teachings of

231

their church he presently found it impossible to remain along with them within its fellowship. At a later period in his spiritual development, however, he recognized the debt he owed to them and perhaps even to the humble congregation among whom with his parents he worshipped in those early and formative years. He remained in all his wanderings in close relation with them, realizing that what they were and what they, and especially his mother, did for him "left a permanent mark such as nothing could obliterate or remove." He was, however, to pass through a spiritual crisis which was, no doubt, closely related to the ministries of a deeply Christian home and which he recognized as his conversion.

This "deep inner change" which "changed the very scenery of daily existence" came to him when at the age of nineteen he was about to leave school and enter the University of Cambridge (*op. cit.*, Cap. V). He tells us how "without warning, the strong conviction of sin and of impurity came upon me with overpowering strength . . . and I knew myself as I really was." It might have been the experience of St. Paul or St. Augustine or anyone in any age who is confronted by God and cries, "O wretched man that I am, who shall deliver me?" Then followed with him as with them, when the night had passed and the day dawned, "a new and wonderful sense of peace and forgiveness stealing into my life at its very centre and bringing infinite relief." It is a story often told and never stale or common, the rebirth of a soul. It is necessary that we should set forth as central to the whole significance of Charles Andrews's life this event and what it meant to him. To omit it would be to omit the key to all he did and was. Again and again he bears witness through all the labours of his life to its centrality and to the power of a new life that it brought to him and that was constantly renewed at its source. Forty years later, describing in his spiritual autobiography what happened to him on that night of revelation, he writes, "Christ has been the living Christ to me ever since. . . . I have known the secret of his presence here and now as a daily reality. . . . It was the love of Christ within my heart which now began to constrain my life and mould my whole character. This is, essentially, what I owe to Christ" (*op. cit.*, pp. 95, 103).

These passages from his own account of what happened to him on that fateful night and morning can never be left out of account in any estimate of what C. F. Andrews did in the service of mankind or of what he was in his own inner being. *"Ecce Deus,"* he could say, *"fortior me qui veniens dominabitur mihi."* The source of the power over him of this experience has been sufficiently indicated, but it may further guide us in our understanding of how the experience entered into and shaped him if we note two comments with which he himself concludes the chapter in which he unveils his own secret. "There was no need for me," he writes. "to formulate this in a creed. It was spiritual consciousness that had come to me, not an intellectual definition; and whenever I have gone aside from that spiritual basis in order to define in metaphysical terms what I believe, it has seemed to me to bring weakness instead of strength, uncertainty instead of truth." These words make clear to us his characteristic attitude to this revelation that had come to him and that was to come again and again.

From this revelation there followed as its consequence then and always the realized and accepted duty of service, the service of love. "Almost the next day," he goes on, "I began to put this new found joy into practice. Near the church wherein I had worshipped . . . there was a slum quarter where drunkenness and vice were forced upon the poor by their very poverty itself. Never before had I even dreamt of visiting these homes or seeing these poor people. But now they became very dear to me for Christ's sake. . . . In this way the weeks and months went by, and the vision of Christ remained with me all the while" (*op. cit.*, pp. 103-4).

❧

He had won a scholarship at Pembroke College, Cambridge, and in October, 1890, his college life began. It becomes evident from this time on—and increasingly as the years pass—that it was personal relationships of admiration and affection and the ties that they created that meant most to him in his life. From such relationships in large measure he derived his strength, and to them, no doubt, he owed some of his limitations. In the relationship into which he came with his divine Lord, as he himself has described it to us—a relationship of personal devotion—we find the archetype of his life. He lived by the giving and receiving of affection and his spirit was always open to this traffic. It was indeed, as we have just heard him declare, "a spiritual consciousness, not an intellectual definition," that came to him at his conversion.

Cambridge opened wide to him doors of friendship that enriched this new experience and guided and shaped his course. There he had, he tells us, "the unique good fortune" at the very beginning of his university career to have as his college tutor, Charles Hermann Prior. To him Andrews owed much during the years when "the old naïve beliefs of his childhood" were passing away and his life was being reoriented. Chief among the trials that he had to face was the breach with his parents when he found it necessary to abandon elements in the faith which he had taken over from them and to shape a new course for himself. At this crisis in particular he was greatly assisted by another friendship that was granted to him, that of Basil Westcott, the youngest son of that bishop of Durham who holds so high a place among Johannine scholars. Basil Westcott was, he tells us, "the dearest companion I had in the world among those of my own age at college." The Westcott family became from this time on one of the most potent influences of his whole life.

By the time that Andrews had finished his studies in Cambridge he had made up his mind to be ordained to the ministry of the Church of England. It was also clear to him that his sphere of work, wherever it was, must be among the poor. His tutor, realizing that he was "too much of a dreamer," arranged that he should go as a lay worker to one of the most poverty-stricken districts of the Durham diocese, Monkwearmouth. There he would have to face "the concrete realities of practical life." His apprenticeship for the life of service of the poor that awaited him began here accordingly in

1895 and was continued in the Pembroke College Mission, Walworth, where he was among "the poorest and most neglected of London's poor" (*op. cit.*, pp. 123, 136).

When this period of training was completed he was ordained to the Anglican ministry, though he tells us that he had many doubts and hesitations to overcome concerning some of the "articles of religion" which he was required to sign and some of the duties that he would have, as a clergyman of the Church of England, to discharge. The recitation of the "cursing psalms" and the use of the Athanasian Creed in some of the church services caused him much searching of conscience; but when he looked from these things to the work that he had been enabled to accomplish among his poor parishioners he saw there "higher marks of ordination than any man-made articles of subscription." Nevertheless his misgivings were not overcome. The strain that this conflict created resulted in chronic ill-health, and when in 1900 an offer came to him to return to Cambridge as a fellow of his college and vice-principal of Westcott House, "it became evident to all," he says, "that the doctor's verdict must be obeyed and I must give up the college mission work" (*op cit.*, pp. 143, 145).

During these years the influence of the bishop under whom he served at Monkwearmouth was a dominant factor. "In those earlier years of my life," he writes, looking back over thirty years, "when 'hero-worship' was a second nature to me" (as indeed it continued to be to his life's end), "it was the greatest privilege of all to be allowed to stay with him and go for walks with him each afternoon." They talked often of India, which was beginning to cast its spell on Andrews as it had already done on several members of the Westcott family. He remembers that time spent in such company as "golden days," and they were so especially because they were shared with his intimate friend Basil Westcott, who presently left to join the Cambridge Mission at Delhi of which his father had been one of the founders. There were two channels in particular by which, we can see, the influence of this gracious family touched him at this time and moulded his thoughts and plans. One of these was their interest in India, an interest which had already sent three of their sons to serve its people as missionaries, while a fourth, Basil, was about to join 'hem. The other centred in the Gospel of St. John, to the study of which the bishop had devoted his great gifts of insight and scholarship. His interpretation confirmed Andrews in a love of this gospel that throughout his life continued to sustain and inspire him. There was also, he tells us, another "sacred memory" of those early days, associated with the elder sister of his friend Basil, "a frail invalid lady," whose heart was almost more in India with her brother than in England. "In her invalid's room, from which she never went out, the whole living world seemed to be present" (*op. cit.*, p. 134).

These two interests—St. John's Gospel and India—which to him appeared to form in certain respects a harmony, continued to hold his heart throughout his whole life. From the time of his conversion onward, this gospel, he tells us, meant more to him than any other part of the New Testament and his references to it in his writings confirm this indebtedness. That the influence of Bishop Westcott had its part in making him so "Johannine" in his Christian outlook cannot be doubted; so also the parallel interest in India that began to lay hold of him at this period was greatly reinforced by his close relation with the Westcotts. His thoughts turned more and more to that land as the sphere for the exercise of his vocation. Thus it came about that, when Basil Westcott died in Delhi of cholera after a very brief period of service as a missionary, this came to him as a personal challenge that could not be set aside. His ties with Pembroke College and Westcott House could not bind him any longer when his friend's death called him. "It was clear to me," he writes, "that I must go out and take his place." On March 20, 1904, which he always, he tells us, looked back to as "a second birthday in his life," he set foot on Indian soil and began his new life in the East (*op. cit.*, pp. 148, 152).

❧

Andrews was thirty-three years of age when this second birth came to him. Looking back nearly thirty years later he says that he was one of the "twice-born," so sharply was his life "cut in two" by his entrance into this new environment. That does not mean that there was any break in the continuity and consistency of the two portions. He was aware, he tells us, from his first day in India that he had entered "a different world of human thought," but in spite of this contrast he later on realized the unity that lay beneath. Nor did he himself change. His character and his aims had been already determined and they continued in their course, gaining new hues and new dimensions, but fundamentally the same in their source and their direction. Christ became in India "not less central but more central and more universal; not less divine to me but more so, because more universally human" (*op. cit.,* p. 153).

It is not intended to provide here a full biography of this man but to see him as a great Christian and, just for that reason, as a revolutionary, one who interpreted Christ and Christianity by his acts in such a spirit of devotion and of resolve as to give his life an exceptional significance in the times in which he lived and for the people who took note of him. In the first thirty years the lines of his character had been laid, the sources of his strength had been discovered, the goal of his efforts had been descried. Thenceforward he ran a straight course to the end and lived by one faith. For that reason, once the framework of the thirty strenuous years that remained for him has been outlined, it should be possible to proceed to consider more fully what his life's aims actually were and what was its ultimate achievement.

We have seen that Andrews, as soon as he landed in India, became aware that he had entered a different world of thought from that of his past environment. He had entered as well, as he must soon have realized, a land where a gulf had already begun to open—and was rapidly widening—between the Indian people and their British rulers. The Viceroy, Lord Curzon, was in the last year of his office, and in spite of his great qualities he had failed to understand India and had only increased the alienation of the two races from each other. G. K. Gokhale, who was the first of the popular leaders to win Andrews's admiration, had withstood the Viceroy in his council with unflinching courage and consummate ability year after year, while other popular leaders, such as Lala Lajpat Rai and B. G. Tilak, were awakening and extending the spirit of rebellion among the common people. Gokhale, reviewing Curzon's seven years of rule after the Viceroy had left India, pointed unerringly to the cause of his tragic failure when he said that he lacked "a sympathetic imagination without which no man can ever understand an alien people."

In St. Stephen's College, Delhi, Andrews was at one of the focal points of this mounting agitation. He was among students, always ready even in Cambridge to harbour insurgent thoughts, and it was not likely that in India such thoughts in those he was brought into contact with would be hid from his discerning eyes. How eager he was to enter into the heritage that India offered him and to understand its genius and appreciate its aspirations was presently revealed in a little book published by him in 1914 called *The Renaissance in India*. There he hails Mahadev Govind Ranade as, by his "largeness of vision and magnanimity of character," one of the chief architects of the India that was then emerging from the shadows. It was peculiarly appropriate that it was Mr. Gokhale, disciple of Ranade and heir of his spirit, who launched Andrews in 1913 upon his public career as friend of India and brother of her poor.

In the years from 1904 to 1913 his first duty was to the college in which he taught, and he was not long there before he found even within its walls both friends to bind to himself and evils that had to be redressed. The first of the friends he made there was one, among so many who during his life were granted him, whom he always reckoned and declared to be the most valued and beloved of them all, Sushil Rudra. When Andrews left St. Stephen's College in 1914 Rudra, who was then principal, wrote of him, "No single personality has had so great an influence in the development of the college as Charles Freer Andrews." Andrews could have said no less truly that no single personality had so great an influence upon himself as this friend. "It was an intense joy to me," he says, "to be able to serve under him."

The association of these two men, by the testimony of their colleagues, "largely transformed the college and gave it some of the characteristic features it has since then possessed." It was, indeed, mainly through the efforts of Andrews that Rudra was chosen as principal. This was the first step in a process by which the college divested itself in large measure of its foreignness and became a truly Indian possession, rooted in the soil of the land. The work of collaboration between these two friends proceeded until, by the time Andrews's service at the college came to an end, it possessed a constitution setting it free from many of the limitations that its foreign origin placed upon its influence and granting it what was virtually complete autonomy. What these reforms meant, because of the spirit that they embodied, may be summed up in the testimony of one of his British colleagues, Professor C. B. Young. It fully confirms what, as we have seen, Principal Rudra wrote of him when he left the college. At the time of Andrews's death, in a tribute that he contributed to the college magazine, Mr. Young wrote, "Far above particular contributions stands out as his supreme gift to our college his passionate belief in a human brotherhood which overleaps all barriers of race and creed." This was embodied, for example, in the constitution of the college referred to above, with its emphasis on "inter-racial and inter-credal unity." "More than any other man," Mr. Young goes on, "he built up that tradition of close personal association between the different communities and races which has been one of the greatest contributions made by St. Stephen's to the national life. His own intimate friendship with Rudra was the starting-point and the incentive of a series of almost innumerable friendships between men of different creeds and races of which the college has been the kindly foster-mother." "Thus a distinctive mark of St. Stephen's College has been the spirit of friendship of which Andrews was supremely the living embodiment" (*see* the articles by Professors Young and Spears in *The Stephanian*, June, 1940).

What was happening to Andrews during these first ten years of his Indian life was that he was testing his powers and gradually discovering the sphere in which they were to be exercised. The milieu of St. Stephen's first gave him his opportunity and he made use of it. He took his place beside his friend Rudra in protesting against the imposition of the Thirty-Nine Articles and the Athanasian Creed on the young Indian Church, placing upon its neck "a yoke which neither our fathers nor we were able to bear." He fought against sectarian narrowness and came, in consequence, into collision with his bishop, a saint and scholar whom he venerated. Mr. Young, though a Baptist missionary, had been invited, largely through the persuasion of Andrews, to become a member of the staff of this Anglican college and had agreed to do so. Andrews's character and his distinguished career as a scholar gave him a dominant influence in college life and he used it to achieve those aims of brotherhood which he felt himself called upon both to extend in their range and to strengthen. He was conscious already of the urgency of the duty that was laid upon him in such matters. Writing of the dominant influence that he exerted in the college, Mr. Young makes the comment that "this masterfulness was not due to the self-assertion of egotism (than which nothing could be more unlike Andrews) but to the natural and inescapable prominence of a man who in powers of mind and heart was a giant among pigmies." One more quotation from Mr. Young's tribute may complete our view of what he effected in St. Stephen's College, which he never ceased to bear in his heart through all the years given by him to later and larger activities. "All that he thought and said and did in St. Stephen's and outside was the embodiment or application of his commanding passion for unity." This ideal of racial and credal unity furnished "the basal principles of his work in and for India." "He and Rudra in partnership," Mr. Young goes on, "made of this place a school of friendship transcending creed and race, a place where, in the phrase of another and even more famous of Andrews's friends 'life is not broken up by narrow domestic walls' " (*op. cit.*, p. 36).

❧

The time had arrived, however, when a challenge came to him to exercise in a wider sphere the gift of reconciliation that had been entrusted to him. It was G. K. Gokhale who actually laid this burden upon him, and no one in India could do so with more authority than he. He was the outstanding figure at that time in the public life of his country, a leader, as we can see to-day, of great wisdom and moderation. He may be described as the second in the line of India's liberators during the final stages of her progress towards the status of a free nation. He followed in the steps of M. G. Ranade, to whom he looked up with reverence as the pupil looks up to his teacher, the disciple to his *guru*. The third in that succession, M. K. Gandhi, claims for himself a similar relation to Gokhale. Both Gokhale and Gandhi were engaged at this time in a struggle which to them appeared to concern vitally the honour and self-respect of the Indian people. This was a struggle against the imposition on Indian labourers, under a system of indenture, of what Gokhale described as a "life which, if not one of actual slavery, is at any rate not far removed from it." This system was brought to an end there when in 1917 the government of India stopped all further recruiting, but its consequences still continued and caused intense feeling throughout the land. In 1913 the Viceroy himself expressed "the sympathy of India, deep and burning, . . . and of all lovers of India for their compatriots in South Africa in their resistance to invidious and unjust laws."

The particular instance of this abuse which Mr. Gokhale and Mr. Gandhi were bringing to the notice of the Indian government for redress was that of the Indian "coolies," as they were called, who were recruited for labour in the coal mines of Natal. Gokhale had returned from South Africa, where he had gone to negotiate on behalf of the Indian government, while Gandhi was still there engaged in organizing a movement among the miners demanding justice from South Africa.

It was when matters had reached a crisis and Gandhi was leading the first of his "passive resistance" marches that Gokhale, in November 1913, sent Andrews a telegram in-

viting him to go out immediately to South Africa "in order
to help the Indian community which was suffering from an
intolerable wrong." Andrews at once consented, and in
January 1914 he arrived in Natal. This was the first of the
many journeys in the cause of the oppressed or the unhappy
that occupied so much of his life from this time on. Like
the "second birth," as he calls it, that came to him at the
age of thirty-three, this was a notable hour in his life, when
he set himself to a task of emancipation and put away all
aims except the fulfilment of his call. It was at this time,
apparently, that Albert Schweitzer's example and the message of his book, *The Quest of the Historical Jesus,* came to
him, "enkindling," he says, "with fresh ardour [his] droop-
ing heart." He received a new call and took a new decision.
"The greatest break in my life came," he writes, "when I
decided at last to leave the Cambridge Mission Brotherhood
and abandon direct ministerial work under a bishop in order
that I might launch out on an unknown sea and set sail for
a wider and ampler world" (*What I Owe to Christ,* p. 213).
At the same time, in order that he might be in no way en-
cumbered but be ready for "the crisis of a last hour," he
not only surrendered his employment but "gave away his
life's savings and became a wanderer." His friend Hoyland
adds: "I do not think that any of his friends knew how
Charlie was supported financially during those strenuous
years. . . . He certainly lived on the barest minimum both
during the anti-indenture struggle and afterwards" (Hoyland, *C. F. Andrews,* pp. 41, 50).

The anti-indenture struggle—if we include in that description not only the agitation to obtain the abolition of the
indenture system itself but also that for the abolition of other
evils and injustices that remained as its consequence after it
was abolished—occupied a large part of the years that followed upon this first journey; for as David Livingstone crossed
and re-crossed Africa to save Africa from slavery, so Andrews
crossed and re-crossed the oceans of the world to save the Indian "coolies" from this "near-slavery" which laid its burden
of bondage upon them. South Africa, Fiji, the West Indies,
British Guiana—these were only some of the lands to which

Indians had gone under indenture to work in sugar-planta-
tions or in mines; and wherever there was need of a champion to call attention to injustice done to them or cruelty
endured by them Andrews was at their service. Not restlessness but the imperious call of human need sent him posting
over land and ocean without rest. He mentions in one place
that at the time when he was writing—in 1932—he was on
his way to South Africa for the seventh time. His friend
H. W. Peet calculated that his book, *What I Owe to Christ,*
must have been written "in four out of the five continents
and while crossing and re-crossing one or more oceans."

On this first journey he was not alone. His companion—
not on this journey only but on several other similar ones
as well—was W. W. Pearson, who shared his deep sympathy
with the Indian poor as well as his admiration for such distinguished Indians as Rabindranath Tagore. He went with
Andrews to South Africa and to the Fiji Islands and thereafter gave himself to work at Santiniketan under the leadership of Tagore. When he died by a fall from a railway train
in Italy Andrews suffered, he says, "one of the greatest blows
that I had in my life."

On the wharf at Durban the two friends found Gandhi
awaiting them. This was Andrews's first meeting with one
who thenceforth was to have so great a part in his life. Looking back on it long afterwards, he writes, "Our hearts met
from the first moment we saw one another and they have
remained united by the strongest ties of love ever since."
"To be with him," he goes on, "was an inspiration that
awakened all that was best in me and gave me a high courage, enkindled and enlightened by his own" (*What I Owe
to Christ,* p. 246). Gandhi had not yet, of course, won for
himself the position that as "mahatma" and as the recognized champion of India he held later in the hearts of the
Indian people, but he had already shown his willingness to
suffer with them and for them. The march of passive protest
against injustice that had set out for the Transvaal under his
leadership had been broken up, and Gandhi and his wife
had been cast into prison at Bloemfontein. By the time that
Andrews and Pearson arrived on the scene a temporary

accommodation had been arrived at with the South African Government and Gandhi had been released.

During the time spent in South Africa Andrews was making deeper discoveries of what was required of a Christian, and in this Gandhi was by his personality as well as by his acts his chief teacher. He learned with a new conviction two things that remained with him always and shaped the course his life took. One was the conclusion he drew from his observation of Gandhi's character. He tells us, "Even when I was trying to help Mahatma Gandhi at the height of the strain of conflict I was subconsciously occupied in thinking out the meaning of his personality—so entirely 'Hindu' and yet so supremely 'Christian.'" The other came from his painful experience of how so many who professed themselves to be Christians and represented the Christian Church treated Gandhi because he did not belong to the white race. "When I reached Natal," he writes, "I found a racial situation within the Church almost exactly parallel to that against which Paul so vehemently contended. . . . I must not for a moment shrink back from the issue but boldly meet it. Like Paul I might have to withstand to their faces those who would bring racialism within the Christian Church" (*op. cit.*, pp. 252, 239, 257). These two standpoints had from this time forward to be his.

In this way his spiritual education was proceeding, and during this period his relation to the Christian Church and especially to the Church of England was exercising his mind. He was not one who shut his eyes to facts, however grim, or hesitated to draw conclusions from them and act accordingly. For that reason, looking back seventeen years later on what he learned during these months, he can speak of "the strain mingled with a buoyant happiness" that this experience under Gandhi's leadership brought to him. Presently, however, news came to him of his beloved mother's death and, a settlement of the Indian question having been reached, he found himself free to visit England. His brief stay there confirmed him in the decision that he could have no more to do with a "colour-ridden Christianity" and must take steps to show that this was so.

On his return to India he took up his residence at Santini-ketan—"the Abode of Peace." "The poet," he writes, "in his great-hearted generosity took me just as I was," but, until he had carried his decision into action and surrendered his ministerial status, he felt that he could have no peace of conscience but was living a life of untruth. It is not, of course, to be supposed that he wholly abandoned the Church of England, much less Christianity. He remained "a communicant of the Anglican communion" till his death, but looked upon himself as a layman. "From that day to this," he wrote in his spiritual autobiography, "the thought has been present with me that the true ministry for which I was fitted and prepared by God was prophetic rather than priestly" (*op. cit.,* pp. 268, 270).

Another conflict that made Santiniketan at first less to him than its name signified concerned his attitude to the first great war with Germany that had just burst upon the world. This period of perplexity ended when, to quote his own words, "I saw that I had very nearly betrayed Christ, my Master, when I had allowed the war-fever to get possession of me. Now . . . I was back in my right mind. The relief that came to me with the decision was very great, and it was never regretted afterwards." In this decision, as in so many others, he acknowledges the help given to him both by Tagore and Gandhi. Whether either of them was in the full sense of the word a pacifist is doubtful, but Gandhi's *Satyagraha*—literally "truth-force" but usually taken as equal to "passive-resistance"—and Tagore's ultimate attitude to that war in particular are associated by Andrews in his own case with the authority for him of Christ who, he was confident, "beyond a shadow of doubt," condemned war. "Christ's own war on behalf of the down-trodden peoples all over the world had to be fought and he was calling me to enlist in his service" (*op. cit.,* pp. 276 *ff.*).

Perhaps "the acute inner suffering and trial" that he passed through in this connection was one of the causes of an illness that followed when, in May 1915, he had a severe attack of Asiatic cholera. It appears to have been while he was slowly recovering his strength in Simla that it became "as clear as daylight to him that he was called to go to Fiji to fight in behalf of the Indians employed there under indenture." Not for the first time this summons came to him through a waking dream. At the close of his period at Cambridge he tells how "a moment of luminous vision" enabled him to keep fast hold of unseen realities and remained long with him as a source of spiritual strength. So it was on this occasion also, and on his recovery from his illness he set forth for Fiji under the constraint of this experience.

As on the visit to Africa in the previous year, he was accompanied by William Pearson. This was the first of three visits that he paid to Fiji, the others being in 1917, when he went alone, and in 1936. On the first two occasions his purpose was, as it had been in South Africa, to help those Indians who had gone to Fiji under indenture. His unwearied championship of those suffering under this system did much to expose its evils and to bring about its final abolition—not only in Fiji but in all the British colonies—on January 1, 1920. His third visit was made at the invitation of the Indian community in Fiji in order that he might help them to defend their citizen rights. In the preface to his book, *India and the Pacific,* he gives a summary of his efforts in behalf of the Indians there and in many other parts of the world who were in such great need of a champion. "During the years 1913-1936 I have visited not only Fiji but also nearly all the other colonies where Indians have settled. Everywhere I have received the warmest welcome and have learnt at first hand what handicaps Indians have suffered. Thus a great part of my life has been occupied with these problems."

෴

The method that this ambassador felt to be necessary was that of personal contact with those whom he sought to aid. He did not seek to stir up trouble but to allay it, and to do so by such understanding and sympathy as only a full knowledge of each situation could create. So he passed from South Africa to the Fiji Islands, where his method was carefully tested by successive visits. We find him next in East Africa which became—because of its nearness to India, on the one hand, and of the demands that the European settlers were making on the other—the scene of a conflict of critical significance. That was why Srinivasa Sastri, one of the wisest and most patient of India's political leaders, said to Andrews in reference to the struggle for equality of treatment between Indians and Europeans, "If Kenya is lost all is lost." Andrews explains that "if racial discrimination in favour of the white race in Kenya was finally imposed by the Colonial Office no self-respecting Indian could remain within a commonwealth that was nothing more than a sham and a fraud." We see the long shadows from that dispute stretching down to to-day when the question of the "colour bar" is more than ever darkening our skies.

Andrews, accordingly, when he journeyed from colony to colony was an ambassador of inter-racial friendship through the whole world, but especially of an abiding friendship between India and Great Britain. It is difficult to trace his itinerary as he traverses the continents. To protect from injustice Indians settled in British Guiana and British Columbia he found it necessary to visit in person those lands, while the dangerous policy of a "white Australia" sent him to that dominion, whose future, as Andrews realized and as we all realize more clearly than ever to-day, cannot be separated from that of Japan and India. Concluding in 1937 his book *India and the Pacific* he writes, "The Pacific Ocean with its long sea borders and its numberless islands is likely to become at no distant date the centre of fresh prospects for all mankind; and in this process of the ages India with its intellectual and spiritual background will have an important part to play" (p. 206).

It is impossible to do more than name some of those regions to which Andrews's labours in this cause summoned him. From them he returned from time to time to England or to India to have his physical strength renewed or his ardour rekindled. There were other ways of serving India besides placing himself beside the friendless children of her dispersion. He must enter into closer relation with the land itself. It was apparently in London in 1911 that, listening to

W. B. Yeats as he read poems of Tagore from the *Gitanjali,* he first became convinced that he must "move amongst the people of India as one of themselves," that he must "be bound up with the life of India in every respect" (*What I Owe to Christ,* p. 267). India had subdued him to herself, and had done so pre-eminently through the ties of affection and reverence that united him with two Indians, Mahatma Gandhi and Rabindranath Tagore.

In what respects these two great Indians influenced him and affected his whole attitude to India will be considered more fully later. Meantime it is to be noted that from the time of his return from his first visit to South Africa in 1914 his home, in any sense in which this world-wanderer can be said to have had a home, was Santiniketan, the home in Bengal of the Bengali poet. It was more than Tagore's personal home, for his father, by taking up his residence there at the close of his career as one of the noble line of theistic reformers of Bengal, had made it a sacred place. An Indian sage was traditionally supposed to retire to such an *ashram* for religious study and meditation when "his hair had grown white and he had seen his son's son." After his father's death Rabindranath Tagore made this place in a wider sense a centre for religious culture and the nucleus of an ambitious dream he cherished of founding an international university. From this place Andrews set out on his errands of mercy across the seas. What it and its master were to him during the last decades of his life can be indicated by two quotations. He tells us that, on his last journey to Fiji, "the memory of the peace of Santiniketan and [Tagore's] home there, where he sat each morning long before the break of day in quiet meditation, was a wonderful comfort in times of utter loneliness and bitter hostility." And again he tells us that, living with him between his voyages, his reverence and love grew deeper year by year. "There at Santiniketan I learned to understand the spiritual beauty which underlies Indian life, keeping it sweet through all the ages in spite of cruelties and wrongs which have gone unredressed" (*op. cit.,* pp. 292, 302).

It was mainly through the medium of these two great

Indian personalities—so different in some of their fundamental outlooks upon life but so united in their devotion to
their common motherland and to what they believed to affect
her honour—that Andrews looked at India and appraised
her greatness. Through them and others of their quality he
would have foreigners see India and recognize (as he says)
her "inner moral beauty." The ties of reverence and affection
that bound him to them bound him to India. Andrews accompanied Tagore in 1916 to China and Japan and was with
him in Great Britain and in America on other occasions,
but it was the peace of Santiniketan and the poet's own
"serene and beautiful spirit" that made him look forward
from his arduous wanderings "with a fond and eager joy" to
his return there. "A quiet haven had been entered," he says,
"and the vessel of my life found its anchorage" (*Christ in the
Silence,* pp. 18, 20-21).

The demands that Gandhi made upon him were usually
of another sort. The contemplative needs of his nature found
what they needed in the Abode of Peace and in the fellowship it offered; but he could not long remain inactive and
he must be at Gandhi's side exercising *Satyagraha* along with
him; or watching over him as he by his fasts staked his life
on the justice of his cause; or again, beside him in London
supporting him at the round-table conferences. These two
mentors represented two sides of his nature, both of which
needed to be satisfied, and we may conclude that during the
years of alternating action and contemplation the *ashram* of
Gandhi and the *ashram* of Tagore found an equilibrium that
brought to him fulfilment.

Nor does that sum up the duties that sent him during the
busy and troubled years "between the wars" on errands of
mercy to the ends of India and of the earth. It might be
earthquake or flood or famine or clashes on the North-West
Frontier or the last sickness of a single forlorn Indian student
in Germany—this "brother of the poor" could not shut his
ears to the call. He must be up and away,

Doing the King's work all the dim day long,
In his old coat. . . .
Smoked like a herring, dining on a crust.

But as the crowded years went past and his strength grew less his still unwearied spirit had to find other means than those of travel by which to serve his fellow men. His pen had never been inactive at any time, but when he found it necessary to seek more often the quiet of Santiniketan or Selly Oak or Pembroke College he used the opportunity in new ways. It is true that his spiritual autobiography, *What I Owe to Christ,* was written in the midst of many journeyings—as he says, "in the midst of the struggle rather than in retirement and retreat"—but other books that followed and were written with the same aim were, it is evident, the product of times of enforced leisure and the fruit of a desire to strengthen young people especially "in their faith and love for Christ."

Thus his labours for his fellow men of every land continued and expanded. His appeals, whether these were made by his acts or by his pen, issued always from a heart overflowing with an affection that was personal and, indeed, individual in its direction and that was glad and even gay. So when he lay dying in a hospital in Calcutta he was still, as ever, "surrounded by an atmosphere of love, joy and inward peace." There, on April 4, 1940, this good soldier of Jesus Christ obtained his discharge and his voyagings their end.

2

THERE are three aspects of C. F. Andrews's life and his achievements that deserve to be more closely studied, for the message that they "placard" before the modern world and the example that they show to it. These may be represented by three titles that describe what he was and the kind of service that he set himself to render to his fellows. He was pre-eminently a friend, overflowing in his friendship and fellowship with men, and especially he was a friend of India. That he was that in India in his relations with men of every class and creed and colour, no one can deny. The other two titles of honour that were bestowed on him were tributes paid by the multitude in India who loved him and watched him at work there. It was Gandhi that first gave him the designation *Dinbandhu,* which means "Brother of the Humble" and suggests many enterprises of help for the despised and the suffering that draw him like a magnet. He was also frequently described by Christian Indians and, more significantly still, by non-Christians, reinterpreting his initials, as "Christ's Faithful Apostle." He was probably right when he said of himself that the ministry for which he was fitted and prepared was prophetic and not priestly; that it was, if we may express the distinction from another point of view, dynamic and not static. But, as the word prophet has its associations with the Old Testament rather than the New, he may more fitly be described as "an apostle," and an apostle of the order of his most beloved teacher, St. John.

Through these three aspects of his service of mankind runs the silken cord of friendship holding them together and giving to them a peculiar sheen. He was first and last a friend. In India they have a name which means "Friend of All the World," *Jagad-mitra,* and surely there was never anyone to whom it would have been more aptly given than to Andrews. But his was not a vague cosmopolitanism; his friendship had, as all friendships to be real must have, a centre: or we might more truly say, two centres—one a centre of reception and the other a centre of distribution. Of the source from which his great power of affection was derived we must speak later, for to leave that out would be to leave all out. But from him radiated forth a warmth that kindled a responsive glow, like a household fire, in hearts and homes wherever he went, but that glowed nowhere more comfortingly than in the land that itself so conquered him. "I longed," he says, "to be bound up with the life of India in every respect, . . . to be among them as one of themselves, and not an alien and a foreigner." The range of that affection was unlimited. He was a friend of India first: but he was at the same time a friend of all the world."

That is the primary fact that has to be realized in regard to Andrews. In the capacity for friendship he was unique. He had other great qualities without which this central source of strength would have been inadequate to the tasks he undertook and accomplished. But here lay the citadel of his personality, and of its range and power we have to be convinced if we are to do him justice. Professor T. G. P. Spear, one of his British colleagues in St. Stephen's college, writes of him: "Andrews' life was a catalogue of friendships; each stage is marked by a new friend, each one, as he would characteristically say, dearer than a brother. His capacity for new friendships remained fresh to the last and while he was constantly making new friends he never lost an old one" (*The Stephanian*, June 1940, p. 4). That is a remarkable testimony but it is confirmed by all we know of him. If each friend he made was "characteristically" described by him as "dearer than a brother," is there not exaggeration in these professions? One remembers how Martin Luther said that the dearest of his children was the one that was at the moment on his knee. So it was, it would seem, with Andrews. When in his thought and imagination he summoned one of his friends before him, his whole heart warmed and glowed, as Luther's did. Was he, then, a sentimentalist? Here is what Professor Spear says of his work as a peacemaker in labour disputes: "On the surface it seemed as though the gentle sentimentalist had little chance in bargaining with hardboiled industrialists and matter-of-fact officials, but when they met it was the prophet in homespun who was fit to get the better of the men of the world. His intellect retained the keen edge of its Cambridge days, his memory was a storehouse of facts and he added to both an intense perception of broad moral issues. To the innocence of the dove he united the wisdom of the serpent and the unexpected combination often produced inspiring results" (*op. cit.*, p. 20).

To a reader of his books Andrews's expression of his affection may sometimes seem so unrestrained as to sound exaggerated, but when his words are tested by his deeds there

can be no doubt of their sincerity. No one can be dismissed
as a sentimentalist whose emotion proceeds at once to action
and finds its fulfilment in unswerving purpose. When he was
converted he set himself at once—"almost next day," he says
—to the service of the poor and the ignorant round about
him in Birmingham and in the college mission at Walworth,
and so it was wherever he might be all his life long. As he
himself says, "a fugitive and cloistered virtue" never had
any attraction for him. He believed, in words that he often
quotes, that "love's strength standeth in love's sacrifice." A
word of Christ's that evidently meant much to him—and
that was given to him, he tells us, by his father—was, "Ye
are my friends, if ye do whatsoever I command you," and his
emphasis is placed upon the doing. Some lines quoted in
the memorial appeal issued by his Indian friends after his
death from a poem by Andrews himself reveal how central
this union of emotion and duty was in his religion:

> " 'Who loveth much'—the Master gave the meed,
> Not by the rule of indolent belief,
> Not by professing sympathy with grief
> Without the act. Nay, by the living deed
> He fixed for man Love's everlasting creed."

This was his "everlasting creed" and to make it real once
more as it had been in the early centuries was one of his
most significant services to his time.

The scene that he chose, or rather that was chosen for him,
for this demonstration was India. He became, in a sense true
of no other foreigner, a friend of India. But India was not
for him an abstraction: she was men and women and children of every class and kind, and the way to their hearts,
as he himself repeatedly emphasizes, was opened for him
through his friendship with his first Indian friend, Sushil
Rudra. As a result of his own experience he was always
urging upon those who desired to understand and to serve
the people of India that they should have one or two Indian
friends whom they could grapple to themselves. Because of
the intimacy of his relation with Rudra "the first newness
of India," he says, "passed into closest contact with its peo-

ple." "Many have greatly wondered how I came so quickly
to understand the people of India and to be understood by
them. The answer is quite simple and the secret is easily
told. Such a close friend as Sushil Rudra is very rarely given
in this life to any man" (*What I Owe to Christ*, pp. 157,
161). He repeatedly tells us indeed that of all his many
friends Rudra was the dearest. We have seen that he took
a leading part in securing the appointment of his friend as
the first Indian principal of St. Stephen's College. It was
largely through his insight and his freedom from all self-
interest that Sushil Kumar Rudra was chosen for this position for which he was eminently fitted, and so the custom
of reserving it for an Englishman was abandoned. St. Stephen's has never had reason to regret the course it then took,
and Andrews by this act had set his foot on the road of
India's vindication along which he was to travel so far in
the years to come.

But notable as was his friendship for Rudra, and fruitful
as was that early relationship in moulding his whole future
course, it is with two great non-Christian Indians, the greatest of their time, that Andrews is associated in the eyes of
the world, and it was above all through his fellowship with
them that he both received from India and gave to India
what made him India's friend and helper. These were
Mahatma Gandhi and Rabindranath Tagore. With these
two men, so different in their gifts but so representative
each in his own way, of India at her highest, Andrews maintained, all through his career from the time when he left
St. Stephen's College onwards, an intimacy which neither
their engrossing tasks nor his distant journeyings were able
to disturb, and one which they prized no less than he. To
have kept this close fellowship fully alive and active with so
much acknowledged profit on both sides through so long a
time was in itself a remarkable achievement, especially so
when it was a relationship that had to overcome both racial
differences and the hostility that conflicting national interests might arouse. That this was achieved is itself a convincing evidence of the high spiritual quality of these men, each
so remarkable in his own nature and gifts.

To tell the story of Andrews's relations with Gandhi is to tell the story of India's political struggles during the last twenty-five years. That story cannot be told in any detail here but only as it reveals the mind and heart of Andrews and the significance of the life he lived in India's service. The two men (almost of the same age) felt themselves at once akin, and a partnership was inaugurated which had notable consequences for each of them and for the country to which they had already dedicated their lives. Andrews has described the meeting at Durban at Easter 1914 and its effect upon himself. "Our hearts," he writes, "met from the first moment we saw each other, and they have remained united by the strongest ties of love ever since. To be with him was an inspiration which awakened all that was best in me and gave me a high courage, enkindled and enlightened by his own. His tenderness towards every slightest thing that suffered pain was only a part of his tireless search for truth whose other name was God" (*op. cit.*, p. 246).

It is not so easy to estimate how far Andrews on his part may have influenced Gandhi and modified his policies. To read the enigma of the Mahatma's character and pronounce any judgement on his career can hardly be attempted with any confidence as yet. At the same time some of the qualities that make him so great a figure can be recognized and the strong attraction that Andrews felt to him fully understood. Of the depth of his compassion for the poor and the down-trodden in his own land—and, indeed, as Andrews says, "for every slightest thing that suffered pain"—there can be no dispute, and that would be matched by a similar compassion in Andrews's heart. There has been much compassion in India from the days of Buddha onwards, but a compassion that flies from pain rather than, as it was in the case of these two mahatmas, one that takes it upon the heart and strives to heal it. Another quality that is unmistakable in Gandhi is his courage, and we have seen already that, with all his gentleness, Andrews was by no means lacking in that either.

Andrews, in a passage just quoted, describes one of the sources of the inspiration that Gandhi awakened in him as "his tireless search for truth." Here also one must agree that the claim is justified. Gandhi must be recognized to have constantly sought to build upon a foundation of reality, and, still more evidently, to have been wholly sincere and honourable in his dealings. Compassion and courage and fundamental truthfulness are qualities of nobility that can hardly be surpassed in their significance for any man and especially for a politician, and they justify the title of Mahatma, or Great Soul, that India has bestowed upon its leader. It is not to be wondered at that Andrews's kindred spirit should greet in him such moral greatness.

Gandhi was scarcely less grateful to Andrews for what this friendship meant to him. Thus, after Andrews's death, he recorded in his organ *Harijan* how close the bond between them was. "Nobody probably knew Charlie Andrews as well as I did," he wrote: "Gurudev [Tagore] was *guru*—master —to him. When we met in South Africa we simply met as brothers and remained as such to the end. There was no distance between us. It was not a friendship between an Englishman and an Indian. It was an unbreakable bond between two seekers and servants." That need not imply that they were in all respects in full agreement. For example, Gandhi's asceticism and some of the consequences that followed from it in his policy and his public acts Andrews seems to have sometimes frankly opposed and criticised. This was one of the respects in which he was more in accord with "the less puritan ideals of Santiniketan" (*Mahatma Gandhi's Ideas,* p. 331). In this respect, as in others, Gandhi represents the Hindu tradition, with its negation of life and life's rewards. What counterbalanced for Andrews this defect in Gandhi was "an amazing sweetness and child-like innocence" that he found in him and that makes him trace "an illuminating parallel with Francis of Assisi." "I could easily imagine Gandhi preaching to the birds," he writes, and as a matter of fact one whom we may call a spiritual ancestor of Gandhi, Tukaram, a very gracious poet saint of three centuries earlier, gathered the birds about himself in this very fashion. Tukaram and Gandhi represent, indeed, the flower of one strain in Hinduism, but Andrews was "brought up against inassimilable features also" (*op. cit.,* p. 344).

One of these "inassimilable features" was Gandhi's "fasts unto death," announced by him as such in 1932 and 1939, to which Andrews seems to have been strongly opposed. That "terrible phrase," he calls it, "which seems to me morally repulsive"; and for a time, at least, Gandhi appears to have recognized that such a method of bringing about his aim of "converting the hearts of Englishmen" would not prove successful. "It is easy," Andrews wrote to him, "to get their sympathy with the removal of untouchability"; but "it is *not* easy to get sympathy with the idea of committing suicide by fasting unto death. The horror and repulsion are too great." Gandhi was willing to admit that "it looks certainly barbarous," but this did not prevent him from announcing yet another fast of this kind five years later.[1] His less drastic fasts, such as the one for twenty-one days at Delhi in 1924 he viewed differently. That fast was undertaken for his self-purification: in Gandhi's own words, "the prayer of a bleeding heart for forgiveness for sins unwittingly committed." He felt himself involved in the guilt of the terrible outbreaks of violence that followed upon one of his non-co-operation experiments. To Andrews he seemed to be "bearing the sins and sorrows of his people," but "to put his life in the scales" as he did when he announced that he would "fast unto death" went, in Andrews's opinion, beyond anything that he had a right to do (*op. cit.,* p. 308).

There were other matters on which they were in sharp disagreement, when neither of them was willing to give way to the other. One of these was the burning of foreign cloth.[2] Their relation to each other is vividly revealed in their arguments on this subject, and Andrews's letter, as given by Gandhi in the weekly paper *Young India,* deserves to be quoted in full.

"I know," he wrote, "that your Burning of Foreign Cloth is with the idea of helping the poor, but I feel that you have gone wrong. There is a subtle appeal to racial feeling in that word 'foreign' which day by day appears to need checking and not fomenting. The picture of your lighting that great

[1] These quotations are from letters written in 1933 and from *Harijan,* April 15 of that year.
[2] This seems to have been about 1921.

pile, including delicate fabrics, shocked me intensely. We seem to be losing sight of the great outside world to which we belong and concentrating selfishly on India; and this must (I fear) lead back to the old, bad, selfish nationalism. If so, we get into the vicious circle from which Europe is trying so desperately to escape. But I cannot argue it out. I can only say again that it shocked me, and seemed to me a form of violence; and yet I know how violence is abhorrent to you. I do not at all like this question of foreign cloth being made into a religion.

"I was supremely happy when you were dealing giant blows at the fundamental moral evils—drunkenness, drug-taking, untouchability, race arrogance, etc., and when you were, with such wonderful and beautiful tenderness, dealing with the hideous vice of prostitution. But lighting bonfires of foreign cloth and telling people that it is a religious sin to wear it; destroying in the fire the noble handiwork of one's own fellow men and women, of one's own brothers and sisters abroad, saying it would be 'defiling' to use it—I cannot tell you how different it appears to me! Do you know I almost fear to wear now the *khaddar* that you have given me, lest I should appear to be judging other people, as a Pharisee would, saying, 'I am holier than thou!' I never felt like this before.

"You know how, when anything that you do hurts me, I must cry out to you, and this has hurt me."

Gandhi's comment on this letter indicates once more how close was the intimacy between them. "Whenever he feels hurt over anything I have done," he writes, "(and this is by no means the first of such occasions) he deluges me with letters without waiting for an answer. For it is love speaking to love, and not arguing." But Gandhi was not to be easily moved when he had made up his mind. He goes on: "I remain just as convinced as ever of the necessity of burning." Yet another instance of divergence in their convictions is seen in regard to questions relating to war and Gandhi's inconsistent attitude in encouraging recruiting for the first world war. He found himself, he says, "in painful disagreement" with his friend but he could not convince him in this case any more than in the other that what he was doing was contrary to the spirit of *Ahimsa* (*Mahatma Gandhi's Ideas*, pp. 133, 146).

Two of the principles that guided Gandhi and that in theory—though not always in Gandhi's application of them —were accepted with enthusiasm by Andrews are what are called *Ahimsa* and *Satyagraha*. The essential harmony between his mind and Gandhi's is due to their agreement in what these two "practical religious ideals" of Gandhi signified for Gandhi himself and the reinforcement that they brought to Andrews in his labour in the cause of India (*op. cit.*, Caps. VII, XIII).

Ahimsa is a Sanskrit word with a long religious history which implies abstinence from inflicting injury on any sentient being, and for the most part it has been understood in that negative sense. Thus for the followers of the Jain religion, as well as for many Hindus, the often quoted sentence "Ahimsa is the highest religious duty (*dharma*)" has a limited ethical range. But for Gandhi, as he tells us, "it has a world of meaning and takes me into realms much higher, infinitely higher." Gandhi was not the first in India so to deepen and enlarge the significance of the word. Mahadev Govind Ranade, the reform leader, who was, as we have seen, Gokhale's *guru,* equated Ahimsa with love, just as Gandhi does, and in the Hindu theistic tradition called *Bhakti*—to which both Ranade and Gandhi belonged—such an interpretation would not be strange and such an ideal was not infrequently proclaimed. But as Gandhi knew, and indeed discovered from his own experience (when, for example, he mercifully destroyed a suffering calf), his interpretation of the word often aroused violent opposition and anger among orthodox Hindus.

Satyagraha goes along with Ahimsa in Gandhi's philosophy. It is a word—apparently coined by himself—which means "truth force" or perhaps rather "holding to truth." He explains a Satyagraha-struggle as a "fight on behalf of truth consisting chiefly in self-purification and self-reliance." He often translates it also as "soul-force." Along with Ahimsa it implies a programme of what is often called "non-violent non-co-operation," though that description hardly conveys its positive character. It was a weapon such as had often been resorted to in the West as well as in the East when the weak have had to face the strong. Gandhi himself tells us how it first came to him. "It was the New Testament," he is reported as saying in his early years in South Africa, "which really awakened me to the rightness and value of passive resistance. The *Bhagavadgita* deepened the impression and Tolstoy's *The Kingdom of Heaven is Within You* gave it a permanent form" (quoted in. *Renascent India,* by H. C. E. Zacharias, p. 77).

How deeply religious this Ahimsa-Satyagraha teaching was, as Gandhi interpreted it, and how central in determining his actions, can be seen clearly from a passage which Andrews quotes in his *Mahatma Gandhi's Ideas* (pp. 225 f.). Gandhi is writing, apparently, in 1920, and referring to "the non-co-operation struggle in order to right the Khilafat and the Punjab wrongs and to win *swaraj.*" This is what he calls his *Dharma Yuddha* or "War of Religion."

> "My confidence," he says, "is unshaken that, if a single satyagrahi [that is, follower of Satyagraha] holds out to the end victory is certain. This is the beauty of Satyagraha. It comes up to us; we have not to go out in search of it. There is a virtue inherent in the principle itself. A war of righteousness in which there are no secrets to be guarded, no scope for cunning and no place for untruth, comes unsought, and a man of religion is ever ready for it. . . . A war of righteousness can be waged only in the name of God and it is only when the satyagrahi feels quite helpless, when he is apparently on his last legs and finds utter darkness all around him, that God comes to his rescue. God helps us when we feel ourselves to be humbler than the very dust under our feet. Only to the weak and helpless is divine succour vouchsafed."

The fact that Gandhi sees himself always waging a religious war, which this passage makes evident, awakens suspicion of him in many minds. They may admire his self-dedication to his aim, but they are aware of a danger that lies in the very intensity of his beliefs. For Andrews, on the contrary, these facts awaken his reverence. Even when he disagrees with Gandhi he is conscious that Gandhi has reached the conclusions which he holds so strongly by arguments "that have been tested and examined in his personal experience by his own pure spirit," and therefore no more can be said. "No saint," says Mr. H. N. Brailsford of Gandhi in *Subject India,* "has ever lived his creed more faithfully." That is a tribute of the highest order, and it can be paid no less truly to Andrews's fidelity to his creed. If the two creeds were closely similar—as they in considerable measure appear to be—then no more would need to be said, but perhaps Andrews was deliberately silent in regard to some of the differences that were indeed there all the time because their agreement was of so much greater significance in the circumstances of the struggle Gandhi was waging for his country's freedom. This was what mattered supremely at the moment.

Yet he can say with no reservation as he looks back years afterwards at what Gandhi did in South Africa, "He had then put us Christians to shame; and his example had ever since set me seriously thinking. What he called Satyagraha or Truth Force was obviously Christian; while the savage brutality of war was the reverse" (*What I Owe to Christ,* p. 277).

There was another aspect of Gandhi's character that bound Andrews to him no less closely than did his faithfulness to Ahimsa and Satyagraha—his compassion for the poor. He rejoices to see Tagore and Gandhi more fully at one in this matter than in any other. They both hold strongly "that God is to be found among the lowliest children of the soil." Andrews tells us in one place how, one evening while he was with Gandhi at their devotions in Gandhi's *ashram* at Sabarmati, Gandhi asked him to read a poem by Tagore and he read the poem that begins with the words, "Here is Thy footstool and there rest Thy feet, where live the poorest and lowliest and lost." He goes on: "It seemed to me that in that company of Mahatma Gandhi and his chosen band of followers the presence of God was almost visibly near at hand in the cool of the day there in that *ashram* where the poor were so loved and revered. Long years afterwards I heard Mahatma in a deeply moving way refer to that evening worship and that reading from Rabindranath Tagore, and realized that he had felt, as I had on that occasion, the mysterious presence of the Eternal."

It was such deep elements of agreement in their attitude to life and its duties that made the relationship between

Andrews and Gandhi so intimate and their harmony so close. The materials are not available that would enable us to estimate with any exactness the part that Andrews played in "the long, slow agony" of the as yet unfinished struggle for India's political emancipation. In that struggle the personality of Gandhi far more than anything else determined—and still determines—India's attitude. Andrews believed without reserve in the spirit that guided Gandhi in his struggle; it was in the main the same as that which guided himself. His primary concern was to see to it that the war for India's independence was maintained at a consistently high moral level. He quotes in one place words of Gandhi himself in which he describes Tagore as "a sentinel warning us against the approach of enemies called Bigotry, Lethargy, Ignorance and other members of that brood." Andrews could no less truly be called a sentinel, though the enemies that he kept at bay might bear other names. His championship of India's cause in South Africa when the summons first came to him was a championship of such a kind, and his outlook upon the distresses of India and of the world in its essentials never changed. He saw, writ large in India's relation with Great Britain, the moral evil of subjection. He had seen this evil at its acutest in the case of Indians settled in British colonies or dominions, and he found much the same situation within India itself. Foreign domination, there, as elsewhere, "creates in the rulers a domineering spirit and implants in the ruled a subservience that destroys all moral standards. Race feeling with bitterness on both sides becomes intensified" (*Britain and India,* p. 92).

In all these moral aims that were of the first consequence for him in determining political strategy he found himself able to support Mr. Gandhi. "I can trace every day more clearly," he says, "how this prolonged subjection to a foreign rule is injuring something vital in [India's] soul" (*op. cit.,* p. 65). Looking at the problems of India and the sorrows of her poor peasantry as well as the eager demands for freedom of those who felt themselves to be in bondage and despised, he says, "No doubt if I had been born in India and had passed through all those difficult years I should speak exactly as Mahatma Gandhi does." Sometimes we may feel that he surrenders too much of his critical faculty in his desire to identify himself with a people whose cause he believes in and whose poverty and distress he sees so vividly, but his deepest conviction was that what was needed in India was "to set the moral value of things right," and it is certainly true, as he claims, that "Gandhi has done more than any other living soul to bring this new moral emphasis into prominence" (*op. cit.*, p. 153).

For these reasons Andrews was always ready to give to Gandhi the sympathy and comradeship that meant so much to him. What actual assistance in political action he rendered we cannot be sure. Gandhi tells us how when he issued an open letter "giving concrete shape to the Khilafat claims" his "revisionists were Rudra and Andrews," and how "non-co-operation was conceived and hatched under Rudra's hospitable roof" (*Mahatma Gandhi's Ideas*, p. 99). No doubt Andrews would be there and we know that he was in full sympathy with that particular policy. But it was much more for his affection and encouragement in times of suffering and crisis that Andrews's personal presence was desired by Gandhi and his support valued. His home in India—in so far as this wanderer can be said to have had a home there or anywhere—was at Santiniketan, but when a cry for help came to him from Gandhi he never failed to respond. "This was especially the case," he says, "when he [Gandhi] had any dangerous illness. On two such occasions—in the year 1918 and in 1924—I was with him night and day while he was very near death" (*op. cit.*, p. 18). In 1924 he was with him both while recovering from the operation that he had to undergo while he was in prison in Poona and also when, later in the year, he undertook a twenty-one days' fast at Delhi, "as an act of penance on behalf of the sins and infirmities of his own people." The special sin for which the Mahatma undertook this act of vicarious suffering was that of Hindu-Muslim antagonism and for a while it seemed as if this heroic effort at conciliation might succeed. But the high hopes that were at first aroused were not fulfilled. "Evils," Andrews writes, "that are centuries old cannot altogether be overcome by a single act" (*op. cit.,* p. 319). That fatal fissure within the unity of the life of India remains unhealed, and still prevents her full attainment of the status of a free nation.

Again when Gandhi went to London in September, 1930, for one more of the efforts to bring about a solution of the Indian problem, Andrews was there with him, acting we may say, as a liaison officer between the two lands both of which he loved and whose reconciliation he so much desired. Once more there was failure. But though the same failure has been repeatedly experienced since then, Andrews as long as he lived neither slackened his efforts in the cause of India nor weakened in his confidence in the achievement of the aims that for him were embodied in the'person of Mohandas Gandhi. Gandhi tells us that he said to him on the bed from which he was never to rise, "Mohan, *swaraj* is coming."

In the last years before the end came to his long campaign Andrews was more in England and less in India than he had been in the preceding twenty years. In one of the books of devotion that in these later years occupied his attention alongside of the cause of India he can still bear witness to the nearness to his heart of Gandhi and what Gandhi represented. "Mahatma Gandhi though absent in India," he writes in the preface to his book *Christ in the Silence,* "has been very near in spirit to me, both by his letters and personal friendship. He has interpreted, through his actions, much that I have tried to write about at first hand in this task. For in ways often difficult to understand but amazing in their supreme sacrifice he has shown me the meaning of that 'greater love' whereof Christ speaks, when a man lays down his life for his friend." There could hardly be a greater tribute than that to this friendship which bound Andrews not only to Gandhi but also to the cause of liberty and peace, of Ahimsa and Satyagraha, which in his eyes Gandhi so supremely represented.

Gandhi evidently hoped that what he calls "Andrews's legacy" might be a renewed effort to reconcile India and England. "Not one of the heroic deeds of Andrews," he wrote after his death, "will be forgotten so long as England

and India live. If we really love Andrews's memory we may not have hate in us for Englishmen of whom Andrews was among the best and noblest. It is possible, quite possible, for the best Englishmen and the best Indians to meet together and never to separate till they have evolved a formula acceptable to both. The legacy left by Andrews is worth the effort. That is the thought that rules me whilst I contemplate the divine face of Andrews and what innumerable deeds of love he performed so that India may take her independent place among the nations of the earth" (*Harijan*, April 19, 1940).

✥

But Gandhi's great gift to Andrews of his friendship and the contagion of his passionate purpose in the service of India must not stand by itself as interpreting Andrews's secret to us. There must be placed beside it the great debt —complementary in large measure to the other—that he owed to Rabindranath Tagore. One sometimes asks oneself the question, To which was he indebted most? But perhaps Andrews himself could not have answered. Each contributed something to him that he needed and that he valued greatly: the one what we may describe in Andrews's own words as "that stress upon action that comes from crisis"; the other the need for peace, the peace of Santiniketan, the Abode of Peace. He loved them both, but of Tagore he always speaks, not with love alone but with reverence.

Between these two friends of Andrews there was a contrast that was superficial but at the same time deeply significant. The fundamental harmony that overcame the discords was due to their common devotion to India and to the heritage of Hindu culture which they possessed so fully and valued so highly. But their homes were separated by the whole breadth of India and they spoke different languages. The one, Tagore, was an internationalist and a humanist; the other, Gandhi, was a nationalist, not in the sense of having any antagonism to other nations, but in that of what he called *Swadeshi* ("I confine my attention to the land of my birth"), and he was also an ascetic. Gandhi again must be described as a politician, while Tagore writes of himself,

"I pray that I may never die a patriot or a politician but as a free spirit; not as a journalist but as a poet" (*Letters from a Friend,* p. 168).

One could go on accumulating antitheses in regard to the two men and yet at the end we would have to admit that their agreement was nearer to the truth about them than their divergence, the essential harmony than their superficial discord. Between them they go far to represent the real unity that behind all differences makes India one nation. Andrews was fortunate in having grappled so close to himself two such representatives of India's infinite variety.

Tagore had his spiritual descent from Raja Ram Mohan Roy, that great herald of the dawn in India of whom Indians, looking back to his shining figure leading his people forward in the early years of the nineteenth century, could fitly say in the words of Emerson, "He first cut the cable and gave us a chance at the dangers and the glories of blue water." His father, Devendranath Tagore, the *Maharshi* or "Great Sage" as he was called, has a place only less significant in India's spiritual emancipation. His autobiography Evelyn Underhill ranks with "the few classic autobiographies bequeathed to us by certain of the mystics and saints." His son, Satyendranath, describes it in his introduction as "a record of the struggle of a soul striving to rise from empty idolatrous ceremonial to the true worship of the living God." The Maharshi was an Indian theist and could say, "The Nirvana-salvation of the Upanishads did not find a place in my heart" (*The Autobiography of Maharshi Devendranath Tagore,* p. 165). "Seekers after God," he says in another place, "must realize Brahma in these three places. They must see Him within, see Him without and see Him in the abode of Brahma where he exists in Himself. When we see Him within our soul we say, 'Thou art the innermost soul of the soul; thou art my Father, thou art my Friend, thou art my Comrade.' When we see Him without us we say, 'Thy royal throne is in the infinite sky.' When we see Him in Himself, see the supreme Truth in His own sanctuary, then we say, 'Thou art in thine own Self supreme Goodness and Peace; One without a second'" (*op. cit.,* p. 150).

That was the heritage into which Rabindranath Tagore entered, which helped to make him the poet and the deeply religious man that Andrews revered and loved. He could not but be a world citizen but he lived in an age of nationalism when love for his own land and people seemed of necessity to set him at variance with many who passed India by or despised her. In his letters the resentment that this arouses is constantly being expressed. "Ram Mohan Roy," he writes in a letter to Andrews from New York, "was the first great man in our age who had the profound faith and large vision to feel in his heart the unity of soul between the East and the West. I follow him though he is practically rejected by my countrymen" (*Letters to a Friend*, p. 109). One of the minor conflicts and irritations that arose between Tagore and Gandhi was caused by Gandhi's depreciation of Ram Mohan Roy as "a pigmy" compared with the more "swadeshi" saints Kabir and Nanak, who owed nothing to the West. "If he is not understood by modern India," Tagore sorrowfully recognized, "this only shows that the pure light of her own truth has been obscured for the moment by the storm-clouds of passion." "The idea of non-co-operation unnecessarily hurts that truth. It is not our hearth-fire but the fire that burns out our hearth and home" (*op. cit.*, pp. 165, 163).

Thus there was a deep division in his soul, a wound that could not be healed and that carried continual pain into his heart. He could not "tune his mood of mind to be in accord with the feeling of excitement sweeping across the country." A voice says to him, "Your place is on the 'seashore of worlds' with children; there is your peace and I am with you there." He can recognize the value of what Gandhi was doing, "calling up the immense power of the meek that has been waiting in the heart of the destitute and insulted humanity of India" (*op. cit.*, pp. 129, 128). He recognized its value and its necessity but he had to remain outside of it all.

So he does not appear to a reader of the *Letters to a Friend* as he appeared to that friend himself, the messenger of peace, the dispenser of "calm wisdom." The same disquiet sounds through these letters as we hear in Amiel's *Journal*, and behind what we may in both cases describe as this buddhistic undernote of restlessness there is a deep longing for peace, but seldom, except in nostalgic memory, its attainment. He calls it the shadow of his own egotism, and the psychological insight of many of his spiritual ancestors among the poet saints of India diagnosed in themselves the same disease. When Andrews speaks of "his serene and beautiful spirit" we must suppose that in Santiniketan the peace they both so often longed for indeed abode, but we find it easier to recognize Tagore's chief role in Andrews's description of him as "the great Sentinel on guard for the integrity of his country."

We can see Andrews turning from one to another of these two men, entering with full understanding into the spirit of each and seeking to hold together the two halves of truth that between them they represent. He found the harmonizing element in "the universal principle of Ahimsa" to which both these great Indians equally adhered, and which Gandhi sought to keep at the centre of the national movement. The difference between them in temperament and outlook, that he was constantly seeking to harmonize for the good of the India they both desired so much to serve, evidently had a great, and sometimes a painful interest for him. In *Mahatma Gandhi's Ideas* (p. 343) he quotes a suggestion of Romain Rolland that Tagore is the Plato of our time and Gandhi the St. Paul. With the second parallel he is in agreement to this extent, that Gandhi experienced "a great upheaval of conscience such as we imply by the word conversion," and further that Gandhi had a strong sense of sin and could cry like the Apostle, "Unhappy man that I am, who shall deliver me from the body of this death?" The parallel between Tagore and Plato evidently appeared to him to be nearer the truth, for, he says, "there is in Tagore all the catholicity and the passionate love of ideal, spiritual beauty which the name of Plato connotes." He goes on: "There is much more also: and I have seen in Tagore that which his own wonderful countenance portrays, the serenity which is found in the Gospel picture of Christ. No one has taught me more of that

divine character than Rabindranath Tagore has done by his
own life and example."

Quite evidently, as has been already suggested, Tagore in
Andrews's eyes stood for serenity and peace and his home,
Santiniketan, beckoned to him from across the seas as indeed
the Abode of Peace. But to read Tagore's letters to Andrews
and Pearson hardly confirms this view of him. We see him
there on almost every page as a man deeply divided in spirit
by a conflict that his time and its problems had created
within him. "My India," he writes to Andrews, "is an idea,
not a geographical expression. Therefore I am not a patriot
—I shall ever seek my compatriots all over the world. You
are one of them and I am sure that there are many others.
My solitary cell is awaiting me in my motherland. In their
present state of mind they will have no patience with me
who believe God to be higher than my country" (*Letters to
a Friend*, p. 123). So it is he rather than Gandhi who cries,
"Unhappy man that I am," and who, in the spirit of St. Paul,
could even say, "My heart's desire and prayer to God for
India is that she may be saved," or, as he would rather put
it, "that she may understand the true meaning of emancipation."

❧

It would be foolish to attempt to assess the value of the
contribution that each of these two remarkable personalities
made to Andrews's understanding of India and to his vivid
appreciation of her distresses and her demands. He rejoiced
in what each gave him, and through their friendship he
found a way that led him into a deep intimacy with the
essential spirit of their people and made it possible for him
to help them as no other foreigner could. With Tagore as
with Gandhi the acknowledgement of what Andrews did for
him personally, as well as for his people, is grateful and sincere. In his preface to Andrews's posthumously published
little book *The Sermon on the Mount*, he pays noble tribute
to what he owed to his friend whose love, he says, "I believe
to have been the highest blessing of my life." "Such a rare
companionship of soul was a gift of God beyond all price.

No lesser explanation on the human plane will suffice to account for it. In it there was no taint of selfishness, no stain of ambition, only a simple-minded offering of the spirit to its Lord. The question in the Kena Upanishad came into my mind unbidden: 'By whose grace was this soul sent to me, in what secret is rooted its life?' "

And what Andrews was to this great representative of India he was towards the whole of the people of the land. "He did not," Tagore goes on, "pay his respects to India from a distance with detached and calculated prudence. He threw in his lot without reserve in gracious courtesy with the ordinary folk of this land." In the realization and acceptance of all that this involved for him, an Englishman, he showed, Tagore goes on, "the moral strength and purity of his love. . . . He came to live with us in our joys and sorrows, our triumphs and misfortunes, identifying himself with a defeated and humiliated people." Andrews tell us in another of his books how that epithet of "a defeated people" hurt the sensitive nature of the poet when, on the occasion of a visit of Tagore to Japan, the Japanese newspapers warned their country against this "prophet of a defeated nation." They had discovered that his mind was not racial and national like theirs, and that he hated war.

There were many others who were similarly bruised and humiliated among the people of India and to them the sympathy and understanding that Andrews's sensitive spirit was always able to supply brought consolation and strength for which they were deeply grateful. There may not have been many in India who were quite as sensitive as Tagore, but one such writes in his autobiography of what Andrews did for him. Jawaharlal Nehru does not seem to have been among his most intimate friends, but he tells us how moved he was by Andrews's "imaginative insight into the mind and heart of a hurt and helpless people." In a pamphlet that Andrews had published in 1920, called *Independence—the Immediate Need*, Nehru found, he tells us, "the feeling of the humiliation of India, a fierce desire to be rid of it and to put an end to our continuous degradation." "It was wonderful that C. F. Andrews, a foreigner and one that belonged to the dominant race in India, should echo that cry of our inmost being."

"Andrews," Nehru goes on, "had written that the only way of self-recovery was through some vital upheaval from within. The explosive force needed for such an upheaval must be generated within the soul of India itself. . . . It was with the intense joy of mental and spiritual deliverance from an intolerable burden that I watched the actual outbreak of such an inner explosive force as that which actually occurred when Mahatma Gandhi spoke to the heart of India the *mantram* [3] 'Be free! Be slaves no more!' and the heart of India responded."

The succour and strength that Andrews brought to the Indian people by his identification of himself with their cause is manifest in such testimonies as these in which Tagore and Nehru tell with deep feeling of what Andrews's life with and for them achieved. It was something imponderable that he bestowed on India but it was none the less rare and precious on that account, and it was given quite simply, as Tagore declares, by means of "his rare gift of spontaneous, universal friendship."

3

WE HAVE SEEN already from many instances how much the sorrows of India, and—more than anything else because it lay at the root of so many of these sorrows—its poverty, lay heavy upon Andrews's heart, as it did upon the hearts of his two friends, Gandhi and Tagore. Because so many in India saw that that was so, it came about that everywhere he became known as *Dinbandhu*. The title means "Brother of the Poor" or "of the Humble." In either sense the name could fitly be applied, but it is true that for him as for Mahatma Gandhi the poverty of India in the simple sense of the physical hunger of so many multitudes of

---

[3] That is, we may say, "the word of power."

its people is a basal fact in the appeal that India makes to them. Andrews was *Dinbandhu* in the literal sense of his willingness as a brother to share in the poverty of India's poor. So it also was with Gandhi. Whatever we may think of the economic value of his emphasis on the *charka* or hand spinning-wheel and upon hand-spun and hand-woven cloth, we cannot deny that in making them the symbols of his crusade he is placing at its centre what is India's central problem, the relief of the poverty of her peasantry. Andrews in an editorial in *Young India* makes this statement: "If the question is asked, What is the sum and substance of the charge which Mahatma Gandhi laid against the British government in India? it may be summed up in a single phrase. He charged them with the oppression of the poor." If that is considered too severe a charge to bring against a government that has done so much for India we may accept instead the much more moderate statement of the Viceroy, Lord Wavell, in his first address to the central legislature at Delhi: "We must lift the poor man of India," he said, "from poverty to security, from ill health to vigour, from ignorance to understanding, and our rate of progress must no longer be at the bullock-cart standard, but at least at the pace of the handy and serviceable jeep." Does not this imply a judgement upon past neglect?

But this Brother of the Poor was not content to limit his responsibility to bringing charges against the government of neglect of its duty of taking measures to relieve the physical poverty of India. He interpreted the word and his duty in a wider sense. Wherever he found Indians—for Indians had a special claim upon his sense of brotherhood—in any condition of distress that he could do anything to relieve, he placed himself at their disposal. We have seen how the first challenge of this kind that came to him was that which confronted him when he went to South Africa to stand by Gandhi in his championship of the indentured Indians there. "When Gandhi began his struggle in South Africa," Andrews tells us, "he found the name of India so sunk in public estimation that he himself and all his companions were commonly called 'coolies' even by men of education like General Botha. Within twenty-three years he raised the name of India to such a moral height that he left South Africa amid the generous farewells of Europeans who expressed their deep respect for him and his compatriots" (*Mahatma Gandhi's Ideas*, p. 293). A similar vindication of the rights and the reputation of other Indians overseas was now to be one of Andrews's first duties and one which was to occupy much of his time and strength during the rest of his life.

What the evil of indenture was may best be summed up in the measured words in which G. K. Gokhale described it in a speech to the Imperial Legislative Council of India denouncing the system: [1]

"Under this system those who are recruited bind themselves, first, to go to a distant and unknown land, the language and usages of which they do not know and where they have no friends or relatives. Secondly, they bind themselves to work there for any employer to whom they may be allotted, whom they do not know and who does not know them, and in whose choice they have no voice. Thirdly, they bind themselves to live there on the estate of the employer, they must not go anywhere without a written permit, and must do whatever tasks are assigned to them, no matter how irksome these tasks may be. Fourthly, the binding is for a certain fixed period, usually five years, during which time they cannot voluntarily withdraw from their contract and have no method of escaping from its hardships, however intolerable. Fifthly, they bind themselves to work during the period for a fixed wage which invariably is lower, and in some cases very much lower, than the wage paid to free labour around them. And sixthly and lastly, and this is to my mind the worst feature of the system, they are placed under a special law never explained to them before they left the country, and which is in a language which they do not understand, and which imposes on them a criminal liability for the most trivial breaches of the contract, in place of the civil liability which usually attaches to such breaches. Thus they are liable under the law to imprisonment with hard labour, which may extend to two or sometimes to three months, not only for fraud, not only for deception but for negligence, for carelessness, and . . . for even an impertinent word or gesture to the manager or his overseers. . . ."

[1] These passages in Gokhale's speech are taken from Hoyland's *C. F. Andrews*.

Mr. Gokhale goes on to describe how those simple and illiterate people are recruited by "the unscrupulous representations of professional recruiters who are paid so much per head for the labour they supply." He goes on to show in detail the iniquity of the system, the suffering it caused, which is made evident by the numerous suicides of workers, and the degradation it imposed on those subjected to it. He declared that it condemned the indentured labourers to "a life which, if not one of actual slavery was at any rate not far removed from it." He demanded that the government should bring the whole indenture system to an end so far as India was concerned.

That was the conflict in the cause of India in which Gandhi found himself involved in South Africa and it was in the course of that conflict that he discovered and used that weapon of Satyagraha which he was to wield so often in later years in a wider field. There Andrews discovered for himself in association with Gandhi, a mission from which he could not turn aside and a method of fulfilling that mission which he received as "a new religious truth which yet was not new but as old as the everlasting hills." He found in South Africa a way of helping India that led him out in many directions and laid upon him many burdens but that he could rejoice in, for he was throwing in his lot with the down-trodden and despised.

Gandhi was successful in his struggle in behalf of his country and his people and an agreement was arrived at with South Africa in 1914 which vindicated the reputation of Indians from the contempt which the name of "coolie" and the treatment of them as coolies had brought upon them. General Smuts, who came to this agreement with him, recognized Gandhi then and always since then as "a great man, one of the great men of the world, dominated by high spiritual ideals."

This was not, however, the end of the troubles of Indians in South Africa. In his book *What I Owe to Christ* Andrews speaks, apparently in 1932, of his being engaged in writing that book on a ship which was bringing him to South Africa for the seventh time and he adds that East and Central

Africa had become almost as well-known to him as South Africa was. Nor was that his final visit. It was indeed inevitable that he should encounter in Africa challenges that he could not ignore that affected not Indians alone. Africa was the headquarters for the whole world of that race-hatred which Andrews saw threatening to poison the springs of humanity in all the relationships of men. While he defended Indians against its cruelties he found it necessary sometimes to defend Africans against Indians as well. He had to guard against any partisanship in his championship of Indians. Tagore tells how when the Indians in South Africa tried to keep the Kaffirs at a distance and treat them with contempt Andrews could not tolerate this and, in consequence, "the Indians of South Africa once imagined him to be their enemy" (*The Sermon on the Mount*, p. x).

Nevertheless the first claim upon him was that of oppressed Indians wherever they might be, and soon he was on his way on a similar errand to Fiji. Two things in regard to the Indians who had gone under indenture to that colony which he felt demanded investigation without delay were what he calls "the appalling statistics of suicides" among them and the fact that the same moral evils existed there as in Natal but that in Fiji they had gone far deeper. This latter condition was due to the sex-disproportion among them, since not more than forty women were recruited for indenture for every hundred men so recruited.

His first visit was paid in 1915 and a second followed in 1917. The report that he and W. W. Pearson, who accompanied him, submitted after the first visit strongly condemned the indenture system "as leading inevitably to moral degradation." On his second visit he found, he tells us, that the state of things was much worse than before; and an agitation was set on foot in India which aroused strong feeling throughout the country and so impressed the government of India that it accepted the popular will and brought recruiting to an end. On January 1, 1920, this whole system of recruiting Indian labour was finally abolished. A third visit was paid by Andrews to Fiji in 1936, when he was able to judge of the progress made by the Indians who had remained there during the sixteen years that had elapsed since they had been set free from the semi-slavery of indenture. He found that things had gone steadily forward. "In spite of indebtedness," he writes, "in spite of insecurity of tenure, in spite of a thousand other evils, the advance made . . . has meant a triumph of character whose value is very hard to over-estimate; for the change . . . has not only given good economic results; it has also provided a new social structure" (*India and the Pacific,* p. 37). "On all my journeyings among Indians abroad I have never seen such a complete transformation. It reveals a remarkable power of initiative." Even the old religion, he finds, has recovered its vitality, under the guidance of the reforming Arya Samaj and the "family life is being built up again on its old religious foundation."

Perhaps his estimate may be suspected of reflecting his own natural optimism, but he was aware that there remained serious problems to be solved. Are the races to be unified or are the racial boundaries to be kept sacrosanct? How long must the franchise remain as heavily weighted on the side of the European as it now is? He classes the governments of Kenya and Fiji as both forming anomalies in British constitutionalism, with racial supremacy established and the colonial civil service kept racially exclusive as well. These and other problems presented by Indian settlements overseas similar to those found in Fiji are bound up with the major problem of India's own future within or outside of the British Commonwealth of Nations. What Andrews was doing there had its own significance for the solution of that immense problem.

Andrews was fully aware of this, and ends his book, *India and the Pacific,* on this note (p. 214): "The struggle for freedom and independence in India cannot be separated for a moment from the struggle that is always going on in the most distant colony where Indians are domiciled. A victory there is a victory for India itself. A defeat on the other hand, brings with it the deepest sense of humiliation." His hope in regard to this colony, as in regard to every one of the others with whose welfare he identified himself so fully, was that "the freedom that every Englishman has inherited as a birthright" would be handed on to them.

∼✺

If that can be said of a distant outpost such as Fiji, and if the future of the Indians there has importance for India itself and India's future in relation to Great Britain, how much more shall we find this to be the case when we turn ιo Kenya, which is just at India's door. The aim of the English settlers there was, as one of them frankly described it, that "since South Africa has closed the back door into Africa, so that no Indian may enter Durban, in the same manner the British in East Africa must close the front door at Mombasa." They have been successful in establishing a complete colour-bar for the highlands of Kenya, reserving them exclusively for Europeans, but they sought to go further and turn the whole of Kenya into a "white oligarchy."

It was in connection with this struggle that Andrews came to know Kenya so well, for in 1923 intense feeling was aroused in India by a resolution adopted by the Kenya Europeans threatening an armed revolt if the names of the Indian settlers were placed on the voters' roll. In the hope of finding a solution of this dangerous situation a delegation of Indians, headed by the distinguished Liberal, Mr. Srinivasa Sastri, went to London in 1923. Their request for a general electoral roll in Kenya for all persons capable of passing a minimum test of civilization might have been accepted as a just demand by the Colonial Office but in the end white prejudice once more prevailed. The question that then arose is one that is of crucial importance for the future of the British Commonwealth of Nations. Is it to be a commonwealth of free and equal peoples? Or are there to be those within it who on account of their colour are relegated to the position of "second-class citizens" and so to be subjected to the dominance of the members of the white races? It was in connection with this ominous decision in Kenya that Mr. Sastri used the words that are often quoted by Andrews, "If Kenya is lost all is lost." This was, it seemed to him, the "acid test of the British Empire" and it remains so now when the question still hangs in the balance whether or not a free India will enter the British Commonwealth.[2]

At the same time it is right to remind ourselves that an agreement was reached in 1927 between the Union of South Africa and India as to the position of Indians in South Africa. This is the Cape Town Pact, by which "assisted emigration" was to be stimulated by a high bonus but to remain entirely voluntary, that in the case of Africa-born Indians who insisted on making South Africa their own country the Union government pledged itself to assist them in every way to attain the white standard of life in the Union. The significance of this compromise agreement—unsatisfactory as it is—is all the greater when we remember that it was negotiated on the one side by General Hertzog, "an extreme Boer nationalist," and on the other by Mr. Srinivasa Sastri, an Indian of great distinction and high culture. Mr. Sastri, we are told, captivated the Hertzog cabinet and a sequel to this achievement of his statesmanship was that he returned to South Africa, at the request of the Viceroy, Lord Irwin, and of Mahatma Gandhi, as the first "Agent" of the Indian government in that country. The "coolie" nation had to this extent at least been vindicated. It was not long, however, before it became evident that trouble was brewing again in South Africa, and Andrews in the last months of his life felt grave anxiety as to the future of Indians there.

There remains at the same time the danger, not yet by any means averted, that in British East Africa the principle of racial equality will be openly abandoned as it has been in South Africa. In Andrews's opinion the racial segregation of the Kenya highlands for European occupation, outside the townships, is "the worst blow that has been dealt against equal racial treatment for the colonies for a whole century."

His visits to colonies where "ex-indenture" Indians were to be found reveal his readiness to put himself to any inconvenience in their cause and demonstrate how fully he earned the title "Brother of the Poor." British Guiana, Trinidad, Jamaica, Mauritius, were among these. He tells us that half the population of Trinidad and British Guiana came origin-

[2] H. C. E. Zacharias, *Renascent India*, pp. 226 ff.

ally from India. The question arises in regard to such groups
whether they should continue to look to India as their home
and turn to it in any time of distress for help, or should
rather make a wholly new life for themselves where they
have cast their lot. Thus in his report on his visit to British
Guiana, Andrews tells how he found the Indians there suffering from a period of economic depression, with the result
that their thoughts turned back to India and they desired
to return there. Andrews had to tell them that Indian
living conditions were on the whole even worse than those
they were passing through and that at Calcutta he had found
"a mass of stranded repatriates who were only too anxious
to come back again to Demerara." In spite of this warning,
he says, "the cry went on that it was better to die in India
than to die in Demerara."

Andrews's account of his visit to British Guiana reveals
how much hardship has to be undergone from time to time
by colonies like this which suffer from periodical vicissitudes
in their fortunes, and how much need there is that, as is now
being realized in some measure in Great Britain, much more
must be done than has been done in the past to assist those
who have settled in these lands to achieve and to maintain a
more satisfying life. Andrews also gives a grave warning of
the consequences in such a colony as British Guiana of injustice that has been done to Indians elsewhere. "It is absolutely true to say . . . that Kenya and Natal have 'fouled
the pitch' for Demerara." He concludes his report with the
words, "When people leave their mother country to come
abroad and make great sacrifices of habit and tradition in
order to do so, it should at least be accepted as an axiom
that the material conditions to which they come by immi-
gration are superior to those they left behind in their mother
country."

But it was not only Indians overseas whose conditions outraged Andrews's sense of justice and touched his compassionate heart. They were often, indeed, as in the case of the settlers in British Guiana, better off materially than their fellow

countrymen in India. It was the political injustice inflicted
upon a people who were looked down upon as uncivilized
and degraded, rather than their poverty in the literal sense
of the word, that moved him to champion their cause. He
never forgot that in taking the side of Indians unjustly deprived of their rights as well as of their good name he was
at the same time vindicating the liberal traditions of his own
land and maintaining its honour. In the case of "the poor"
within India's own borders the case is in some respects different. They too, in common with all the Indian people
whether they are at home or abroad, have certain rights that
they demand and certain wrongs that have been inflicted
upon them, but in their case the source from which their
poverty comes is more complicated than with those who have
gone to seek their fortunes overseas. We have accordingly
to look more closely at their woes and the causes of them.

That India suffers tragically from economic poverty is a
fact beyond argument. That "India—along with China which
is almost on the same level—is by all reckoning the poorest
country in the world" and that its poverty "to-day seems to
be increasing," Andrews affirms without any qualification:
but we cannot accept a generalization as a fact when we have
not sufficient data either to affirm or to deny. It remains
unquestionably true, nevertheless, that India's poverty is
extreme, that it is the basal fact of the human problem of
its people, and that far more than has been done could be
done and should be done to remedy it. That statement
applies not only to the evils that come directly from undernourishment but also to those that are caused by diseases
due to undernourishment or aggravated by it. These sorrows
of the land may be said to be in part inflicted by man and
in part by nature. Such a famine as that which has caused so
much death and destruction in Bengal recently was due, as
we can say without hesitation, to both of these causes un-
happily coming together at a tragic moment in India's history. There are other catastrophes, such as earthquake and
floods, that come with no human cause at work that we can
discern, while others again are the results entirely of human
cruelty and crime. All of these causes of suffering operate in

India and of them all Andrews was well aware, and of the suffering that they brought upon the innocent as well as upon the guilty.

In the case of some of the worst of the evils that afflict India Andrews did not feel called to deal as directly or to assign blame for them as outspokenly as he did in the case of others. These were the evils that India's own people have inflicted, evils springing from old and warped traditions or religious beliefs that are wrong or have been perverted. Some evils, for example, spring from the very Ahimsa—the "non-injury"—that, as interpreted by Gandhi, Andrews saw to be so noble. But when Gandhi, untrue to this partial truth when a higher truth guided him, put an end painlessly to the misery of a poor calf, a leader of Hindu orthodoxy threatened to shoot him. Andrews recognizes that an example emerges here of a problem that needs a higher wisdom than Hindu orthodoxy for its solution, and so he touches only lightly upon it. Gandhi had a full right to go further in vindicating a true Ahimsa than anyone not born a Hindu could, but he feels himself helpless before the spectacle of the holocausts of sheep and lambs slain for sacrifice at Kalighat in Calcutta. "I must go through more self-purification and sacrifice," he writes, "before I can hope to save these lambs from that unholy sacrifice. It is my constant prayer that there may be born on earth some great spirit, man or woman, who will deliver us from this heinous sin" (Gandhi, *My Experiments with Truth*, Vol. I, p. 548).

The case is similar with the evils that spring from the ancient and intolerable wrong of "untouchability." These evils must be condemned—as Andrews condemns them—and must be cured, but on the whole he himself leaves such evils alone in the belief that an India now awakened, or awakening, will itself carry through their cure. He recognizes how Christian missions in the past "rescued many thousands of these depressed classes from a life-long degradation that had sunk almost below the human level." "But," he goes on, "things have now entirely changed. Hinduism with inner faith and hope and courage is reforming itself. . . . The whole outlook has changed radically from what it was a century or even sixty years ago" (*The True India*, p. 148).

This tremendous problem, with the consequences that any real solution of it would bring to the unhappy people involved as well as to the reputation of India in the eyes of the world, probably weighed more heavily on his heart than any other of the woes of India. That this was so, and that he was aware that he could not take any effective part in bringing about that solution, is evident from a remarkable letter that he wrote to Gandhi in May, 1933. Gandhi was in prison at the time and had announced a twenty-one days' fast which was to be "a heart prayer for purification of myself and my associates for greater vigilance and watchfulness in connection with the Harijan ['untouchable'] cause." With this fast and its object Andrews was in entire sympathy and he wrote to Gandhi from England this very significant letter to say so. Then he goes on:

> "Haven't you been trying to serve two masters and if you have given your life as a hostage for 'untouchability removal' does not that mean entire concentration on that issue for the whole remainder of your life without turning to the right or to the left?
> "I want to work that out and 'think aloud' as you rightly put it. You staked your life itself on this one issue—removal of this curse. Can you now go and use that life in other secondary issues? I want you to answer that question. I am quite unworthy even to put it, because I haven't risked my life at all and am living here in comparative ease. . . .
> "You may say—and it may be right—that without Purna Swaraj [complete independence] you will always be blocked on this very question by some obstruction from an alien government. I can understand that argument. . . . But there is another moral argument that you have used again and again. It is this: 'We are not fit to attain Purna Swaraj while we go on treating our Harijan brothers and sisters like this.' You have all the moral force behind you if you are led to take this course—to say to the world, 'My life is now entirely a hostage for the Harijans.' "

Gandhi's reply need not be given with any fullness; we are not concerned with him except in relation to Andrews, whose plea he puts aside on the ground that his life "is an indivisible whole." "I can't devote myself entirely to untouchability and say, 'Neglect Hindu-Muslim unity or Swaraj.' All these things run into one another and are interdependent." But it seems plain that Andrews was afraid that, as another great Indian, Swami Vivekananda, once confessed of himself, "I have become entangled," so it was with Gandhi. Politics had drawn him aside from what should have wholly absorbed him. Andrews, so far as we know, acquiesced in Gandhi's decision and put aside his doubts; but it is significant that he had doubts. His opinion quoted above that the whole outlook on untouchability had changed was certainly too optimistic. Immense difficulties had to be overcome and no one was equipped as Gandhi was to overcome them.

The entire removal of this blot from Indian life in the course of the present generation—which, he says, is the aim of educated India—would indeed be a miracle, as he recognizes; but, he adds, it is not impossible. Gandhi's example in this matter is visible to all India and it may work that miracle. Certainly every Christian who seeks the good of India will desire that this end may come and come speedily, and every Christian ought, as Andrews urges, "to welcome this advance from within Hinduism as a true movement of the Spirit of the living God" (*op. cit.*, p. 148). But Andrews's hopes for an advance from within Hinduism need not have prohibited him, or anyone who shares his desire for India's welfare, from helping up from the depths these submerged and outraged millions, in the name and by the power of Christ.

Concerning another indigenous evil, child marriage and the tragic consequences that follow, Andrews also makes his position quite clear. He stands side by side with India, seeking to divest himself of his foreignness and yet aware at the same time that he cannot wholly do so. Just because he is a foreigner, when he deals with evils that the people of India have themselves created, he cannot speak to them as frankly as Gandhi, for example, does. He tries to see, and does see, the explanations and extenuations that we ought to take into account when we blame them. We must remember, for example, that one cause of a high mortality in maternity cases is "the grinding poverty of the poor."

"I can well understand," he says, dealing with this subject, "that I am risking the inference being left by my words, that I am making light of acute human suffering of a very unbearable kind and taking the sting out of the stern warnings which nature gives, so that they fail to have their full effect · of goading the public conscience of India into concerted action. . . . But to goad the public conscience effectively is like an act of surgery. And surgery needs a very skilful hand. . . . Nothing in the world does more harm than to wound sensitive public feeling by harsh incisions made in wrong places" (*op. cit.,* p. 125).

We must, we recognize, tread gently when we approach such ancient wrongs, and realize our own unrepented sins. Andrews has a chapter in *Mahatma Gandhi's Ideas* on "untouchability" to which he gives the title "Our Shame and Theirs." The phrase is Gandhi's and has reference to his sense of India's humiliation in the presence of that evil. Andrews in this chapter deliberately set side by side as similar, and as being India's shame on the one hand and our shame on the other, "the caste feeling in India and the race prejudice in South Africa." We shall deal later with the shame that Andrews felt when he realized in South Africa that this race-prejudice had even become embedded in the Church at its very centre.

❧

Something must now be said of how Andrews sought to help those suffering from such calamities as earthquakes and floods, and from the consequences that come from men's hostility and suspicion as we find them at work among the hilltribes of the North-West Frontier of India. These will have to suffice as illustrating how he responded to many other demands upon his sympathy and help.

Earthquakes and floods are not infrequent in India but the earthquake of which Andrews wrote a brief account was of exceptional severity and destructiveness. The number of deaths that it caused, actually accounted for and recorded,

according to the official figures, was over 10,000. A leading
Indian who took a large part in the organization of relief
considered that the number could hardly be less than 20,000.
It took place in North Bihar in January, 1934. Andrews was
in London at the time but he did all that he could to make
the calamity and its gravity known and to secure funds for
the relief of the extreme necessity of a peasantry always living on the verge of destitution. Miss Agatha Harrison, who
visited the stricken area with Gandhi, reports a striking estimate of the severity of the situation as she saw it: "It was said
that the poverty of the men and women was at zero; the
earthquake had divided this by ten."

As Andrews was not able to arrive till late in the year he
had no actual experience of the famine that followed, and
his help was mostly given from a distance. Even when he
arrived, to find that an abnormally heavy monsoon had
caused further miseries, his own ill-health limited the personal help he was able to render. He bears witness, however,
to the fact that the desperate human need for a time at least
overcame the dissensions that at other times caused in this
province so much strife and division. Gandhi, Miss Harrison
reports in a letter to Andrews, "Never commiserated with
them in their misery. He presented them with a challenge:
'What has this calamity taught you? This is no time for differences between Congress and Government, between Touch-
able and Untouchable'." And in some measure at least this
unity was achieved.

Another seemingly intractable evil, due in this case to
human factors and not to the forces of nature, has long confronted India, and of it and Andrews's attitude to it something must be said. This is what, in the title of a book published by him in 1937, he calls *The Challenge of the North-
West Frontier*. He describes the solution that he proposes in
that book as "a contribution to world peace." He felt, it is
evident, the urgent pressure of this subject on his heart and
conscience because of the new method of dealing with frontier raids that the government of India had recently adopted.
This consisted in the bombing of frontier villages from the
air. The sharp controversy that had been aroused in India

in consequence of the adoption of this method, and the resentment that the allegation of the bombing of women and
children created, had some effect on the government, causing
it to consider how retaliatory methods of repression could be
modified and remedial methods adopted instead. These criticisms came to a head when the subject was debated in the
Legislative Assembly in 1935.

Events that have happened since then in the second world
war, the hideous devastation that has been caused by the
bombing of cities, increase the urgency of the whole problem
here involved and justify more than ever the sombre antici-
pations of Andrews. He reminds us that the action of the
British government at the Air Disarmament Conference in
1933 in demanding that "air-bombing for police purposes in
certain outlying districts" should be exempted from abolition, had "blocked," as he alleges, the efforts of the conference in the cause of peace and deprived Great Britain of the
moral initiative that she had previously held in that cause.
In the Spanish civil war, "the murderous horror of the in-
cendiary bomb shocked the civilized world," and we know
how all that has happened since has deepened this horror.
Perhaps the civilized world is by this time benumbed, but
no one can put a limit to the ruin that threatens the whole
world if the methods that were made use of on the Indian
frontier, with the utmost moderation and for the ends of
justice and the prevention of greater evils, were to become—
as they have become—the instruments of unrestrained violence and passion. If it be indeed true that, as H. M. Tom-
linson, whom Andrews quotes, affirms, we threw away the
opportunity of preventing such a menace as this has proved
to be "because we required a few bombers for a private purpose among hills so remote that most of us do not know
exactly where they are," then we may well deplore the limitations of human foresight.

Another aspect of the situation on the Indian frontier that
influenced Andrews greatly in setting forth his plan in 1937
was his confidence in the pacific disposition of the chief
frontier leader at that time, Khan Abdul Ghaffar Khan, and
the influence that he believed that Gandhi and his principle

of Ahimsa had upon him. "Of one thing," Andrews writes, "I can speak with certainty at first hand, namely about the character of Khan Abdul Ghaffar Khan himself." "To find a Pathan leader," he says again, "practising Ahimsa or Non-Violence, enjoining it upon his followers and implicitly taking instructions from Mahatma Gandhi, reads almost like a legend or romance, but in reality it is a solid fact in modern Indian history." The "Frontier Gandhi" as this remarkable man has been called, declares in the strongest terms his devotion to non-violence. "I want the Pathan," he says, "to do to others as he would like to be done by. It may be I may fail and a wave of violence may sweep over my province. I shall then be content to take the verdict of fate against me" (*The Challenge of the North-West Frontier*, pp. 80, 84).

One cannot help suspecting that Andrews here, as in other instances that we have noted, may be too sanguine in his estimate of the possibility of so speedy a change, that mankind "of ancient crooked will" cannot be transformed all at once by the presentation to them of an ideal, however lofty. He wants that the traditional line of thought which India has inherited and can still reproduce should have full freedom of development in public policy. Khan Abdul Ghaffar Khan himself—and indeed Andrews also—have doubts of the success of the introduction of a Hindu principle among people so different from the Hindus as the Pathans of the frontier are. We are told that even the adherence of the North-West Frontier province to the Congress policy for India shows signs in the last year or two of weakening. Abdul Ghaffar is no longer a leading member of the Congress and his brother, who has succeeded him on the Congress working committee, has probably less influence over his fellow Muslims. Congress control of the Frontier Province seems now to be definitely interrupted.

Thus it is possible that Andrews's confidence in the possibility of applying Ahimsa to this province by the action of the Muslim people would not be confirmed by events. That does not, however, affect the validity of the policy that he presses upon the government of India. He links up his plan with his claim that India should be free to govern herself, and the question as to how in these circumstances the frontier is to be controlled would be a question for the independent Indian government to decide for itself, and such a government may not feel that the method of Ahimsa is applicable there. Andrews himself admits that there may be something to be said for approving even the policy of "police bombing" in very exceptional circumstances when peaceable methods had been tried and police work was found to be necessary.

Apart from this, however, the general policy of bringing such an area under humane and enlightened administration and endeavouring to win the goodwill of the inhabitants is what Andrews is here urging upon the attention of those, whoever they may be, British or Indian, who are responsible for the government of this area. Whether that policy is called by such a name as Ahimsa or by any other name, a measure of persuasion is surely better than one of brute force, and one that remedies abuses than one of retaliation. The present government of India has always recognized this, though it has pursued its aim at too slow a pace and with too little steadfastness of purpose. Andrews in advocating "a revised frontier policy" reminds us that this trouble is one that is not found on the Indian frontier alone, that it has yielded elsewhere to economic measures freeing people in similar circumstances from a life of poverty and enabling them to obtain a better living from their barren soil. He cites as a single example of the influence humane and skilled treatment can exercise upon such wild tribesmen the work that Dr. Pennell ("Pennell of the Frontier" as he was called) did among them by means of his hospital at Bannu. He quotes an English colonel, who knew the frontier well, as saying that "to have Dr. Pennell was worth a couple of regiments, so great a peace-maker he had become." He might also have quoted what Sir John Maffey, formerly governor of the Frontier Province, wrote of Mrs. Starr, a nurse in a mission hospital in Peshawar. She went, at the governor's request, unarmed and unprotected, far into the mountains of Tirah: and because she was known for her work all through that turbulent region she was able to do so in perfect safety and to bring back an English girl who had been kidnapped. "By what she did," wrote Sir John, "she made a British mark upon the heart of Tirah that was better than the drums and tramplings of an army corps." It was more than a British mark; it was a Christian mark. A policy inspired by such a spirit as these instances exemplify is the true alternative— whether it be called by the Indian name of Ahimsa or by any other name—to the policy of "police bombing" or of frontier expeditions.

4

THERE STILL remains for examination an aspect of Andrews's life and work which is indicated by the title of "Christ's Faithful Apostle," a title given to him because it fitted his initials and at the same time was true to what he was. By whom the name was first given is not apparently known, but when it was suggested it was at once recognized, not less by non-Christians than by Christians, as entirely appropriate and was frequently cited as such both during his life and after his death. Non-Christians never doubted that this was the fundamental fact in regard to him, explaining all else. It accordingly provides us with an appropriate opportunity of attempting a general appraisal of the abiding value of his life and of measuring it by a standard which he himself would have chosen. From the first day when he set foot on Indian soil, as he himself tells us, a new life began for him, and from then onwards he was a friend of the land and a brother especially of its humble people. But central to all that he was and did, "making it fair and like a lily in bloom," was his Christian faith and his Christian apostolate.

That this is true of him there can be no doubt at all and whoever first gave him this designation described him in a relationship which he sought to have, above all else, as the controlling factor in his whole life and service. In *What I Owe to Christ,* which is certainly the most notable of all his writings and has been recognized as a religious classic, looking back on the time when his life in India was opening before him, he sums up his religious experience. "After thirty years of life spent in the East," he writes (p. 152 *ff.*), "certain great facts in my own religious thinking stand out in the foreground. By far the greatest of these is this—that Christ has become not less central but more central and universal; not less divine to me but more so, because more universally human. I can see him as the pattern of all that is best in Asia as well as in Europe."

At intervals throughout his life when occasion to do so arose he publicly declared anew the central spring of renewal that he had first discovered when he was nineteen years old. Thus in 1927 he wrote at the request of a Japanese newspaper a statement of the faith that had sustained him through the years from that early experience. "Since that time," he says, "during more than forty-three years of incessant struggle, journeying to and fro throughout the world I have never lost the assurance of Christ's living presence with me. . . . He is no imaginative dream but a living Presence." Twelve years later, when his last illness was drawing near, he wrote a little book, *The Sermon on the Mount,* which was published after his death. In it he tells once more of this secret that so long before had first become his possession and that he had so often tested in the strain of living. "Christ has been the living Christ to me ever since and all my deepest thoughts have sprung from him." There could hardly be a more consistent life than that which he lived from that first day to his last.

It is true that a breach occurred in his religious belief and practice which in some degree turned it aside from the course that it had been pursuing, and which to some seemed to mean the actual abandonment of Christianity. Andrews passed during several years through an inner conflict as to his duty to the Church of England, of which he was an ordained minister. The conflict began early in his Indian career. He was himself in those days a high-churchman, but

C. F. ANDREWS

when he realized how such views as that attitude implied "separated him from those he loved in Christ Jesus" and made the deepest Christian fellowship, as represented by the partaking together of the Holy Communion impossible, he felt he could not hold that position any longer. He became aware of other difficulties as well when his friend Sushil Rudra protested against the Thirty-Nine Articles of English churchmen being imposed upon Christians belonging to the Indian tradition. He learned of these differences of outlook through his close friendship with Rudra and by seeing them through his Indian eyes. Again, his new sensitivity to his environment and its claims was further aroused at a Christmas Day service which was overshadowed for him when he heard the children reciting in Urdu the grim clauses of the Athanasian Creed. He was learning the lesson that never ceased to guide him through his Indian life, that he must see and feel through the eyes and the hearts of the Indian people and not remain imprisoned in his Englishness. The sense of his "bondage"—as all this seemed to his friend Rudra— under what in these matters his Church required of him became more and more intolerable. He had not yet, however, reached the stage of active revolt.

That stage was reached later when in South Africa he came face to face with grave evils, especially that of "the colour bar" and of racial discrimination, which he found to be "poisoning the wells of the Christian faith in almost every land abroad, leading irresistibly to a divided Christendom." It was in South Africa, as we have seen, that this became fully realized by him when he saw how Gandhi and others among his Indian friends were refused admission to many of the Christian churches. And yet these "were better Christians than we." "I had to stand on their side and not with those who were keeping alive the spirit of racial and religious exclusion." He wrote in a religious quarterly of his Church protesting against the moral evil that "threatened the Christian brotherhood principle." "The race cleavage," he declared, "has become embedded in the Church at its very centre—in the Sacrament," but his protest hardly stirred an echo in return (*What I Owe to Christ*, pp. 257, 263).

Finally, on his return from South Africa to Santiniketan, "when I saw," he says, "the pure face of the poet looking into mine I knew at once . . . that a final decision had there and then to be made." It was really no hasty step but the conclusion of a long moral struggle that had now lasted for several years. He wrote to his bishop, "telling him simply why I could not any longer conduct the Sunday services at Burdwan." "Since then," he goes on, "I have not taken any ministerial duties under a bishop, feeling that the subscription that I once gave to the Articles and the Book of Common Prayer no longer holds good. But I have remained throughout a communicant at the Anglican communion wherever I have gone" (*op. cit.,* pp. 268-9).

That was written probably in 1932. To complete the story of his emancipation from what he felt to be the bondage of beliefs which he had accepted when he took orders in the Church of England but which he was now no longer able to accept, a passage from an article that appeared in the magazine *Young Men of India,* in May, 1940, must be quoted. The writer tells how a day or two before Andrews underwent the operation which was followed by his death he wrote a letter to a friend in order to remove misunderstanding as to his Christian position and his final attitude to his own Church. In this letter he explained that the matters—or at least some of them—that had raised a difficulty of conscience for him many years before no longer caused such a difficulty because of the revision of the Book of Common Prayer "as now used in India," and in consequence he had been able "to resume the full duties of the Christian ministry."

❦

But whether it was as a priest of the Church of England or as a prophet of the living God that Andrews discharged his ministry no one can deny that he bore the marks, if ever any man did, of a Christian saint. St. Francis Xavier,[1] a forerunner of his in India, along with much that was in strong contrast with what Andrews felt himself called to be and do in India, was in some of his qualities of sainthood strikingly

[1] *The Life of St. Francis Xavier,* by Edith Ann Stewart [Mrs. Robertson].

like his modern successor. "He went barefoot," it is said of St. Francis, "with a poor torn gown. Everyone loved him dearly." We have seen how like Andrews was to that picture. It could as well be said of him as was said of the earlier saint that he was "like a whirlwind of love." We sometimes feel as if no man could love so many with such a warmth of love as he was aware of within his heart. But there are some who, whether by nature or by grace, are furnished with a greater capacity for this divine quality than others, and among those he must take a high place. Continually in India, he tells us, "it is as if I saw Christ in the faces of those I met." We need not try to explain this quality of his saintliness otherwise than by his possession of that insight and the heart to respond to it. It was that quality which, as we have seen, made it possible for him to be so great a friend.

Another of the marks he possessed, identifying him as belonging to the great succession of the Christian saints, was the spirit of joy that accompanied him in all his toils. We have seen how "eager people" came to Andrews asking him for the secret of "his evident joy and gladness." This was a quality that he himself was aware of as welling up within him, and he could have testified with Tertullian that the Holy Spirit is a glad Spirit. He tells us in one place how when the long weariness and strain of watching by the sickbed of an Indian student in Germany ended at last, "after the hurricane had passed over me and the deep waters had wellnigh overwhelmed me, the dear presence of my Lord and Master came like sunshine into my life, filling it once more with gladness" (*Christ in the Silence*, p. 37). It could certainly be said of many young Indians, brooding and unhappy, that they found their way to him, as it is said that St. Francis Xavier's brother Jesuits did to him also, and were made happy again by looking on his face.

There is yet another characteristic of some Christian saints that he possessed and that he shared with this earlier apostle to India. It is said that once Francis was heard in his sleep to cry out "More, more, more," and it was found that in his dreams he had been asking that he might suffer more and yet more for Christ. So it seems to have been with Andrews.

He cannot be described as an ascetic, and in this respect he found himself opposed to Gandhi, especially to Gandhi's emphasis upon celibacy. "The human body," he writes, "to Gandhi is an evil not a good." He notes the difference between him and Tagore in this respect, Tagore affirming in a well-known poem, "Deliverance is not for me in renunciation," while Gandhi is possessed by the negative aspect of sin, "which has to be rooted out by an almost violent self-discipline." The contrast in this respect between the two men is striking and we have seen already how it often caused estrangement. In this matter Andrews was in agreement with Tagore rather than Gandhi. It was not austerity but love that guided him as it guided St. Francis. A sentence from the Sermon on the Mount that meant much to him was the question, τί περισσὸν ποιεῖτε; (Matt. v. 47), which he translates, "What do ye to excess?" Have you given, that is, as he explained it, to the extreme limit of love? He had these words in the Greek original on his study table when he was a student in Cambridge and fifty years later he was asking himself the same question in the last book he wrote. He saw in this "the tremendous test which Christ puts on our allegiance when he tells us, 'For my sake go even to this excess of love, and be prepared even to love your enemies.'" He saw then with clear vision the loftiness of Christianity, how it possessed, as he says in this final utterance of his mind, "a distinctive and precious quality which has made it unique among all the religions of the world." That was the level at which (and he testifies that it was so in his own experience "at periods, however brief") "every exercise and sacrifice of the will appeared to be joyfully possible" (*The Sermon on the Mount,* pp. 135, 136, 137).

These are some of the qualities of Andrews's religion that reveal the sources of energy that lay behind a life so strenuous and so selfless—a life also that drew men to him by its ardour and its attractive power. One other aspect of his religious life, that was written across it all from first to last and that proclaimed past all doubting its sincerity, was the way in which for him belief and action were inseparably bound together. In the preface to *What I Owe to Christ* he states this with an emphasis of strong conviction. "Christ . . . seeks from us deeds not words. Devotion to him is in the first place not sentimental but practical. . . . If [the Christian faith] has no power to restore or recreate the human will leading on to deeds of unselfish service, then it stands self-condemned" (p. 15). Such a passage as this—and all that so fully confirms it in his life—is a sufficient answer to the charge of sentimentalism so often brought against Andrews. Such "theopathic saintliness," as William James describes it,[2] was not his. We have here indeed a feature of the witness that Andrews's life bore to his Christian belief which reached very deep in its significance and spoke to India—indeed, we may say, to the world—with something like apostolic power. It is this element in his influence which might well be called revolutionary, for the need for it is urgent in those who profess the Christian religion and preach it. It was indeed this which once turned the world upside down and which may do so again to-day if Andrews's example is followed.

The unmistakable reality of Andrews's religion and this power that it possessed "to build above the deep intent/The deed, the deed" commended it to those who watched him in India and wherever he went. Gandhi has frequently urged upon Christians, and especially upon Christian missionaries, to refrain from telling India about Christ and instead to live the Christian life; but Andrews, while agreeing with his opinion, did not confine himself too closely within its bounds. He certainly "told" the Christian message by his life in every province of India, and that message was never proclaimed more effectively than it was by him. His theory of leaving the Hindu to his own religion is difficult to reconcile with his affirmations, one of which has just been quoted, of the uniqueness of Christianity among the faiths of the world; and none of his friends, certainly not Gandhi himself, was unaware, when they called him, as they so often did, a true Christian, how high a place they were giving him. This "reality" that spoke so loud in his life, as well as the happiness that accompanied it, and that shone from him, drew to him young people everywhere. His own experience

[2] *Varieties of Religious Experience*, p. 345.

was that "radiance" shone upon him just in proportion as the test of seeking to do God's will in daily life was sincerely applied. So, as we have seen, young people came to him asking him for his secret of joy. He himself sought to appeal to "the energizing joy of youth as a gift gloriously meet for the Master's use." For that reason he was able to remain in close touch with "the young student world" all his life, for he had within himself the life of Him who, as an early Christian document expresses it, "is born at all times young in the hearts of the holy."

In "the young student world" whom he drew to himself and to whom he was drawn irresistibly there was no section that he desired more to serve and whose need of his glad spirit was greater than the students of India. They often asked him of the religious source of the radiance that they saw in him and coveted, and he, we can be quite sure, was never unwilling to tell them in plain words what that source was. He tells us how he found on his return to the West after long absence that "joy had entered into human life once more." He found it "in the Oxford Fellowship, in the World Student Federation, in the youth movements and the colleges of many lands." But there were many sections of youth among whom he must have found that this joy was something passionately desired but not yet attained. That was so at the time of which Andrews was speaking, namely about 1932, among the youth of Germany, and that was, and is so, also among the youth, especially the student youth of India. The causes which brought about this loss of what may be said to be a vital necessity for the young were largely the same in both lands. In 1931 there were in Germany, we are told, "about forty thousand unemployed university people" who, in consequence, could no more look into the future with anything like happiness or confidence. "The same situation had about the same time cast a deep shadow over the lives of the students in the universities of India. And behind that fear there lay in both cases still deeper causes for despair. The young intellectuals of both countries had for years been undergoing a process of disintegration and disillusionment. The past and the present had fallen apart and a chasm had opened between them. Thus they found themselves forlorn individuals in a nation into which they were unable fully to integrate themselves and in which they had little hope of building up such a fellowship as was essential to the fulfilment of their lives. With what that situation has developed into in Germany as a result of the appeals and promises of Hitler we have no concern here, but what young Germany needed and what the Leader who arose among them claimed to give them was what Indian students also needed and still need and in their souls desire. They need "a new conception of their value and of their place both in the cosmic order and in the world around them." [3]

In India not a few of the students who became acquainted with Andrews seem to have turned to him as representing what they felt so deeply that they lacked. His was a manifestly integrated life; fellowship was a precious reality to him and he gave it freely to them out of his abundance. He lived as one who possessed an assurance of "his place in the cosmic order," or—to express it in religious language—of his place in the divine purpose of love, as a member of the family of the divine Father. These religious convictions formed the living spring from which flowed the unfailing happiness and joy that they longed to possess as he possessed it.

Rabindranath Tagore's sensitivity of nature reveals what was felt by so many and he may be taken as representing their spirit—half resentment and half longing—at its finest. We have seen already how deeply hurt he was by the taunt cast at him in Japan of belonging to a defeated nation. The West drew him but he felt himself bound up with the East and sharing its sorrows and its humiliation. "This has been the reason," he said, addressing an audience in London, "why the West has not yet come home to our heart, why we struggle to repudiate her culture. It is because we ourselves are under the dark shadow of her dominance." The conflict, reflected in the clear mirror of Tagore's magnanimous nature, embittered many hearts among the young people of the land. And for them, as even for Tagore himself, Andrews became a symbol of an attainment that seemed, because of

[3] E. Amy Buller, *Darkness over Germany*, p. 158; also p. 119.

their lack of freedom and of the self-respect that accompanied freedom, to be beyond their reach. "There are screens between us," Tagore wrote to his friend, "which have to be removed—possibly they are due to the too great inequality of circumstances and opportunities between the two parties. . . . I cannot tell you how thankful I feel to you, who have made it easier for me to love your people. For your own relationship with India has not been based upon a sense of duty but upon genuine love. It makes me feel sad when I see this lesson of your life being lost—when it fails to inspire our people with the realization that love of humanity is with you far truer than patriotism" (*Letters to a Friend,* pp. 181 *ff.*).

He saw the lesson of Andrews's love being lost because its full depth was not realized. There were screens between them, barriers that the love of a single Englishman could not overcome. The young people he spoke to with such warmth of feeling could not hear all that he had to say because of the tumult of their patriotism in their own ears. As Tagore says in another of his sorrowful surveys of the situation, "The East was not ready to receive the West in all her majesty of soul. We have not seen what was great in the West because we have failed to bring out the great that was in ourselves.[4] Once at Oxford, Andrews tells us—once of many times, it is quite evident—an Indian student asked him what the source was of the spiritual power by which men could sacrifice themselves for others gladly. "I could only tell him," Andrews says, "from my own experience that it was the daily presence of the living Christ claiming them by His love that had wrought this love in return" (*What I Owe to Christ,* p. 305). What more was there to tell? But the chasm remained.

There we see "Christ's Faithful Apostle" seeking to do for the youth of India what has been done elsewhere so tragically amiss, showing to them from his own experience what could transform their dull tasks and could give their little existence a cosmic significance and an eternal destiny. Andrews saw clearly that the political situation in India at

---

[4] Quoted in *India and Britain,* p. 37.

the present thwarts the efforts and blights the hopes of the youth of the land, making their lives dull and insipid and meaningless. That was what made him take up their political cause with such fervour and conviction. On our part the debt of honour that we owed had to be paid and the shadow that darkened the sun for them had to be lifted. He championed the good elements in Hinduism and in Islam—sometimes, perhaps, too blindly—just because religion was bound up with so much that still brought comfort to their lives. But he saw beyond that partial good quite clearly their orphaned condition in a universe that had only a dim and shadowy deity shining bleakly and remote upon them. After telling of the question that the Indian student asked in Oxford and of his answer he goes on to affirm that "human life would sink back incredibly far, beyond all recovery whatsoever if it were not for the supreme miracle of grace that Christ's presence has brought to mankind" (*op. cit.*, p. 307).

This brings us to the duty of examining Andrews's conception of his apostolate or, to put it otherwise, his missionary vocation, and what it involved. Did he put it aside when he surrendered his priestly ministry under a bishop but retained his prophetic ministry as that for which he was "fitted and prepared by God"? We needed, he believed, to become "first-century Christians" once more (*op. cit.*, pp. 270, 209). What did that involve for him in India, as for Albert Schweitzer in Africa, whose example moved him so much? What he says on "proselytizing" and on the relationship to each other of the religions of the world opens up great questions on which Andrews's sincerity and devotion give him a right to speak and which have crucial importance for the Church of Christ. They cannot be dealt with fully here but they cannot be passed by.

For his knowledge of Hinduism Andrews was in the main indebted, it is evident, to his friendship with Mahatma Gandhi and with Rabindranath Tagore. Neither of these could be counted an orthodox Hindu. Gandhi belongs by his family tradition to the *bhakti* or devotional Hinduism of the Vaishnavas, which is a theistic type of Hinduism that has a long history down the centuries. Tagore belonged to the modern eclectic theism of which his father and Raja Ram Mohan Roy were the first architects and which is indebted both to the *bhakti* tradition and to Christianity. It is not necessary to add anything to what has been already said of the lofty religious character of both these men nor to emphasize the fact that in each case the religion is a deeply realized, inward and ethical experience. It would be true also to say that each of them, while—in Gandhi's case certainly and probably also in Tagore's—claiming to be a Hindu, was a quite exceptional Hindu. Tagore could be more accurately described, as his Hibbert Lectures, *The Religion of Man*, make clear, as a humanist, though belonging to what Professor Irving Babbitt has described as "the least humanist of lands." The negations of Vedantic Hinduism were abhorrent to him much more than they were to Gandhi for whom, as we have seen, asceticism has a peculiar—and a peculiarly Hindu—attraction. Gandhi says of Tagore that he had "a horror of everything negative. His whole soul seems to rebel against the negative commandments of religion." That horror is really a consistent theist's horror of the barrenness of monistic Hinduism. It is to be found in Andrews as well as in Tagore, for with his conversion he escaped, he tells us, from "the impossibility of worshipping an unknown God who can only be described by negatives" (*op. cit.*, p. 101). But when Hindu negations are in question Tagore is more ready to express his "horror" than Andrews. Tagore indeed says frankly that monistic Hinduism "is not a religion" (*The Religion of Man*, p. 117).

When, therefore, Andrews speaks of Hinduism as he saw it in the religion of his two friends he is not really speaking of what we may call central Hinduism. Even putting aside, as he, of course, deliberately does, and as they do also, all idolatry, the religion by which they lived and which he saw in them represents only a fraction of the highly diversified Hindu system. Nevertheless he often generalizes in regard to what he calls Hinduism when what he says is only relevant to a part of it. To take a single but important example—in *Mahatma Gandhi's Ideas* he has a passage which deals with the Hindu conception of God. "The word 'God,' " he writes (p. 34), "without any further connotation, is well-known in every Indian language and is constantly on every Hindu's lips. The name of God is written on every Hindu's heart and when he thinks of God he thinks of him as One and Supreme. In all my intimate talks on religion with Mr. Gandhi, amid many divergences and shades of contrast, I have never felt that there was any real difference between us with regard to this intimate belief. Here we were on common ground. In this sense Mr. Gandhi is a theist and so am I; to both of us belief in God is as certain and immediate as our own personal existence."

What Andrews says here of Gandhi's conception and his own being closely akin is, no doubt, true, but when he takes for granted that the same can be truly said of the conception of God that is behind "the word that is constantly on every Hindu's lips," that is far indeed from being the case. Gandhi himself would not make any such claim. He admits frankly that while Hindu, Musalman and Christian all believe in God "we may each of us be putting our own interpretation on the word 'God.' . . . But what does that matter?" (*op. cit.,* p. 95). A Christian surely thinks—and Andrews certainly thought, as passages already quoted show—that it does matter.

That there is no doubt of this in the case of Andrews's own religious convictions is clearly shown if we turn to what he wrote three years later of the character of God as revealed in Christ compared with what the word "God" conveys in other religions. In *What I Owe to Christ* he writes (p. 218): "No one can know the Father as [Jesus] does or reveal him as Jesus can, because—that is his great secret—he and his Father are one. He is the Son of God, not in any narrow, abstract, metaphysical sense, which has no moral meaning, but in a deep, spiritual sense of oneness: one in mind, one in will, one in purpose, one in character itself. Herein, in the character of God, is the profoundest religious change that Jesus offers to all human estimates and values. It is a change so deep, so original, so incredibly simple, that it makes the Christian faith a new religion indeed—not a compendium merely of what had gone before but startling in its originality, and in its outward results nothing less than a fresh beginning in human history."

In the two passages quoted Andrews is speaking of the same thing—the character of God—as seen by Hinduism and by Christianity respectively. Can it be said that they are the same? "The narrow, abstract, metaphysical sense" of the word God, "which has no moral meaning" is the prevailing Hindu view which affects even the ordinary Hindu deeply and influences his whole life, and Andrews, of course, repudiates it, as Tagore would have repudiated it. Even Gandhi does so. Bal Gangadhar Tilak, the powerful popular figure who preceded Gandhi in the remarkable influence that he exercised all over India, was not a theist like Gandhi. He was an orthodox Hindu, a Vedantist, a man of great learning and high personal character. But Gandhi says of him: "He used to challenge my view of life and bluntly would say truth and untruth were only relative terms but at the bottom there was no such thing as truth or untruth, just as there was no such thing as life or death." Gandhi was, of course, poles apart from the purely metaphysical conception of God's nature which lies behind that view of life and which certainly has no moral meaning. There can be no harmony between a religious life which is built upon that foundation and the religious life that is built upon the revelation of God the Father that comes to us by Jesus Christ, His Son.

There is in Indian legend a famous story told by a Hindu poet of the sixteenth century called Tulsi Das, a story which Andrews more than once uses to illustrate his own religious outlook. The story tells how a seeker after God turned away from Brahman, "the unbegotten, the indivisible, the immaterial"—that is to say, the wholly negative—saying, "This lays no hold of my heart." "Tell me," he said, "how to worship the Incarnate," that is, the personal deity Rama. He desired worship, not speculation. There is, in contrast with this, another more modern Indian tale of a *sannyasi* or Hindu ascetic, a typical product of Vedantic orthodoxy, who when he was dying a violent death looked up at his murderer and said, "And thou, too, art He." That conception of the nature of God, with its resulting identification of God and man, is what some Hindus suppose Jesus meant when He said, "I and my Father are one." But neither Andrews nor any Christian would agree with them for a moment. A conception of the nature of God which, denying the difference of good and evil, places Him or it beyond them both is of course the very negation of the Christian faith. It has, however, a powerful position in the religious thought of India and has done much to mould Indian character.

Enough has been said to make it clear that Andrews's generalizations in regard to Hinduism have to be accepted with caution. It cannot be of this widespread and powerfully influential doctrine of monism, so destructive of moral effort, that he was thinking when he wrote, "The East represents the Eternal Divine Spirit . . . as unmanifest, yet he is mirrored by the pure in heart in the depth of the human heart." It is hard to find "the clue to the organic unity of the religious history of man in the East and West" which Andrews tells us he was seeking (*op. cit.*, pp. 156, 301), when we realize the flat contradiction between the Christian faith and this acosmic monism of which he was undoubtedly aware and which he from time to time specifically condemns. He had a favourite Shakespearian quotation which we can appropriate as applicable here. In the terrible words of Hamlet we have come "between the fell, incensèd points/Of Mighty opposites."

What Andrews is really pressing upon our notice is not so much a theory of the unity of all religions as a warning against what Gandhi once called "doing a religious thing in an irreligious way." He is warning us against seeking to win a victory for Christianity by un-Christian and even anti-Christian methods. He is denouncing what Tagore bitterly described as being "like a coolie recruiter trying to bring coolies to his master's tea-garden." No doubt there are more reputable disguises that proselytizing often adopts and everyone who takes up the high vocation of being an apostle of Christ has to be on his guard against them all. A friendship made with a saintly Musalman, such as Munshi Zaka Ulla, if it was made with a view to winning him to the Christian faith, would have seemed to Andrews a deceit, an act of treachery to love. And yet we may be quite sure that, if his friends asked him—as many of his non-Christian friends did —to unveil to him the most precious of his spiritual possessions, he would have done so, and surely he would have rejoiced if his friend came to share with him in that Supreme Good "which is death to hide." The word "proselyte" applies to unworthy methods of presenting the Christian message and securing adherents to it, methods of pressure or enticement that are themselves denials of a true love and a true reverence for human personality. These methods he denounced and his recoil from them sometimes seems to carry him further than is necessary or even right. But in such matters as these what is chiefly demanded is a tender and very sensitive conscience, true to the obedience that we render to the Lord of our lives and to His spirit which we proclaim and seek to represent. That, we are well assured, is the tribunal before which Andrews set his own conduct and tested his own motives.

There can be no doubt, of course, as he, and Gandhi also, were continually pointing out, that, in Andrews's words it is "infinitely more important to act out silently the Christian faith than to make professions about it"; but to proclaim the Christian message is a somewhat different matter and it is for that that the apostle is sent forth. That proclamation is indeed most effectively made through the fragrance of a truly Christian life, as Rudra held and as Andrews's own life demonstrates for all to recognize. Such silent influence is "worth all the propaganda teaching in the world." Nevertheless for Andrews, and for everyone who is entrusted with the good tidings of great joy which shall be for all people, silence cannot be, and was not even in his own case, the rule. Andrews, indeed, disliked, and refrained from, argument, and it has to be recognized that argument is often unprofitable in this kind of situation. This is especially so when, as with Andrews, the faith by which he lives and to which he testifies, is, as he says it was, "a spiritual consciousness, not an intellectual definition" (*op. cit.*, pp. 21, 165, 103). But witness has to be borne to the message and to the experience that accompanies it, and Andrews did not deny himself that privilege.

In all Andrews's warnings against "aggressiveness" in this matter one thing that is always restraining him is his sense of the nationalist spirit that was abroad in India and the inhibitions, as well as the sensitiveness to any suggestion of inferiority, that that spirit created in the minds of his Indian friends. At the same time these warnings were addressed to the foreigner, because Andrews saw as one of the most serious faults of at least the British foreigner his tendency to *impose* truth rather than to share it, to present his message, even when it was the message of the divine love, as if it was *his* gift rather than God's.

These reflections should cause us to consider anew the methods we should use so as to secure that the Christian message is conveyed to India and to every non-Christian land in a fully Christian way. But that concern must not preclude us, as Andrews, one feels, allowed it sometimes to preclude him, from recognizing and condemning evils that in India have issued, in part at least, from wrong thoughts of God and life and duty. Of that enough has been already said. It is indeed true that the reformation of gross abuses in India must be achieved by the children of that land themselves, and any denunciation of them by us must be restrained and must make full allowance for the failure of us all to live up to our professions. Just as we recognize that failure, and stand beside them, as Andrews did, encouraging them, they will feel the more free to denounce the evils in their society and to search out the roots in their own ancient doctrines from which these evils have sprung. Such doctrines as that of *Maya,* or the unreality of all life and duty, and that which declares—in a common popular saying—that "the doer and the Causer to do are one," with its resulting fatalism, are deadly breeding grounds for social wrongs and miseries. When one thinks of the sorrows of India one desires to see arising in that land not only those who demand her freedom but also many like those leaders in social reform whom India has had and still has, who, knowing what those evil roots are, will denounce them with even Voltairian violence and call upon their countrymen, as Voltaire did, "*écraser l'infame.*"

Andrews did not conceive that he was called to that duty, and in the circumstances of India at the present time it was probably not his duty. His duty, as he saw it, was to see that justice was done to India in her political and economic life and that liberty and self-respect were restored to her. He saw clearly that the sense of their wrongs and of their being, as Tagore bitterly described them, "a defeated and humiliated people" had created deep bitterness and resentment. He accordingly gave himself without reserve to the removal of these evils and he sought, to that end, to identify himself in every respect with them and with the new hopes and aspirations that were awaking within them. He gave them these things through the exceptional power of affection that he possessed and that was profoundly deepened and irradiated by the love of God that had come to possess him and govern him.

❧

Looking back across the life he lived for nearly forty years in India's cause we realize afresh the consistency and unwavering courage of it and see their only explanation in the Source from which they issued and to which he always ascribed whatever in him was of worth. Rabindranath Tagore, because of his finely sensitive nature, was able perhaps better than any other of his friends to interpret his spirit. He saw how much Andrews gave up for India and how "out of his English tradition he brought to India his English manhood." His life had nothing in it of complaint for this exchange. He believed himself to have been richly rewarded and few indeed have won so rich a prize as was his in India's affection for him.

Andrews was no *deraciné* Englishman. There was what someone in another connection has called "a passionate ambivalence" in his life as he toiled for India and looked back to England. Both lands were in his heart and he sought that both should remain united in friendship and in a deeper understanding than they had yet reached. This is one goal to which he looked that is not yet attained.

But surely Tagore was right when he said of him, "His love for Indians was a part of that love of all humanity which he accepted as the law of Christ." The name that fits him best of all is, as we have seen already, an Indian name, *Jagadmitra,* "Friend of All the World." So it is fitting that the final word in regard to him should be with his friend Rabindranath Tagore whom he called *gurudeva,* "revered teacher," and who shared with him his love of humanity. "This," he said, "is what I would say to you in solemn confidence at the moment when his lifeless body is being committed to the dust—his noblest gift to us, and not only to us but to all men, is a life which is transcendent over death itself, and dwells with us imperishably."

NICOLAS BERDYAEV

by

Evgeny Lampert

Mark 1:9-11

EVGUENY LAMPERT. Born in 1914. Educated in Russia, Germany and France. Graduate of the University of Strasbourg and of the Russian Theological Academy in Paris; doctor of philosophy of the University of Oxford. Mr. Lampert, who is a member of the Eastern Orthodox Church, now resides in England and is a lecturer for the Oxford University Delegacy for Extra-mural Studies.

310

1

THE personality and thought of Nicolas Alexandrovich Berdyaev takes us back to the spiritual movement in Russia towards the beginning of the twentieth century. This was a time of a stirring of creative forces, of great spiritual and intellectual awakening and searching. Whole new worlds seemed to be revealed in those years. It is now clear that this period marked a true cultural renascence in Russia, a renascence of philosophy, literature, art; and above all a very great intensification of religious consciousness. Russian culture has never burnt with such a flame as then. Men of extreme sensitiveness and openness to every breath of the Spirit appeared on the horizon of Russia's life. There occurred violent and sudden transitions from Marxism to Idealism, from aestheticism to mysticism and religion, from atheism to Christ and the Church, from materialism and positivism to Christian metaphysics and Christian philosophy. It is true that, alongside genuine religious searching and the awareness of deep spiritual crises, there was also a fashion for "bogus" mysticism, for occultism and all kinds of pseudo-religion. Yet there undoubtedly emerged a new type of man, with a tremendous realization of the depths of life. This inner reorientation was connected with the change from an exclusive concern with the "things of this world," prevalent for so long among the Russian intelligentsia, to a rediscovery of "other worlds" and other dimensions. And there began a passionate struggle in the name of this new vision.

The spiritual crisis was bound up in the first place with a disintegration of the traditional outlook of the Russian intelligentsia, of its exclusively social bias: it was the final break with the Russian "Enlightenment," with positivism in the wide sense of the term. Minds began to be freed from the bonds of purely utilitarian values. During the second half of the nineteenth century a type of Russian became prevalent in whom the whole religious energy inherent in the people of Russia was concentrated in the social problem. There was a great truth in this concern: yet the spirit came to be too much absorbed in the waging of the social struggle. Towards the beginning of the twentieth century, however, an almost sudden change took place: the wholeness of a merely social world-outlook was broken up, and war was declared for the rights of the spirit and the inner life, for the spiritual and spiritually creative nature of man, and his ultimate independence of social utilitarianism and social progress. Of course, this did not mean that the social problem ceased to disturb men's minds. On the contrary. But a kind of revaluation came about, as a consequence of which the social problem itself was faced in a freer and more creative way.

At the head of this movement were two outstanding men, who may without exaggeration be called the prophets of the spiritual renascence in Russia: Nicolas Berdyaev and Sergius Bulgakov (the latter is now a priest and the most prominent theologian in the contemporary Russian Church). Berdyaev was born in Kiev in 1874 of an aristocratic military family and was educated in a military school. While a student he was expelled from the university owing to his socialistic views and activties. At the age of twenty-five he was exiled for the same reason from Kiev to the north of Russia, and early in 1917 was again threatened with banishment. He opened his literary career in 1900 with a work on *Subjectivism and Individualism in Social Philosophy*. After the October Revolution he was appointed to the chair of philosophy in the University of Moscow, but after twice undergoing imprisonment was expelled by the new government.

Berdyaev seemed to have an almost irresistible personal charm; it was somehow quite impossible not to be delighted to meet him—a fact I observed in many people, even amongst those whose views were strongly opposed to his.

This was due to the exceptional warmth of his heart, his great kindness and generosity, although personally he often seemed reserved and reticent. One never felt in him any sign of ambition and rivalry, which is such a rare quality in the literary world. Yet he never failed to advocate his own spiritual convictions strongly and even passionately. It was strange to think that beneath the outer calm and harmony there lay hidden a "wandering" soul, for ever agitated by moral and intellectual problems, by struggle and disquietudes.

Berdyaev's house in Clamart (Paris) was a model of cordiality and hospitality, and a real intellectual centre for French as well as Russian circles.

Berdyaev and Bulgakov first proclaimed their message, together with other Russian thinkers, S. Frank, P. Struve, M. Ternavtsev, M. Gershenzon and others, in a symposium of articles under the general title *Landmarks*. It was a kind of manifesto, and produced a real revolution in thinking Russian circles. Previously to this, on the initiative of the same persons and with close collaboration of the writer Dmitry Mereshkovsky (died 1940), a whole series of so-called "Religious Philosophical Societies" were founded in Moscow, Petersburg (Leningrad) and Kiev. The meetings of these societies, at which extremely lively discussions on the most burning religious, philosophical and social questions took place, had a remarkable response and attendance, although the government looked with a great deal of suspicion on them.[1] The book *Landmarks* and these societies became one of the most vivid expressions of the spiritual ferment in Russian society, and the channel for the thought of that time.

❧

[1] Berdyaev recounted how much later, after the October Revolution, the meetings of one of these societies, which had by then assumed a rather different character, attracted such a number of people that he as president received a warning from the authorities that the floor of the university hall in Moscow where they took place was threatened with collapse. Mereshkovsky gave his impressions of the meetings: "It was as if the walls of the hall dissolved, and revealed endless vistas; this comparatively small meeting became the threshold of the Universal Church. Speeches were made which sounded like prayers and prophecies. In this fiery atmosphere it seemed that all things were possible: a miracle was about to happen; the barriers dividing men would collapse, and the reunion and integration of all would come about. . . ."

This spiritual renascence had several sources. However strange it may seem, one of them was Russian Socialism and Marxism of the 'nineties—at first, critical rather than orthodox Marxism.[2] Berdyaev himself was a Marxist, and himself experienced a change from Marxism to Idealism, and then to Christianity. This Marxism of the 'nineties, as Berdyaev himself has explained, already presented itself as a crisis in the consciousness of the Russian intelligentsia. It revealed a great cultural intensification and awakening of spiritual and intellectual interests unknown to the older intellectuals, who were infected with many evils of West-European positivism. This became manifest above all in philosophy. Some of the Russian Marxists with a deeper intellectual culture had from the very first adopted the idealistic philosophy of Kant and the neo-Kantians, and tried to combine it with the social system of Marx. This line of thought was represented by Berdyaev, Bulgakov, Struve and several others. Marxism by its very nature cleared the way for the creation of broad and integral historical and philosophical conceptions. In his first book, *Subjectivism and Individualism in Social Philosophy*, Berdyaev already tried to formulate a synthesis of Marxism and Idealism. And more than any other Marxist of his school he professed a kind of messianism of the proletariat. Nevertheless, although Berdyaev belonged sociologically and politically to the extreme left and revolutionary wing of the Marxists, he was in fact never a thoroughgoing materialist. "I never believed in a 'class-truth' or 'class-justice,' " he says. Then, as always, Berdyaev's attitude to truth was, so to say, an absolute one; and all his religious and philosophical aspirations are a search for the Absolute. Berdyaev is truly a *pèlerin de l'absolu*, "pilgrim to the Absolute," to use an expression of the Catholic writer Léon Bloy (whom, incidentally, Berdyaev greatly admires). "Truth and justice are absolute and are rooted in the transcendent; they are not of social origin," he wrote in one of his first books, *The Problems of Idealism*. But Berdyaev attempted to build up a

---

[2] *Cf.,* "Russian Religious Psychology" in *The Russian Revolution*. This is a very valuable essay, which discusses some of the processes described in the present chapter.

theory according to which the psychological and social consciousness of the proletariat (as the class free from the sin of exploitation and itself exploited) is pre-eminently open to transcendent reality, to the realities of absolute truth and justice. This psychological consciousness, in its turn, was defined in his view by economic and class conditions. In this way he attempted to overcome the materialistic element in Marxism and to combine the latter with a belief in the absolute truth and meaning of life. He had often on this account to defend himself against the attacks of his political collaborators, especially Lunacharsky, Bogdanov and Plekhanov, later outstanding leaders in the bolshevik revolution of 1917. He was accused of heresy, and it was predicted that he would end in religion and Christiantiy. These prophecies were fulfilled.

Another source of the cultural renascence was literature and the arts. By the end of the nineteenth century the Russian public had changed its attitude towards art and aesthetic values. Nihilism in relation to art (*e.g.,* Pisarev and his school, who rejected art altogether or admitted it only as "useful for the purpose of educating a scientific intelligentsia") was finally overcome, and artistic creativity was freed from mere social utilitarianism. Volynsky, Mereshkovsky and Shestov were some of the first in this re-orientation. It expressed above all a new attitude to the Russian literature of the nineteenth century, which the earlier social and literary criticism was never able fully to appreciate. Philosophical and religious-philosophical criticism now became prevalent. The enormous importance of the work of Pushkin, Tolstoy and Dostoevsky was realized, and their decisive influence on the Russian consciousness and idealogical tendencies began. Berdyaev himself was greatly indebted to Tolstoy [3] and, especially, to Dostoevsky.[4]

The artistic revival very soon assumed a specifically Christian colouring. The main problem which had to be faced was that of the Christian justification of art and culture in gen-

[3] *Cf.,* his article on Tolstoy in *Put* ("The Way"), No. 11, 1928.
[4] A very interesting study by Berdyaev of Dostoevsky has appeared in an English translation. See list of books.

eral. In 1902 new societies were organized in Petersburg, at which there even took place meetings between writers and the clergy of the Russian Orthodox Church.[5] Besides subjects relating to literature (in particular Tolstoy and Dostoevsky) a whole series of problems associated with the name of Rozanov were raised. Vassily Rozanov, the peculiar and original Russian counterpart of the English D. H. Lawrence, was a prophet of the religion of life, of vitality, and sought for a Christian justification of love, sexuality, culture, art— in short, of the "flesh," as he called it.

At the same time the influence on Russian literature and on the Russian reading public of Western elements began to be felt: French Symbolism, Ibsen, Wagner, and especially Nietzsche. The last-named, interpreted in a peculiarly Russian way, was in fact one of the inspirers of this whole movement, which fact may have given it a certain amoralistic tinge.[6] Strangely enough, Berdyaev was particularly influenced by Ibsen among the Western writers, not so much by his artistic genius (which is negligible) as by his general feeling for life. It was above all by Dostoevsky and Ibsen that the acute awareness of the problem of personality and the personal destiny of man was aroused in Berdyaev. It may be noted here that from the very beginning these problems had a religious connotation for him and became the very heart of his whole outlook.

❧

Finally, the third source of the renascence was the nineteenth-century Russian religious philosophy, to whose traditions many returned. This philosophy was represented primarily by the Slavophils,[7] who in their turn were to some

[5] A specially prominent member of the Russian clergy was Sergius Starogrodsky, then archbishop of Finland, now patriarch of Moscow and head of the Orthodox Church in the Soviet Union.

[6] *Cf.*, Shestov's *Dostoevsky and Nietzsche* (German translation, Marcon Verlag, Cologne, 1924).

[7] The Slavophils represented that movement in Russia which expressed the belief that Russia has a unique endowment and mission in world history, because she had received the pure tradition of Christianity and an essentially Christian culture. They did not consider Russia in any way superior to, but merely different from, the West, and Russia's universal duty was to be herself and not to imitate Western civilization, as their opponents the *Westerners*

extent influenced by the German romantic philosophers, especially F. G. Schelling, F. Baader and others. The Slavophils created the first original school of philosophy in Russia. This philosophy tried to overcome the abstract rationalism and idealism of Western thought, and aspired to build what may be described as a philosophy of concrete, organic realism. The names of Alexis Khomiakov and I. Kireevsky, Nicolas Feodorov and Vladimir Solovyev (the latter two being only indirectly associated with the Slavophils) are perhaps the most outstanding in this connexion. At the beginning of the twentieth century the works of these philosophers began to be read again, and Khomiakov and Solovyev left a special mark on Berdyaev. Among the German philosophers, he was mainly influenced by F. X. von Baader, through whom he came to know Jacob Böhme, the German mystic of the end of the sixteenth century, the meeting with whose works, as Berdyaev himself repeatedly states, was a great event in his life. We shall see later that in some respects this meeting was the cause of considerable ambiguities in Berdyaev's Christian philosophy.

The age of positivism and hostility to metaphysics, still flourishing in the West, had closed in Russia. Much of what was later said by Max Scheler, N. Hartmann, M. Buber, and other so-called "existential" philosophers was expressed long before by Russian thinkers in the early years of this century. Actually, positivism never had a really decisive import on the more important thinkers in Russia; but it was only from the beginning of the twentieth century onwards that Christian problems began to determine their whole manner and style of thought.

The thinking Russian returned to Christ: a real "pilgrimage" to the Church had begun. Yet the return was to the Church and to Orthodoxy as restated by Khomiakov rather than as represented in official theology. And this meant a kind of novelty in Russian Orthodox soil. Khomiakov was

wanted her to do. Some of the Slavophils saw in Russia the germs of a new culture that was to displace the disintegrating rationalized civilization of the West. They to a large extent anticipated the ideas of Oswald Spengler (*cf.*, *Untergang des Abendlandes*), without however sharing his simplifications and onesidedness.

surely a "modernist," an innovator, even a reformer. His teaching on the catholicity (*sobornost*) of the Church is not strictly traditional, though his concern is deeply of and with the Church. His Orthodox and Russian consciousness had assimilated and absorbed the experience of European humanism, transcended and transformed: this is evident particularly in his teaching about freedom in the Church and in his rejection of external authority in Christian life.[8] All this is very close to Berdyaev's outlook, and is felt throughout his whole work.

Nevertheless the "modernistic" character of this whole movement is profoundly different from Western Modernism or Liberalism in the Roman Catholic, Anglican and Protestant Churches. Its *motifs* were not to adjust Christianity to the level and demands of contemporary science, or even merely to translate it into the terms of modern thought. Its *motifs* were religious, mystical, and even eschatological. There was, above all, as it were an expectation of a new outpouring of the Holy Spirit in the Church and in the world, and hence the revelation of a positive Christian attitude to culture and social life, the revelation of the truth about the "earth," and of the Christian meaning of human creativeness: it comprised a new vision of the mystery of God-manhood, of which Solovyev had already spoken, the vision of God in the world, in history, in man, and the vision of the world and man in God. And ultimately these aspirations sprang from a deep realization of complete rootedness in the life of the Church.

[8] Khomiakov's doctrine of the Church, so important for the understanding of the paths of Russian theology, is expounded exhaustively in Gratieux's admirable study, *A. S. Khomiakov et le Mouvement Slavophile*, vol. II, published in the series "Unam Sanctam," Editions du Cerf, Paris, 1939. *Cf.*, also *The Church of God*, an Anglo-Russian symposium (S.P.C.K., 1934); Bulgakov, *The Orthodox Church* (The Centenary Press, 1935); and Zernov, *The Church of the Eastern Christians* (S.P.C.K., 1942). The Russian word *sobornost*, which is a key-term in Khomiakov's ecclesiology and, indeed, in the religious thought of nearly all modern Russian thinkers, while roughly corresponding to the English noun "catholicity," contains a wealth of meaning not found in any equivalent English word. It suggests the idea of "all-togetherness," of "congregationalism," of catholicism as a spirit in which all work together creatively and to which all contribute. It is certainly not new, but rather a rediscovery of a fundamental Christian conception, but it is very important for the understanding of how Russian Christians approach the problem of the relations between the individual and society.

In the Russian philosophy of that day various trends and shades can be distinguished. There was in the first place a strong tendency to return to the tradition of Platonism and the Eastern church fathers, which had been to a large extent forgotten by official Russian theology. Actually Solovyev had already experienced a reorientation in the Platonic direction; but now there was an attempt at giving it a more patristic and Orthodox foundation. This trend was represented by P. Florensky, a brilliant theologian and mathematician,[9] and by Sergius Bulgakov, who began as a free religious thinker and publicist, but later gave his philosophy the character of a theological system. This school of thought expressed what may be termed a *cosmic* outlook, which is probably altogether typical of Orthodoxy, and in particular of Russian Orthodoxy. So-called Sophiology is bound up with this cosmic orientation.[10] Its main concern is with the problems of the transfiguration and deification of the world, of the meaning of creaturehood, of God transcendent and immanent, etc.

Berdyaev did not actually range himself with this Platonic sophiological school. His thought was always *anthropological* rather than cosmological in emphasis: his fundamental problems are freedom, personality, creativeness. This was, however, strictly but a matter of emphasis, in so far as both points of view are quite inseparable and mutually dependent. It merely points to the fact that the new religious thought was in no way a uniform and finished "school," but a very complex movement. Most of the Russian thinkers of t⸳is time had several features in common. They were concerned with the problem of the cosmic destiny of man and his supreme relatedness to God. They all recognized that there is some kind of affinity and ultimate "commensurability" between God and man; they all visualized the drama of salvation as related to and linked up with the drama of divine and cosmic life. They all opposed rationalism (which allows the expression of the mysteries of divine and human life through the medium of purely intellectual concepts) a kind of intuitive,

[9] *Cf.*, "The Successors of Solovyev" (Trubetskoy, Bulgakov and Florensky), by N. Lossky in *Slavonic Review*, No. 7, London, 1924.
[10] See Bulgakov's *The Wisdom of God* (Williams & Norgate, 1937) for a general introduction to Sophiology.

mystical knowledge, and emphasized the great paradox and dialectical character of the Christian revelation.

❧

This religious renascence had its limitations, and its weakness lay above all in the lack of a real social basis. It remained to a great extent within a cultural *élite*, without touching the broader masses of the people. And this solitude grew as time went on. Even in the past the path of Russian culture has been intensive rather than extensive: there has seldom been a broad enough cultural environment and tradition; each decade has usually taken a new direction. And though it seemed that the youthfulness of Russia's culture foreclosed any possibility of decadence, yet, owing to the gulf between the upper and lower layers and a kind of uprootedness of the cultural *élite*, it now became possible for decadence to manifest itself. Such disparity is equally, and perhaps even in a greater degree, true of modern Western Europe— a fact which, as we shall see later on, Berdyaev has shown in his diagnosis of West-European culture. A very typical representative of such decadence in Russia was the exceptionally brilliant writer and symbolist Vyacheslav Ivanov. Even Berdyaev and his collaborators were carried away. People seemed to live in different, separated worlds, on different planets. There was, indeed, a tremendous intensification of thought and spiritual sensitivity, but no firm concentration of the will on a real transformation of life.

The Russian revolution at once revealed this terrible disparity. The masses of the people changed from a more or less naïve Orthodox faith to a naïve materialistic and atheistic one; and the cultural centre was simply overthrown. There occurred a disruption of Russia's cultural heritage, a break of cultural tradition, such as was unknown even in the French Revolution. It is only in the last few years that Russia has begun to rediscover her cultural sources and treasures. Many of the old *élite* were unable to withstand the spiritual crisis of the revolution: they veered wildly to the "right." All the complex religious problems raised at the beginning of the century disappeared, and were replaced by very elementary reactions against the persecution of the Church and Christianity, which in point of fact, in spite of all its horrors, was to a great extent inevitable and providential. Reactionary and nihilistic apocalyptic moods began to hold sway among Christians. Many were unable to grasp the positive religious meaning of the revolution and its inmost inevitability in the destiny of Russia. Berdyaev was one of the few exceptions in this new predicament. Through the experience of the revolution he withstood all decadent leanings, and became aware of the new problems of social reconstruction; he came to realize that (in his own words) "the problem of bread is not only a material, but a spiritual one." And the discovery of the universal meaning of the revolution became one of the main themes in the subsequent development of his social thought.

In the autumn of 1922 Berdyaev, together with a group of professors and writers, was expelled from Russia. He went to Berlin, where he founded the Religious Philosophical Academy, which was meant to carry on the tradition of the "Religious Philosophical Societies" in Russia, but now in a completely new environment, in exile. A new epoch began. Russian religious thought came out, as never before, to meet the West-European spiritual world. The organic bond with the spiritual and cultural past of Russian thought was kept alive, so far as this was possible in the difficult conditions of exile, and at the same time something new emerged out of the catastrophic experience of the immediate past and the encounter with the West. In this new situation it was Berdyaev who played a most outstanding, indeed prophetic, part.

2

PHILOSOPHICAL works are of two kinds: some lead us through intricate systems, like hitherto unknown lands; others bring us into direct personal contact with the philosopher himself. The books of Nicolas Berdyaev have always been of the second kind. In all his intellectual approach and manner of thought he is nearer to such thinkers as Pascal, Kierkegaard or Nietzsche than to such as Aristotle, St. Thomas Aquinas or Kant. Every book of Berdyaev's (and there are twenty-seven of them, not counting essays and articles) is a kind of philosophical confession, in which the author expresses himself. Instead of separate themes, "objects" and fragments of reality, it presents an integral, vital, personal vision of the world in its relatedness to God and to man. To use Berdyaev's own language, all his books, and indeed all his thought, are not "objective," but "existential." Each one of them is a stage, the present moment of his own spiritual destiny. They are characterized less by any particular subject than by the angle of vision from which the author's living thought, ever moving, yet remaining fundamentally true to itself, views the world. That is why there is no more adequate and attractive introduction to Berdyaev's philosophy than himself; to understand him and enter his spiritual world one should read his books.

Thought such as this does not prompt "criticism." The reader of Berdyaev's books may be conscious of disagreeing with him in many things. He nevertheless will consistently feel the power and integrity of Berdyaev's philosophy and will realize that it is thought and lived out to the end, so that any particular affirmation which may provoke disagreement is bound up with his fundamental feeling for life. Now, it is hardly possible to maintain that this feeling for life is actually wrong or unsound. It may perhaps be said that it is one-sided, as all human prognostications are. It may be opposed by another point of view, equally one-sided: but this will not render it less valuable or important. Berdyaev's thought is such that it imperatively demands a response, an answer: "demands," precisely because it presents a challenge to that indivisible part of us which is both *conscience* and *consciousness.* Perhaps no one among modern Christian thinkers arouses, moves and inspires us in this way more than Berdyaev.

His manner of thought is defined by the fact that in his

NICOLAS BERDYAEV

own works he as it were discovers for himself that which God has bid him discover. "God expects from me a free creative act," he writes in the introduction to his *Freedom and the Spirit.* "My freedom and my creative activity are my obedience to the secret will of God, who expects from man something much more than what is usually meant when we speak of his will. . . . All the forces of my spirit and of my mental and moral consciousness are bent towards the inward understanding of the problems which press so hard upon me. But my object is not so much to give them a systematic answer, as to put them more forcibly before the Christian conscience . . ."

Thought, then, is above all the unfolding of the thinker's own awareness of life, of his own experience, and witnesses to his own relation to the sources of being: it is not a construction of concepts or ideas, but search and acceptance, question and response, challenge and counter-challenge.

Here Berdyaev not only follows the path of contemporary "existential" philosophy, but shows his affinity with the Russian philosophical tradition, which literally grew out of such questionings of the human spirit.

Berdyaev has emphasized more than once the "antinomic" and paradoxical character of his writings (*e.g.,* in *Freedom and Slavery of Man*), and thus expresses one of the fundamental characteristics of his thought. It often includes affirmations which appear to be logically contradictory; yet it is just this which seems to make it true to life, which is wholly pervaded by contradictions, conflicts and unevennesses. May it not be that the meaning of Christian life consists in the power to experience and resolve such tragedies and contradictions, and the task of Christian philosophy to give them expression? But neither the paradoxical character of Berdyaev's philosophy, nor, incidentally, the wide range of problems (religious, philosophical, ethical, sociological, political, historical, aesthetic, literary, etc.) which he explores in his books, breaks its essential unity. His books are not "scientific" works, nor are they written according to any specific philosophical or theological method. They belong to no school of theology or philosophy; they are, to use his own language, "prophetic" rather than "scientific." Berdyaev deliberately avoids the terminology of the schools. His work is what he calls "free prophetic philosophy," with all the partial and incomplete utterances of a prophet. "I have deliberately overstepped," he says, "the limits of philosophical, theological and mystical knowledge, so dear to the Western mind, as well in Catholic and Protestant circles as in the sphere of academic philosophy" (*op. cit.*). Altogether, if by philosophy be understood a systematic or historical inquiry into the nature of certain laws and principles of knowledge, of being, substance, cause, etc., then Berdyaev is not a philosopher at all: which does not prevent him from being a great and original thinker.

This unsystematic character of his thought is enhanced by his peculiar style, which some have described as "tautological": he hammers out his thought by constant repetition of the same ideas and even the same words and phrases, which incidentally makes it extremely difficult to translate him adequately into any foreign language. Yet this style acts like the repeated blows of a sculptor's chisel cutting out the complete and finished embodiment of an idea.

∾

Berdyaev can hardly be described as a "Russian Orthodox theologian," for which he is often taken in the West; neither is he an "official" representative of Orthodox church-doctrine. In the first place, it is extremely difficult to attach any meaning whatever to terms like "official representation" and "officially representative" of the Church, particularly from the point of view of the Orthodox conception of the Church. Moreover, the Orthodox Church has (maybe fortunately rather than unfortunately) no "official" philosophy. But above all Berdyaev philosophizes and speaks about God, about Christ, about man, and not as it were in the capacity of a "handmaid" of theology; he propounds philosophy not as a kind of instrument for use in pursuit of aims established by religious dogma—in other words, not as an apologist does, but rather as an advocate of the God-willed, creative cognitive activity of man, emphatically as an advocate of human philosophy, of human love for the truth, of the creative gift of man to surpass himself and partake of this truth. In Berdyaev this attitude is bound up with the fundamental idea of *God-manhood,* to which we shall return later on, which is for him a witness to the calling of man to creative interaction with God both in life and thought. "No theology can regulate the process of my knowledge from outside and impose a norm: knowledge is free. But I cannot any longer realize the purpose of knowledge without . . . undergoing a religious initiation into the mysteries of Being. . . ." (*The End of Our Time.*)

Thus he is neither a theologian who, as some have suggested, cannot get away from philosophy, of which he imparts more or less strong doses into his theology, nor on the other hand a secular or "pure" philosopher who probes into religious problems; he is a thinker who quests for and questions about ultimate realities: about God, man, and man's transcendent destiny.[1] Herein lies, I believe, a profoundly Christian characteristic of Berdyaev's thought, though some may contest this. For Berdyaev, as well as for many other Russian religious thinkers, Christian truth is the revelation of God's movement towards man and, simultaneously, of man's movement towards God, of the humanity or human likeness of God and the divine likeness of man, and, consequently, also of the supreme truth and justification of human questionings, of human problems and human philosophy.

Berdyaev's thought attains a great intensity where he turns to concrete problems of human life. It breathes love to man along with a passionate concern for his struggles, sufferings and tormenting quests, and at the same time faith in man's call to great deeds. Hence Berdyaev's bitterness against any smooth, comfortable and untragic interpretation of Christianity, so often based on the division of the world into those being saved in the bosom of the Church, where everything is supposed to be delightful, bright and happy, and those perishing in the world where all is darkness, misery and torment. Any sense of safety and security is for him equivalent

---

[1] Russian critics have called him (sometimes ironically) a "seeker after God" (*bogoiskatel*), a term very much in vogue forty years ago.

to insensitiveness and indifference to the tragic fate of mankind[2]; it blocks the vision of life and of life's great and unforeseen possibilities. Hence also Berdyaev's strictures on *"bourgeois"* mentality, which he associates primarily not with any particular class—the capitalist class, for example— but rather with a particular spiritual attitude, with smugness, middle-way mentality and lack of courage, with general well-being and self-satisfied well-doing. "The *bourgeois* lives in perpetual fear that his assured and peaceful existence will be abrogated. He is above all an optimist and believes in happiness solidly achieved in a finite world; he inclines to pessimism only when it is a question of other people's misfortunes and sufferings or of improving the social condition of the worker" (*Spirit and Reality*). Berdyaev himself would probably feel exactly the opposite: he would feel "optimistic" about men's responsibility towards their fellow human beings and "pessimistic" about man's individual destiny: "pessimistic," because he is so much concerned to bring to light the tragic sense of life which the *bourgeois* so easily dismisses. Moreover, he believes that even Christianity has succumbed to *bourgeois* mentality and has become for many a means to "safeguard" and "consolidate" human life, and to cut man off from the supreme responsibility of sharing in the tragedy of stricken mankind.

In a novel of the French writer André Gide, *Le retour de l'enfant prodigue,* which is a free literary interpretation of the gospel parable, the prodigal son, to the question as to what he did while away from his father's house, replies "I suffered." This answer might equally be given by many to-day who are far, and probably farther, away from their Father's house than the son in the parable. Berdyaev warns Christians against indifference to the fate of these prodigal children, who in one sense or another are sharing in the

---

[2] I shall offer no apology for using here and elsewhere such seemingly vague and much misused words as "tragic," "tragedy," "tragic sense," and so forth, because their meaning is fundamental to a comprehension of Berdyaev's point of view. What is meant by these words is a kind af awareness of the polarity of human life, of tormenting opposites and cleavages which no human reasonableness and common sense can resolve, which must be experienced and lived through to the end in order to lead man to a higher, transcendent unity.

agony of Christ himself. "Does he not also love a Nietzsche who fights against him?" he asks. I do not know of another Christian thinker (with the exception perhaps of Dostoevsky) who is such an untiring advocate of the unique and indeed tragic fate of man as is Berdyaev. Such advocacy evidently does not consist in a mere desire to bring man back to the truth, or to "convert" him to the Christian Church, but above all in a kind of identification with him and with the problems arising out of his predicament. In fact, Berdyaev believes that Christians can learn a great deal from man thrown into the raging storms of the world to-day. Christianity can and does save modern man, threatened as he is with destruction, only if it is acutely sensitive to all the experiences of his life, to his temptations and his questionings: but never as a mere *Deus ex machina*. To this end Berdyaev is prepared to accept openly and without reserve the whole content of modern life as at least a "negative revelation" of the Christian truth. He is not afraid of secularism; in fact, he prefers it to merely rhetorical ecclesiasticism and conventional Christianity.

Berdyaev does not stand on "solid ground," he does not know or believe in stable forms and patterns of life. The earth beneath him is on fire, he lives and thinks in all respects, spiritually and socially, in an age of revolution and carries within him the principle of some great overturn. This is manifest in the notably intense apocalyptic and eschatological tone of his thought. The Apocalypse, the last book of the Bible, the revelation of the things to come which will transform the universe, is a present reality to him no less than it is for Russian popular imagination: he is essentially concerned with the ultimate issues of life, and is continually seeking to surpass the limits and boundaries of this world. Hence the anarchical element in his outlook, particularly in his social outlook—a desire to break away from all restraints and standards of society and civilization. If his books often abound in references to the historical past, his thought nonetheless turns constantly to the future, and it is not in the laws of gradual evolution and progress but in the ultimate transcendent realities that he sees the purpose and meaning of history. Yet, despite the value which he attaches to the last things, his mood is not a passive but an active and creative one.

∾

Up to now I have endeavoured to characterize Berdyaev mainly as a thinker and philosopher. But there is another side to him: Berdyaev the *fighter*. This is partly due to the general tradition of Russian philosophical thought, which had but little taste for mere speculative and abstract knowledge, and is partly a matter of necessity, of the environment in which Berdyaev came to live during the time of his philosophical activity. But it is above all in keeping with the very style of his thought. Many of Berdyaev's books and almost all his articles are controversial and polemical: and he fights primarily for *freedom*. He defends that which is particularly threatened and everywhere defenceless to-day, even in the supposedly free Russian "emigration" in the midst of which Berdyaev spent the most mature years of his creative work. Whenever (especially within the bounds of the Russian spiritual world) there is a theoretical or practical onslaught on the freedom of man, of his spirit or thought, Berdyaev strikes relentlessly, giving full vent to his fighting temperament; and he delivers no foul blows. Many feel that he is, in fact, more convincing and penetrating in his destructive than in his constructive judgements. He remorselessly pursues and exposes every violation of man and human freedom, every congealing and hardening of the spirit in all spheres of life—cultural, social, scientific, religious and ecclesiastical. In his fight Berdyaev often forgets the self-limitations laid on themselves by philosophers and theologians, and is occasionally capable of saying things which in the eyes of some may even place him outside the Church. In point of fact however even thus he is fulfilling an invaluable part of the Church's work. Such are, *e.g.*, his memorable utterances in connexion with the condemnation of Bulgakov's Sophiology by certain hierarchs of the Russian Church.[3] Such is his unceasing struggle in the Russian "emigration" for the value of spiritual freedom

[3] For all the documents relating to this controversy, including Berdyaev's comments, see *Orient and Occident*, new series, No. 1, March, 1936.

against the blind political reactionism of *émigré*-psychology. Such are his calls to national and social repentance, to awareness of the inner positive meaning of the events in revolutionary and post-revolutionary Russia, and to the realization of the new problems raised by the revolution. Much that has been said and written by him in this connexion recalls the bold French Catholic writer Joseph de Maistre, who regarded revolutions as a divine judgement and the French *émigrés* of his day as impotent mischief-makers—with the difference that Berdyaev lives in an age at once more radical, more complex, more tragic, and more intensely threatened by elemental forces.

This combination of philosopher and fighter in one man must be the despair of every lover of classification who still hopes to give Berdyaev's thought a formal definition. Yet it is in fact but a sign of the dynamism and vitality of his thought, which does not pertain to the realm of abstract speculations but presents a whirlpool of living and acutely relevant ideas.

3

THE concept *God-Manhood* summarizes the quintessence of Berdyaev's thought. He begins and ends his reasoning not with God or man, but with God *and* man, with the God-man, with Christ and God-manhood. This defines both the content and "style" of his thought. Without bearing this in mind it is hardly possible to discern the inner motives and trace the complex thread of his argument. "Both philosophy and theology should start neither with God nor with man, but rather with the God-man. The basic and original phenomenon of life is the meeting and interaction of God and man, the movement of God towards man and of man towards God" (*Freedom and the Spirit*).

Men have seldom been able to realize fully the fundamental fact of religion, namely, that God is both the wholly

"Other One," transcendent and utterly beyond the world and man; and yet creates and reveals himself to man, enters into him and becomes the inmost content of man's very existence. How can that which is transcendent to man be equally immanent in him, and consequently in so far not transcendent at all? How can that which is immanent in man be transcendent and wholly beyond him? In face of such a dilemma there seems to be no other solution than to reject either the one alternative, viz., God-in-the-world and man (this view is sometimes called *dualism*); or the other, viz., God-beyond-the-world and man (*monism*)—with all the far-reaching and disastrous consequences of both points of view.

This paradox indicates how the problem of religion presents itself to Berdyaev. Both points of view he regards as a witness to the limits and impotence of discursive reasoning, which is incapable of comprehending the mystery of the living correlation of God and man, of the transcendent and the immanent, of the absolute and the relative, of the one and the many, of the whole and the part, and so forth. If we understand all these concepts as static and immovable entities, as it were congealed into logical crystals, then God himself must needs appear to be a sheer misunderstanding, evident to anyone familiar with the elements of logic: he is, so to say, hot ice, bitter sugar or a round square. Yet logical contradiction and impossibility is no evidence of actual impossibility. Life itself is such a contradiction and impossibility to Berdyaev; and these contradictions, which he seeks to bring to light and to transcend in all their implications, point to the mystery of God-manhood, to the mystery of the vital meeting and all-pervading mutual penetration of God and man. God-manhood is in fact that *coincidentia oppositorum* (to speak in the terms of the mediaeval theologian Nicolas of Cusa), the coincidence and unification of opposites, of God and man and God and the world, which unites what discursive reasoning is incapable of uniting, and renders every moment and atom of life and being a witness to the supreme simultaneous oneness and duality of God and man.

Berdyaev's intention is not to propound a metaphysical

doctrine; he wants to describe as it were intuitively a mystery which belongs to the very depth of being and is revealed in existence itself. The mystery of God-manhood is, indeed, unfathomable, irrational, inexpressible in terms of the objectivized world, where one object displaces the other, where all things are extraneous to one another and mutually exclusive. And only in as much as the grip of this objectivized world is loosened, only in so far as man is freed from the world of divided and isolated things and objects, can he become aware of true life in its unity and multiplicity, in its absoluteness and relativity, in its transcendence and immanence, in its agony and bliss—in other words, in its God-manhood.

The idea of God-manhood is clearly of primary importance for Berdyaev's teaching about God and man, on which we shall dwell in more detail presently. But it has also more general implications. It does not merely denote a special understanding of the relation between God and man, but in general expresses a particular feeling for an *ethos* of life; an *ethos* which above all finds itself up against any static attitude to life where everything tends to become fixed, divided and "extrinsic"; where all things remain impenetrable substances, opposing unsurmountable barriers to one another and creating estrangement and limitations. God-manhood is to Berdyaev the revelation of the way out of the isolated state of the "natural world." It gives birth to striving for the infinite, for fullness and boundlessness of life, where nothing is external or "extrinsic," as in the world of lifeless things and objects, but all is *within* and all is known from within. In fact, for Berdyaev nothing in life is "objective" at all, but all is profoundly "subjective," *i.e.*, all is inherent in the knowing, experiencing and living subject; in other words all is *existential*.

Thus the idea of God-manhood leads us to those elements in Berdyaev's thought which he himself describes as "existential," partly under the influence of certain modern philosophical currents.

So-called existential philosophy, as well as theology, goes back on the one hand to the phenomenological school

(Husserl), and on the other to Søren Kierkegaard, and is without doubt one of the most significant movements in contemporary thought. To begin with, it breaks with the abstract tendency of philosophical thinking and seeks a more immediate, concrete, "intuitive" vision of life. We have already noted that this was the concern of the Russian philosophical tradition in the early twentieth century and before, with its radical criticism of West-European abstract, idealistic thought and its claim to a more realistic, intuitive world-outlook. Modern existential philosophy moves on the same lines. Its main concern is to view the essence of being not in general, abstract principles and ideas, but immediately in man's own personal existence. The unusual categories with which it operates—anxiety, fear, anguish, triviality, death—are taken from the experience of human life and replace the categories of substance, cause, quality, quantity, etc., which are ultimately mere abstractions. Yet phenomenological and existential philosophy as it is expressed by its most brilliant representatives, like Hartmann and Scheler, either denies man, his activity and creativeness (*cf.*, Scheler's *Vom Ewigen im Menschen*)—the same, though in a different sense, applies to the school of so-called dialectical theology, which to some extent derives its origin from the "existential" movement—or denies God and is openly atheistic (*cf.*, *Heidegger's* sensational book *Sein und Zeit*, whose popularity, however, is due more to fashion than to real appreciation), Berdyaev is pre-eminently a *Christian*. Christ the God-man is the vital pivot of his thought. Furthermore he is a *humanist*, in the deepest and true sense of the word. He believes in and seeks for the truth of man.

∾

In the first place it is important to elicit how Berdyaev's existential philosophy states the problem of knowledge. How do we approach reality? What is the relation between "thought" and "being?" Berdyaev's answer may be summarized in the following way: as long as the knowing subject and the known object are conceived as divided, as long as reality presents itself to us "objectively," or rather in an objectivized way, so long must knowledge needs remain inadequate to reality, *i.e.*, a knowledge pertaining to disparate, disintegrated being (*cf.*, *Solitude and Society*, the title of whose Russian original is *I and the World of Objects*). True cognition presupposes unity or oneness of "being" and "thought," a unity which transcends the very differentiation and opposition of subject and object. And this unity is initially present in the creative act of knowledge. Moreover, Berdyaev seems to deny the very problem of traditional epistemology in as much as it is concerned with the question as to whether one should or should not recognize the known object as a primary independent reality. As is well known, this problem finds its classical expression on the one hand in scholastic and Thomist "realism," for which the known object must have a primacy over the knowing subject; and on the other hand, in "Idealism," which tends to deny objective reality and reduce it to concepts or sensations arising in the mind of the knowing subject.

Berdyaev does not admit that knowledge is at all determined by the opposition of "subject" and "object," or of "thought" and "being," in as much as they face each other in an extraneous way. The very fact of cognition is for him an event in being, a revelation of its ontological nature. Being can never be objectivized or exteriorized, whether in theory or in practice; it is revealed in man's very existence, from within; it is co-inherent and co-existent in man.

We are naturally inclined to identify reality with objectivity; and to prove the reality of something usually means to prove its objectiveness and extrinsicality. While this may be true to some extent (in fact, to a very limited extent) of purely external things accessible to our empirical perceptions, it cannot be applied at all to spiritual realities. "The discovery of reality," says Berdyaev, "depends on the activity of the spirit, on its intensity and ardour. We cannot expect that spiritual realities will be revealed to us in the same way as objects of the natural world, presented to us externally, such as stones, trees, tables, chairs, or such as the principles of logic . . . In the realm of spirit reality is not extraneous, for it proceeds from the spirit itself" (*Freedom and the*

Spirit). Thus it is not objectivity which is the criterion of reality, but, paradoxically enough, the criterion is the reality itself as revealed in man's existence.

In this way Berdyaev hopes to guard knowledge from "ossification," from the conversion of its content into static "things," which to a large extent has come about in so-called scientific thought. He regards cognition as an integral, creative act of the spirit, which does not know anything external at all, for which everything is its own life, everything is *within*, "in the depth." [1]

The question however arises as to whether such a theory of knowledge does not render cognition objectless altogether, and consequently devoid of content. Is it not threatened by "evacuation," and thus by becoming a knowledge of nothing at all? Does not Berdyaev assume that there is nothing transcendent to and beyond man, or if so, only as an "object" or "thing," *i.e.*, as something ultimately false and unreal? The inner logic of his thought in no way suggests such an inference, although some of his utterances, particularly in the discussion of the more practical implications of his epistemology, might lead to such conclusions. Berdyaev's theory of knowledge is indeed "objectless," in the sense that the object of knowledge is not fixed into "thinghood," that its content does not denote a "something" which exists on its own account, in isolation, out of vital relation with concrete human existence. But it is surely not objectless in the sense that it precludes anything but the knowing subject, which is actually one of the worst forms of Idealism and subjectivism, and which, as we have seen, Berdyaev explicitly repudiates. Moreover, his existentialism even presupposes man's self-transcendence—to God, to other men and to the world. Yet such self-transcendence is an *inward* process, not an outward one into the world of isolated, extraneous things. Man becomes aware of other reality than himself only in awareness of its relation to his own being, in self-awareness; and this latter is the initial fact of his self-determination to

[1] Berdyaev is fond of the spatial symbol of "depth," which he seems to regard as the most fitting to express the enigma of life. This shows his tendency to mysticism, about which incidentally he has written some very striking pages (*cf., Freedom and the Spirit* and *Spirit and Reality*).

anyone or anything. The relation of man to God and to man is an event within his very existence, in his inmost profundity; it is an inherent part of his own destiny. "Return into oneself and self-awareness," says Berdyaev, "imply outgoing to the other one and self-transcendence" (*The Meaning of Creativeness*). Such is the Copernican discovery of his existentialism, not less significant than the "Kopernikanische Tat" of Kant.

All this makes the fundamental difference of Berdyaev's thought from every kind of psychologism and solipsism. Psychology regards man as cast into the objectivized world: the "soul," "*psyche,*" remains a solitary, self-contained unit, an unrelated and isolated being. To this Berdyaev opposed what he calls *pneumatology*, which considers man above all as a spirit, equally personal, free and self-determining, yet always open, continually surpassing itself, and vitally correlated with God, other men and the world at large. "Man's spirit is not an inert substance, self-contained and self-sufficient" (*Freedom and the Spirit*). In fact Berdyaev does not recognize it as a "substance" at all, if substance means a limitable, finished, static reality. "Spirit is existence," *i.e.*, a reality which transcends all limitations and divisions, all fixity and immobility.

This theory of knowledge has far-reaching implications for Berdyaev's religious outlook and his philosophy of the Christian revelation.

In the first place, his existentialism precludes a thorough distinction between so-called natural and supernatural knowledge. This distinction in itself he regards as a product of objectivized thinking, in as much as it implies that men can think of God out of direct relation with and so to say in abstraction from, the Christian revelation. If the Christian revelation is an event within human existence, in the very depth of being, which it is indeed pre-eminently, it must be recognized as intensely relevant at the initial stage of our knowledge of God and the ultimate meaning of life. An act of faith is thus implied not only in the realm of "supernatural" revelation, but in all true knowledge. Only return to the ultimate depth of being renders philosophical thinking a possibility at all. The two ends of the chain of human thought must be integrated into a single existential intuition. "One cannot arrive at God, to him there are ultimately no 'ways'; one can only go out from God; he is not merely at the end: he is at the beginning" ("The Russian Religious Idea" in *Problems of Russian Religious Consciousness*). "I am the way, the truth and the life" (John xiv. 6).

In this sense Berdyaev almost identifies philosophy with mysticism. Their difference is as it were of a quantitative rather than qualitative nature. The true difference lies not so much between mystical and philosophical knowledge, as between what he calls the "mysticism of perfection," or "elevation of the soul to God," and the mysticism of penetration into the mysteries of being, of divine and human life, or of philosophical *gnosis,* a kind of second-sight or insight into the supreme meaning of all things. In this latter sense Berdyaev regards as mystics such men as Jacob Böhme, Baader, Dostoevsky, Solovyev, Léon Bloy, who were, however, all more or less far from being "perfect." He even defines mysticism as "knowledge which has its source in vital and immediate contact with the ultimate reality . . . It is derived from the word 'mystery,' and must therefore be regarded as the foundation and source of all creative movement" (*Freedom and the Spirit*).

The other religious implication of Berdyaev's existentialism is his belief in the reciprocity of every act of God's revelation to man. "In as much," he says, "as revelation is an event within man, in the very depth of human destiny, it presupposes not only the one who reveals, but the one to whom the revelation is made too; in other words, it implies man's active and creative participation. Revelation cannot operate on man automatically and mechanically, independently of who and what he is" (*The Meaning of Creativeness.* Cf., *Freedom and Spirit*).

Berdyaev repudiates the traditional theological view that revelation is based on belief in the "moderately normal," unchangeable, natural human being, who belongs to an eternal natural order. Any idea of finiteness, of a finished objective order, be it supernatural or natural and social, he regards as primarily responsible for the false and disastrous conservatism of certain forms of Christian consciousness, wherein man is left with only one task—to conform to and obey this order, the very permanence of which is considered to be a preordained condition of revelation. Moreover, revelation itself is believed to be an entirely "objective" act, independent of any creative participation of man in it. To this view Berdyaev opposes the idea of man's free creative relation to God and his call to interaction with him. Such opposition to any fixed permanence of both the "supernatural" and "natural" orders marks Berdyaev's revolutionary, dynamic, and active Christian consciousness, which looks to the things to come and expects man to change creatively the outer and inner conditions of life.

∼

The idea of divine-human interaction brings us back to the fundamental assumption of Berdyaev's philosophy, that of God-manhood, which we shall now endeavour to analyse in its main elements.

It has already been noted that Berdyaev is not concerned to frame a rational doctrine of God and man, and that he does not attempt to co-ordinate or synthesize the divine and human principles in a rational system. He thinks of God-manhood not conceptually, but rather *mythologically*. "Christianity is entirely mythological, as indeed all religion is; and Christian myths express the deepest and most central realities of the spiritual world. It is high time to cease being ashamed of Christian mythology and trying to strip it of myth. No system of theological or metaphysical concepts can destroy Christian mythology and it is precisely the myths of Christianity which constitute its greatest reality; for it becomes an abstraction as soon as it is freed from them" (*Freedom and the Spirit*).[2] And he adds that materialism and

---

[2] It is scarcely necessary to point out that here myth and mythology do not mean the inventions of human imagination or the delusions of primitive mentality, or, indeed, anything that is opposed to reality, as is suggested by the use of these words in common parlance. "Myth," says Berdyaev, "is the concrete recording of events and original phenomena of spiritual life symbolized in the natural world and engraved on the memory, language and creative work of man" (*op. cit.*). A myth represents within this world the

positivism equally live by myths, whether they be those of
material nature or of scientific knowledge.

What, then, is the content of the myth of God-manhood?
This is described by Berdyaev as the "drama of love and
freedom between God and man; the birth of God in man
and the birth of man in God." "Spiritual experience shows
us that man longs for God, and that God longs for man
and yearns for the birth of man who shall reveal his image."
This fact finds its fullest and most concrete expression in
Christianity, in which "the humanity of God is revealed and
the divine image of man." [3] Berdyaev sees the depth of true
life in this primordial divine-human mystery, in the meeting
and mutual relatedness of God and man. He does not conceive of religious life (just as in his analysis of knowledge)
as a confrontation of an unchangeable, static and ultimately
lifeless religious "subject" with an equally changeless and
static religious "object," and is in consequence compelled to
recognize a reciprocal relation and interaction between God
and man, that is, precisely "the birth of God in man and the
birth of man in God, and the revelation of God to man and
of man to God."

> "Within the depth of spiritual life there is unfolded before
> us the religious drama of God's dealings with man and man's
> with God. Without God and within human nature alone there
> can be no spiritual life. That quality of life which is called
> spiritual can only exist in man if there is something to deepen
> his life, something to which he can transcend himself . . .
> On the other hand, if there were nothing but the divine
> nature, if God had, as it were, no other self except himself,
> there would be no original phenomenon in spiritual life, and
> all would disappear into an abyss of divine selfhood and un-
> differentiated abstraction. God must limit himself and go out
> into the other self, that is into the being of man."

Berdyaev distrusts all systems of rational theology; he accuses them of disregarding the problem of God-manhood
and thus leading to an objectivized, "idolatrous" conception

realities which transcend the world; it brings two worlds together in images
and symbols.

[3] I refer here for the most part to *Freedom and the Spirit,* as the most
"theological" of Berdyaev's works.

of the relation between God and man. He describes in rather horrifying words the notion of God prevalent in some of these systems:

"God conceived as a metaphysical transcendent being, as an immutable inert substance, represents the latest form of idolatry in the history of the human spirit. Monotheism can in fact be a form of idolatry . . . Man in bondage to the objectivized world conceives of God as a great exterior force, as a 'super-natural' power in every respect comparable to a 'natural' power. God is merely the highest and most perfect of all forms of power, or in other words a projection of natural being. This supreme power demands to be appeased. The transcendent God avenges himself like the gods and man of the fallen world." But "Christianity appeared in the world to conquer decisively both idolatry and servitude. It affirmed the religion of the Trinity, in which God revealed himself as Love and the Beloved."

Berdyaev, then, does not think of God except in relation to man. Surely this does not imply that God *per se* is not at all, or that man supplies something which is lacking in God. Yet since God is Creator, since he created man, the living personal being related to him who is the living personal Creator, he cannot but be himself supremely related to man, for every living and personal act becomes real only in this relatedness. The fact that God "longs for man, for his other one, for the free response of his love," shows not that there is any insufficiency or absence of fullness in the being of God, but on the contrary the superabundance of his plenitude and perfection (cf., *Freedom and the Spirit*). Just because God's life is "agreement of contraries," he embraces both the perfection of his eternal transcendent being and the distinct and vital experience of man's relation to him. In this sense every act of God's revelation to man, and of man's participation in it, does not concern and affect man alone but also God, *i.e.*, it is an essentially divine-human act. Berdyaev is even bold enough to refer to the amazing words of the Catholic mystic, Angelus Silesius, who says, "I know that without me God could not endure for a moment. Were I brought to naught, he would yield up the ghost for lack of me" (*Der Cherubinische Wandersmann*)—words which may well disturb and alarm us. But this utterance expresses for Berdyaev a truth of innermost spiritual experience—an existential truth, not a metaphysical proposition. As such it does not necessarily lead to pantheism (which has become the bogy of rationalist theologians). Hence the abundance of symbolic and mythological language in his theology, which is "safer" and indeed more adequate to express the mysteries of divine-human life than abstract metaphysics. "To speak of God-manhood, of God's reciprocal relation to man, is a mythological representation and not a philosophical proposition; it is to speak the language of the prophets of the Bible rather than that of the Greek philosophers."

✖

Three fundamental problems are bound up in Berdyaev's thought with the idea of God-manhood: the problems of *creativeness*, of *freedom*, and hence of *evil*.

God-manhood is the call to mankind to manifest the image of the Creator in human life. *Man is a creator*, in virtue of his divine-human (theandric) nature and of the image and likeness of God in him. This is the ontological and ethical basis of Berdyaev's teaching about man. And he takes on the task of discovering, defining and justifying the image of the Creator in man. In the world to-day, in which the image of man is threatened with destruction, man-creator is and must become the supreme Christian ideal. Berdyaev is no doubt justified in his profound dissatisfaction with the traditional Christian attitude to this problem. Christians have too often reduced the whole issue to a mere submission of the creative act of man in all spheres of cultural and social life to religion and religious authority. Here the creative act—whether cognitive, artistic, ethical, social or technical—was regarded as of essentially secondary significance, as of inferior quality and even harmful from the religious point of view. A sharp distinction was drawn between the "sacred" and the "profane," which resulted to begin with in Christians living in two different rhythms, the religious rhythm of the Church, governing a limited number of days and hours in their life, and the unreligious rhythm of the world, governing a greater number—in other words in secularization; and finally this involved man's rise against religion as a tyranny, in an attempt to establish autonomy for his creative dignity and achievements. To the idea of a mere subordination of the creative act of man to a hierarchically superior power, Berdyaev opposes the idea of the *intrinsic* religious value of this act in its free realization, the idea of its existential meaning. "God expects from man a free creative act," for truly "My Father worketh hitherto and I work," and "the works that I shall do he [man] shall do also; and greater works than these shall he do" (John v. 7; xiv. 12).

It must be understood that Berdyaev's apologia for creativeness has little or nothing in common with the modern ideas of "activism." The technical and economic processes of our civilization demand of man that he should always be "doing" something: a perpetual frenzied activity and the use of every moment of time for action. Such activism threatens to eliminate all contemplation from life. This means that man will cease to *pray*, that he will have no longer any relation to God, that he will no longer believe in the possibility of disinterested knowledge of truth. Yet man is determined in relation not only to time, but also to eternity. He cannot be absorbed in the flux of time, in a ceaseless actualization of every instant, in the mad precipitancy of the temporal process. Man is called to recollect and to bethink himself in utter silence, to realize the depth of life revealed in his relatedness to life eternal. In as much, then, as the creativeness of modern activism is a denial of life eternal, in as much as it *binds* man in time, Berdyaev rejects such creativeness. No doubt man is called to activity and work—he cannot and should not remain simply a contemplative, for neither God nor the world is a spectacle: he must continue God's own original creative act; he must transform and organize the world. Yet man is above all a meeting-point of two converging worlds, the eternal and the temporal, and hence is not only vitally related to time but also to eternity. This, too, pertains to the supreme existential truth about man. When man is turned into the tool or object of an impersonal activistic process in this world he is no longer a free personal human being; in fact, he ceases to be creative. For true creativeness frees man from the flux of time; it turns his gaze to Heaven, it reunites human existence with its sources in God-manhood, and modifies the natural configuration of things.

Many are alarmed and repelled by Berdyaev's exaltation of creativeness, and objections have been raised from all sides to the very understanding of man as creator and as called to creativity. It may seem however that his critics, who accuse him of over-valuing and divinizing man, of "titanism" and humanism, have largely misunderstood the particular way in which he posits the whole problem. After all, to have a high idea of man as creator and as called to participate in God's creative action is in itself far from being an invitation to proud and egocentric independence, for man bears primordially and irrevocably the seal of God's creative power who made him "in the beginning." "It is strange to think," says Berdyaev, "that God could have created something small and insignificant as the crown of his creation. It is impious and blasphemous to have a low opinion of God's idea, and to hold it in contempt as despicable and of no account" (*The Meaning of Creativeness*). Man's creativeness is therefore not his autonomous right or claim, but rather his duty before God and the fulfilment of his will: not to be creator and not to live creatively, not to take part in God's unceasing creative action in the world, is disobedience to God, and in the last resort rebellion against him. Such is Berdyaev's approach to the problem. It may be asked whether Christianity has freed Prometheus from his fetters, or has chained him still more heavily. I believe that it has freed him, for he was chained not by God, but by the demons of nature with whose power he was wrestling.

Berdyaev himself wrote a great deal about the falsehood of humanism, in which man has asserted himself without and against God and has gradually cut himself off from the sources of being; moreover he has shown that this led in its turn to a denial and destruction of man, for "Humanism has destroyed itself by its own dialectic" (*The End of Our Time;* cf., *The Meaning of History*). But to the question as to where the falsehood of humanism lies, why it is impotent, why it is experiencing such an overwhelming crisis to-day, he answers not that it has overstressed the dignity and calling of man to creativeness, but that it has not done this enough, and so has in fact resulted in man's degradation and denial. It did not give man his full dignity, which reaches to the heavens, to God, and thus fatally under-estimated him. Berdyaev wants to overcome humanism, not against man, in order to degrade him, but in the name of the God-man, and hence in the name of man. Most of the anti-humanistic tendencies of to-day, on the other hand, imply derogation of man and dehumanization of life and thought. So-called dialectical theology (Karl Barth, E. Brunner and others, *see above*) is particularly interesting and significant in this respect. It has shown not only an acute and just reaction against humanism, but also a revolt, an almost demonic revolt, against any link and vital relation between the creature and his Creator: hence a revolt against the eternal mystery of God-manhood, which is revealed in Christ and must be revealed in Christ's humanity.

Berdyaev stands firm in his conviction that Christianity is *human,* that, in fact, herein lies its distinctness, though many Christians have maintained, and continue to maintain, the contrary. His vision of man in the light of the mystery of God-manhood has rendered his thought essentially and profoundly Christian.

The most important works of Berdyaev are devoted to the problems of ethics; and he once said that he considered his ethics to be Christian in as much as he has succeeded in showing them to be human. Even the *Destiny of Man,* one of his most abstruse, complex books, which is largely inspired by the themes of eschatology, by the agony of pondering on the problem of evil and Hell, is actually about the simple truth of *being human,* which many modern theologians are so much inclined to despise. He has shown the emergence of a morality which paves man's way to Hell, paves it by its devotion to the "good," to moral principles and ideals, and heralds a path which would free man from this hell of goodness. And he is ready to place himself beyond good and evil in order to ask whether that which has long been held to be good and evil is really good and evil.

❦

We turn to the second problem connected with the idea of God-manhood, that of *freedom*. This problem in general, as well as in the particular context of Berdyaev's philosophy, is bound up with very complex metaphysical presuppositions and implications, which in view of the nature of the present essay cannot be expounded: I shall therefore confine myself simply to a few hints as to how Berdyaev formulates the problem.

In common speech, and even in philosophies, the concept of freedom has two different connotations. There is freedom as a way, freedom as choice, choice between good and evil, freedom by which truth or God is recognized and accepted, but which in itself is undetermined by anything or any one. And there is freedom as an aim to be achieved, freedom in the truth, freedom that is in God and a gift of God. When we say that man has acquired freedom because his higher nature has conquered the lower, because reason has come to control his passions, we are speaking of freedom in the latter sense. It is the freedom of which the gospel says, "Ye shall know the truth, and the truth shall make you free" (John viii. 32). Here truth brings freedom, and freedom is as it were not first but second. When, on the other hand, we say that man freely chose the path of life and in freedom came to truth, we are speaking of freedom in the former sense, of freedom which is "first" and not "second."

Now this first kind of freedom may issue not only in good, but in evil as well. It bears no guarantee of goodness, no certainty that man will follow the right path and will come to God. Moreover, as Berdyaev says, this freedom has a "fatal tendency to destroy itself, to turn into its opposite and precipitate man into anarchy, which in its turn brings slavery and tyranny" (*Philosophy of Freedom*). "We know in our own experience that the anarchy of passions and the lowest impulses of our nature, which live each for its own ends, bring us into a real state of slavery, deprive us of the freedom of the spirit, and end in disintegration" (*Freedom and the Spirit*). This applies equally to personal and social life. Freedom which remains "formal," objectless, incapable of positive choice, indifferent to truth, leads to the disintegration of man and of the world. Thus, taken in itself, the first kind of freedom is powerless to preserve and maintain true freedom, and always threatens man with destruction.

Berdyaev maintains the distinction between the two freedoms. But the defectiveness, or rather the potential defectiveness, of the first kind of freedom does not lead him to an unqualified upholding of freedom in the second sense, of freedom that is in truth and goodness, of freedom which is regarded as identical with truth and reasonableness. For him the will to self-determination must have the primacy over reason. He is aware that a mere freedom of reasonableness too may destroy itself, may bring about the power of compulsory goodness and give rise to a religious and social life in which freedom turns out to be a child of necessity. If the first kind of freedom may lead to anarchy, the second may lead to theocratic or "totalitarian" despotism. This is witnessed to by innumerable pyres lit by Christians and non-Christians alike to burn heretics in the name of truth and its liberating power. Such freedom does not know what Dostoevsky expressed in the striking words of the Great Inquisitor to Christ: "Thou hast desired the free love of man. The freedom of his faith has been dearer to thee than anything else . . . In place of the hard and ancient law, man was to decide for himself, in the freedom of his heart, what is good and what is evil." In these words Berdyaev's own faith may be discerned. Like Dostoevsky, he rejects "miracle" and "authority" as violations of human conscience, as the denial to man's spirit of his freedom.

> "I can receive the supreme and final freedom from truth alone, but the truth cannot force or compel me: my acceptance of the truth pre-supposes my freedom, my free movement in it. Freedom is not only an aim but a path. . . . Freedom has brought me to Christ, and I know no other path leading to him. Nor am I the only one who has passed through this experience. No one who has left a Christianity based on authority can return to anything but a Christianity which is

free . . . I admit that it is grace which has brought me to faith, but it is grace experienced by me as freedom. Those who have come to Christianity through freedom bring to it that same spirit of freedom" (*Freedom and the Spirit*). "A man who has achieved a definite victory over the seductive temptations of humanism, who has discovered the hollow unreality of the divinization of man by man, can never hereafter abandon the liberty which has brought him to God, nor the definite experience which has freed him from the power of evil" (*ibid.*). And finally: "When man returns to God after an experience of apostasy, he knows a freedom in his relations with him untasted by one who has passed his life in the peace and security of his traditional faith, and who has remained within the confines of his spiritual inheritance" (*ibid.*).

What, then, is Berdyaev's answer to the question of the relation between the two forms of freedom? Sometimes their relation appears to him a continuous irreducible conflict, for "man moves from the first kind of freedom to the second, and from the second to the first, but everywhere freedom is poisoned from within and dies" (*Freedom and the Spirit*). Life itself is a proof of such constant conflicts.[4] In fact there is no solution *save in the coming of Christ the God-man.* "Only the New Adam can take from freedom its deadly effect without compromising freedom itself . . . The grace of Christ

---

[4] The difficulty of the problem has led Berdyaev to what is probably the most disastrous conclusion in his whole philosophy; and one which seems in fact in no way warranted by his own fundamental presuppositions: I mean the doctrine of *Ungrund*, which he has taken over from Jacob Böhme. I cannot expound here this complex and even confused point. Berdyaev's main contention is that in a certain sense freedom is not created at all, but proceeds from the *Ungrund*—a kind of primordial void, non-being, which precedes both Creator and creation, over which no being has power: it remains impenetrable even to God. Hence the boundless and unforeseen possibilities of freedom. Thus man seems to be only "partly" related to God (as well as God only "partly" related to man); in other part he belongs to that void, to "nothingness" (which sometimes, in spite of all his reservations and qualifications, becomes for Berdyaev a "somethingness"): he therefore renders man capable of confronting God in utter independence on or rather unrelatedness to him. This view, which is put forward to explain the boundless good as well as evil possibilities of freedom, and man's rebellion against God, implies dualism and is ultimately a rationalization, against which Berdyaev himself wages such a righteous struggle. It appears to me to be thoroughly unexistential and un-theandric. If Berdyaev claimed to have built up a harmonious philosophical "system" this doctrine would be a real *rent* in it. Fortunately his philosophy is no such system, and this particular doctrine is a wrong answer to an intensely relevant and real problem. As such it may even retain its positive value. Side by side with the Böhmian *Ungrund* we find in Berdyaev another answer, which is less rationalized but more satisfactory, at least from the Christian point of view.

is the illumination of freedom from within and hence knows no outward restraint or coercion. It differs from the truths of this world and from the truths of the 'other world' as understood by sinful man, which all seek to organize life by constraint and end by depriving him of the freedom of the spirit. The light of Christ illuminates the dark irrationality of freedom, without, however, imposing limitations upon it." The very nature of Christ's grace is shown by Berdyaev as both divine and human, for it proceeds not only from God but from the God-man, from God's eternal God-manhood. Hence man has a part in it and shares it freely. In the power of the mystery of God-manhood God meets the beloved creature, and the reciprocation of his love is infinitely and supremely free. (It may be noted in parenthesis that this view has nothing in common with Pelagianism, which seems to be a typically Western heresy: its very approach to the problem of the relation between God and man is alien to Berdyaev, being as it is the result of an incipient disintegration of the Christian myth of God-manhood.)

Here are a few truly inspiring passages from *Freedom and the Spirit* where Berdyaev presents his Christian interpretation of freedom:

> "It is Christianity alone which can comprehend the fundamental mystery of human freedom, which is inseparably linked with the union of two natures in Christ the God-man; a union which, however, does not in any way annul their distinction. The source of man's freedom is in God, and that, not in God the Father, but in God the Son, while the Son is not only God but man . . . that is, Eternal Man. The freedom of the Son is that in which and by which the free response to God is effected. It is the source of the freedom of the whole human race, for this freedom is not only that of the old Adam but also of the spiritual Adam, that is, of Christ. It is in the Son that the free response is given to the call of divine love and to God's need of his other one, a response which is heard in the heavenly and spiritual sphere and which is re-echoed upon earth and in the natural world . . . The whole generation of Adam is in the Son of God, and it finds in him the inner source of its liberty, which is not only a freedom like God's, but freedom in relation to God and in its attitude towards him. To receive the freedom of Christ is not only to receive

the freedom of God but to receive also, by partaking of Christ's human nature, that freedom which enables man to turn to God." And further, speaking about the Cross: "God the Son, veiled beneath the form of a crucified slave, does not force recognition of himself upon anyone. His divine power and glory are manifested in the act of faith and free love. The Crucified speaks to the freedom of the human spirit, for without a free act on the part of the spirit there can be no recognition of him as God. A crucified God is hidden as well as revealed. The constraint exercised by the natural world wholly disappears in the act of divine revelation, for everything turns on the existence of inner freedom. Man, obsessed by the forces of the external world, sees nothing in the Crucified but a human being suffering torture and humiliation, and the consequent defeat and annihilation of truth so far as this world is concerned. Divine truth seems to be powerless . . . But the religion of truth crucified is the religion of the freedom of the spirit; it possesses no logical or juridical power of compulsion and is revealed as love and liberty."

The mystery of freedom, then, and the solution of its inherent tragedy must be sought for in the Christian revelation of God-manhood, in Christ the God-man, crucified and risen.

Nonetheless the light that proceeds from Christ and illuminates all the paths of human freedom does not render Berdyaev in any way insensitive to the overwhelming power of evil, sin and suffering born from this freedom, and does not make him content and happy in an easy-going optimism. In fact, as we have already seen, awareness of evil and sin in the world and the capacity for suffering and compassion are for him pre-eminent signs of a true Christian spirit. "Man is a creature who suffers and is compassionate, who is sensitive to pity, who in these ways proves the dignity of human nature" (*Spirit and Realty*). In the face of the evil and agonies in the world Berdyaev refuses to accept any conception of God's providence which establishes a rational or moral expediency and "final causality." "In this world there are irreconcilable good and evil, unjust suffering, the tragic destiny of great and just men. It is a world in which prophets are stoned and unjust men, the persecutors and crucifiers of the just, are triumphant. It is a world in which innocent children and innocent animals have to suffer. It is a world in which death, evil and anguish reign supreme. Is Divine Providence effective in this world?" (*ibid*.).

∾

In this very question we feel Berdyaev's deep awareness of that terrible age-long action brought for their sufferings by stricken mankind against God—a challenge to the Hidden God to reveal himself. At one time Berdyaev was a convinced atheist; but, like many other people who have seriously and deeply questioned about the meaning of life and have sought the truth, he was an atheist, not because of intellectual difficulties which stood in the way of his belief in God, but for moral reasons, because spiritually he could not solve the agonizing problem of theodicy, *viz*., of the "justification" of God in face of the tragic strickenness of the world and man. And may it not be that the overwhelming fact of boundless evil and innumerable sufferings in the world is indeed the only serious objection to faith in God? This is surely why, among the rebels against God, there are people of a deeply sensitive conscience, imbued with the thirst for truth and justice. The historical destiny of the Russian people is a striking witness to this.

Thus no optimistic teleology is capable of facing, not to speak of solving, the problem of evil. To solve it one must first of all taste the tragedy of evil; evil must be lived through, or rather lived out from within; one must experience all the paths and possibilities of freedom. "Good," says Berdyaev, "is revealed and triumphs through the ordeal of evil." He answers the argument against God from the existence of evil in the world by affirming that the very existence of evil is a proof of the existence of God. "If the world consisted wholly and solely of goodness and righteousness there would be no 'need' for God, for the world itself would be God. God is, because evil is. And that means that God is because freedom is" (*Dostoevsky;* cf., *Freedom and the Spirit*).

Berdyaev as it were offers man the way to light through darkness, through the abyss and chasms of freedom. It almost seems that he, not unlike Dostoevsky and other Russians, wants to *know* evil, so that in the experience of this knowledge it may be overcome. This is a dangerous truth (and what truth is not dangerous!); it is a truth only for the really free and spiritually mature. Only a slave or a spiritual infant could understand it to mean that one must consciously take the path of evil in order to be enriched and to arrive happily at the good. Berdyaev is no evolutionist for whom evil is but a moment in the development of good—such a point of view is fundamentally untragic and optimistic (besides being morally vicious), and for this reason alone quite alien to him. "Only the unmasking of evil, only deep suffering from evil, can raise man to greater heights. It is precisely self-satisfaction in evil which means utter ruin . . . Evil is the tragic path of man, his destiny, the trial of his freedom. But it is not a necessary moment in the evolution of good . . . Man may be enriched by the experience of evil, become more acutely conscious; but for this he must suffer, realize the horror of perdition, expose evil, cast it into the fire of Hell and expiate his guilt" (*Dostoevsky*).

Evil, then, is overcome from within, through living it out, through deep inward awareness of its meaning, through inner illumination—in other words, existentially. "And the light shineth in the darkness; and the darkness comprehendeth it not" (John i. 5). This is the path of Christ's redemption. God who came down to earth and became man shared the destiny of stricken and sinful humanity, and in this sharing redeemed it. "Christ has died, and we must freely accept death as the way to life and as an interior moment of it" (*Freedom and the Spirit*). The cross of Christ is the revelation of the meaning of evil and suffering, and the only adequate answer to the question, "Is Divine Providence effective in the world?" God does not explain or justify the anguish of life, but takes it on himself, tastes its full horror, and in so doing illuminates it. Thus the problem of evil points as well to the twofold mystery with which life is bounded—to God-manhood, in whose power tragic existence becomes and is Christian existence.

"The transfiguration of the life of the world into eternal

life is the supreme goal of all things. The way which leads
to it involves the free acceptance of the cross, suffering, and
death. Christ is crucified above the dark abyss in which
being and non-being blend one with the other. The light
which shines from the Crucified is a light shining in the
darkness. It is this light which both illuminates the shadows
of being and overcomes the darkness of non-being" (*op. cit.*).

4

IT HAS already been pointed out
that Berdyaev cannot conceive of true Christian life which
does not share in the fate of the world, and that for him all
that happens even in the non-Christian and anti-Christian
world is not only the concern of Christianity, but ultimately
an event within it, and cannot remain external to it. History is not a meaningless void into which man is placed only
to be hurled into another world, but is the realm of God's
providence and man's interaction with it. And in a truly
prophetic spirit Berdyaev wants to make the human soul
aware of the momentous and eternal issues which history reveals and which are in themselves decisive.[1]

The world to-day stands in the shadow of a crisis, a crisis
which has equally deep-seated social, economic, international,
cultural and spiritual implications. This crisis is also one
of Berdyaev's central problems, and he summons Christians
to become aware, from within Christianity itself, of the
tragedy in which the modern world is plunged, and to grasp
the meaning of the present historical predicament as an event
intensely relevant to Christianity.

The world is in a flux; little solid is left in it; and both
inwardly and outwardly it is passing through an age of

[1] *Cf.* his most illuminating attempt at a Christian philosophy of history in
The Meaning of History.

revolution. Man to-day lives in *fear:* his life is as it were suspended over an abyss and he is threatened on all sides. He has lost the hopes which so recently he tried to substitute for the Christian faith. He no longer believes in progress, in humanism, in science, in salvation to be brought by democracy and democratic civilization; he knows the injustice of capitalism, and has become disillusioned about the utopias of ideal social-orders; he is eaten away by cultural and spiritual scepticism. In this atmosphere there have arisen new forms of pessimistic and nihilistic philosophy, in comparison with which the romantic pessimism of the past seems extremely comforting and harmless. Such was already Karl Marx's well-known *Verelendungstheorie,* according to which health, that is, the socialist collectivity of the future, had to be the result of the shocking state of the proletariat under capitalism; things had to get worse and worse in order that they might be better. Such is the philosophy of Martin Heidegger, to whom being itself is essentially fallen, though there is no one and nothing from whom it can have fallen away: the world is desperately depraved, but there is no God. Anxiety and throbbing fear are at the very heart of man's existence. Such too are the sinister philosophies which propagate the "necessity of desperation." The mind of Europe is under the sway of the melancholy, obscure and tragic Kierkegaard. His teaching of trembling and fear is spreading more and more, and it reveals the contemporary state of the world and man. A similar mood is shown in the school of dialectical theology and Barthianism, which are possessed by a deep consciousness of the terrible sinfulness of life and man, which are in radical reaction against the liberal humanism of the last century and proclaim a negatively eschatological Christianity. A similar reaction against liberalism, romanticism and modernism is to be found in the Roman Catholic Church in the form of a thoroughgoing return to St. Thomas Aquinas, a return which is not only theological but also inspires a whole cultural movement.

Berdyaev's thought expresses the same disruptions and disquietude. It seems to be in fact in the tradition of Russian thought to understand and give expression to such things (*cf.*, Herzen, Dostoevsky, Solovyev, Leontiev, Feodorov and others); and Russia's historical destiny itself revealed, before anyone in western Europe was aware of it, that the earth is crumbling away under our feet and that, in Berdyaev's words, "we can see all things naked and undeceiving." This became manifest above all in the Russian revolution of 1917, in which all the hopes of modern man in the idols of humanism, materialism, economism and all the other "isms" which constitute the faith of the average European, reached their limit and showed their true face: not only their truth, but also their demonic falsehood. "The Russian people," says Berdyaev, "in full accordance with their particular mentality, offered themselves as a burnt-offering on the altar of an experiment unknown to previous history: they have demonstrated the extremest consequences of certain ideas. They are an apocalyptic people and they could not stop short at a compromise, at some 'humanitarian state': they had to make real either brotherhood in Christ or comradeship in Antichrist. It the one does not reign, then the other will. The people of Russia have put this choice before the whole world with awe-inspiring force" (*The End of Our Time*). It will, however, be convenient to postpone a fuller account of Berdyaev's views on Russia to the end of this chapter.

It should be noted that although many idols of the past have been cast down by the forces of modern history, yet those forces have also created new idols. Man is constituted in such a way that he can only live either by faith in God or else by faith in idols and ideals: he cannot be a thoroughgoing, consequential atheist. Moreover, the creation and worship of idols pertain to all spheres of his life: they can be found in science, in culture, in our national social and spiritual existence. The awareness of such tendencies renders Berdyaev highly critical of the nihilism, fear and feeling of doom characteristic of the above-mentioned spiritual currents. However inevitable and even necessary these reactions may be, and however justified the disquiet which inspires them, Berdyaev does not seem to believe that they are really capable of saving the situation in which stricken man finds himself. In fact, he perceives behind them the reverse side of the same chaos and dislocation of the world. And as in modern social and political movements fear and insecurity drive man to the principles of force, authority and the suppression of freedom, so in some contemporary religious aspirations he sees a disastrous tendency to authoritarianism and the debasement of man. Man seems to have grown tired of freedom, and is ready to renounce it for the sake of solid force, which he wants to shape his inner and outer destiny. He has become tired of himself and disappointed, and longs for the moment which will abandon him completely either to supra-human social collectivity or to a supra-human transcendent divine power. Both are to Berdyaev heresies against God-manhood, the truth of which he so eloquently and diversely defends.

∼∽

There is one phenomenon in respect of which he believes man to be still full of a strange optimism: *modern man believes in the might of technology and the machine.* Here we come to a very remarkable prognosis of Berdyaev's thought, on which it is important to dwell more fully. He has devoted a special essay to this theme—one of the most brilliant of his shorter works, in which he has attained to a great depth of insight into the spiritual destiny of modern man (cf., *Man and the Machine;* also the corresponding chapters in *The Meaning of History*). He considers the crisis of our time to be largely determined by technology, which has given us a colossal power, but which in the last resort we are unable to control.

For a long time the sphere of technology was regarded as quite neutral and indifferent from the religious point of view, remote from any spiritual issue and, so to say, innocent. Russian thought seems to have been the first to realize fully that this is not so. Nicolas Feodorov, that strange and almost enigmatic thinker, author of the amazing *Philosophy of Common Work,* already perceived it in the early nineteenth century. Berdyaev too has come to realize that technology is fundamentally a spiritual problem, a problem pertaining to the inmost destiny of man and his relation to the world and to God, and that it has created an entirely new spiritual environment. Technology has put into man's hands a terrible and unheard-of power, with which he aspires to unleash the hidden forces of nature and exploit them for his own ends. But at the same time it has proved stronger than man himself; it has subdued him, it brings him bitterness and disappointment, it threatens him with destruction, and by its power the final cataclysm of the world may come about. Berdyaev views technology in the first place as the change in human existence from *organic life* to *organization*. In the past man lived in an organic order, linked up with the cosmos, with the earth, with nature. The great cultures of the past were encompassed by the life of nature and evolved within its rhythm. Closeness to the earth gave birth to what Berdyaev calls "telluric mysticism" (a term borrowed from the work of the German mythologist J. Bachofen, *Das Mutterrecht;* cf., *Spirit and Reality*): man felt himself one with the earth and the living organism of nature. This was displayed even in religious life, and has created religious myths and symbols. The life of social units, of the family, of the state, of the religious community was conceived as essentially organic and resembled a living organism.[2]

But technology made its appearance, and cut man off from nature. It as it were transferred him to the plane of universal space and imbued him with the feeling not of the cosmic but of the material, spatial and "planetary" character of the earth. It showed itself as a power hostile to all organic incarnations and plunged man into a new cold, metallic atmosphere, charged with electric power, but devoid of cosmic warmth and the throb of living blood. "Man in the technical age of civilization ceases to live amongst animals and plants." The power of technology has, moreover, brought with it a weakening of the "psychic" element in human life, of human emotions, of tenderness, sensitiveness and lyricism. In short, technology has killed all that is "organic" in life, and instead has placed human existence under the banner of "organization." Berdyaev tells us with great

2 In more recent times the Russian people in particular have been inclined to conceive life in terms of organism rather than organization; hence the doctrine and practice of *sobornost.* Cf., John Maynard's interesting study, *Russia in Flux* (London, 1941).

power and eloquence how the machine, with cold and cruel ruthlessness, tears asunder the bonds of the spirit with the living and organic flesh of life. "The heart of man shrinks from the hard blows dealt to it by the machine; it loses blood and gradually wastes away." The process of technicization, mechanization and materialization seems almost inevitably to end in the death of life.

Nevertheless in the last resort Berdyaev welcomes this process. He believes that the spirit can transform and revivify it and enter a new and integral life. Technology faces man with a reality which is more significant and of greater value for his final destiny than the conditions which defined his life in the age of organic, cosmic unity. Berdyaev does not want, nor does he like, mere romantic reaction whether it be the reaction of the nineteenth [3] or of the twentieth century. Romanticism was in fact quite powerless in its reaction against technology and could not solve the problem—or maybe solved it in much too easy a way. Berdyaev does not aspire to a mere return to former patterns of organic life, to a patriarchal structure of society and old forms of agricultural and artisan civilization; he is equally opposed to the conversion of life and nature into a mere instrument of technical exploitation. He wants man, and quite particularly Christian man, to define his attitude to the new environment in a creative and positive way. And in the very experience of technical civilization he perceives hidden possibilities for a greater intensification and purification of the spirit, and for a power which steels and tempers heart and mind. Man can and should be technical and capable of "organizing"; he can and should become maker and master of technical forces, which does not in itself and of necessity imply the mechanization and rationalization of life. In fact true creativeness renders life mysterious in its unforeseen possibilities and points to the "irreducible, irrational element of being," whose vision has so much contributed to Berdyaev's originality.

[3] John Ruskin in his rejection of the machine would not even reconcile himself to travelling in a train, but used to drive demonstratively in a carriage alongside the railway.

Another side of the process which has given birth to the crisis of the modern world is seen in the entry of vast human masses into the sphere of culture, in the "democratization" which is taking place on such a large scale to-day. Berdyaev distinguishes two elements in cultural life: the "aristocratic" and the "democratic." The former denotes the principle of qualitative selection, of deepening and intensification, without which culture could never attain perfection; [4] the latter denotes the quantitative principle. Cultural life spreads outwards, and continuously absorbs new social strata. This inevitable and necessary process can be observed particularly in Soviet Russia, whereas Western culture suffers acutely from self-isolation, from loss of inner unity, of integral co-ordination between the upper and lower layers, and the *élite* seems to be increasingly less aware of its call to serve the common cultural whole. The idea of service has weakened since as far back as the Renaissance, and has been gradually replaced by the ideas of liberalism and individualism. Berdyaev shows how one-sided "aristocratism" must inevitably result, and in point of fact has resulted, in a general disintegration and atomization of life and man in a whole series of cultural processes in Europe—in literature, art, science and politics (cf., *The End of Our Time*). An integral conception of life is a Christian conception: it was characteristic of the middle ages. And Berdyaev arrives at the conclusion that the way to cultural integration lies in a creative re-discovery of the middle ages, or, as he calls it, the "New Middle Ages" (cf., *The End of Our Time*).

These ideas had been expressed before in Russian thought. In particular, Vladimir Solovyev was the prophet of the New Middle Ages. The idea of an integral culture with its underlying principle of service has re-appeared in a new and powerful, though blurred, form in Russian Communism, which Berdyaev therefore believes to be the actual forerunner and anticipation of the New Middle Ages. In his book, *The End of Our Time,* he has made an extremely profound

[4] Berdyaev has dealt with this subject in his book, *The Philosophy of Inequality* (1923), which was written largely under the impression of the general cultural levelling which came about in Russia in the years immediately following the Revolution.

statement, the significance of which cannot be over-estimated: "In considering Russian Communism we must not rely on the categories of modern history, humanism, democracy, or even humanistic socialism, nor may we speak of liberty or equality, understood according to the spirit of the French Revolution. In Bolshevism there is a passing of all bounds, a flood, an agonizing attainment of something most superlative; its tragedy is not enacted in the full day of modern history but in the darkness of medieval night. In communist Russia one can travel only by the stars, and to understand the revolution modern astronomy must be put aside for medieval astrology . . ."

There occurred in Europe a fatal dissociation of the "aristocratic" element in culture from the "democratic," and the cultural *élite* has proved powerless to give the masses the ideas and values which could inspire them. This Berdyaev explains as being due to a kind of cultural over-refinement and fragility, which prevents the *élite* from meeting the movements of the masses creatively and draws it into self-isolation and particularism. The masses, on the other hand, easily assimiliate a vulgar materialism and external technical civilization, and in view of the particular environment of their own existence they are not open to a higher spiritual culture, and so easily pass from a religious world-outlook to atheism. (It may be added in parenthesis that this last danger is enhanced by the disastrous associations of Christian churches with the ruling classes and with the defence of an unjust social order.) In any case no ideas of cultural and intellectual refinement can exalt, inspire or dominate the heart of the masses. What can and does inspire them are images, myths or symbols ("archetypes," to use a term belonging to modern psychology) which express the deep and all-pervading hopes and fears of mankind; in other words, *beliefs,* beliefs of a religious or anti-religious, social-revolutionary or national-revolutionary nature. Hence Berdyaev does not see any solution of the conflict between the "aristocratic" and the "democratic" elements, between quality and quantity, between "height" and "breadth," based on the idea of a neutral, secularized, symbolless and mythless culture, for such a culture is doomed to powerlessness and exhaustion. What is needed is a resuscitation and new awareness of Christian myths and symbols which in themselves are a symptom of both religious and cultural intensity. The restoration and re-integration of culture must emerge from within Christianity. The very symbol of God the Father as revealed in Christianity sums up and integrates the "aristocratic" and "democratic" principles, for it is both a call to highest "quality," to "heavenly perfection," to realization of the dignity of God's children and to common life and fellowship, to service and integration. "In Christianity," says Berdyaev, "the problem of culture is integrally bound up with the problem of society . . . The fate of culture depends on the spiritual and material condition of the working masses; it depends both on whether their hearts are inspired by the Christian truth or by atheistic materialism, and on whether their labour and their material problems are recognized as of supreme and transcendent spiritual significance or as neutral and profane" (*Put,* No. xxxv).

With the growth of technology and the mass-democratization of culture Berdyaev associated another important problem of modern life which is particularly disturbing for the Christian conscience, namely, that of the individual and society. As a result of the spreading technicization and democratization of life man's personality comes to be more and more crushed by society. This situation is shown by Berdyaev to be pre-determined by the capitalistic social order with its individualism and materialism, its Mammon-worship and economic autonomy, its stock-exchange and "anonymity"; all this did much to produce a general levelling-down and to kill personality (Cf., *Christianity and the Class War*). Materialistic Communism (and in fact all totalitarianism), which in some sense has justly risen against capitalism, finally crushes personality, absorbs it completely into the machinery of the social collective, and rejects on principle man's unique and transcendent personal destiny.

In this new conflict man is either forced into himself, into self-isolation, and remains out of any relation to the community, or else is utterly subjected to and dissolved in the collective; and it presents to Berdyaev the conditions which as it were negatively point to the Christian truth about man, finding in this truth its own solution. Christianity alone is the supreme affirmation of man's free personality and his unique eternal value, and does not permit him to be converted into a mere tool for the ends of social life. The very fact that man is imbued with awareness of the mysterious, boundless depth of his own personal existence establishes the limit of society over him. Yet at the same time Berdyaev's personalism, or even subjectivism (in the true sense), does not preclude, but in fact implies, a call to common life, to service, to the union of every "I" and "thou" in "we," to *communism,* no more and no less (Berdyaev says that he is quite ready to label himself a Christian communist, although for some this is a contradiction in terms). Only in Christ and in the life of his divine-human body is realized the innermost integration of personality and society: man and society are existentially correlated and thus each comes to the fulness of its life.

I shall dwell more fully later on the constructive ideas of Berdyaev's social ethics. I will merely note here that the problem of personality and society raised by the present crisis must in Berdyaev's view bring about a structure of social life which he describes as *personalistic Socialism.* This will include all the truth of Socialism and repudiate all its falsehood, its false world-view, which denies not only God but ultimately even man. But Berdyaev is far from "optimism" about the future. After all, no one who has lived consciously through the last thirty years can cherish roseate and encouraging dreams in this respect. Yet the knowledge of the evil forces opposing the emergence of a new society does not paralyse his power to confront creatively the urgent tasks of social re-integration. Moreover, with all his thoroughgoing faith in man and man's free creativeness, he never loses the living awareness of God's action upon the world and of the grace of Christ quickening those who fulfil his work in this world (It is, in fact, hardly fair to Berdyaev to speak of merely "not losing the awareness of Christ's grace," considering the nature of the reality involved). "Not for anything in the world would I be free from God; I wish to be free *in* God and *for* God. When the flight from God is over and the return to God begins, when the movement of aversion from God becomes a movement towards Satan, then modern times are over and the middle ages are begun. God must again be the centre of our whole life—our thought, our feeling, our only dream, our only desire, our only hope . . . " (*The End of Our Time*). And it is this meeting and encounter with God which is for Berdyaev the supreme solution of man's predicament to-day.

The modern world is experiencing above all the crisis of man: not only the crisis *in* man and in human life, but over and above this the crisis *of* man himself.

This crisis is to Berdyaev the betrayal of God-manhood by Christian Europe. Sinful human nature has never been able to realize the fulness of this mystery. Even within Christianity itself it seems to have been insufficiently recognized or brought to light; whence the truth about man too has remained unrealized. This made the appearance of humanism inevitable. "Humanism arose in the midst of the Christian world because Christianity had not fully realized the truth about man . . . because it was given neither expression nor sanctification . . . But humanism in modern history is to be clearly distinguished from the humanism of antiquity, since it could only arise in a Christian period of history. It is connected in some way with a Christian problem which seems so harassing and insoluble" (*Freedom and the Spirit*). Berdyaev describes humanism as a "great, providential and inevitable test of human freedom," as a test which has a profoundly Christian significance. "It is the pathway of the freedom of man, in which his creative forces are tested and human nature gains its self-awareness" (*ibid.*). He perceives in humanism a "partial truth," the truth of the divine-*human* nature of the Christian revelation.

Yet humanism gave rise to a process fatal in its results. There began a theoretical and practical disintegration of the Christian myth of God-manhood. To begin with one half as it were was cast aside, namely, the reality of God.[5] But the other "half" remained, *i.e.*, the reality of man and the Christian idea of man. A striking example of such half-truths is, according to Berdyaev, the anthropocentric philosophy of Ludwig Feuerbach, who repudiated God but so to say preserved the divine likeness of man. This applies to other humanists who have not yet directly encroached on the image of man.

The destruction of the myth of God-manhood, however, went further. As humanism evolved in isolation from God, it *ipso facto* threatened to destroy the other "half" as well, namely the reality of man. The betrayal of God led to the betrayal of man, for "where there is no God, there is no man . . .—that is what we have learned from experience" (*The End of Our Time*). "The turning of humanism against man constitutes the very tragedy of modern times. Humanism destroyed itself by its own dialectic . . . for the putting up of man without God and against God leads to man's own negation and destruction" (*ibid.*). The most characteristic representatives of this stage in the fate of European civilization are Marx and Nietzsche, who have both violated man. For Marx the supreme value is no longer man, but the social collective. A new myth arises—that of the messianic mission of the proletariat. "Marx," says Berdyaev, "is a direct outcome of humanism." [6] On the other hand there is Nietzsche, who also denies the supreme value of man by substituting for him the super-man, the man of the elected race (*"Die blonde Bestie"*): man is expected to surpass himself, yet this is in the last resort equivalent to his annihilation. The same applies to the theory and practice of National-Socialism, which has replaced the value of man by that of an impersonal, biological entity.[7] Nietzsche is the other outcome of humanism.

[5] I am fully aware that no such arithmetical phraseology is adequate to express this complex process: neither God-manhood nor man's living relation to this mystery can be dissected in such a way. I am using these terms only to describe Berdyaev's point of view more briefly and more lucidly.

[6] *See,* however, his more qualified interpretation of Marx in the next chapter.

[7] It may, however, be pointed out that Nietzsche would probably be horror-struck by his contemporary Germanic adepts.

Modern man has entered an epoch which knows neither God nor man: atheistic Communism, racism, capitalism and many other "isms" seem to join hands in a demonic struggle against God-manhood.

❧

I now turn to Berdyaev's views on Russia.[8] He has an amazing insight into the social and religious currents which have determined his country's historical destiny; moreover, he is himself Russian to the very core of his being. His thought cannot be understood outside the context of Russian life, and from him much may be learned of the Russian mentality. All his problems express the preoccupations of the Russian mind—not the notorious and on occasion nauseating *âme slave*, but of that mind which speaks in the great literature of Russia, in the questionings of her intelligentsia, and indeed in the fate of her whole people, with its burning disquietude and searching for the utmost truth in the world, with the breadth and boundlessness of its vision, with its limitless and truly Christian faith in God and man.

"Russia," writes Berdyaev, "remained outside the great modern humanist movement; she has had no Renaissance" (in the European meaning of this word). The uniqueness of Russia's destiny lies in that "she has never been able wholly to accept humanist culture, with its rationalist concepts, formal logic and law, neutrality in religion, and general secular compromise." "But the Russians took over the last fruits of European humanism at the moment of its decay, when it was destroying both itself and the divine image in man" (*The End of Our Time*). Moreover, it would seem that no other people has gone so far on this path of humanism, or has drunk so deeply of its poison. To this the Russian Revolution is evidently the most striking witness. Russian humanism is described by Berdyaev as that of the heroes of Dostoevsky's novels, of Kirillov and Piotr Verekhovensky in *The Possessed*, and Ivan Karamazov in *The Brothers Kara-*

8 Cf., *The Soul of Russia; The Fate of Russia* (essay on the Psychology of War and Nationhood); *Dostoevsky;* "The Russian Religious Idea" in *Problems of Russian Religious Consciousness;* and also *The Russian Revolution* and *The Origin of Russian Communism*.

mazov, which has in the last resort but little in common with the classical humanist spirit of the West and its secularized, neutral culture and civilization. This is largely due to certain distinct features of the Russian character, which Berdyaev describes as being possessed by the feeling that the world is always on the brink of some apocalyptic cataclysm; that life, which is governed by standards of civilization, of worldly goods and *bourgeois* virtues, is of doubtful value; that history is intolerably slow; and that truth and justice, or false-hood and iniquity (as the case may be), cannot be half-hearted and can suffer no delay or compromise (Cf., *The Fate of Russia* and "The Russian Religious Idea," *op. cit.*).

As regards the relations of Russia with the West Berd-yaev ranges himself beside Solovyev and Dostoevsky, but goes considerably further. He was much stimulated in this respect by the war of 1914-18 and later by many years spent abroad in contact with Western culture. He has entirely freed him-self from the spiritual and historical provincialism which was to some extent characteristic of both the Slavophils and Westerners in their tendency radically to oppose Russia and Europe.

"We are entering on an epoch which at many points makes one thing of the age of Hellenic universalism. If there have never been such divisions and such enmities, there have on the other hand never been, at least throughout the course of modern history, similar *rapprochements* and attempts at world-unification. For the murderous strife of the war has contributed to a coming-together and fraternizing among the peoples, to the unifying of races and cultures; it drew Russia out of its state of isolation. Nationalities are ceasing to keep themselves apart from one another; and this is in accordance with their destiny; all will have to depend upon all. To-day the organization of each people affects the state of the whole world. What occurs in Russia has repercussions in every coun-try and upon every race. There has never before been such close contact between the Eastern and the Western worlds, which used to live so markedly separate. Civilization is ceasing to be European and is becoming 'of the world'; Europe will have to renounce her pretension to a monopoly of culture. . . . And Russia, situated midway of East and West, in a terrible catastrophic way has taken on the most considerable significance of all nations: the eyes of the whole world are on her" (*The End of Our Time*).

The above quotation shows a striking revival of certain characteristic elements of nineteenth-century Russian thought. *Gentilhomme russe citoyen du monde!* Berdyaev develops in a new way the traditional theme of Russia's special historical path and mission, which lies at the basis of the slavophil philosophy of history. In the coming period of history and culture, which, as we have seen, Berdyaev describes as the "new middle ages," "a quite special place will belong to Russia" because she "looks to the future" more than does any other country, because she is free of the fetters of standardized civilization and protected against the development of the *forms* of life at the price of its *content,* because the Russian people is the most universalist nation and the most deeply penetrated by a burning desire for the coming of the Kingdom of God on earth.[9]

Such is Berdyaev's faith in Russia; but he is also aware that on this path to a renewal of life and spiritual rebirth the Russian people will have to go through the purifying fire of national repentance and undergo a stern self-discipline of the spirit.

5

IN THIS chapter I describe some of Berdyaev's positive social ideas. It must however be borne in mind that most of his writings on social questions are of an intentionally polemical character, both as to matter and manner, and his constructive affirmations are consequently to a large extent only implicit in his negations. Moreover, Berdyaev is not a sociologist in the strict sense of the term,

---

[9] *Cf.*, Dostoevsky's famous speech in praise of Pushkin, in which he spoke of the Russian people as possessing a special gift for realizing the idea of the unity of all mankind: "the task of coming generations in Russia will be in the end, perhaps, to utter the final word of the great universal harmony of the final, brotherly meeting of all peoples in Christ's gospel-word."

and the social problem is for him primarily a matter of ethics rather than of economics and politics. Charles Péguy, one of the most profound of French Catholic writers, once drew a distinction between "politics" and "mysticism," a distinction which clearly differs from the commonly accepted use of these terms. To his mind this distinction coincided with that of falsehood and truth, of mere opportunism and a genuine attitude to life. It is well known that Péguy was in considerable sympathy with the French politician Jean Jaurès so long as Jaurès' socialism seemed "mystical," but ceased to sympathize with him when that socialism turned out to be only "politics."

Now it can be said that Berdyaev too approaches the social problem from the point of view of "mysticism" rather than "politics"—which, however, does not at all mean that he denies the value of politics or economics, of the state or the nation, etc. His "mysticism" denotes a particular evaluation of man and his place in society and he judges the process of social life above all from the point of view of the Christian value of human personality. He is up against any autonomy and self-sufficiency of the various spheres of social existence and their conversion of man into a mere means and tool for social development, for the power of the state or of the economic collective. And this leads him to the consideration of the most important problem of "ends" and "means" in social life.

Is it possible to attain social freedom by means of force; unity by compulsion; love through hate; truth through falsehood; in other words, to attain the "Kingdom of God" by the means of the "Kingdom of Cæsar"? This question is indeed exceedingly disquieting and can fail to disturb only the spiritual *bourgeois* who is hypnotized by the norms of secular utilitarianism.

When Vissarion Belinsky, a famous Russian social writer and publicist of the last century, was carried away by the idea of Socialism, he was filled with boundless love for humanity, and, while proclaiming the slogan (since proverbial among Russians) "Sociality, sociality or death!" was quite prepared to destroy half mankind with fire and sword in order to make the other half happy. He in fact anticipated the ethics of "totalitarianism," although he was originally moved by compassion and love for man. Berdyaev observes a similar psychological process whenever good ends are bought at the price of evil means, and annihilation is required for the sake of these ends. However, it is common knowledge that the way to Hell is paved with good intentions. "Ends" are too often mere abstractions, which may cover anything. From Berdyaev's "existential" point of view the decisive thing to know is not abstract principles and "ends" which govern the life of so many, but the quality of life itself, *i.e.*, what life actually is. And it is force, hatred, cruelty and falsehood, or (as the case may be) love, compassion and truth rather than abstract ends and principles, however exalted, which are decisive for the evaluation of life; in other words, *means* are symptomatic of the real quality of life, of its spirit and its content. "What is it to me," exclaims Berdyaev, "that man aspires to freedom while his whole life is full of violence; that he aims at brotherhood while his life is full of hatred; that he desires the triumph of the Christian Church while his whole life is permeated with anti-Christian deeds and feelings; that he strives for the good of his country while in its name he oppresses its people?" It may be noted that Leo Tolstoy was already acutely aware of the importance of the question of "ends" and "means." But his post-conversion rationalism and insensitiveness to the tragedy of history prevented him from really facing it, though his very concern and disquietude were extremely edifying and significant. Both the Christian and the anti-Christian worlds have been led astray and have stumbled precisely in the sphere of "means." While continuing to regard as "ends" the Kingdom of God and salvation, or the good of mankind and a perfect society, they have too often calmly committed all sorts of crimes and injustices as occasion arose.

As has already been noted, Berdyaev does not deny the value of the state or politics with their "means," which are often inevitably evil; but he is concerned to show them as essentially relative values, subordinate to man, as having not a "substantial" but a "modal," functional meaning. This is in his view the main social imperative of Christianity, which, however, Christians are so much inclined to forget. He has no doubt that the living, personal human being stands above the state, economics and even society at large: these he admits only as functions of concrete personal human existence, as a content of man's personal life which he must master and integrate. The possible objection that society is after all "greater," and in any case stronger and consequently more decisive, than man, Berdyaev meets by pointing out that in our sinful world the things of the greatest value are seldom in possession of the greatest strength. It is rather the other way round: coarse and hardened matter appears to be mightier than the Almighty God. The state always has more power than man; but this is just because it is of less and not of greater value. Evidently society forms a larger unit, into which man is placed as a much smaller unit; and in this sense human personality seems to be absorbed by society and wholly dependent on it. But from the existential point of view, as well as from the point of view of the hierarchy of spiritual values, it is not the personality which is part of society but rather society which is a part of personality, or, so to say, its (personality's) realization in a direction outside itself; and the depth and absolute, eternal value of personal existence will remain impenetrable to society.

I must repeat that Berdyaev approaches the problems of social life, not from the point of view of "politics" and of naturalistic sociology with its laws and standards (as such his position must, no doubt, appear to be meaningless), but above all from that of the supreme value of human personality, which may even sometimes involve opposition to the social order and its sociological assumptions. Such a position becomes particularly significant against the background of certain contemporary social phenomena: nationalism, state-worship, totalitarianism and economism have overthrown the hierarchy of values and have resulted in all the calamities of universal disintegration. Berdyaev longs for idols to be shattered—in the name of the living God and living man. Hence his call to what he terms a "personalistic revolution." "The world has yet to see a great and unheard of revolution: the revolution of the human personality" (*Freedom and Slavery of Man*). "Man is an end in himself and cannot be used as a means" (*ibid.*). If social harmony is reached by using him as an end, it is not harmony but an antheap. Revolution in the name of man and human personality is the only revolution which can be called Christian.

❧

But Berdyaev's faith in such revolution by no means implies what in the nineteenth and twentieth centuries came to be known as individualism; it is in fact its very opposite, and even demands that it should be overthrown. It is precisely individualism which destroys personality, and leads in practice—however paradoxical this may seem—to the domination of society over human personality, and in the last resort to the slavery of man. This is particularly manifest in economic life, in capitalism. If Berdyaev is intensely disturbed, as indeed he is, by the position of the proletariat in a capitalistic order, it is because the personality of the working-man, rather than his class, suffers and is humiliated. From the sociological point of view the victim of individualistic capitalist economy is the working *class,* which is deprived of the means of production and forced to sell its labour like goods; but from the existential Christian point of view the working-class is a pure abstraction with no capacity for suffering or joy, and it is *man* in the working-class who suffers or rejoices.

For Berdyaev's social ethics nothing is more ambiguous and cynical than the so-called "freedom of the individual" in a capitalist democratic order. And to this individualism he opposes, not the negation of personality or its subjection to the social collective, but the affirmation of the personality of every living human being, who is levelled down and crushed by the unreal and fictitious individualistic system. Berdyaev accuses capitalist society of never being really concerned with the value of man's personality, of never having defended its dignity: it has been concerned not with man, but with "economic man," with a quasi-human being conducive to economic power and expansion. It is indeed advantageous, according to capitalist ideology, that man, or rather "economic man," should be guided in economic life by individual interests and be entirely autonomous in his economic initiative. But this is valuable not because capitalism believes in the creative initiative of man and its place in the life of the community, but because such initiative is a useful means to increase production, creates channels for inordinate acquisitiveness and justifies insatiable lust. The process of production itself has hardly ever considered man as such, otherwise there would never be that discrepancy between production and demand which is so characteristic of a capitalist society. And the defence of freedom and economic individualism is ultimately nothing but the self-protection of the exploiters and holders of economic power, and seldom or never the protection of those who are exploited and deprived of this power, so that the real freedom of the greater part of mankind remains quite fictitious.

In Berdyaev's analysis the individualistic, capitalist system is equivalent to the domination of the "whole," of the anonymous impersonal economy and the autonomous power of economics over the "particular," *i.e,* over living personal human beings. A human being, however, is for him emphatically not a "part" of anything, either of society or of the world at large. It is itself a whole, and hence the relation of man and society cannot be conceived in terms of "whole" and "part." If it is desirable, as indeed it is, to limit the scope of economic individualism and autonomy, Berdyaev envisages such limitation not for the sake of the state and society or the "whole," but for the sake of personal human beings, their real freedom and right to economic justice. "Economic man must be limited in the name of man's integral and sacred personality."

If individualists and liberals in economic life believe that man must be given full economic freedom and autonomy of economic initiative and that he must be guided by personal interests, they are primarily concerned with the advantages of maximum production or of national prosperity and expansion; they are hardly determined by any faith in the

unique and supreme value of the human personality. Berdyaev on the other hand believes in this value, and consequently maintains that society should be organized on this
basis rather than on that of a powerful state and national
prosperity; whereas the individual should be guided by the
ideal of social service, of self-sacrifice and self-limitation. In
other words, the individual must think of society, of others,
whilst society must think exclusively of the individual. Such
a view may even imply a wide scheme of economic socializa-
tion, which in fact Berdyaev welcomes; yet this should be
brought about, not for the sake of society, but in order that
man may be secured the possession of real freedom. "Freedom
cannot exist only for a privileged group; it must exist for all
or for nobody. It must exist for every living human being"
(*op. cit.*).

It may be relevant to refer here in more detail to Berdyaev's attitude to Marxism. He has brought to light certain
aspects of Marx's teaching which are, even from the Christian point of view, strikingly superior to impersonalistic and
inhuman capitalist ideology. He has shown how in Russia
a revolution on a grand scale could come about under the
banner of Marx just because the liberal-democratic creed
which gave birth to capitalism was universally spent and
powerless to inspire anyone.

Marx gave a definition of capital which exceedingly surprised and even shocked economists. He defined it as the
social relations of men in the process of production: he regarded capital not as an objective material reality (*Verding-
lichung*), but as a symbol of the relations between living
beings. He dissolved the motionless, objectivized economic
categories and recognized them as historical. Behind the
lifeless material goods he perceived living people, their toil,
their struggles and their vital relations with one another.
Here economics ceases to be conceived as having a substance
of its own: its "substance" is people, human labour, conflict.
It is only capitalism which turns people into "goods," sees
goods where in fact there is concrete human existence.

Berdyaev regards such an interpretation of capital and
capitalism as Marx's most remarkable discovery and con-

tribution. But at the same time he is fully aware that this discovery is reduced to an absurdity by Marx's own materialism: for it is precisely materialism which objectivizes all things and disregards acts and living relations as the primal reality of being. Hence capitalism too is thoroughly materialistic.

～

Both to capitalism and materialistic Marxism Berdyáev opposes a *personalistic socialism,* which, so far as economics is concerned, is nevertheless Marxist. He believes that Marx's attitude to the capitalist system corresponds to an existential philosophy of life rather than to materialism; for it is the existential philosophy which perceives human existence, human destiny, and vital human relationships behind the world of objects, things and goods. The very concept of labour is an existential one. Marx's materialism, on the other hand, like all materialism, belongs to the *bourgeois* world, to a world which has enslaved man by its lifeless economic categories and material objects. "A true liberation of human existence from the fetters of the *bourgeois* world will signify above all the freedom from material *things* and from the rule of economics" (*Christianity and Class War*).

Personalism in social life is essential for Berdyaev if only because man is irrevocably endowed with the image and likeness of God, which cannot be said of the state, the nation or the social collective as such. The latter have a transcendent value only in the power of man's relation to God, *i.e.,* of the image of God in man. "Christ," says Berdyaev, "suffered and died on the cross for the salvation of every human being, rather than for the state or the social collective; indeed, it is they which have crucified him." Berdyaev is far from denying the religious value of social life, or that the Kingdom of God itself is a society (or rather community), but this latter is conceived by him as essentially personalistic, *i.e.,* based on existential personal relationships, and has but little resemblance to the state. It is indeed not by chance that the whole of after-Christian history is a crying witness to a continuous conflict between Church and state. Caiaphas said: "It is expedient for us that one man should die for the people, and that the whole nation perish not" (John xi. 50). The state, even the so-called "Christian state," always speaks as Caiaphas spoke at that greatest moment in history. But the Christian truth is a "personalistic revolution" in the world: its relation to social life is determined by the supreme and all-pervading vision of the absolute and transcendent value of human personality. And when Christianity ceased to be a revolution in that sense it took the fatal path of opportunism, and its fall drove men away from it. "The very existence of personality," says Berdyaev, "signifies a discontinuity in the world, as it were a break in the world process, and witnesses to the fact that this world is not self-sufficient . . . Personality is the convolution of two worlds" (*Solitude and Society*).

I should like to emphasize again that it would be a great mistake to identify Berdyaev's point of view with social individualism, as some of his interpreters have tried to do (*Cf.,* J. F. Hecker, *Religion and Communism,* New York, 1930). He rejects individualism altogether as being based on a completely false conception of the relation between man and society, a conception which creates extraneousness and estrangement between the members of the social community and leads either to the isolation of the individual within himself or to the subjection of personality to the extraneous collective, which is (as history has sufficiently shown) the reverse side of the same thing, *i.e.,* it leads in both cases to disintegration. Berdyaev's personalism, on the other hand, presupposes both man's self-existence and his out-going and relatedness to God and men. It implies awareness of man's universal and cosmic nature, to which nothing is external, whose very existence is to be in community and togetherness (cf., *Solitude and Society*).

This explains Berdyaev's strictures of democracy, in which he seems to carry on the tradition of Russian nineteenth-century publicists.[1] He thinks it a great mistake to believe that liberal-democratic ideology expresses or guarantees the principle of personality and personal freedom. In fact it

---

[1] Cf., *The End of Our Time, Christianity and Class War, The Fate of Man in the Modern World,* and other works.

ignores the real nature of man and man's personality, and conceives of freedom as a product of society. "The Declaration of the Rights of Man," he writes, "cannot be said to have given much attention to 'man'; he was rather put in the background by the 'citizen,' who was understood as a political animal and his rights as formal rights. So the declaration easily degenerated into a charter of protection for *bourgeois* interests" (*Christianity and Class War*). This is evidently based on the primacy of social values over personality. Moreover, Berdyaev regards the very concept of freedom in democracy as formal, abstract and wholly rooted in the secularized mentality which is so characteristic of West-European civilization.[2] "Democracy is individualist in principle . . . and this leads it to a dead-levelling of human beings. Democrats talk a lot about liberty, but no respect for the human spirit and personality is entailed: it is a love of liberty expressed by people who are not interested in truth . . . There was probably more real liberty of the spirit in the days when the fires of the Spanish Inquisition were blazing than in the middle-class republics of to-day" (*The End of Our Time*).[3] Berdyaev believes that it is just because of its lack of real content and of a positive attitude to truth that modern democracy is passing through a grave crisis. It is threatened on all sides, above all by Socialism, which, unlike democracy, is primarily concerned with the truth (whatever socialists may believe this to mean), and does not leave Pilate's question "What is truth?" to the counting of votes and the possible results of the clash of party—and economic interests. Not unlike some of the more anarchically thinking Slavophils, Berdyaev believes that it is time for men to

[2] Nevertheless he does not deny the existence of a genuinely Christian tradition of democratic liberalism: in England in the seventeenth and ninteenth centuries (and even now to some extent); in the nineteenth century in France (Lamennais and Lacordaire) and in Russia (some of the Slavophils and particularly Solovyev). But he doubts whether this tradition has been as yet of decisive importance for the destiny of Europe, though this may be so at present and in the future (cf., *Put*, No. ix).

[3] He recalls an anecdote attributed to Louis Blanc. A well-to-do man was walking past a cab and said to the driver, "Are you free?" (*i.e.*, disengaged). "Free," was the reply. "Long live freedom!" exclaimed the passer-by and went on his road.

challenge republic, legislation, representation and all the ideas regarding the citizen in his relation to the state.

∽

Berdyaev makes a very important distinction which, no doubt, he also owes to the Russian Slavophils and their teaching of *sobornost,* namely that of *society* and *community.* "Man," he says, "has need not only of society, to which moreover he often belongs simply by the force of circumstances; but also, and even more decisively, of community" (*Solitude and Society*). Yet community cannot be created by the way of external organization which so often defines the structure of societies. Though perhaps it may be possible and even necessary to create just social conditions by means of external planning and organization, the life of the community functions in other ways: it presupposes fellowship, *i.e.,* personal or personalistic relationships.[4] Berdyaev insists on the fact that it is quite fatal to separate personal and social acts: every personal act in human life has a social projection and is bound up with the relation of man to man. Behind every social act stands a series of personal acts and the quality of any social activity is ultimately determined by the quality of the relations between the living human beings who inspire it. It is impossible to create a perfect society from imperfect human material, as it were abstracting it from the living people who make it up. And it is likewise impossible to attain personal perfection while upholding an unjust social order, while committing social crimes, violating and exploiting one's neighbour. This point of view is in the last analysis assumed also by Communism, which both holds in high esteem the human material out of which communist society is to be built up, and seeks to create not only new and just social conditions, but also fellowship and common life. Its fatal mistake lies, however, in that it holds the possibility of creating a community by the same means as are used to organize society or the state. Berdyaev has but little faith in these means and he can conceive of true community only on the

[4] This thought has lately been put forward very forcibly by Dr. J. H. Oldham and the Christian News-Letter; cf., *Real Life is Meeting* (C.N.-L., 1943).

basis of the Christian, existential truth, which reveals the supreme and integral synthesis of personal and common life among men.

This life derives its origin not from a class, nor from the state, nor from a race, nor even from society: it springs from the living waters of Christ's body. It belongs to the truth of God-manhood, in which all things are equally personal and in common; in which man constitutes not a mere unit of the universe or a part of a machine, but a "living member of an organic hierarchy, belonging to a real and living whole" (*The End of Our Time*). Such was, if not in practice, at least in purpose the great epoch of the middle ages, and such the new middle ages will be, in which the Christian truth about man and the world will have the decisive power and significance. For these new middle ages Berdyaev longs with all the thirst for and love of things to come so characteristic of him —*amor futuri!* "Christians must will the creation of a Christian society and culture, putting before all things the search for the 'Kingdom of God and his righteousness.' Much depends on our freedom, on man's creative efforts . . . I have a presentiment that an outbreak of the powers of evil is at hand . . . The night is coming and we must take up spiritual weapons for the fight against evil, we must make more sensitive our power for its discernment, we must build up a new knighthood . . . *We* are men of the middle ages, not only because that is our destiny, the doom of history, but also because we will it. *You,* you are still men of modern times, because you refuse to choose . . . " (*ibid.*)[5]

[5] It is interesting to note that Berdyaev's "personalistic socialism" is represented, though quite independently of him, by a group of French Catholics (who have come out of Péguy's "school"), particularly associated with Emmanuel Mounier and the review *Esprit*. Their moral and social outlook, which marked a real Catholic revival in France, has developed along spiritual lines similar to those of Berdyaev. *See* Mounier's *Personalist Manifesto* (Sheed & Ward).

6

As I write these lines historical
events are taking place in Russia which will decide her fate
for a long time to come. There is no doubt that the future
shape of Russian culture is closely bound up with the catastrophic events of the war. Nonetheless I venture to suggest
that the main motifs of her cultural development go deeper
than the external events of to-day, or for that matter than
those of the last stormy twenty-five years of her history.
Every external historical factor is preceded and to some extent predetermined by deeper spiritual processes: and the
outer factors of Russia's life, in spite of all its recent disruptions and dislocation, have deep spiritual roots in her
historic destiny. To understand them we must be aware of
these spiritual roots and of the elements which in one sense
or another prepared the soil for the present harvest. Here
the Russian religious thought of the years before the revolution is the first to arrest our attention. It may be legitimately
asserted that while the revolution, as it issued in radical
social economic changes, occurred in 1917, it was preceded
by another revolution in the spiritual and cultural sphere—
the revolution at the beginning of the twentieth century.
This was described in the first chapter as a spiritual renascence. It struck a note of expectation of great things to come,
of a renewal of life and of the liberation of man. The figure
of Nicolas Berdyaev is a symbol of the great vision and courage which inspired this revolution.

◆

The present book presents studies of the lives and thought
of "Christian Revolutionaries." What is revolution and how
are we to define it?

The notion of revolution used *ad nauseam* as a slogan

hardly bears scrutiny. Its true meaning, however, may be most comprehensively described as an *eruption,* as a radical change, a break-up and turning upside down. And though revolutions often mature slowly within the life from which they have emerged, they nevertheless burst into our gradual and continuous daily existence as something sudden, as something new and unheard of, and so cut asunder the course of time.

The spirit of Berdyaev's philosophy, with its ideas of man's calling to co-operate in the cosmic realization of God-manhood, with its ideas of creativeness and freedom, with its faith in the impossible, with its contempt for causal necessity, utilitarianism and conformism, is a spirit of novelty and change, of hope in the new things to come, and thus a spirit of revolution. He is a Christian and Russian heir of the ancient, mysterious Heraclitus who saw existence in perennial flux, in the process of becoming, as a continuous emergence of new forms of life.

Yet Berdyaev's call is not to mere external revolution, but above all to a revolution *within.* Our moment of history, in fact, demands that the primacy of spiritual life should be proclaimed over the long-dominant external and largely fictitious values of the "kingdom of this world," because these values have spent themselves and do not inspire anybody. In order to uncover the springs of regeneration it is imperative to turn inwards, to deepen our awareness, to attain to a more meaningful attitude to life: one which will free us from bondage, hardening and inanition of the spirit. To turn inwards does not, however, mean to abandon the burdens and responsibilities of the world for the sake of a comfortable, sheltered inner life; it is rather a movement to a greater activity, a greater potency and intensity of the spirit.

If sin speaks of man's loss of freedom, slavery, and the bondage of the spirit, then salvation is and will be not submission to an outer order of society, not the worship of the present or of any future external forms of life, but the acquisition of freedom, meaning, depth, of true humanity, love and creativeness, in other words a new vision of the mystery of God-manhood. Berdyaev's thought is a signpost on the way to true inwardness, to a creative return of man's spirit to the divine-human sources of being.

∾

It has frequently been pointed out that Berdyaev is more concerned with man than with God, that his circling round man and subjective human existence has considerably narrowed down his philosophical and theological outlook, to the exclusion of more general and universal problems on which other thinkers have pondered for centuries. Are we not doomed here to fruitless anthropomorphism, which disregards the existence as relevant values of supra-human and supra-personal realities and the perennial objective forms of being? When we read Berdyaev's passionate denunciations of every sign of "objectivization" and falsification of life when projected on to the "objective" plane, in cultural, social, and scientific spheres, in the symbolic forms of religious and historical traditions, when we are faced with the terrible panorama of the defeats of the spirit, we may perhaps be justified in asking how it is possible to believe in the spirit's future victory. Is not history thus deprived of any power and purpose of realization? And though Berdyaev is an untiring advocate of creativeness, does this creativeness not remain for him as it were torn away from its own creations, from that in which it is embodied and objectified? In other words, does it not cease to be a true creative *act*, which must of necessity turn outward towards its object, and become a mere creative impulse, an aspiration without aim or content, so that man's creative energy is scattered to the winds and lost in space? Following Berdyaev past the graves of the mummies of objectivization (or "things," as he would say) which he has laid low, many may well ask: What about the more evident creative achievements in the "objective" sphere of culture? Do the creations of Sophocles, Shakespeare, Pushkin, Beethoven still live and preserve their spiritual "existential" power? If we admit any value in these, we cannot help, it seems, going further still in the rehabilitation of objectivized values, even in the sphere of social life and civilization: is not each of them capable (granted, of course, a creative attitude towards them) of being a positive contribution and enrichment?

I have deliberately given voice to these doubts in an interrogative form, for I do not believe that they actually present relevant objections to Berdyaev's view, in spite of the fact that his occasional waywardness and contradictions may justify them. Some of these doubts have already, I hope, been dispelled in the previous chapters. I shall confine myself here to a few observations.

Berdyaev's emphasis on the "existential" nature of life does, in fact, never imply mere preoccupation with the self-isolated human being, with the *solus ipse*. He is preeminently concerned with existence as *correlation*, with life as the vital relatedness of man to God (God-manhood) and of man to man (community, *sobornost*). Man's life is viewed as authentic only in his freedom from the bonds of individualism and self-sufficiency, in his encounter with God, with the world and with other men. Though he is summoned to discover the meaning of life in personal, creative inwardness, yet such a discovery is as much a movement from within *outward* as one from without *inward*, and thus presupposes objective reality outside man. But this reality has no meaning as a separate, divided "objectivized" sphere of life. It has meaning only as an inherent part of man's own personal existence, of which he must be at all times conscious. Hence Berdyaev's strong belief in common, corporate salvation, in the integration of all humanity and the whole world into a united, transfigured cosmos. Even the processes of objectivization, as Berdyaev sees them, may be a positive activity of the spirit, in so far as they fulfil man's active task of the shaping of life, and truly embody his creative energies. As soon, however, as the spirit loses its inwardness and submits to the determinism of its own external creations they become its defeat and ruin.

≈

Berdyaev's philosophy, like all true philosophy, epitomizes the historical situation of his time, with its peculiar needs and problems. I have already shown that this situation has issued in modern man's feeling of fear and insecurity, not only in the social sphere, but in the very depth of his life. Yet with all the awareness of the perils threatening human existence to-day, there is in Berdyaev a strong faith in the supreme underlying meaning of this predicament: it is a great opportunity in which man's destiny is being worked out and his soul is growing deeper, more complex and more mature. Berdyaev perceives in the agonies of stricken human existence the seeds of new life—an eternal, not only human but divine-human answer to and atonement for all that has happened to modern man. To Berdyaev applies what Dostoevsky said of himself: "It is not as a child that I believe and confess Christ Jesus. My 'hosanna' is born of a furnace of doubt." And Berdyaev's merit lies in that he is one of the few who have found the Christian answer, and yet do not cease to question with those whose lives are still torn asunder by disbelief, doubt and sufferings; one of the few who dare to be, as thinkers, Christians and, as Christians, thinkers. He belongs to those watchmen who look out into the gathering darkness: "He calleth to me out of Seir: 'Watchman, what of the night? Watchman, what of the night?' The watchman said: 'The morning cometh and also the night: if ye will enquire, enquire ye . . .' " (Isaiah xxi. 11-12).

BIBLIOGRAPHY

SØREN KIERKEGAARD

References to the standard lives of Kierkegaard and to his own writings are shown under the following abbreviations:

L—*Kierkegaard.* By Walter Lowrie, D.D. (Oxford University Press, 1938).

L2—*A Short Life of Kierkegaard.* By Walter Lowrie, D.D. (O.U.P., 1943; Princeton University Press, 1942).

J—*The Journals of Soren Kierkegaard.* Edited and translated by Alexander Dru (O.U.P., 1938).

U.P.—*Unscientific Postscript.* By S. Kierkegaard (1838). Translated by David Swenson & Walter Lowrie (O.U.P., 1941).

P.F.—*Philosophical Fragments by Johannes Climacus.* Translated by David F. Swenson (O.U.P., 1936).

P—*From the Papers of One Still Living.* By S. Kierkegaard (1838).

S.D.—*Sickness unto Death.* By S. Kierkegaard. Translated by Walter Lowrie (O.U.P., 1941; P.U.P., 1941).

P.A.—*The Present Age.* By S. Kierkegaard. Translated by Alexander Dru and Walter Lowrie (O.U.P., 1940).

R.—*Repetition.* By S. Kierkegaard. Translated by Walter Lowrie (O.U.P., 1942; P.U.P., 1941).

St.—*Stages on Life's Road: Studies by Various Writers.* Collected and edited by Hilarius Bookbinder (1845).

C.D.—*Christian Discourses.* By S. Kierkegaard (1848).

P.V.—*The Point of View for My Work as an Author.* By S. Kierkegaard (1859).

T.C.—*Training in Christianity by Anti-Climacus.* Edited by S. Kierkegaard (1850).

S.E.—*For Self-Examination.* By S. Kierkegaard (O.U.P., 1941).

Attack upon Christendom. Translated with an introduction by Walter Lowrie. Princeton, N. J., Princeton University Press, 1944.

Christian Discourses and The Lilies of the Field and the Birds of the Air, and Three Discourses at the Communion on Fridays. Translated with an introduction by Walter Lowrie. London, New York, Oxford University Press, 1939.

The Concept of Dread. Translated with an introduction and notes by Walter Lowrie. Princeton, N. J., Princeton University Press, 1944.

Concluding Unscientific Postscript. Translated from the Danish by David F. Swenson, completed after his death and provided with an introduction and notes by Walter Lowrie. Princeton, N. J., Princeton University Press, for the American Scandinavian Foundation, 1941.

Edifying Discourses. Translated from the Danish by David F. Swenson and Lillian Marvin Swenson. Minneapolis, Minn., Augsburg Publishing House, 1943-45.

Either/Or; a Fragment of Life. Translated by David F. Swenson and Lillian Marvin Swenson. Princeton, N. J., Princeton University Press; London, H. Milford, Oxford University Press, 1944.

Fear and Trembling, a Dialectical Lyric. Translated with an introduction and notes by Walter Lowrie. Princeton, N. J., Princeton University Press, 1941.

A Personal Confession. European quarterly. London, 1934, v. I, p. 115-120. Translated by A. Dru.

Stages on Life's Way. Translated by Walter Lowrie. Princeton University Press; London, Oxford University Press, 1940.

Training in Christianity and the Edifying Discourse which Accompanied It. Translated with an introduction and notes by Walter Lowrie. London, New York, Oxford University Press, 1941.

G. K. CHESTERTON

The Defendant, Dent, 1901.

Twelve Types, Humphreys, 1902.

Browning, Macmillan, 1903.

The Napoleon of Notting Hill, Lane, 1904.

Heretics, Lane, 1905. Sheed & Ward.

The Club of Queer Trades, Harper & Brothers, 1905.

Charles Dickens, Dodd, Mead & Co., 1906.

The Man Who Was Thursday, Dodd, Mead & Co., 1908.

Orthodoxy, Lane, 1909. Dodd, Mead & Co.

The Ball and the Cross, Lane, 1909.

Tremendous Trifles, Methuen, 1909.

George Bernard Shaw, Lane, 1910.

What's Wrong with the World, Cassell, 1910.

Wit and Wisdom of G. K. Chesterton, Dodd, Mead & Co., 1911.

A Defense of Nonsense and other essays, Dodd, Mead & Co., 1911.

Manalive, Lane, 1912.

Magic: a comedy, G. P. Putnam's Sons, 1913.

Victorian Age in English Literature, Butterworth, 1913.

The Flying Inn, Lane, 1914.

The New Jerusalem, Hodder & Stoughton, 1920.

The Superstition of Divorce, Chatto & Windus, 1920.

Irish Impressions, W. Collins Sons & Co., Ltd., 1920.

Eugenics and Other Evils, Cassell, 1922.

The Man Who Knew Too Much, Cassell, 1922.

What I Saw in America, Dodd, Mead & Co., 1922.

The Ballad of White Horse, Dodd, Mead & Co., 1924.

The Everlasting Man, Dodd, Mead & Co., 1925.

William Cobbett, Hodder & Stoughton, 1925.

The Outline of Sanity, Methuen, 1926.

St. Francis of Assisi, Hodder & Stoughton, 1926.

The Catholic Church and Conversion, Macmillan Co., 1926.

The Innocence of Father Brown, Cassell.

The Incredulity of Father Brown, Dodd, Mead & Co., 1926.

All Things Considered, Methuen & Co., 1926.

R. L. Stevenson, Hodder & Stoughton, 1927.

Generally Speaking: a book of essays. Methuen & Co., Ltd., 1928.

The Judgement of Doctor Johnson, a comedy in three acts, G. P. Putnam's Sons, 1928.

The Thing, Dodd, Mead & Co.

The Poet and the Lunatics, Cassell, 1929.

Four Faultless Felons, Dodd, Mead & Co., 1930.

Come to Think of It, Methuen, 1931.

All Is Grist: a book of essays, Methuen & Co., 1931.

Chaucer, Faber & Faber, 1932.

St. Thomas Aquinas, Hodder & Stoughton, 1933. Sheed & Ward.

Avowals and Denials: a book of essays, Methuen & Co., Ltd., 1934.

All I Survey, Dodd, Mead & Co., 1933.

Autobiography, Sheed & Ward, 1936.

As I Was Saying: a book of essays, Dodd, Mead & Co., 1936.

Collected Poems, Methuen, 1937. Dodd, Mead & Co.

The Coloured Lands, Sheed & Ward, 1938.

The End of the Armistice, Sheed & Ward, 1939.

The Father Brown Omnibus, Dodd, Mead & Co.

The Scandal of Father Brown, Dodd, Mead & Co.

ERIC GILL

Art Nonsense. Twenty-four essays. Cassell, 1929.
> (Quotations herein are from the pocket edition, 1934.)

Clothes. Cape, 1931.

Beauty Looks After Herself. Thirteen essays. Sheed & Ward, 1933.
> (Quoted herein as *Beauty*.)

Unemployment; an essay. Faber & Faber, 1933.

Money and Morals. Three essays. Faber & Faber, 1934.
> (Quoted herein as *M. & M.*)

Art and a Changing Civilization. (In the Twentieth-Century Library.) Lane, 1934.
> (Quoted herein as *Art*.)

Work and Leisure. Three essays. Faber & Faber, 1935.
> (Quoted herein as *W. & L.*)

The Necessity of Belief. Faber & Faber, 1935.
> (Quoted herein as *Belief*.)

Work and Property. Eight essays, Dent, 1937.
> (Quoted herein as *W. & P.*)

And Who Wants Peace? (Pax Pamphlet No. I). James Clarke, 1938.
> (Quoted herein as *Peace*.)

Social Justice and the Stations of the Cross. James Clarke, 1939.
> (Quoted herein as *Stations*.)

Sacred and Secular. Six essays. Dent, 1940.
> (Quoted herein as *S. & S.*)

Christianity and the Machine Age. (Christian News-Letter Books, No. 6.) The Sheldon Press, 1940.

    (Quoted herein as *Machine Age.* This is an excellent summary, in seventy pages or so, of Eric Gill's beliefs and teachings.)

Autobiography. The Devin-Adair Company, 1942.

    (Quoted herein as *Auto.*)

Last Essays. Nine essays, Cape, 1942.

Architecture and Sculpture. Manchester: G. Falkner & Sons, Ltd., 1927.

Art and Prudence. The Golden Cockerel Press, 1928.

Art in Relation to Industrialism. American review. Camden, N. J., 1936.

Engravings; a selection in wood and metal. Bristol: D. Cleverdon, 1929.

Engravings, 1928-1933. London, Faber & Faber, Ltd., 1934.

An Essay on Typography. London, Sheed & Ward, 1931.

In a Strange Land. London, J. Cape, 1944.

It All Goes Together. New York, The Devin-Adair Co., 1944.

Sculpture; an essay on stone-cutting. Ditchling, Sussex, At St. Dominic's Press, 1924.

C. F. ANDREWS

The Relation of Christianity to the Conflict between Capital and Labour. (Burney Prize Essay, 1894.) Methuen, 1896.

North India. (Handbooks of English Church Expansion.) A. Mowbray, 1908.

The Renaissance in India. The United Council for Missionary Study, 1912.

The Oppression of the Poor. Madras, Ganesh & Co., 1921.

The Drink and Opium Evil. Madras, Ganesh & Co.

Indians in South Africa. Madras, Ganesh & Co., 1922.

Non-co-operation. Madras, Ganesh & Co.

Terence MacSwiney and the New World Movement. Triplicane. Madras, S. Ganesan, 1922.

Christ and Labour. Student Christian Movement Press, 1923.

Letters to a Friend. By Rabindranath Tagore. Edited by C. F. Andrews. Allen & Unwin, 1928.

Zaka Ullah of Delhi. Heffer and Sons, Cambridge, 1929.

Mahatma Gandhi: His own Story. Edited by C F. Andrews. Allen & Unwin, 1930.

India and the Simon Report. Allen & Unwin, 1930.

Mahatma Gandhi's Ideas. Allen & Unwin, 1931.

Mahatma Gandhi at Work: His own Story Continued. Edited by C. F. Andrews. Macmillan Co., 1930.

What I Owe to Christ. Hodder & Stoughton, 1932.

Christ in the Silence. Hodder & Stoughton, 1933.

Sadhu Sander Singh: A Personal Memoir. Hodder & Stoughton, 1934.

India and Britain: a Moral Challenge. S.C.M. Press, 1935.

The Indian Earthquake. Allen & Unwin, 1935.
John White of Mashonaland. Hodder & Stoughton, 1935.
India and the Pacific. Allen & Unwin, 1937.
Christ and Prayer. Harper & Brothers, 1937.
Christ and Human Need. Hodder & Stoughton, 1937.
The True India: a Plea for Understanding. Allen & Unwin, 1939.
The Rise and Growth of the Congress in India. With Girja Mookerjee.
   Allen & Unwin, 1939.
The Good Shepherd. Hodder & Stoughton, 1940.
The Inner Life. Harper & Brothers, 1940.
The Sermon on the Mount. Macmillan Co., 1942.

NICOLAS BERDYAEV

All the books listed below are in Russian. Translations in English, or failing this in French or German, are mentioned when they exist. Works marked * are specially important for the understanding of Berdyaev's thought.

F. A. Lange and the Critical Philosophy. Moscow, 1900.
Subjectivism and Individualism in Social Philosophy. A Critical essay on N. K. Mikhailovsky. St. Petersburg, 1901.
Sub Specie Aeternitatis. Philosophical, sociological and literary essays. St. Petersburg, 1907.
The New Religious Consciousness and Society. St. Petersburg, 1907.
The Spiritual Crisis of the Intelligentsia. Essays in social and religious psychology. St. Petersburg, 1910.
Philosophy of Freedom. Moscow, 1911.
A. S. Khomiakov. Moscow, 1912.
The Soul of Russia. Moscow, 1915.
* *The Meaning of Creativeness.* Essay in Justification of man. Moscow, 1916. (German translation, *Der Sinn des Schaffens,* Verlag Mohr, Tubingen, 1927.)
The Fate of Russia. Essay on the psychology of war and nationhood. Moscow, 1916.
* *The Meaning of History.* Essay on the philosophy of human destiny. Berlin, 1923. (English translation by George Reavey, The Centenary Press, 1936.)
Philosophy of Inequality. Berlin, 1923.
The World-Outlook of Dostoevsky. Prague, 1923. (English translation by Donald Attwater, "Dostoevsky," Sheed & Ward, 1934.)
"The Russian Religious Idea" in *Problems of Russian Religious Consciousness.* Berlin, 1924. (French translation "L'idée religieuse russe", in Cahiers de la Nouvelle Journée, No. 8, Bloud et Gay, Paris, 1927.)
The New Middle Ages. Berlin, 1924. (English translation by Donald Attwater in "The End of Our Time," which includes four other essays: The End of

the Renaissance; The Russian Revolution; Democracy, Socialism and Theocracy; and the "General Line" of the Soviet Philosophy. Sheed & Ward, 1933.)

Leontiev. Paris, 1926. (English translation by George Reavey. The Centenary Press, 1940.)

* *Philosophy of the Free Spirit.* 2 vols, Paris, 1926. (English translation by O. F. Clarke, "Freedom and the Spirit," The Centenary Press, 1935.)

* *The Destiny of Man.* Essay on paradoxical ethics. Paris, 1931. (English translation by Nataly Duddington, The Centenary Press, 1937.)

On Suicide. A psychological essay. Paris, 1931.

Russian Religious Psychology and Communist Atheism. Paris, 1931. (English translation by D. B. in "The Russian Revolution," Essays in Order, No. 6, Sheed & Ward, 1935.)

Christianity and Class War. Paris, 1931. (English translation by Donald Attwater, Sheed & Ward, 1933.)

Christianity and Human Action, in the Christianity on the Atheist Front Series. Paris, 1932.

* *Machine and the Machine* (in Put, No. 38, 1933.) (English translation, including other essays, in "The Bourgeois Mind," Sheed & Ward, 1934.)

* *I and the World of Objects.* Essay on the philosophy of solitude and common life. Paris, 1934. (English translation by George Reavey, *Solitude and Society,* The Centenary Press, 1938.)

The Fate of Man in the Modern World. Paris, 1934. (English translation by Donald Lowrie, S.C.M. Press, 1935.)

* *Spirit and Reality.* The foundations of theandric spirituality. Paris, 1937. (English translation by George Reavey, The Centenary Press, 1939.)

* *The Origin of Russian Communism.* Published only in French and English. (English translation by R. M. French, The Centenary Press, 1937.)

* *Slavery and the Freedom of Man.* Paris, 1940. (English translation by R. M. French to be published by The Centenary Press.)